RETURN TO THE SCENE OF THE

CRIME

RETURN TO THE SCENE OF THE

CRIME

A Guide to Infamous Places in

CHICAGO

Richard Lindberg

Cumberland House
Nashville, Tennessee

Published by Cumberland House Publishing, 431 Harding Industrial Drive, Nashville, Tennessee 37211-3160.

Maps courtesy of American Map Company.

Cover and text design: Unlikely Suburban Design
Typesetting: Mary Sanford

Library of Congress Cataloging-in-Publication Data
Lindberg, Richard, 1953–
    Return to the scene of the crime : a guide to infamous places in Chicago / Richard Lindberg.
      p.   cm.
    Includes bibliographical references and index.
    ISBN 1-58182-013-5 (pbk. : alk. paper)
    1. Chicago (Ill.) Tours.   2. Historic sites—Illinois—Chicago Guidebooks.
3. Crime Scenes—Illinois—Chicago—History.   4. Criminals—Illinois—
Chicago—History.   I. Title.
F548.18.L495   1999
917.73'110443—dc21   99-27633
                                               CIP

Printed in the United States of America
   4 5 6 7 8—04 03 02 01

Other Books by Richard Lindberg

- *Stuck on the Sox,* 1978
- *Who's On Third: The Chicago White Sox Story,* 1983
- *The Macmillan White Sox Encyclopedia,* 1984
- *Chicago Ragtime: Another Look at Chicago 1880–1920,* 1985; reprinted in paperback as *Chicago by Gaslight: A History of the Chicago Netherworld 1880–1920,* 1996
- *To Serve and Collect: Chicago Politics and Police Corruption from the Lager Beer Riot to the Summerdale Scandal 1855–1960,* 1991; reprinted in paperback, 1998
- *Passport's Guide to Ethnic Chicago,* 1992; second edition, 1997
- *Stealing First in a Two-Team Town: The White Sox from Comiskey to Reinsdorf,* 1994
- *Quotable Chicago,* 1996
- *The White Sox Encyclopedia,* 1997
- *The Armchair Companion to Chicago Sports,* 1997

In addition, Lindberg was a contributing author to the following:

- *The Encyclopedia of World Crime* (1990)
- *The Baseball Biographical Encyclopedia* (1990)
- *American National Biography* (1999 revision)
- *The Encyclopedia of Major League Baseball Team Histories* (1990)
- *A Kid's Guide to Chicago* (1980)

CONTENTS

· T o u r 5 ·

North by Northwest: Kenilworth to Barrington   229

For many years it was acknowledged that the farm communities and
suburbs linked by the railroads to the city held the key to a safer
lifestyle and an escape from crime.

· T o u r 6 ·

West Side Stories   263

With its residential neighborhoods moving outward from the city, the
West Side mirrors the remarkable growth of Chicago from its days as a
frontier garrison to the imposing industrial metropolis it soon became.

· T o u r 7 ·

Residences of Organized Crime: The Western Suburbs   325

The movement of heavy industry out of crowded Chicago neighborhoods in the early years of the twentieth century heralded a population
exodus from the city to the suburbs.

· T o u r 8 ·

South Side Sinners   351

Whatever else one may say about Chicago's South Side, it is undeniable
that the importance of the Windy City was shaped by urbanization
south of Madison Street.

ACKNOWLEDGMENTS

A number of people assisted in making this book a reality, beginning with Carol Jean Carlson, whose skilled editing, words of encouragement, and research assistance allowed me to complete this manuscript in a timely fashion. Without Carol's sense of direction, the task would have been much more difficult.

A number of fellow writers and crime historians provided useful tips, and helped fill in the blanks concerning puzzling aspects of some of the crime stories included in this volume. I owe a tremendous debt of gratitude to William J. Helmer, America's foremost authority on John Herbert Dillinger and Depression-era outlawry. Bill is far too modest and self-effacing to own up to the significant contributions he has made to the genre of true crime writing over the years, but his published works speak volumes. No armchair detective's library is complete without at least one Helmer work.

Tamara Shaffer, one of the original members of the Merry Gangsters Literary Society, has spent years studying and writing about the slaying of the Grimes sisters and the Schuessler-Peterson murders. I doubt that there is anyone in Chicago, or elsewhere, who has devoted more personal time to tracking down fresh leads and following up on the loose ends of these puzzling child murders from the 1950s. For Tamara, the work has been largely a labor of love, and I thank her for her contributions to this project.

Pat Butler of the Lerner Newspapers was of help on the Adolph Luetgert sausage-vat mystery. This is a classic Chicago crime, and Pat is well versed in all of the Luetgert lore and gore. John O'Brien of the *Chicago Tribune* assisted me with old newspaper clippings. John covered the crime beat for more than thirty years before retiring in 1999. He is the last of that venerable breed of big city reporters that is cognizant of the "real" Chicago beyond north Michigan Avenue and the Water Tower.

Paul Davis Newey, former Chief Investigator for the Cook County State's Attorney in the days of the late Ben Adamowski, provided personal insights into the character and background of the man known as Dick Cain. Wise and generous, Paul understands Chicago from the perspective of the criminal justice system.

John Touhy, headquartered in Washington D.C., shared fresh insights with me about a man who coincidentally has the same last name, Roger Touhy. Biart Williams, who contributed so much to my earlier Cumberland House entry, *The*

Armchair Companion to Chicago Sports, supplied essential details for several crime vignettes. Bill Hersh of the Uptown Chicago Commission provided rich anecdotes about the Uptown nightclub district. Jeannette Callaway at the Chicago Crime Commission was as always helpful and supportive as I tracked down loose information, and Cheryl Besenjak coordinated the graphics arrangement with the American Map Company. I wish to also thank Christina Carlson, who trained her expert camera lens on the crime scenes, showing us how these landmarks from the netherworld appear today. Gera-Lind Kolarik and Art Bilek supplied additional photographs. Bill Tyre of the Prairie Avenue Foundation filled in a few missing details.

I am, of course, very grateful to Ron Pitkin and Mary Sanford at Cumberland House, who shepherded the manuscript through production. And finally, I would like to thank my agent, Margaret Graham Tebo, who took a concept that had been swimming in the back of my mind for nearly seven years and committed it to print when others had suggested that I forget it and refocus on some other subject. A book begins and ends with the agent and the publisher, and this volume is a reflection of their confidence in my abilities as an author and historian.

INTRODUCTION

"A façade of skyscrapers facing the lake and behind the façade, every bit of dubiousness!"

E. M. Forster

What is it about this city that inspires the pundits, thinkers, and social critics to extol the outlandish and revel in the odd and the fantastic?

"I give you Chicago! It is not London and Harvard," exulted H. L. Mencken, renowned observer of the American scene and resident of Baltimore. "It is not Paris and buttermilk. It is American in every chitling and sparerib. It is alive from snout to tail." Things move fast in Chicago, and Mencken and others witnessed in the hurly-burly of city life the energy, vitality, and affirmation of the American spirit.

Others tended to view the city, not in heroic terms, but as a breeding ground of crime—a place of savage, unrelenting violence and miserable slums. From its earliest days, the frontier city lying in the fertile crescent along Lake Michigan's western shore was a study in moral contradiction. Chicago sought to emulate the highest ideals of mankind through the sermons of clergy and the genteel examples set forth by its prairie aristocracy. The reform movements of the postbellum era, when the city rose from the ashes of the 1871 conflagration, impressed upon the wellborn the indefatigable virtues of thrift, self-reliance, entrepreneurship, sobriety, and moderation; while the great mass of common people struggled with their own conundrum: If liquor, dice, cards, and the other lowbrow Levee attractions were such *reprehensible vices,* why did they seem to have such universal appeal among all social classes?

No less than the great social arbiter Al Capone stumbled upon the Holy Grail, the real meaning of it all, when he bluntly declared, "Chicago has never been legit!" Far be it from the current generation of politicians, image-makers, and civic boosters to contemplate replacing the official city motto, *Urbs in Horto* (City in a Garden), with Capone doggerel, but in light of the events of recent years, it might make perfect sense to revisit the issue.

In the days of "Long John" Wentworth, Chicago's bungling antebellum mayor, the city existed as a paradise for adventurers, fools, and vagabonds staggering off of the bumboats and paddlewheel steamers churning the tepid waters of the Mississippi and Ohio Rivers. They drifted northward to Chicago, this great human tempest of bounders, panders, cardsharps, bunko-steerers, and world-weary cynics poised for one last kill on the jumpin' prairie flats.

For all the pretentious bombast and blather from the champions of decency; the Law and Order Leagues, Civic Federations, soothsayers, editorialists, Sunday preachers, and Committees of Fifty and Fifteen; none of them could have possibly forestalled the social forces unleashed upon the city by the "dangerous criminal classes"—a grimly archaic nineteenth-century code word for the impoverished, the foreign-speaking, and those deemed likely to cause problems and draw blood. By their sweat, toil, and petty larcenies, the great mass of working people helped fulfill the manifest destiny of the city.

Chicago is many things. It is Pabst Blue Ribbon Beer, the Friday night fights, Polish sausages, the Dill Pickle Club, open fire hydrants in August, and the slot machines in the back of Joe's Tavern. Alas, Chicago. It will never become a stuffy white-pants Sunday ice cream social for country-club idlers. From "snout to tail," it is a city that would rather revel in temptation than yield to righteousness.

* * * *

Chicago is a city with a past. My interest in its more notorious aspects was kindled many years ago inside the darkened auditorium of the Roosevelt Theater, a vintage 1920s movie palace that was a part of the State Street nightlife that Frank Sinatra rhapsodized over in musical verse in his film *Robin & the Seven Hoods,* a Chicago gangster spoof. The color and vitality of downtown Chicago ebbed after the lamentable disappearance of the Roosevelt and its sister theaters, the Oriental, McVickers, Woods, State & Lake, Loop, and a collection of smaller "art houses" and burlesque halls lying south of Van Buren.

My visit to the Roosevelt Theater that July afternoon in 1967 awakened me to the other side of Chicago with a violent episode drawn from the crime files of city history that Mrs. Green, my fourth-grade teacher, had managed to overlook during her hero-filled discussion of the early days of Fort Dearborn.

Even now, I get a kick out of watching Jason Robards on late night local television as the distinguished actor chews the rug portraying Al Capone in *The St. Valentine's Day Massacre.* It was certainly not method acting or even *cinema vérité,* but the swagger and the fury of this crisply narrated drama depicting one of the goriest moments in Chicago gangster history enchanted me.

Mesmerized by the celluloid depiction of gangster life in the Roaring Twenties, I hopped aboard the Clark Street bus bound for Lincoln Park. I was intent on locating the garage at 2122 where Al Capone's men massacred seven rival gangsters in the early morning hours of Valentine's Day, 1929.

Chicago's most famous landmark to crime turned out to be a rather shabby, uninspiring warehouse dwarfed by the Gold Coast apartment hotels rising before me in the distance. The faint outline of lettering advertising the services of the "S.M.C. Cartage Company" was barely visible on a pane of window glass.

Whatever the company's initials once symbolized to the proprietor, they connected me to a past far removed from the reality of my daily life on the far northwest corner of the city. That afternoon, as I peered intently through the grimy glass and pressed my hand against the weather-beaten bricks, I imagined the seven men lined up against the wall moments before the clatter of the Thompson submachine guns ended their lives.

Questions raced through my mind. I asked myself: Why were Bugs Moran's men there in the first place? What was it they were waiting for that morning? Maybe they were hatching some fantastic scheme aimed at overthrowing Capone. What were their dinner plans for that evening? I have often wondered about these things since.

Did Al Capone actually expect his hired assassins to calmly waltz through an open front door, line up seven of Bugs Moran's associates, and spray them with machine-gun fire? Or was it maybe just an accident of history waiting to happen; the unintended outcome climaxing the bloodiest and most chaotic crime period in this nation's history?

Later that year, I read in the newspaper that the S.M.C. Cartage Company was slated for demolition. The city took the position that the disappearance of this squat, ugly little building frozen in time on Clark Street would erase rancorous memories of the embarrassing gangland murders that sealed Chicago's reputation as the crime capitol of mid-America.

The bricks from the massacre wall were privately sold to a collector of antiquities and carted off to Canada for display in a discotheque. Developers planted greenery, covering over the site with a patch of shade trees and a senior citizen's high-rise; but 2122 N. Clark would never become as anonymous as Mayor Richard J. Daley or the Chicago Office of Tourism might have hoped for or anticipated. Curiosity seekers by the thousands have tramped past 2122 N. Clark since 1967, re-creating in their mind's eye the blood-soaked images of the massacre.

Local ghost hunters even say the spirits of the restless dead haunt the place. Devotees of the supernatural snap photographs as the tour buses roll past. The site gives the Merry Gangsters Literary Society of journalists and true-crime buffs something to analyze, debate, and ponder over highballs in a tony downtown restaurant, leaving only the City of Chicago and the cultural high brows to fuss and fume over the inappropriateness of it all.

Indeed, Chicago affords its visitors a splendid, majestic lakefront; breathtaking views of an architecturally singular skyline; an unparalleled collection of impressionist masterpieces housed in one of the finest art museums in the world; and an internationally recognized opera company. Other cities can be justifiably envious of Chicago's record of civic accomplishment and its abundant harvest of culture, art, and commerce. We are truly blessed, those of us attending a night at the opera in Chicago. Indeed we are.

By the same token, however, let us not forget that within this spectacular mosaic of uplifting culture and commerce, the City of Big Shoulders has also spawned some of humanity's worst rejects—Herman Webster Mudgett, the "42 Gang," Dion O'Banion, the Levee, Randolph Street river pirates, white slavers, Leopold and Loeb, and Adolph Luetgert. Where else but in Chicago? I ask you. It is the dark side of this great city that visitors find so fascinating, and that is what this book is essentially about.

Living in Chicago all these years, and afflicted with a historian's curiosity and obsession with the past, I have been afforded a rare glimpse of the city as it was through the preparation of this volume and my earlier books dealing with aspects of city crime and politics, *Chicago by Gaslight* and *To Serve and Collect.*

I have returned to the scenes of hundreds of crimes, both famous and obscure and tragic and absurd, since my visit to the S.M.C. Cartage Company that afternoon. My neighborhood sojourns helped me to better understand the social milieu of Chicago and to feel the surging pulse of the city as I began to think seriously about recording my impressions with pen and paper. As I toured both the historic and commonplace locales where average people carry on their daily lives against the backdrop of some hideously revolting crime or jarring event reported in the newspaper, I soon realized that it takes many years to erase toxic memories.

Then as I began to explore some of the most stratified neighborhoods in the city, I soon realized that infamy lives on long after the residents who were old enough to remember the event, or to have heard faint recollections, have moved to the suburbs.

Infamous buildings are reduced to piles of rubble or recycled in curious and sometimes bizarre ways. The McCready funeral home on Sheridan Road where John Dillinger's remains were shipped following his violent death at the Biograph Theater has become someone's private domicile. The signs were taken down, and a security gate was built around the property. Only when you closely examine the exterior architecture of this stately old building do you suddenly realize, that yes, it does resemble an old-fashioned funeral home.

Then consider the 5100 Club at Broadway and Carmen up on the far North Side of the city. It was an important stopover on the Vaudeville circuit in the 1930s and 1940s. Comedian Danny Thomas launched his stand-up career playing at the 5100 to packed houses. The razzle-dazzle show lounge became a Western Tire and

Automotive Supply Store outlet by the 1960s. As such, it was the favorite target of the nocturnal cat burglar Richard Morrison, who cleaned out the stockrooms at the request of eight thieving Chicago police officers, who guarded the front door just in case an honest cop happened to stroll past. Today, with memories of Summerdale and Vaudeville mostly obscured, the nondescript building at 5100 N. Broadway is a grocery store peddling soft drinks, lottery tickets, and fast-food snacks to the Asian-American residents of Uptown.

Revitalization dramatically alters the physical appearance of city neighborhoods from one generation to the next, and often in dramatic and unexpected ways. Because so many famous crime scenes evolve into contaminated and neglected brown fields overrun with weeds and garbage, while gentrification of nearby areas goes forward unimpeded, I am convinced that these sites are tragically cursed.

In 1984, as I began preparations for my third book, *Chicago by Gaslight,* I journeyed into the heart of the former South Side Levee in order to gain a perspective on the city's most illicit den of early twentieth-century vice. Where there was once a scarlet parade, I found automobile graveyards, buckled and torn pavement blocks, and grass sprouting up through cracks in the sidewalks. An eerie silence permeated the acres of abandoned properties in the vicinity of Cullerton and Dearborn Streets—the broken bones of the old Levee.

The illicit trade in this area gradually disappeared after World War I, and the gaslight-era criminals, opium peddlers, and flesh merchants were uprooted and driven out of the district by powerful, mobilizing social forces and the thrust of technology. As these gaudy palaces of sin were plowed under, the local residents living east of the district discovered to their great consternation that the city had no effective plan to commercially redevelop the Levee properties.

The Levee decayed. Within a few years, the western edge of the district was a ghost town. It remained a desolate patch in a run-down and isolated corner of Chicago up until the 1990s, when the Chinatown business community planned for the redevelopment of the empty lots lying north of Twenty-second Street.

Even today, as townhouse developers push the envelope on new residential construction along South State Street, portions of Clark Street, Wabash Avenue, and Dearborn down to Roosevelt Road, there are patches of the old Levee that are likely to remain in a state of neglect for the foreseeable future.

Which brings to mind the contentious debate over Block 37, and its uncertain future. This two-and-a-half-acre parcel of real estate in the heart of downtown Chicago has remained an open field since the late 1980s. The demolition of Block 37 occurred during a period of frenzied, but ill-advised, speculation. The popcorn palaces, restaurants, and dingy retail emporiums lining Block 37, between State

RANDOLPH STREET LOOKING WEST FROM STATE STREET IN 1945—VAUDEVILLE, MOVIE HOUSES, AND A SENSE OF DOWNTOWN VIBRANCY THAT IS LOST TODAY.

(Courtesy of the Chicago Historical Society)

RANDOLPH AND STATE—BLOCK 37—AS IT LOOKS TODAY. A PUBLIC SKATING RINK IS ONLY A TEMPORARY ATTRACTION UNTIL THE CITY OF CHICAGO FIGURES OUT WHAT TO DO WITH THE TROUBLED SITE.

(Photo by author)

Street (east) and Dearborn (west), and bounded by Randolph Street on the north and Washington Street to the south, were taken down, one by one. A gleaming 1.2 million-square-foot office tower and retail complex designed by the renowned architect Helmut Jahn was to be the key to the rebirth of State Street following twenty lean and sluggish years in the 1970s and 1980s when the visible signs of neglect threatened the once famous shopping and theater district. However, the proposed deal that would have added a world-class Jahn creation to the graying skyline of the inner Loop fizzled during an unexpected shakeout in the local real estate market.

The city puzzles over the future of Block 37. The value of the land remains high, but the market is depressed, and no one seems willing to go beyond the discussion stages in committing scarce dollars toward its improvement.

FJV Ventures and JMB Realty, the investment consortium with title to the property, floated a scheme that would have added a $100 million-dollar mixed-use retail, hotel, and office complex to the vacant Loop land. The Macy Department Store chain expressed interest, then withdrew its offer from the table when the city refused to grant concessions.

In rebuffing the big money boys from Michigan Avenue and Wall Street, the city took the cavalier position that the proposed development failed to recognize that "this is State Street, not Main Street."   •

There is another possibility. Could it be that Block 37, one of Chicago's historically cursed brown fields, is haunted by its forgotten criminal past?

During the Civil War, the south side of Randolph Street bordering State was a disreputable rooming house and dance hall district known as the "Hairtrigger Block." It was reported in the street journals of the day that thieves and gamblers lounging in the sporting houses along Randolph would draw their weapons and fire at the slightest provocation. Garrotings, strong-arm assaults, and nightly saturnalia went unreported because this property had a fearsome reputation as a bastion of violence and iniquity. It was assumed that in a "segregated" vice area such as this one, violence predicated by licentiousness would occur, and far better for the decent citizens of Chicago that it should happen here rather than somewhere else. Thus, the city police exercised great caution and noninterference in the administration of justice for purely self-serving reasons.

For a period of about fifteen years, the Hairtrigger Block owed its existence to the parasitical relationship formed with the corrupt city police, and it thrived as a center of commercial vice activity. Bounty jumpers, copperheads, and wanted criminals were provided safe haven in this red-light resort. In the second floor lodging rooms overlooking the bucket-of-blood concert saloons of Randolph Street, the gamblers and their women entertained till dawn. The bluecoats turned a blind eye to the badger games and crooked cons run by "Cap" Hyman, Jack Haverly, Roger Plant, Mike McDonald, and other early crime bosses of Chicago who possessed the means to pay bribe money.

During the latter stages of the nineteenth century, what we now call Block 37 had evolved into "Gambler's Row," and was an emerging downtown Mecca for Vaudeville song pluggers and live performance theater. Working out of small offices overlooking the street, Tin Pan Alley transplants composed many of the familiar and forgotten sentimental ballads of that era at 64 West Randolph.

Even in the salad days of the early 1900s, when the luminaries of the Orpheum Circuit trod the boards at the famous Randolph Street theaters, there remained an unsavory underworld element lurking behind the glittering facades. The same gang of swindlers operating the bordellos in the South Side badlands also owned the objectionable downtown wine rooms, which were fronts for prostitution.

In the 1940s, syndicate taverns—concealing slot machines and games of "21"—and "B-girls" hustling customers for drinks in the Randolph Street dives were a public nuisance and an embarrassing eyesore in the very shadow of City Hall. These petty forms of vice gradually gave way to an even more unsightly aggregation of all-night pinball arcades; Baer's Treasure Chest; the Holloway House; peep shows; a Greyhound bus station that was an overnight haven for pimps, hookers, cons, soul savers, and hustlers; and $1.95 steakhouses east of Dearborn. One could also find a boarded-up coffee shop, wholesale electronics shops stocked with tourist kitsch, and a magazine outlet promoting lurid adult books. This is how Randolph Street—Block 37's northern exposure—appeared to the rest of the world in the mid- to late 1970s.

Districts such as this one often remain in dispute for decades, and the swarm of media publicity attending the Block 37 controversy in recent years failed to take note of the earlier patterns of crime and vice segregation as likely predictors of future land usage.

There are many such places that I have located in Chicago, pointing to the inescapable fact that crime and criminal activity of historic proportions forever stigmatize neighborhoods long after the perpetrators responsible for the outrage move on.

* * *

Return to the Scene of the Crime is neither a celebration of the great deeds of the men and women who inhabited America's most representative metropolis, or a glorification of their villainy and misbehavior. Rather, it is a historic compilation of unhistorical events; and a roadmap to places and events you are not likely to find listed in the pages of *Fodor's* or the *Michelin* guide.

You will read the unvarnished accounts of famous crimes that inspired Hollywood motion pictures and calamitous events from city history with world-wide repercussions. From the luxurious high-rises of the Gold Coast to the squalid slums of the neighborhood once known as "Little Hell," you will find the incidents and personalities of Chicago's sensational and criminal past lurking behind every "dubious façade."

Chapters correspond to the geography of Chicago and its surrounding suburbs. It is impossible to cover so vast an area on foot, or in one day. Unlike the island of Manhattan, traveling beyond the downtown area of the central city and the Near North Gold Coast requires public bus or elevated train, or a private automobile.

Within the main segments, the reader will find many other addresses of sites related to the crime scene, or germane to the central focus of the story. Anecdotal information and interesting historical vignettes are offered for consideration as "Side Trips."

I have also provided practical street maps pinpointing the approximate locations of the crime scenes with this word of caution. Many of these localities, particularly in the oldest and most dilapidated residential neighborhoods of the West and South Sides of the city, lie within the boundaries of dangerous, crime-ridden zones. Exercise proper caution when attempting to explore these areas on your own.

For those readers who do not wish to venture out alone—which is perfectly understandable because dubiousness does indeed exist behind every façade as we shall soon see—I sincerely hope that you will enjoy this informal excursion into the heart of darkness from the comfort and safety of your own living room.

Richard C. Lindberg

RETURN TO THE SCENE OF THE
CRIME

On the Waterfront:

Downtown Chicago

Not long after the Great Fire of 1871 had reduced the temples of commerce, the great hotels, and the retail promenade of State Street to ruins, a gathering of real estate speculators from the South and West Divisions of the city descended on the City Council. The promoters opened their valises and revealed stacks of crisp, newly minted bills to an unscrupulous cabal of city councilmen.

"A moment of your time gentlemen! Just a moment of your time!" is all they asked.

When it was revealed what these scalawags were up to, the *Chicago Times,* a Democratic paper, scolded its Republican rival, the *Chicago Tribune,* for lending support to their oily scheme to rebuild the downtown area in suburban Hyde Park—six miles to the south.

After a fractious debate, it was decided that Chicago's downtown would remain centrally located, surrounding the confluence of the Chicago River and Lake Michigan. The railroad lines and nautical traffic that flowed in and out of the city with these destination points mandated that the new urban grid of post-fire Chicago would remain essentially the same as before. In a rare and stunning moment, which one does occasionally encounter while plumbing the murky depths of Chicago politics, common sense prevailed over greed and self-interest.

The location of the future metropolis of Chicago was neither coincidental nor haphazard. The sandy marsh at the foot of the river was of strategic military importance to the U.S. government. A permanent military garrison was established there in 1803. That garrison, known as Fort Dearborn, anchored the frontier community for the next thirty-three years, until the Government closed the installation when the threat of Indian attack was removed.

The original city plat of 1829 laid out the conventional grid pattern of streets extending outward from the banks of the Chicago River. The city grew quickly, but not always wisely. Streets were often ankle-deep in muck and mire, and the population was under the constant threat of an epidemic of cholera or some other waterborne disease.

Chicago's early buildings were wood-frame affairs lacking distinction, and the

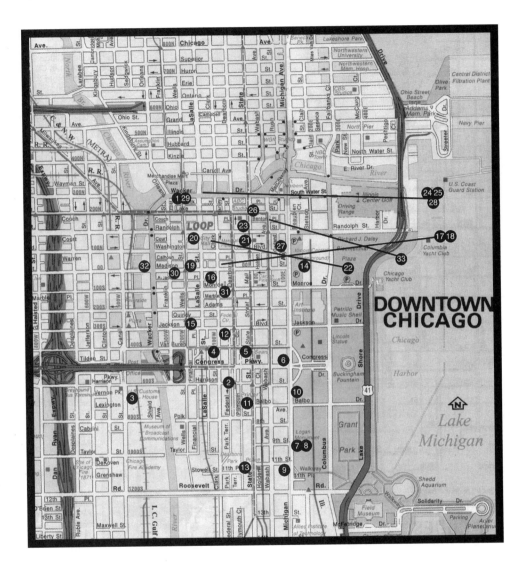

1. Wacker and Wells, where "Action" Jackson was found.
2. First headquarters of Eliot Ness, the Transportation Building at Dearborn and Harrison.
3. U.S. Custom House at Harrison and Canal, the second Ness headquarters.
4. The Armory Police Station was located in the block lying between Van Buren and Harrison and Clark to LaSalle.
5. Whiskey Row, State Street from VanBuren to Polk.
6. The "One Way" Ride began outside the Auditorium Theater at Congress and Michigan.
7. The Karpen Building—910 S. Michigan (at Ninth Street).
8. Statue of General John Logan across the street.
9. Site of the 1864 "Wigwam"; Michigan Avenue between Eleventh and Twelfth Streets.
10. The "Smoke Filled Room," Blackstone Hotel, Balbo and Michigan Avenue.
11. The Custom House Place Levee spread west and south from the Polk Street Train Station at Polk and Dearborn.
12. The Metropolitan Correctional Center at Van Buren and Clark.
13. Chicago Police Headquarters, 1121 S. State (Eleventh and State).
14. Site of Cook County's first jail, Madison Street and Michigan Avenue.

15. The Bank of America Building at LaSalle Street and Jackson Boulevard where the *Wing Foot* crashed.
16. Offices of the Chicago Crime Commission, 79 W. Monroe Street.
17. Tony Lombardo was slain at Madison and Dearborn in 1928.
18. The "Days of Rage" riot occurred 61 years later at this same intersection.
19. The LaSalle Hotel stood at the northwest corner of Madison and LaSalle.
20. Counselors Row Restaurant, where politicians dined, is now the Alonti, across from City Hall between Randolph and Washington.
21. Site of "The Lottery," Crosby's Opera House just west of State on Washington; a casualty of the Chicago Fire.
22. The Lager Beer riot occurred in the Richard Daley Plaza, at Clark and Randolph, when this was City Hall in 1855.
23. The Ford Center for the Performing Arts stands on the site of the doomed Iroquois Theater on the north side of Randolph between State and Dearborn.
24. The steamship *Eastland* capsized in the Chicago River between Clark Street and LaSalle.
25. "Schemer" Drucci was gunned down across the street at Clark and Wacker.

26. "Long" John Wentworth slugged it out with Allan Pinkerton on the corner of State and Lake in the days when Lake Street was the main commercial thoroughfare of Chicago.
27. *Tribune* reporter Jake Lingle was gunned down by the mob in the causeway below Michigan and Randolph in 1930.
28. The *Chicago Democrat*, the city's first newspaper, was located at Clark and Wacker.
29. The building housing the old *Chicago Evening Post* and the *Chicago Times* still stands on Wacker Drive between Franklin and Wells.
30. The first *Daily News* building was located at Wells and Madison; it's a parking lot now.
31. The editorial offices of the *Chicago Inter-Ocean* were located at Monroe and Dearborn, a few doors east of the Chicago Crime Commission.
32. The "Madhouse on Madison Street," where Hearst reporters assembled the *Herald & Examiner* every day, was located at Madison and Wacker; the ugly building was torn down many years ago.
33. The deadly 1977 elevated crash occurred here, at Wabash and Lake.

main roads were virtually impassable in the rainy season and in winter. Worse yet, the waterways, the stagecoaches, and the railroads brought bounders, thieves, and cardsharps, who moved through Chicago's wharf districts and downtown hotels preying on the gullible and unsuspecting.

By 1834, Chicago's first reform movement was already in place. A Committee of Nine was formed to consider the gambling menace and the ways to inculcate religion, sobriety, and respect for the law into the hearts of men who heretofore had only answered to the Goddess of Chance.

Southern "blacklegs" (gamblers) driven out of the Mississippi Valley in the 1840s sought refuge in Chicago, plying their trade on the outskirts of the city, where they were least likely to offend the sensibilities of the laity and advocates of temperance and reform.

Organized crime in Chicago neither began nor ended with Al Capone. It was spawned in the rooming houses and downtown vice districts and took shape well before the Civil War. It was controlled by a syndicate of crime bosses, who exploited the weaknesses and inherent dishonesty of the city police and the elected officials who would consider any reasonable offer.

Commenting on the lax morals of Chicago politicians and the obsequiousness of the politicians as regarded criminal interests, one unhappy loser in the battle to reform the electoral process lamented, "Chicago is unique. It is the only completely corrupt city in America."

In the waning years of the nineteenth century, an army of bunco men and cardsharps worked the elegant lobbies of the Grand Pacific Hotel, the Richmond House, and the Tremont, drumming up business for one Michael Cassius McDonald, the duly anointed czar of the gambling syndicates and the "father" of modern organized crime in Chicago.

McDonald was the first crime leader to form strategic alliances with politicians and police by systemizing payoffs, channeling the graft, and electing his friends and allies to high office. He controlled the city for a period of twenty-five years. Unlike Capone, McDonald never had to contend with rival gangsters taking pot shots at him from passing automobiles, the meddling of the Internal Revenue Service, or the ravages of unchecked venereal disease.

Gambling czar McDonald was a skillful criminal operative, and his deluxe casino emporium at 176 Clark Street (at the intersection of Clark and Monroe Streets) was called the "Store." In the 1880s, captains and kings; politicians and cops; and even the mayor of Chicago, who left the premises with a smile on his face after losing twenty-five dollars at the faro table, patronized the "Store."

"There's a sucker born every minute!" exulted McDonald as he funneled thousands of dollars of gambling profits into the pockets of policemen, judges, the Cook

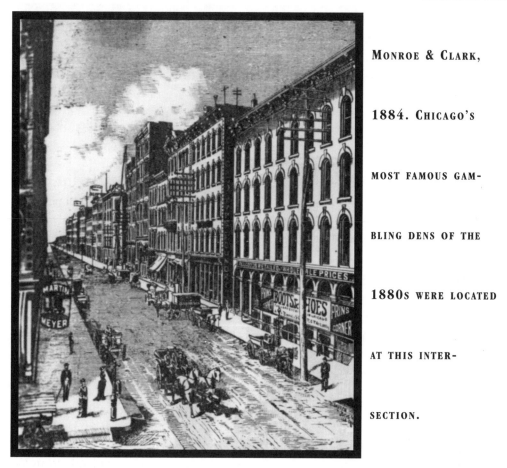

MONROE & CLARK, 1884. CHICAGO'S MOST FAMOUS GAMBLING DENS OF THE 1880S WERE LOCATED AT THIS INTERSECTION.

County Sheriff, and all of their sponsors. He ran a bail-bonding racket from inside the "Store." He bankrolled political campaigns, promoted horse races, owned a newspaper, built a street railway, and erected a luxurious mansion on Ashland Avenue, only a few doors down the street from his friend and ally, Mayor Carter Harrison I—all in an event-filled life.

About the only thing Mike could not do was prevent his feckless second wife, Dora Feldman McDonald, from straying into the arms of a teenaged boy named Webster Guerin. The violently passionate affair ended in murder when Dora stormed into Guerin's office in a fit of jealous rage one morning in February 1907 and shot the young man through the neck. This unhappy occurrence, coming late in McDonald's life, ruined his health and sent him to an early grave.

Mike McDonald left his imprimatur on Chicago, though his infamy was eclipsed by Al Capone, who was only eight years old when the brittle and exhausted gambling boss expired in the midst of a hard-fought legal battle that saved his wife from the gallows.

Randolph Street. "Gambler's Row." "Whiskey Row." Even the sporting houses of the Custom House Levee—which McDonald (whose first wife Mary was a devout Catholic) on principle assiduously avoided—comprised an empire of downtown crime, the wide-ranging legacy of which is discernible even today by the troubling appearance of Block 37 and the ragged-looking areas of the South Loop.

Infamy, it would seem, has a way of transcending time and space.

> We will begin our tour at Wells Street and Lower Wacker Drive. This portion of Lower Wacker Drive can be accessed from Lake Shore Drive at Randolph Street.

THE BODY IN THE TRUNK
August 11, 1961

Sickened by the fetid odor emanating from the mint-green Cadillac, and horrified by the site of the mutilated human remains stuffed inside the trunk, Chicago police officer George Petyo quickly turned away. Covering his nose while desperately trying not to cough up his lunch, Petyo called the morgue. "Send the wagon, I have a dead man here," he said, his voice cracking.

For several days, the cops had been aware of the illegally parked and abandoned car with the flat tire on Lower Wacker Drive. Two parking tickets were tucked under the windshield wipers, but it was that awful smell that finally convinced the curious cop to check things out. The vehicle was registered to one "William Kearney," one of the aliases used by the avuncular juice collector William "Action" Jackson.

In his younger years, Jackson's associates in the Chicago mob called him "Fat Boy," a cruel sarcasm that he deeply resented.

The Cicero gambler, procurer, and part-time loan shark weighed three hundred pounds. He drove expensive Cadillacs and ordered custom-made, white button-down shirts tailored to fit his enormous girth. The mere sight of this plodding gorilla pulling up to the curb instilled fear in borrowers who had failed to keep up with their juice loan payments to his boss, "Mad" Sam DeStefano.

The fleshy gangster finally shed the embarrassing nickname after he was released from prison in 1951. He had served four years for armed robbery, and the boys in the Chicago "outfit" finally accorded him a level of respect he believed he was entitled to all along. They began calling him "Action"—at least to his face.

In mob circles, things have a way of coming apart fast. Alliances are usually only temporary, and the man who is your friend today may stick a shiv in your back tomorrow. "Action" Jackson respected the code of silence. He was not a betrayer of the trust—or a rat, as it is commonly understood in mob parlance. But Fiore "FiFi" Buccieri, "lord high executioner" of the outfit, believed otherwise.

Jackson, a married man with two children, was scheduled to appear before Federal Judge William Campbell in late September on charges of helping to steal $70,000 worth of electrical appliances from the Burlington Railway yards in Cicero, and Buccieri was starting to get the shakes. There was no telling what this "Fat Boy" might say if he wilted under the pressure in open court.

For two weeks the Chicago Police had been seeking "Action" Jackson for questioning in the unsolved slaying of Ralph Del Genio, a truck driver for the Chicago Bureau of Sanitation, who by no small coincidence lived down the street from Jackson in Cicero. Del Genio was in debt to DeStefano, an impossible predicament for anyone to be in for long. It was the fifth unsolved murder linked to organized crime within two months, leading to nervous speculation that the city would soon explode in a bloodbath.

Buccieri fixated on Jackson. He was convinced that "Action" was tipping off the FBI about juice loan activities in the Western Suburbs. Suspecting betrayal, FiFi acted with ruthless abandon. Jackson was lured to a Southwest Side meat-rendering plant to face his destiny. There, Buccieri, James "Turk" Torello, Jackie "the Lackey" Cerone, Dave Yaras, possibly DeStefano, and other unnamed goons were lying in wait.

After securely binding his hands and feet, the outfit heavies impaled Jackson on a meat hook. Howling in pain, Jackson pleaded for mercy. They answered him by whacking the bulky gangster in the kneecaps, before applying a cattle prod to his genitals. "Are you a rat?" they asked. Jackson shook his head no. His sweat and blood formed puddles on the floor of the plant.

In Hollywood, Florida, about a year later, Torello—while the FBI secretly listened in—happily reminisced with his mob pals about the techniques of torture applied to Jackson and his stubborn refusal to 'fess up. "I still don't understand why he didn't admit he was a pigeon."

Jackson had nothing to confess, because he had flatly refused to cooperate with the Feds. He was an outfit guy, not a rat. Why couldn't the "G" (the Government) understand that?

For two harrowing days, Jackson precariously clung to life. His killers inflicted unimaginable tortures, until finally the shock and loss of blood proved to be too much. As they loaded Jackson into the trunk and wiped the blood from their hands, Buccieri glibly remarked, "Jeez, I'm really sorry the big slob died so soon."

No one was arrested for the murder of "Action" Jackson. It was just another unsolved hit, among a thousand unsolved gangland hits, dutifully recorded by the Chicago Crime Commission, record keepers of that sort of thing since 1919. However, this latest example of syndicate handiwork was something all together different. Veteran law enforcement officers, who had examined scores of crime scene photos and had come to view such daily horrors with cynical detachment, were shocked by the savagery of the deed. They talked about it in low, hushed tones for many years to come.

Lest anyone daydream about mob life—the after-hours allure of wise guys, night-clubbing with glamorous showgirls, and driving showy Cadillacs—the black-and-white morgue shots of "Action" Jackson offer convincing proof that the wages of sin can have a terrible price attached.

Each day, thousands of motorists rush by this desolate crime scene, which is engulfed in shadows, dust, and road grime. When the snow and cold and winter winds buffet the streets above, the underground intersection offers the homeless temporary shelter from the storm and a place to bunk in an uncaring world.

Return to Upper Wacker Drive at Monroe and go south to Jackson Boulevard. Turn left (east) on Jackson Boulevard and go east to Clark Street. Turn right (south) and take Clark Street to Harrison Street. Turn left (east) and go two blocks to Dearborn Street.

HEADQUARTERS OF THE UNTOUCHABLES
1928–1932

Eliot Ness was assigned a third-floor office in the Transportation Building at 600 South Dearborn Street overlooking Harrison Street (the southwest corner of Dearborn and Harrison Streets in the Printer's Row neighborhood of the South Loop). In the late 1970s, the commercial office buildings of Printer's Row were largely boarded up and abandoned, properties inhabited by squatters and junkies. The windows of the Transportation Building were blown out. The cracked sidewalks were littered with junk and, from time to time, the cops would be called upon to remove the lifeless form of a vagrant from one of the upper floors of this hopelessly blighted and derelict area. In the early 1980s, the bleak landscape began showing signs of renewed life. Commercial developers bought up the empty buildings lying along the south end of Dearborn Street, in anticipation of a growing demand for upscale housing in a historic urban setting. Printer's Row was rescued from oblivion and is now a chic, trend-setting residential area that is home to a major outdoor book fair in June, which attracts bibliophiles from all over the Midwest. The Transportation Building is a con-dominium development offering the usual collage of late-night convenience stores, a Thai restaurant, and other necessities of yuppie life.

On call twenty-four hours a day, the Bureau of Prohibition agents, which history has recorded as the "Untouchables," were paid the modest sum of $2,300 a year to wage a hopeless battle against bootleggers, rumrunners, and gunmen who operated in open defiance of the Volstead Act.

For the first year of the squad's existence, Eliot Ness, a twenty-six-year-old University of Chicago graduate, reported to George "Hard Boiled" Golding, an unpopular and officious bureaucrat who fouled up one investigation after another. Alexander Jamie, a wartime intelligence operative, who appointed Ness to be his special assistant shortly after the responsibility for Volstead enforcement was transferred from the Treasury to the Justice Department, succeeded Golding.

Eliot Ness was assigned to investigate bootlegging in Chicago Heights. For the first four years, Ness directed his troops from a modest corner office inside the Transportation Building, and did a good job in his initial assignment. But Ness was obsessed with bringing Al Capone to speedy justice in order to enhance his personal reputation and those of his men. Ness's ego and craving for publicity was his Achilles' heel, and ultimately led to his downfall.

Ness demanded unflagging loyalty and honesty from his recruits, who were drawn from universities, military intelligence, and the ranks of federal law enforcement. He preferred serious, unmarried, career-oriented men who were unafraid of danger. More than one Untouchable spoke multiple languages, which aided them considerably in their nightly forays into the immigrant Italian, Polish, and Yiddish neighborhoods.

Ness prided himself on his refusal to compromise his ideals with politicians or gangsters. He could not be bought, sold, or intimidated, and when it was discovered that one of the Untouchables was implicated in a corruptive act, the agent committed suicide. Politicians liked to drop by Ness's office, but they were all turned away, hats in hand.

Go back west on

Harrison Street,

cross the

Chicago River,

and proceed to

Canal Street.

SECOND HEADQUARTERS OF ELIOT NESS
AND THE UNTOUCHABLES
1932–1933

The United States Customs House, occupying the southwest corner of Harrison and Canal Streets at 610 South Canal Street, is a solidly built eleven-story government building opposite the Central Post Office. Both buildings are examples of the classic federal style of the 1930s. The Customs House was designed by James A. Wetmore with Burnham Brothers and Nimmons, Carr & Wright in 1932. The Prohibition enforcement bureau was transferred to the seventh floor of the new Customs House a few months after Deputy Administrator M. L. Harney promoted Eliot Ness to the rank of chief investigator as a reward for helping secure the evidence to indict Al Capone and sixty-eight other gangsters on federal charges. Ness briefly occupied a corner office on the seventh floor, facing the intersection. The office is still in use by U.S. Customs, but the building was carelessly remodeled—and much of its history obliterated—in 1992, when the beautiful marble adorning the walls was removed and carted down to the basement along with the federal eagles affixed to the elevator doors. Down the hall from the Ness office stands the library and courtroom where federal trials involving customs violations were once tried.

With Al Capone pondering his misfortunes from inside the federal penitentiary in Atlanta, there was little else for Eliot Ness to do in the spring of 1932 but shuffle papers in his new role as Chief Investigator for the Prohibition Bureau.

The government transferred him to Cincinnati a year later to chase down hillbillies and other moonshiners violating the Volstead Act. Ness told his biographer Oscar Fraley an apocryphal story about being fired upon by angry backwoodsmen armed with squirrel rifles. He claimed that the mountain men gave him "almost as many chills as the Capone mob."

In 1935, Eliot Ness was given an assignment more to his liking. He was dispatched to Cleveland to direct the Treasury Department's Alcoholic Tax Unit. With a change in mayors in 1935, Ness was named Director of Public Safety.

There occurred in Cleveland around this same time a series of baffling murders that Ness was powerless to solve. Faced with a sly, unseen opponent, who sliced and diced his victims before tossing body parts into the rivers, ravines, and gullies surrounding the city, Ness showed impotence and hesitation in the face of mounting public outrage.

The Torso Killer was never apprehended, and Eliot Ness faded into a life of quiet, lonely obscurity after failing to win the Cleveland mayoralty in 1947. He died exactly ten years later while proofreading the galleys to an autobiography that was about to bestow upon him greater fame than he had ever known in life.

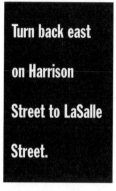

Turn back east

on Harrison

Street to LaSalle

Street.

A FORTRESS OF SOLITUDE: CHICAGO'S
ARMORY POLICE STATION
1872–1911

The Armory Station, the adjoining women's annex, and a fire station occupied a vast municipal compound extending from Van Buren Street on the north to Harrison Street on the south, and from Clark Street on the east to LaSalle Street on the west. In 1911, a printing company was erected on the northeast corner of Harrison and LaSalle Streets, where the First Precinct stationhouse had once stood. That same building is today the U.S. Federal Building at 527 South LaSalle, standing across the street from the LaSalle Street Train Station.

For forty years, the gloomy corridors and dank jail cells of the Armory Police Station were to Chicago what Mulberry Street represented to New Yorkers—the last stop for vagrants, sexual idlers, confidence men, footpads, bunco artists, shoplifters, forgers, murderers, pickpockets, gamblers, and international fugitives. Vice and crime were written all over the place, and the vile basement cells, where the worst criminal offenders were housed, stank of urine, stale tobacco, and human excrement.

When the twisted metal and debris of the Chicago Fire had at last been cleared away, the City Council appropriated $25,000 to construct a stone and brick "bridewell" on blighted land where prostitution had flourished until the very moment the flames devoured the vice district.

Mayor Joseph Medill and the city fathers hoped that the presence of the largest and most imposing police station in the Midwest would discourage the pimps and madams from returning to their former haunts in the nearby Custom House Levee. Instead, the criminal underworld built larger and more opulent bordellos, and business went on as usual under the watchful eye of a succession of Chicago police captains who commanded the district and regulated the nightly payoffs.

Six Armory captains went on to become superintendents of police. Dozens of famous magistrates passed judgment on criminal suspects awaiting a hearing in the Armory "bullpen," and some of the most famous reporters of the day including Brand Whitlock, Finley Peter Dunne ("Mr. Dooley"), Henry Barret Chamberlin, and James Keeley covered the beat for their respective newspapers.

English reformer and magazine editor William T. Stead spent many nights here, chronicling the deplorable conditions and inhumane treatment of inmates for his shocking 1893 exposé, *If Christ Came to Chicago.*

The Armory was the busiest spot along the Chicago rialto, particularly on Friday nights when three hundred men and women, on the average, were locked up. Men of every profession and social strata were herded together, sometimes ten or fifteen in a single cell.

Wife-killers Johann Hoch and Adolph Luetgert (the "Sausage Vat" murderer—see Tour 4) were taken to Harrison Street to be measured and photographed by the Bureau of Identification.

Several hardened criminals contemplated their future behind the somber fortifications of the Armory and decided that suicide was a far better bargain.

Dan Coughlin, convicted of murdering Dr. Patrick Cronin in the first "Clan Na Gael" trial and acquitted the second time around, spent his first night of arrest inside the Armory. Eddie Guerin, who escaped from Devil's Island in a rowboat, was also an occasional overnight visitor. "Molly Matches"; "Grand Central" Pete Lake; Louisa Jordan, "Queen of the Shoplifters"; the Car Barn Bandits; and the Count de Toulouse Lautrec, an international swindler from Montreal, were among the famous ne'er-do-wells of the Gaslight Era to occupy a cot in this unearthly place.

The Armory was reduced to a pile of rubble on June 28, 1911. The English suffragette Sylvia Parkhurst, on hearing of the demise of the Armory, described the building as "a disgrace to humanity."

Continue

east to

State

Street.

WHISKEY ROW
1895–1907

For a dozen years or so, a State Street vice district and rialto known as Whiskey Row extended south from Van Buren Street to Polk Street.

In the first decade of the twentieth century, vice and sin fanned out from the central city in every direction.

"WHISKEY ROW" HAS
REMAINED A BLIGHTED
SECTION OF DOWN-
TOWN. IT SERVES AS A
GRIM REMINDER THAT
THE REBIRTH OF AN
INFAMOUS AREA TAKES
MANY YEARS.
(Photo by author)

Despite angry denunciations, a daily procession of thrillseekers shuffled past the display windows of the great stores and commercial emporiums on North State Street to go slumming with the footpads, vagrants, and other disreputable persons inhabiting Whiskey Row.

No one really knows why the south end of State Street was dubbed "Whiskey Row." It probably had something to do with the "Mickey Finn Special," a potent blend of rot-gut whiskey and knockout drops administered to swells and wealthy out-of-towners by Finn, the larcenous owner of the Lone Star Saloon. After bouncing his dazed and confused victims into the alley, the tough and irreverent barkeep would rifle through their pockets and overcoats, removing the cash and valuables. Finn got away with the scam for years.

Whatever the true origins of the name, Whiskey Row was a curious blend of low-slung, ramshackle buildings housing wine rooms, dope dens, nickel theaters, dime museums, penny parlors, and arcades. The unsavory character of the district annoyed and angered the religious moralists and downtown bluebloods, who pressured the aldermen to rid the central city of such low and vulgar amusements.

Within plain sight of Schlesinger & Mayer's magnificent department store, the Senate, Little White City, Andy Craig's Tivoli, "Mushmouth" Johnson's gambling den at 464 South State, and the Grand Palace advertised a mind-numbing array of lurid attractions and sideshow oddities. It was a real sucker's paradise.

Following police crackdowns in 1905 and 1907, Whiskey Row was abandoned, but the seedy South Loop remained an area of ill repute well into the 1970s.

From his luxurious high-rise apartment at 1000 Lake Shore Drive in the 1960s, mob boss Gus Alex controlled a dozen State Street "bump-and-grind" joints within plain sight of police headquarters and the Pacific Garden Mission.

The Star & Garter Lounge was a State Street pleasure palace for many years. It was the most famous strip club of the South Loop rialto and offered conventioneers a quick fix, $2.50 drinks with a B-girl, and a chance to wager on the ponies. It was named after a legitimate Depression-era vaudeville palace at Madison and Halsted Streets that disappeared after World War II.

The second Star & Garter faced Sears Roebuck's flagship store in Chicago, which served as the nationwide headquarters for the Chicago retailer until the Sears Tower opened in 1973.

Urban renewal and the arrival of the Harold Washington Library finally laid waste to the Star & Garter and the last of the State Street pawn shops, burlesque houses, creep joints, and pornographic bookstores offering X-rated entertainment to lonely and anonymous men.

Take State north to Congress Parkway. Turn east and go one block to Wabash Avenue.

CHICAGO'S FIRST "ONE-WAY RIDE"
November 18, 1904

In 1904, there were 1,420 registered automobiles in Chicago. Motoring was still a novelty and an adventure, and the denizens of the underworld had not yet figured out that the horseless carriage might be used as a practical tool in the commission of a crime. That is, until a chilly November evening, when dashing ladies' man John William "Billy" Bate became the first Chicagoan to be taken for the proverbial "one-way ride." Bate left behind a trail of jilted girlfriends, whose happiness had been shattered by an unfeeling cad last seen chugging south on Michigan Avenue from Louis Sullivan's stately Auditorium Theater with his killer by his side.

He was the first Chicagoan to be murdered in an automobile. At 9:15 P.M., November 18, 1904, a mint-green Pope-Toledo touring car with a high square back turned south on Michigan Avenue from Congress Street. Wearing a chauffeur's cap, goggles, and driving gloves, twenty-two-year-old Billy Bate chatted pleasantly with his passenger, who introduced himself as "Mr. Dove"—perhaps a symbol of eternal peace? That is the way Edwin Slavin, a telephone operator at the Auditorium Hotel, and Chicago police detectives duly recorded the name.

The following morning, a farmer named Peter Freehauf found the car parked on a deserted road near his south suburban Lemont home. Billy Bate was slumped over the steering wheel, shot twice in the back of the head with a .22-caliber pistol.

Hours earlier, Mr. Dove had appeared at the registration desk of the Auditorium Hotel, asking the switchboard operator to telephone a Wabash Avenue garage for a car and driver. He said that he required a vehicle that would accommodate two passengers. After some quibbling, Dove agreed to pay the driver $5 an hour. A call was placed to Dan Canary's garage, where Billy Bate was passing time with the other chauffeurs in a game of coin toss.

Bate, a personable youth who was the son of well-to-do Kentuckians living at 1562 Kenmore (at Buena) on the city's North Side, asked the night manager if Dove was "all right."

"I don't know, and I don't care. Get your money and pick him up," came the sharp reply from Edwin Archer, who answered the phone but couldn't remember much more than the customer's voice quibbling over the rate.

Eyewitnesses described Mr. Dove as a patrician-looking gent attired in evening clothes and a derby hat. A bystander claimed to have overheard angry words exchanged between Bate and Dove as the car sped away from the curb. Beyond that, not much more could be said.

Later, three miles outside the town of Lemont on Archer Avenue in the distant southwest suburbs, a farmhand on his way home after a date observed three people in Bate's car, one of them a woman. Around midnight, Peter Freehauf heard a frightful pounding at his door, then two shots fired in rapid succession. Freehauf and his wife huddled in terror, refusing to open the door. At the crack of dawn, they ventured outside and found Bate, stiff in death's firm grasp. The loyal chauffeur still clutched the levers of his machine. He had been shot in the back of the head on the muddy, deserted road.

Mr. Dove continued on to Joliet by train, wagon, or some other conveyance, pausing at a boarding house to purchase a bottle of benzine to clean his blood-soaked clothes. A kitchen helper described Dove as a chain-smoking nervous wreck who smelled of women's perfume. It was noted that Dove's teeth were small and white, and his voice "as soft as a woman."

Recalling that Bate had a fiancée in Pittsburgh, the police were most interested in learning that Dove confessed to having a Pittsburgh girlfriend. Was the chauffeur slain by a jilted girlfriend posing as a man? The police eventually concluded that Dove was a man, albeit a very feminine-looking man.

Mr. Dove boarded a train in Joliet the following day, vanishing into the silent mists of time.

Lemont police pulled five love letters from the dead man's vest pocket. The next morning Hearst's gossipy *Chicago American* printed allegations that young Bate was keeping company with a wealthy society matron and had left a trail of broken hearts extending from New York to Chicago. One of the more poignant effusions was from a woman named "Rose," who wrote:

> *I understand you have won the love of Bertha, and I presume that you have no further use for me. I hope that your future love will be successful. Of course it is pretty hard on me, but I will let the matter drop and say no more. With Love, Rose*

A posse scoured the countryside for the remains of the second presumed victim in the theory that Bate's killer had ordered him to pick up the woman outside of Chicago. Dove, it was thought, murdered the woman, then turned the weapon on the chauffeur. Dead men, after all, tell no tales. The drainage canal and the roadside gullies were searched with no success. If there had been a woman slain in this peculiar drama, the killer had artfully concealed her remains.

The Bate murder mystery, forgotten and obscure in the annals of Chicago crime, was a subject of titillating newspaper gossip for many days and weeks to come. A female detective—a rarity in those days—was brought in to piece together the essential facts and draw a conclusion, but her theories lacked evidence and the investigation foundered. It was suggested by some that the crime was the last desperate act of a jilted lover. Others believed young Bate was part of a sinister conspiracy hatched by Dove, who betrayed his friend's confidence in the still of a late autumn night. Or maybe Bate was just a lazy idler who fell in with a gang of crooks.

In all likelihood, Billy Bate was the innocent victim of a murder plot hatched well in advance. The handsome young charmer happened to be in the wrong place at the wrong time, as is so often the case.

Chicago Passes Its First Automobile Licensing Law

SIDETRIP

July 1, 1899: A Notice to the Residents of Chicago

"It is proposed to establish a board of examiners, who will for a license fee of 35 cents issue a certificate to each applicant who is able to satisfy the board as to the mental balance, physical condition, reasonable knowledge of mechanical appliances and his familiarity with the parts of the automobile which might become disarranged. The penalty to be prescribed for operating an automobile without a license is a fine of from $5 to $25 for each offense. Speed of the automobile will be limited to eight miles per hour. The vehicles are required to have a fourteen-inch mechanically operated bell and approved brakes. After directing attention to the fact that not only is the safety of the persons in the vehicle as well as the person in the street entirely dependent upon the skill of the operator [we] call attention to the fact that unlike horses the auto-mobiles cannot of themselves avoid danger." (Author's Note: *Chicago recorded its first traffic fatality less than a year later.*)

To continue our tour, proceed east on Congress Parkway one block to Michigan Avenue and turn right (south). Continue to Ninth Street.

THE BATTLE OF MICHIGAN AVENUE
August 10, 1926

Though we cannot say with certainty that Billy Bate, a jilted girlfriend, or even Chicago gangsters invented the "one-way ride" and the drive-by shooting, we are quite confident in the belief that the technique was perfected by rival bootlegging factions during Prohibition. It is hard to believe that staid Michigan Avenue, with its posh retail stores, imposing office towers, and world-famous Art Institute, should serve as the backdrop for a lesser known, but no less significant, drive-by episode from the Roaring '20s. The Standard Oil building at 910 South Michigan was completed in 1911 and opened as the Karpen Building. In 1926, the year that Hymie Weiss caused the city unintentional notoriety and civic embarrassment by helping to expose its criminal-politico connections, the Standard Oil Company, a few doors south of the old YWCA building at 830 South Michigan Avenue, had just had seven stories added to the existing structure. The oil company's headquarters was a hub of commercial activity in 1926, and it was here that many local politicians held court with their bagmen and favor seekers. The petroleum giant moved to a more spacious and modern facility in 1969, letting the 910 building go to seed. Spared the wrecking ball, the functional skyscraper is currently being converted into 267 residential condominiums by Villas Development of Oakbrook.

For two years Vincent "Schemer" Drucci and Earl "Hymie" Weiss played a dangerous cat-and-mouse game with Al Capone and his well-armed gang of South Side racketeers. There was little chance for Dion O'Banion's successors up on the North Side to do much more than maintain the status quo and respect territorial boundaries.

If Drucci had agreed to remain on the North Side, and if Capone were content to rule the Stockyards District north to the Madison Street dividing line, there might have been a semblance of peace in Chicago. But neither side respected treaties, or thought very much of the other side. So, from time to time, there had to be a public airing of differences.

Weiss struck hard at the Capone forces, mortally wounding Johnny Torrio outside his South Side home. Torrio, by now in semiretirement, survived the savage attack but fled Chicago, leaving his empire of crime to Al Capone.

In retaliation for attempting to knock off his former boss, Capone marked the North Siders for death and assigned gunman Louis Barko to handle the job.

"Schemer" Drucci maintained a residence at the Congress Hotel, four blocks north of the Standard Oil Building at Ninth Street and Michigan Avenue. On the morning of August 10, 1926, following a late breakfast, Weiss and Drucci rendezvoused at the Congress and walked briskly toward the Standard Oil Building, where they were to meet with Sanitary District Trustee Morris Eller.

Eller was the mobbed-up boss of the "Bloody" Twentieth Ward and a cheap racketeer disguised in a politician's pinstripes. In 1927 he was promoted to City Collector after gangland returned William Hale Thompson to the mayor's office.

Waiting in Eller's Metropolitan Sanitary District office that morning was the mob's favorite mortician, John V. Sbarbaro, now an assistant state's attorney. (For more about Sbarbaro, see Tour 2.)

Drucci carried in his pocket $13,200 in cash, presumably a down payment on a piece of Chicago real estate, but more likely bribe money earmarked for the North Side gang's Twentieth Ward sponsors.

As the two were about to pass through the neo–Italian Renaissance doors of the skyscraper, Louis Barko and three confederates bolted out of a car on the east side of Michigan Avenue and without warning opened fire. Windows crashed and masonry chips flew as Drucci dived for cover behind the parked cars. Weiss scampered into the lobby of the building, unhurt, but shaken.

The Schemer returned their fire before commandeering a vehicle belonging to one C. C. Bassett, a startled motorist trapped in the crossfire. Drucci's escape was interrupted by the arrival of the police, who dragged him off the running board. It was a bloodless affair, and the shooting was over in less than two minutes. When questioned by police at the South Clark Street Station, the gangster denied ever setting eyes on Barko.

Drucci dismissed it as just one of those "boys-will-be-boys" things. "They told me to kick in with the thirteen grand. They were after my roll," he said.

Hymie Weiss's mother, Mary, posted the necessary bond, freeing her son's pal from the stir.

The meeting in Eller's office, needless to say, was postponed. The indignant undertaker denied even knowing Drucci. "Why drag me in it?" grumbled Sbarbaro. "Just because some hoodlums want to shoot in front of our offices? It looks like if a cat has kittens in this town Morrie Eller gets blamed for it!"

Before another year would pass, both of O'Banion's henchmen would come face to face with Sbarbaro in far less hospitable surroundings than South Michigan Avenue— in the embalming room of his Wells Street undertaking parlor.

THE WHOLE WORLD WAS WATCHING,
BUT WERE THEY PAYING ATTENTION?
August 26, 1968

At the south end of Grant Park, directly across from the Standard Oil (Karpen) Building, where Ninth Street dead ends at Michigan Avenue, stands the towering bronze equestrian statue of Major General John A. Logan. Designed by Augustus Saint-Gaudens, one of the foremost sculptors of nineteenth-century America, the Logan monument was solemnly dedicated by the State of Illinois in 1897, eleven years after this favorite son had expired at age sixty. General Logan, a beloved public figure in his day, served several terms in the U.S. Senate and was a perennial candidate for president on the Republican ticket during the gilded age of American politics. There are many forgotten statues to Civil War heroes tucked away in remote corners of Grant and Lincoln Parks. And while they mean very little to modern-day Chicagoans who race by on their bicycles without giving the matter a moment's thought, to earlier generations they were powerful and enduring reminders of our nation's remarkable resiliency in a time of grave national crisis. The Logan monument, located high atop a knoll overlooking Michigan Avenue, memorialized a time in our nation's history when a great conflict touched the lives of most of its citizens. During the 1968 Democratic National Convention disturbances outside the Conrad Hilton Hotel, a youthful demonstrator, protesting America's involvement in the Vietnam War, scaled the statue and attempted to put a Vietcong flag in the General's raised hand. The symbolic gesture—laden with irony, for Logan was known as the "Great Volunteer" in his day—incited the Chicago Police to madness. To the repeated chant of "The whole world is watching!" the antiwar protesters, who descended on Chicago that week to exercise their Constitutional right of dissent and gain worldwide notice, engaged the cops in a confrontation that a future governor of Illinois would label as a "police riot."

Around suppertime, a bedraggled group of demonstrators, who had earlier that day paraded past police headquarters at 1121 South State Street to protest the arrest of Yippie (the name given to a member of the Youth International Party) leader Tom Hayden, gathered on Michigan Avenue south of the Conrad Hilton Hotel, where the Democratic delegates were headquartered.

A contingency of blue-helmeted Chicago Police in riot gear stood along the sidewalks with their batons poised for action. Edgy and tense, the cops had had their fill of these "punk college kids" spitting in the face of decency and law and order. In Mayor Richard J. Daley's rigid blue-collar union town, the actions of longhaired rebels and pot-smoking draft-card burners did not sit well.

The response of the police to the open rebellion unfolding before them in the streets of Chicago was a mixture of astonishment and uncontrollable rage.

As the protesters marched by, they began a rhythmic chant: "What do we want?" "Revolution!" "When do we want it?" "Now!"

The crowd drifted into Grant Park, circling General Logan's statue. In stony silence the police watched while one college-age demonstrator attempted to climb the statue, then another. Cries of "Ho, Ho, Ho Chi Minh!" and "Pigs!" echoed across Michigan Avenue as a reckless youth flashed the peace sign once he was secure astride the General's horse. After a momentary struggle, the demonstrator succeeded in placing the flag of the Vietcong in the General's hand. With that, a reserve squad of police, who had formed a skirmish line north of the statue, closed in with their batons in the upright position.

The protesters on the statue were forcibly dragged off, some of them kicking and gouging the officers as they responded with terrible force. One of the protestors was hit in the groin. "Fuck you! Fuck this country!" screamed a young man, who broke his arm in a crashing fall. A teenage girl standing nearby was clubbed in the altercation, and when the cop who had hit her noticed a photographer recording the image for posterity, the photographer wisely lowered his camera.

By 5:35 P.M., more than a thousand protesters had assembled outside the Hilton Hotel, egged on by the incendiary speeches of veteran antiwar activist David Dellinger. According to reports, rocks, bottles, and cherry bombs were hurled at police.

The Logan incident was a microcosm of five days of madness that infected the city of Chicago during the "Siege of '68." Far more serious confrontations between police and protesters were to erupt in Lincoln Park and outside the Hilton over the next few days.

By refusing to take a more enlightened view of the situation and grant the kids a permit to sleep in the parks, Mayor Daley exposed his city to unending criticism and ridicule. He drew a hard line and summoned Illinois National Guardsmen to Chicago while his cops ran wild, beating newsmen, TV cameramen, and even a few innocent bystanders like Hugh Hefner, who went for a late-night stroll outside his Playboy mansion, and was cracked over the head.

Chicago American columnist Jack Mabley described the unfolding melee in the streets as a "horrifying view of the police state."

"The force used was the force necessary to counter the mob," retorted an indignant Police Superintendent James Conlisk, who owed his appointment to his father's close friendship with Mayor Daley.

On the other hand, Abbie Hoffman and his legions of hippies and Yippies could not have choreographed the ensuing mob action more perfectly. Yippie leaders came to

Chicago with a premeditated plan to goad the cops and uptight city officials into a public relations fiasco that would never be forgotten. Daley, unknowing, out of touch, and unsympathetic to opposing viewpoints, played right into their hands. The result was chaos.

Daniel Walker, a future governor of Illinois, served as vice president of the Chicago Crime Commission during the time of the disturbances. In his final report to the National Commission on the Causes and Prevention of Violence (the book was published as *Rights in Conflict*), Walker concluded that a "police riot" had occurred in the streets of Chicago, adding, "But while it is clear that most of the protesters in Chicago had no intention of initiating violence, this is not to say that they did not expect it to develop."

Walker's controversial stance offended Daley and the party regulars, but it helped catapult this combative liberal populist into the governor's chair in 1972. He served one term of office and another term in a federal prison after being convicted of bank fraud in 1987.

As the Vietnam War scaled down in the early 1970s, the "movement" fizzled. Was it a lessening of idealism, or did the Civil Rights activists, who for the most part stood on the sidelines during Convention week, sense that once the war ended, the self-styled radicals from Main Street U.S.A. would return to their comfortably secure lifestyles in suburbia?

McClellan Nominated! August 29–31, 1864

SIDETRIP

The Civil War was in its fourth year when Democrats gathered in Chicago. They nominated a "peace" candidate, General George B. McClellan, whose inaction in the face of a hostile Confederate army poised outside Washington, D.C., had compelled President Lincoln to ask for his resignation.

The nation was torn and divided, but Chicago proved to be a good setting for the Democrats because the entire city was filled with Southern sympathizers ("Copperheads") and rebel agents. A plot to free the rebel prisoners of war at Camp Douglas was hatched in Canada as a prelude to a military insurrection scheduled to commence with the opening of the Democratic Convention.

The threatened rebel uprising never materialized. (For details, see Tour 8.) Promising to seek a negotiated peace with the Confederacy, General McClellan and his running mate, George Pendleton, were nominated inside a circular outdoor tent situated between Eleventh Street (then known as Park Row) and Twelfth Street on the east side of Michigan Avenue. Early published accounts describe this makeshift convention hall as the "Wigwam," or the "Amphitheater."

LITHOGRAPH OF THE 1864 "WIGWAM," WHERE THE DEMOCRATS NOMINATED THE "TIN SOLDIER," GEORGE B. MCCLELLAN, AS THEIR STANDARD-BEARER.

(Courtesy of the Chicago Historical Society)

The Chicago Tribune, *a partisan Republican journal, sneered at the extravagant work of the treacherous "Copperhead traitors." "Crowds of visitors throng its extremes and loaf around outside gaping as if they thought the structure would give out the prophet of peace before the appointed time," the paper reported. "They will also be disappointed in the event—a defeat which will endure to all eternity!"*

In 1864, this busy intersection was a public park, a patch of green south of the downtown business district. Today, a commuter rail line slices through Grant Park where the Wigwam was believed to have stood.

The wooden frame tent, designed by O. I. Wheelock and built in record time by John Donlin, accommodated sixteen thousand people and cost the national party sixteen thousand dollars. Its very presence outraged local property owners living along Michigan Avenue, who failed in their efforts to secure an injunction that would block the Democrats from converging in their backyard for their get-together.

The "Tin Soldier," as McClellan was called, inspired intense loathing among the pro-war faction of the party. Delegate Benjamin Harris of Maryland was fuming with disgust when he stormed the dais to harangue against McClellan. "You ask me to go home to bound and persecuted Maryland, which has suffered every injury since the tyrant put his iron heel upon it, and to vote for George McClellan, the very man who destroyed liberties . . . I will never do!" McClellan garnered 202 votes and was nominated by acclaim. He vowed to end the rule of the tax-and-spend Republicans and bring peace to the war-torn land.

In the fall election, President Abraham Lincoln received 212 electoral votes to McClellan's paltry 21.

To continue our tour, return north on Michigan Avenue to Balbo Drive.

THE SMOKE-FILLED ROOM
June 12–13, 1920

Buttressing Chicago's front yard, the stately Sheraton Blackstone Hotel overlooks Grant Park at the northwest corner of Balbo Drive and Michigan Avenue. The twenty-two-story hotel was designed by the architectural firm of Marshall and Fox and opened in 1909. Ten presidential candidates set up their headquarters here in the days when Chicago played host to at least one national nominating convention every four years and the Chicago Coliseum in the 1400 block of South Wabash was the preferred venue for the national spectacle.

From an adjoining suite on the fourth floor of the Blackstone, Ohio Senator Warren G. Harding was summoned to Rooms 408–410 and asked if there was any reason why he shouldn't become the standard-bearer of the Republican Party in the 1920 presidential election. The party bosses wanted to know if there was anything about Harding's moral character that would bring scandal down upon the GOP if it were agreed that Harding should become the "compromise" candidate and break a hopeless deadlock on the convention floor. Entering the smoke-filled suite that reeked of stale cigars and the even worse stench of political wheeler-dealing, Harding, a handsome figure with matinee-idol looks and a yen for beautiful young women, was beaming. "Gentlemen," he said, "there is no reason why I cannot be president of the United States!"

No less an authority on American politics than the distinguished journalist Arthur Brisbane declared Warren Gamaliel Harding of Marion, Ohio, a "middle of the road man, a man who is safe, conservative, and sane." Searching for some notable event or accomplishment to distinguish the Republican nominee from his GOP rivals, who wondered what form of trickery deprived them of the nomination in the waning hours, Brisbane gently reminded his readers that Mr. Harding had delivered a "forceful" speech nominating William Howard Taft for President at the 1912 Convention, also held in Chicago.

Warren Harding was an affable country newspaper publisher, a "Main Street Babbitt," who served as a director of a bank and as a trustee of the Trinity Baptist Church when he was tapped by Ohio party boss Harry Daugherty and Boles Penrose of Pennsylvania to take a stab at electoral politics. Dull, unimaginative and in lockstep with the conservative agenda of the party ideologues, Harding had only his good looks and easygoing nature to fall back on. He was rather like Chance the gardener in Jerzy

Kosinski's satirical novel, *Being There*. Only Warren Harding certainly did not belong there, or anywhere else in the public forum for that matter, other than in Marion, Ohio, attending to his printing presses and church philanthropy.

He came to Chicago having already spent $113,109 on his campaign, but he faced formidable opposition from the party stalwarts. Illinois Governor Frank Lowden, married to George Pullman's daughter, enjoyed the support of the eastern bankers. Major General Leonard Wood of New Hampshire and Senator Hiram Johnson of California were strong contenders with broad-based popular support.

In the blistering heat of early June, the shirt-sleeved delegates failed to achieve consensus. Governor Lowden was vulnerable after two Missouri delegates revealed that they had taken $5,000 in Lowden bribe money. General Wood was considered a tool of big business and unelectable after the press bared details of improper campaign donations received by his backers. The Harding forces pressured the leather-lunged Senator Johnson to release his 140 votes in return for the second spot on the national ticket, but Johnson demurred and a compromise candidate had to be secured.

Meeting in secret at the Blackstone long into the night, Johnson, Henry Cabot Lodge, Medill McCormick of Illinois, and other party leaders agreed upon the harmless Harding, who was ushered forth at 2:11 in the morning.

After Lowden released his delegates the next day, the tide turned to Harding on the tenth ballot. Breaking the deadlock, the "dark horse" stormed to the nomination with 674 votes.

From central Ohio, the candidate's father, Dr. J. P. Harding, expressed fear that his son would be "assassinated," a fear not entirely without substance, as it turned out.

When approached by reporters, Florence Kling DeWolfe Harding, the long-suffering wife who had married Harding over her father's strong objections, told the press with wry cynicism, "I am tremendously pleased of course. But I think my husband is worthy of this honor and I am confident to be in the *reflected* light."

With 61% of the popular vote, Harding easily defeated James M. Cox in the November election. Harding then launched the nation on a conservative course in the areas of taxation, spending, tariff protection, and the rights of labor. But within three years, the Harding administration was besmirched by scandals in the Interior and Navy Departments, the Veteran's Bureau, the Justice Department, and the western oil fields. Harding rewarded Harry Daugherty, his political witch doctor at the Chicago convention, with the job of Attorney General, but Daugherty would be indicted on charges of corruption before his term had run its course.

It is probably no exaggeration of history to say that Harding engaged in extramarital sex with young Nan Britton inside the White House, and that the woman gave birth to the philandering president's daughter out of wedlock. Britton published a memoir of her schoolgirl crush and subsequent affair with Harding. Harding died suddenly and quite mysteriously on August 2, 1923, in his Pullman coach outside of San Francisco, just as allegations of political impropriety involving the administration began to circulate in the national press.

For many years thereafter, the rumor mill churned wildly claiming that Harding was poisoned in order to protect the alabaster reputation of the First Lady. There is little substance to these allegations, but in weighing the merits of the chief executives, most historians concede that Warren Harding, flawed by bad personal habits, was the nation's worst president.

Turn left (west) on Balbo Drive and proceed to State Street. Turn left (south) and go to Polk Street and turn right (west). Go to Dearborn Street.

THE CUSTOM HOUSE PLACE LEVEE
1875–1905

The wicked Custom House vice district sprang out of the ashes of the Chicago Fire and continued to be a blight upon the downtown business area for nearly three decades. Like most "segregated" high-crime areas within large metropolitan areas—places where vice, gambling, and drug trafficking are indulged—the Custom House district thrived on two essential elements: a major east-west railroad corridor connecting the central city to the hinterland, and an alliance with the police, who were headquartered at the Armory Station nearby. The Custom House district existed within the boundaries of the First Ward, between Harrison Street to the north and Polk Street and the Dearborn Station (also known as the Polk Street Station) to the south. Dearborn Street formed the eastern boundary, and Clark Street, the western boundary. However, these were only imaginary lines drawn in 1894 by the English reformer William Stead and based on the observations and learned opinions of Stead's Chicago traveling companion and tour guide, Hank North. The actual boundaries were constantly expanding and contracting with the arrival of each new saloon and disreputable house, and with each police crackdown. In its heyday, the district probably stretched as far east as State Street, where it bumped into "Whiskey Row," and as far south as Twelfth Street. In 1905, the last of the vice merchants were driven into the South Side "badlands" in order for Chicago's business titans to redevelop this end of the Loop for more desirable and practical purposes. Within a few years, soaring loft buildings housing the major commercial printing establishments of the city were built on the vacated lands of the former bagnios, opium dens, and panel houses. Printer's Row, as this area is now called, came into its own as a con-

dominium and rental community in 1979, long after the last of the commercial plants fled to the suburbs, or simply went out of business. The railroad freight yards have also disappeared, and the neighborhood is very quiet now. Only the old Dearborn Station remains, once the eastern terminus for the legendary western rail routes, now the Dearborn Street Galleria.

From its earliest days, Chicago thrived on its notoriety as a "wide-open" town, embracing fortune seekers, grifters, gamblers, and fakers to its bosom. The flagrant and unhampered reign of vice began in the 1850s (perhaps even sooner), when the "Sands" district north of the Chicago River aroused comment and stirred public action against the miscreants who sold sex and salacious amusement to the river men and longshoremen who plied the waterways in and out of the central city.

Commercialized vice flourished in the Civil War period. By 1867 it was estimated that 1,300 prostitutes (a ratio of one prostitute for every 230 inhabitants) roamed the rough, uneven streets of Chicago. Randolph Street, in the heart of the downtown area, between State and Dearborn was awash in bordellos, wine rooms, and cheap dance halls in plain view of the courthouse. It was called "Gambler's Row," because a man gambled with his life if he strayed too far into one of the dangerous clip joints.

The Chicago Fire swept away hundreds of disease-ridden prostitution cribs in the South Loop. City planners, dreaming of creating a modern post-fire "utopia," never imagined that vice in all of its insidious forms would quickly return. When threatened with repression, or even when closed down because of a cataclysmic occurrence like the Great Fire of 1871, the criminal underworld simply regroups and shifts its operation elsewhere.

And so it was in the 1880s when Chicago matured as a city and took its place as the rail center of the nation. Waves of foreigners, speculators, and adventure seekers poured into the city through the Polk Street train station (Dearborn Street Station), one of six major depots in Chicago. The railroads and the coming of the 1893 World's Fair signaled the end of pioneer Chicago, and the birth of the cosmopolitan city. And with them immigrants by the tens of thousands poured into the city.

The purveyors of vice satisfied an immediate demand for the forbidden fruits of life. "Greenhorns" and naive young women stepping off the train at Polk Street were recruited for immoral purposes and lured into the scarlet patch originally known as "Cheyenne," then later as the Custom House, by an army of "cadets" (pimps) plumbing the lower depths for Lizzie Davenport, Mary Hastings, Emma Ford, Flossie Moore, Lizzie Allen, and lesser known madams.

The most infamous bordello of the Gaslight Era was Carrie Watson's place at 441

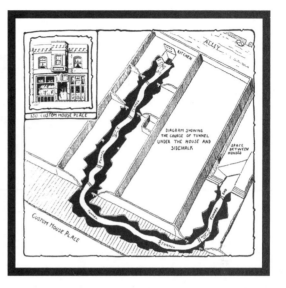

Cutaway view of a

Custom House Place

bordello with tunnels

below (above). Inside a

Levee "resort" (right).

South Clark Street owned and maintained by Caroline Victoria Watson who went into business for herself in 1868. Despite the scandalous circumstances of her life, Carrie is remembered as a cultured woman possessing stunning beauty. When she appeared before Alderman John Comiskey's investigating committee in 1868, she carried her Sunday parasol into the chambers, and was simply dazzling in a diamond-studded white dress. Her brothel enjoyed a worldwide reputation for its ambiance and charm and the cordiality of the sixty women in her employ.

Other "resorts" along the Custom House were not nearly so elegant or refined. Very often a country rube would carelessly stray into a "panel" house, where he would be drugged and strapped to the bed while an accomplice to the swindle, slipping through a hidden sliding wall, stole the man blind and ran off with his clothes. Few of these shame-faced victims would report the crime to the police, lest they suffer a public humiliation by having their names published in the morning papers.

In his published memoir of police life in the Levee, Detective Clifton Rodman Wooldridge drew attention to the dangers of the panel house. "To show the

WILD NIGHTS IN THE CUSTOM HOUSE PLACE LEVEE.

vast extent to which this panel house thieving is carried, it is only necessary to state that $150,000,000 were stolen annually in 1892, 1893, and 1894. Ten thousand dollars may have been taken this way in the levee district in one night."

By the time of the 1893 World's Fair, Chicago had seemingly become the "Paris of

America" for its many debaucheries and illicit attractions. At its very worst, the Custom House Levee was the moral equivalent of the Five Points in New York, San Francisco's Barbary Coast, and the Basin in New Orleans.

William Stead, writing for the English journal *Review of Reviews,* counted thirty-seven houses of ill-fame, forty-six saloons, eleven pawnbrokers, a shooting gallery, and numerous gambling dens, as he researched conditions for his book *If Christ Came to Chicago.*

Clark Street, one block north of Harrison, was for a time Chicago's original Chinatown and "hophead heaven." According to author Charles Washburn, every basement in the block was an opium den or chop suey restaurant. Immigrant Chinese men, who migrated to the United States without their wives or children because of the racist and exclusionary laws of the day, were often forced to settle in close proximity to the flesh peddlers. The Asian community, unwelcome in other quarters of the city, was tolerated by the criminal underworld. The hop joints became a natural extension of the segregated district, and the Chinese immigrants its service providers.

The official city policy toward the segregated vice areas was one of toleration—provided the inmates of the bordellos kept to themselves and the decent element was not harassed or bothered.

But this was never the case. Granted extraordinary latitude by city officials, the vice merchants exploited the situation. Streetwalkers were arrested in the theater district. Pimps solicited female clerks, engaged in socially acceptable (albeit low-paying) professions, with offers of employment as they attended to their customers from behind the sales counters of the large department stores.

By 1903 the conditions were intolerable, and the reformers would no longer stand for it. That year, a wave of indictments, inspired by the municipal leagues, church laymen, and the mayor, sent the resort keepers scurrying for cover—that is, to the emerging South Side Levee at Twenty-second Street and Wabash, where they were warmly received. The Custom House Place Levee vanished by 1910. Commercial printing houses and bookbinderies lining Dearborn Street, Plymouth Court, Federal Street, and Clark Street, which were erected between 1900 and 1915, permanently erased the vice district.

Today, only the ghostly shell of the train station remains where many unfortunate young women stepping off their Pullman coach daydreaming of romantic interludes, theater, and carriage rides through Lincoln Park were accosted by leering pimps standing ready to introduce them to a life of horror and depravity: "Hello deary, what cooks?"

The Chicago Metropolitan Correctional Center

S I D E T R I P

By a strange quirk of fate, the former location of Carrie Watson's ostentatious brothel is now the site of the Metropolitan Correctional Center (MCC), a 1975 Harry Weese design located at Clark and Van Buren Streets. The odd, triangular building houses four hundred federal prisoners awaiting trial. Correctional employees describe the MCC as Chicago's "Club Fed," offering gang members, mobsters, and government snitches all the comforts of home, though Gerry Scarpelli would have probably disagreed, if only he were still around.

There is no need for outside bars because there's no chance of escape. The windows are only five inches wide.

Realizing the hopelessness of his predicament, MCC inmate Gerald Hector Scarpelli covered his face with two plastic bags and hanged himself inside a shower room on the twenty-first floor on May 2, 1989. Scarpelli, regarded as a paid assassin for the Chicago "outfit," saw no future as a jailbird after providing the FBI with sixty-two pages of transcripts describing wise-guy burglaries, contract murders, gambling and juice loan operations from Waukegan south to Calumet Heights.

To continue,

return to State

Street and go

south to

Eleventh Street.

ELEVENTH AND STATE
1928–1999

When the new fifteen-story Chicago police headquarters building opened at 1121 South State Street in the fall of 1928, the beleaguered cops evacuating the horribly overcrowded Harrison Street Precinct could hardly believe their eyes. Six modern high-speed passenger elevators served police, their employees, and the public, with three other elevator shafts constructed for the easy transport of prisoners to their cells and the courtrooms. In its day, Chicago's police headquarters was a spacious, modern facility housing 2,500 inmates in the lockup. The exterior walls of cut stone reached up to the fifth floor, with light buff face brick extending to the cornices. The entrance lobby was constructed of cut marble—a masterful execution, conceived by Deputy Police Commissioner John Stege, who aided Colonel A. A. Sprague, Commissioner of the Public Works Department, as he drew up the final rendering based on practical considerations. Over the years there have been numerous additions and improvements made on the property, including a state-of-the-art communications center installed by Superintendent Orlando W. Wilson in 1961 at a *cost of $3.5 million dollars. Eleventh and State, which has housed the First District for the past seven decades, has reached the end of its useful life, however, and will soon close. The decaying, rat-infested cop shop has seen better days. Toilets overflow. The roof leaks. Cockroaches call the place home. The lockup is cramped (by Year 2000 standards) and fetid. In 1976, someone tried to blow up the building, but the explosive device was found in a trash container and quickly disposed of. A new $65 million police headquarters is nearing completion in "Bronzeville," an up-and-coming neighborhood on the city's South Side once scarred by gang violence and drug running. Site selection was hardly coincidental. Historically, police buildings of this size and scope tend to locate in dangerous, crime-ridden neighborhoods where they form the locus of community life. This was certainly true in the days of the Armory Precinct, built within the boundaries of the old Custom House Place, and at Eleventh and State, which stood only a few blocks north of the cabarets and honky-tonks controlled by the Al Capone interests. Now, the James J. Riordan Chicago police headquarters, housing the John Dillinger death mask among other crime curios of the past, is an intrusion in an up-and-coming part of town. The winos, derelicts, and habitués of the save-a-soul missions a few blocks north on State Street are rapidly being forced out as young urban professional couples, their Shih Tzus, and the downtown lawyers move in.*

The first wagonload of prisoners transferred from detective headquarters at 611 South Clark Street were led through the doors of Eleventh and State on September 14, 1928. Deputy Commissioner John Stege beamed as he surveyed the brightly painted quarters and modern amenities.

"We may miss little things we've always had to do—like running up three flights of stairs every time the telephone rang and such, but it's the finest thing of its kind anywhere and we've needed it for years."

John Stege, the fearless Prohibition-era rackets buster, might well be described as the *only* honest cop in Chicago during the years of the Capone dynasty. He had his hand in everything, including the design plan for the new headquarters building, approved by the voters of Chicago by referendum on February 24, 1925. Designed purely for police activities and court trials, Eleventh and State cost taxpayers $2.5 million, quite a sum in those days.

The war stories are legendary. It has long been rumored that narcotics detectives occupying office space on the unlucky thirteenth floor dangled criminal suspects by their heels outside the window until they cracked.

The most famous criminals of yesteryear were mostly incarcerated in other district

CHICAGO POLICE HEADQUARTERS
AS IT APPEARED IN 1928 AND AS
IT APPEARS TODAY. THE 1960
MODERNIZATION RUINED THE
EXTERIOR APPEARANCE OF THE
CLASSICALLY DESIGNED BUILDING.

lockups. But not all the lawbreakers roaming through the dingy hallways were finger-printed and ID'd by the criminal records bureau. Some of them wore suits and ties and carried briefcases. They were called lawyers.

Traffic court and the high-volume misdemeanor courtroom attached to six Chicago Police Department area headquarters spawned Operation Greylord, a 1980s judicial corruption scandal of unprecedented proportions, even by the earlier standards of graft, which had been honed to near perfection in wicked old Chicago.

"It started out by someone doing a favor, and then some more favors," recalled retired judge James Bailey. "When does a favor become a bribe? Eventually the guy doing the favor says I'm not doing this for the fun of it. I think I should be compensated for it." A stunning cast of crooks—ninety-two judges, bailiffs, political satraps, police officers, deputy sheriffs, defense attorneys, and clerks—was richly compensated over a period of years.

In the dizzying days of the mid-1970s, when this mountain of corruption was tolerated and ignored, there was still a women's court located inside Eleventh and State. It was occasionally the practice for a judge in that court to demand sexual favors of the pathetic junky prostitutes herded into the bullpen following a long night of work on the streets.

One veteran police officer recalled standing at street level waiting for an elevator to convey him to the upper floors of police headquarters. When the doors slid open, a Women's Court judge, well known to the officers and civilian employees assigned to the Chicago Police Department First District, was leaning against the back wall surrounded by giggling two-dollar hookers. One of them was performing a sexual act upon the judge, who was neither surprised nor embarrassed.

"In those days the judges, the lawyers, and the people we arrested were all joined at the hip," the officer reminisced. "It was a brotherhood of corruption where you take care of me, I'll take care of you."

Convicted Greylord judge Raymond Sodini presided over Gambling Court at Eleventh and State in the raucous carnival-like atmosphere where lawyers had to shout at the judge, and each other, in order to be heard above the din of the passing South Side elevated trains. Hot dogs and sausages were grilled on the windowsills while Misdemeanor Court was in session. In the outer corridors, personnel bickered over the split of bribe money flowing into Judge Sodini's courtroom.

Posing as a corrupt state's attorney (code name Leo Murphy), FBI mole Terry Hake triggered the most far-reaching investigation into judicial corruption in this nation's history. U.S. Attorney Dan Webb announced the first nine indictments in Operation Greylord in December 1983. Before it was over, fifteen corrupt judges were convicted on an assortment of bribery charges. Two of the disgraced jurists would take their own lives rather than live out the rest of their days in humiliation.

It was all so sadly reminiscent of Ben Hecht's tongue in cheek *Front Page* spoof of Chicago in the 1920s, except that Greylord was a story without end. It was so typically Chicago.

The Calaboose, 1837

S
I
D
E
T
R
I
P

Chicago's first lockup for criminal malefactors was a crudely fashioned log cabin standing on the edge of Lake Michigan near the present-day intersection of Madison Street and Michigan Avenue. Sheriff John Shrigley, said to be a "clever man with his fists," personally escorted his prisoners to jail on foot.

Go south to Roosevelt Road and turn left (east). At Wabash Avenue, turn left (north) and go to Harrison Street. Turn left (west) on Harrison Street and go to State Street. Turn right (north) on State Street and go to Adams Street. Turn left (west) on Adams Street and go to La Salle Street. Turn left (south) on LaSalle Street and go to Jackson Boulevard.

THE FIERY INFERNO FROM THE SKY
July 21, 1919

The Bank of America Building (most recently the Continental Bank Building) at 231 South LaSalle Street occupies the former site of the Illinois Trust and Savings, where the Goodyear dirigible Wing Foot crashed through the skylight on July 21, 1919. The nation's first civil aviation disaster killed thirteen people. Then, as now, the intersection of Jackson and LaSalle formed the hub of Chicago commerce.

Eight minutes before the close of the business day, a great shadow passed over the marble rotunda of the Illinois Trust and Savings Bank. Inside the bank, 150 tellers and clerks were balancing their cash drawers and were otherwise engaged in the frantic rush to go home.

Overhead, a 153-foot dirigible powered by 95,000 cubic feet of flammable hydrogen hovered over the central business district, when suddenly the craft buckled and plunged to earth. The fuselage of the *Wing Foot* tore through the iron supports holding the glass skylight in place. The twin LaRhone engines and the two gasoline tanks crashed to the floor of the bank, splashing fuel on the bank employees standing within a fifty-foot radius.

Eyewitnesses described the unfolding chaos and panic as a "blast furnace raining hell" upon the unsuspecting. The rotunda was instantly consumed in flames, trapping the tellers behind their wire cages and cutting off their routes of escape. Screaming stenographers, their long skirts on fire, raced toward the exits, but walls of fire blocked their path. Some were burned beyond recognition.

Employees trapped on the second floor of the building plunged to their deaths in a desperate attempt to flee the inferno. The intense heat made rescue work virtually impossible, and the immense size of the curious crowd outside the bank impeded efforts of firemen, ambulance drivers, and undertakers to reach the stricken and the dead.

The death ship was owned by the Goodyear Company of Akron, Ohio, and was engaged in a test and demonstration flight, designed to promote the advantages of lighter-than-air travel to the public, when fate intervened. The craft had taken off from a hangar at the White City Amusement Park at Sixty-third Street and South Park Avenue shortly before 9:00 A.M., and had bobbed lazily across the afternoon skies 1,200 feet above Grant Park, on up to Diversey Harbor.

The *Wing Foot* was piloted by Jack Boettner, a veteran of forty-two dirigible flights, who blamed static electricity and a rush of air from the propellers, which fanned the exhaust flames against the bag. Boettner and his four passengers parachuted off the blimp, but only the pilot managed to escape serious injury or death.

Though never officially charged with criminal negligence, Boettner absorbed much criticism and personal blame after repeatedly contradicting himself during the inquest chaired by future Illinois governor Henry Horner. The Goodyear Company agreed to arbitrate all claims through Horner's three-member committee. The bank chipped in $1,000 for each victim's family and reopened for business the very next day after the disaster. Such was Chicago in its busy, formative years, cranking along at a breathless breakneck speed, never pausing, never looking back.

Five days after the blimp plummeted to the floor of the bank, a race riot erupted on the city's South Side, crowding this story off the front pages of the daily newspapers. But the *Wing Foot* tragedy, and others like it involving lighter-than-air craft, underscored the need for proper safety precautions and, more important, foreshadowed the end of an era. With the crash of the *Hindenburg* at Lakehurst, New Jersey, in 1937, the curtain closed on the dirigible as a means of commercial travel.

The *Wing Foot* disaster is all but forgotten. No plaque or historical marker commemorating this horrible human calamity can be found on the walls of the Bank of America Building. Business, after all, *must* go on.

The First Public Enemies List, 1930

SIDETRIP

In April 1930, the Chicago Crime Commission published the groundbreaking "Public Enemies" list of who was who among the active criminal elite in America. It was no small coincidence that every name on the list was a notorious Chicago gangster.

The list was compiled by Executive Director Frank Loesch with the help of former newspaper reporter Henry Barret Chamberlin, who helped found the civic watchdog agency back in 1919. The concept was copied (actually stolen) by FBI Director J. Edgar Hoover, who insinuated that it was his own pet idea.

The Chicago Crime Commission is the oldest and most venerable of the nation's sixteen citizens' crime commissions. At one point in the 1950s and 1960s, nearly every newspaper reporter and cop in town carried around at least one dog-eared copy of Virgil W. Peterson's annual Report on Chicago Crime. *In those days, it was common practice for investigators to highlight with a felt-tip marker the names of the hoods and the bars, restaurants, and social clubs they frequented. Very often the research data supplied by Executive Director Peterson was of far greater value than the fragmented bits of information assembled by the Chicago Police Department's organized crime intelligence unit.*

Peterson was associated with the CCC continuously from 1942 until 1969. He died in 1989, and the Commission has ceased publishing the hard-hitting, lavishly detailed crime annuals.

However, the Chicago Crime Commission and a dedicated staff of interns continue their worthy mission in a private suite of offices maintained on the sixth floor of the Bell Federal Savings Bank building at 79 West Monroe.

The Public Enemies List

1. Al Capone (died of natural causes in 1947)
2. Tony "Mops" Volpe (died of natural causes)
3. Ralph "Bottles" Capone (died of natural causes in 1974)
4. Frank Rio (died of natural causes in the 1930s)
5. Vincenzo DeMora (alias Vincent Gebardi, "Machine Gun" Jack McGurn, murdered in 1936)
6. James Belcastro (died of natural causes)
7. Rocco Fannelli (died of natural causes)
8. Lawrence "Dago" Mangano (murdered in 1944)
9. Jack Zuta (murdered in 1930)
10. Jake Guzik (died of natural causes in 1956)
11. Frank Diamond (real name Frank Maritote, murdered in 1954)
12. George "Bugs" Moran (died of natural causes in 1957)
13. Joe "Polack Joe" Saltis (died of natural causes in 1947)
14. Joe Aiello (murdered in 1930)
15. Edward "Spike" O'Donnell (died of natural causes in 1962)
16. Frankie McErlane (died of natural causes in 1932)
17. Vincent McErlane (died of natural causes)
18. Danny Stanton (murdered in 1943)
19. Myles O'Donnell (died of natural causes in 1932)
20. Frankie Lake (died of natural causes in 1947)
21. Terry Druggan (died of natural causes in 1954)
22. William "Klondike" O'Donnell (died of natural causes)
23. George "Red" Barker (murdered in 1932)
24. William "Three Finger" Jack White (murdered in 1934)
25. Joseph "Pepy" Genaro (murdered in 1935)
26. Leo Mongoven (died of natural causes)
27. James "Fur" Sammons (died of natural causes)
28. Willie Niemoth (died of natural causes)

To continue, take Jackson Boulevard east to Dearborn Street. Turn left (north) on Dearborn Street and go north to Madison Street.

DEATH IN THE AFTERNOON
September 7, 1928

Tony Lombardo was assassinated in the presence of thousands of downtown shoppers and office workers just one block west of State and Madison, known internationally for many decades as the world's busiest corner. Lombardo headed the 25,000-member Unione Sicilione, an Italian-American fraternal organization considered by many to be a Mafia "front" and a clearinghouse for organized crime's activity in the Midwest during Prohibition. One by one, the leaders of this politically important group were picked off by rival gangs (and each other) with amazing alacrity and ease. Lombardo and a bodyguard were the latest victims. They were shot at point-blank range in front of Raklios Restaurant at the southwest corner of Madison Street and Dearborn, which is now part of the uninspiring First National Bank Plaza erected in 1969. It was 4:30 in the afternoon. Thousands of people had momentarily paused to watch a construction crew raise an airplane up the side of the Boston Store at State and Madison, an impressive seventeen-story steel-frame skyscraper designed by the Holabird & Roche architectural firm in 1915, when the shots were fired. The Boston Store, a family business owned by Molly Netcher Newbury, closed its doors in 1948, but its original terra cotta building at One North Dearborn (northeast corner) remains. The upper floors have been converted into office spaces with an assortment of retail shops serving the public at street level.

Tony Lombardo and his bodyguard, Joseph Ferraro, had called it a day. Switching off the lights in their eleventh-floor offices inside the Hartford Building at 8 South Dearborn Street, the two men came down in the elevator and walked north on Dearborn Street past the Hamilton Club, domain of the city's blueblood elite, and then to Madison Street, where they turned westward.

A third man, named Joseph Lolordo, who had dropped by the office to pay his membership dues and chat with his friends, joined them. Lolordo said he did not know where Lombardo was going, but decided to tag along out of respect to Lombardo, an important cog in the criminal underworld of Chicago.

A year earlier, alert Chicago Police detectives had foiled an ambush plot directed at Lombardo and arrested a team of would-be assassins who had rented a flat directly across the street from his West Side residence at 4442 West Washington Boulevard. The earlier attempt was hatched by a rival Sicilian faction interested in removing Tony Lombardo from the mantle of leadership. Now, the same group had devised a more efficient plan.

Fifty feet from Raklios, an eyewitness reported seeing several men bolt from the doorway of the restaurant. One of the assassins raced up behind Lombardo and discharged two dum-dum bullets into the back of his head. Ferraro was shot in the back by the second gunman and died minutes later, refusing to identify the shooter to a police officer who arrived on the scene.

It was pandemonium as bystanders ran for cover inside the restaurants and stores. With revolvers drawn, the police charged through the crowd in every direction looking for the gunmen, but the killers had already vanished into the throng of people, many of whom were out-of-town guests staying at the nearby Morrison Hotel.

Chicago Police pinned the murder on unknown New York gunmen, whom they believed were avenging the death of Frankie Uale, killed by Al Capone's men two months earlier.

Before his widow could be told the news of her husband's death, Tony Lombardo had already been loaded into a police wagon and taken directly to the Western Casket Company at 226 West Randolph where he was measured for his coffin.

Mrs. Lombardo was preparing the evening meal when she was notified by a newspaper reporter. After confirming the report with detectives at the Central Police Station, the young widow cradled the receiver of the phone and slowly turned to her two children, ages six and three. "Your daddy's dead," she sobbed. "You got no daddy anymore. He won't come home anymore. And I was waiting supper on him."

DAYS OF RAGE
October 12, 1969

The shouts and tumult of the 1960s anti-war movement knew many battlefields. Berkeley. Washington, D.C. Kent State. Columbia University. Chicago. By the autumn of 1969, the movin' and groovin' days of peace, love, and flowers were just about over. After the 1968 Democratic Convention riots, demonstrations against the war in Vietnam turned increasingly violent. The "armies of the night" were on the march, the country was adrift, the Manson "family" had performed their senseless slaughter, and a deep sense of alienation permeated the American spirit. A new decade was at hand. Richard Nixon was in the White House, and the prospects for a negotiated peace seemed hopeless. Meanwhile, the body bags were piling up on airport tarmacs, and the radical Weathermen faction of the Students for a Democratic Society (SDS) threatened armed insurrection and a campaign of domestic terror against the institutions of the "establishment." Were they political idealists committed to the ideals of the sixties, or criminal thugs exploiting the deep divisions in American society? In the "Days of Rage," divisiveness boiled over after a City of Chicago Assistant Corporation Counsel was paralyzed from the neck down while attempting to collar a young demonstrator during a wild melee near the northwest corner of Madison Street and Dearborn across from the First National Bank Plaza. The restaurant, tavern, and other buildings on that block in 1969 were ground to dust. The new Three First National Plaza, a symbol of commerce, big money, capitalism, and all the trappings of the conservative establishment that the Weathermen threatened to annihilate through revolutionary force, stands on the site today.

> *"You don't need a weatherman to know which way the wind blows."*
> *—Bob Dylan*

Repudiating the ideals of peaceful, nonviolent confrontation set forth by the Reverend Dr. Martin Luther King in the early 1960s, the Weathermen, underground campus zealots, detonated four thousand bombs against government and military institutions between 1969 and 1970.

In the fall of 1969, a gust of wind blew into Chicago when the Weathermen precipitated a pointless mob action in a continuing effort to spark a revolution that, for the most part, failed to excite anyone over the age of thirty with a mortgage, a car payment, and a set of responsibilities.

Despite the Wagnerian-sounding appellation, the "Days of Rage" riot in downtown Chicago was a tempest in a teapot; a signpost from the sixties all but forgotten today, except for the liberals and idealists who are left to ponder noble intentions that stalled in the confusion and disillusionment of the 1970s.

It began in Haymarket Square; scarcely a week after a dynamite explosion nearly toppled the statue commemorating Chicago Police Captain William Ward and the bloody events of May 4, 1886. (For details of the Haymarket Riot, see Tour 6.)

SDS organizers promised a peaceful rally and march from Randolph Street and the Kennedy Expressway to Grant Park, where speakers planned to voice their opposition to U.S. military efforts in Southeast Asia.

About 250 marchers suddenly became violent as they turned east on Madison Street from LaSalle Street. The protesters–turned–vandals hurled bricks through a ticket office of the Union Pacific Railroad at that intersection. A volley of stones shattered the plate glass windows of Maxim's Restaurant at 2 North Clark Street.

While midday shoppers watched with a mixture of curiosity, disgust, and apprehension, the slogan-chanting demonstrators exasperated police by splitting into small groups. Armed with small rocks and pipes wrapped inside newspapers, the marchers fended off blows from police batons as they jostled pedestrians and weaved in and out of traffic in their attempts to avoid being tossed into paddy wagons for transport to Eleventh and State.

In the midst of the chaos, Assistant Corporation Counsel Richard Elrod decided to lend assistance to the helmeted cops.

Only a week before the "Days of Rage," Elrod was knocked down in front of the Dirksen Federal Building at 219 South Dearborn and kicked in the head by one of the protestors demonstrating in support of the "Chicago Eight"—on trial for fomenting riots during the 1968 Democratic Convention. "I just wanted to show that I could take a blow as well as any of the uniformed men. Now I'm one of the gang," Elrod joked.

Dick Elrod was the son of Arthur X. Elrod, legendary gambler, saloonkeeper, bail bondsman, criminal court bailiff, and political heavyweight in the Twenty-fourth Ward on the West Side, a syndicate battleground during a rough-and-tumble era of Chicago politics, which had of late become much more "refined."

Young Elrod was at the time a loyal lieutenant in Mayor Richard J. Daley's invincible political organization, and was counted on to move the Machine forward in the coming years. As such, Elrod was designated the city's official "observer" during protest marches. He had been in the thick of the action since 1965, when the period of anti-war and civil rights unrest commenced in the streets of Chicago.

Unafraid of mixing it up with younger, more agile men of nineteen and twenty, the thirty-five-year-old Elrod plunged into the main body of radicals charging east on Madison Street toward Grant Park, when suddenly a voice cried out, "Grab that man!"

Elrod, a former football player at Northwestern University, attempted to tackle a demonstrator hurrying toward a saloon at 56 West Madison. Witnesses agreed that Elrod managed to grab hold of the boy but lost his balance and crashed to the ground at an odd angle. The man he had been chasing allegedly whirled around and kicked the fallen Elrod in the head before breaking free.

Dick Elrod couldn't move. "Help me up," he asked Sergeant Ray O'Malley. Blood trickled out of his mouth, and there was a welt on his forehead. "Let me walk away from this thing like a gentleman." But there was something seriously wrong. Elrod said he had no feeling in his legs. Placed on a stretcher, Elrod was transported to the University of Illinois Hospital where he was diagnosed with paralysis from the neck down.

Meanwhile, twenty-two-year-old Bryon Flanagan, a tall, curly-haired young man from Southampton, New York, was dragged off the pavement and arrested. Flanagan and scores of other demonstrators were taken down to the Cook County Jail at Twenty-sixth and California where they were mixed in with hard-core felons, drug pushers, and murderers from the streets. Flanagan told reporters that his people were "treated very badly," and accused Warden Winston S. Moore of violating their civil rights.

The "Days of Rage" ended with a whimper. Flanagan's sister raised bail, and he ended up a footnote in history—except to Richard Elrod, who endured a painful rehabilitation and would never again be able to walk without benefit of a cane.

An intelligent and personable politician, Elrod parlayed the sympathy vote into success at the polls and was elected sheriff of Cook County in 1970. He was the first sheriff allowed to succeed himself under the terms of a new state constitution, and would complete a record four terms of office before losing to James O'Grady, a former police superintendent, in 1986.

Despite instituting long overdue reforms and modernizing the Cook County Jail, Elrod was blamed for a corruption scandal within his police department dubbed "Operation Safebet." High-ranking vice detectives were accused of accepting payoffs from organized crime figures and the proprietors of suburban strip clubs in return for protecting vice operations, mob-run "chop shops," and illegal gambling games scattered across the more remote areas of suburban Cook County. A four-year undercover FBI sting operation rocked the Sheriff's Police in the mid-1980s. Two senior aides were sentenced to fifteen-year prison terms, costing the out-of-touch sheriff his job.

Elrod was accused of failing to rein in his suburban vice unit and assailed in the press for awarding honorary sheriff's badges and guns to deputies and Chicago ward heelers, whose sole qualifications were their political connections to the administration. It was an ancient custom predating Elrod, but the stench of scandal wafted through the entire department.

Describing the brutal inefficiency of the Cook County Sheriff's Police, the *Southtown Economist* bitterly noted in a 1990 editorial "that while the department has virtually no history of solving serious crimes it has earned the reputation for committing them."

Losing to O'Grady was a bitter personal blow, but Dick Elrod's exile into private life was only temporary. He was appointed a Cook County judge on July 28, 1988.

And whatever happened to Bryon Flanagan, Elrod's adversary for a brief, defining moment during the "Days of Rage"? It remains a mystery. A Chicago jury acquitted him of assault charges, agreeing with defense attorneys that he was blameless for Elrod's crippling injury. Undoubtedly, he has deemed it prudent to steer clear of Daley's Chicago in the intervening years.

In January 1977, Bernardin Dohrn announced the dissolution of the Weathermen after accusing fellow members of "ideological corruption." Dohrn sensed, as did so many others in the movement, that the wind had changed directions in America and the politics of confrontation was passé once the threat of the draft was removed and peace was restored to war-stricken and divided Vietnam. The peace movement atrophied in Chicago and was irrelevant by the time of Watergate.

The former sixties populists can take solace in the lyrics of the old Beatles song, *Revolution*:

> *But if you start carrying pictures of Chairman Mao,*
> *You're not gonna make it with anyone anyhow.*

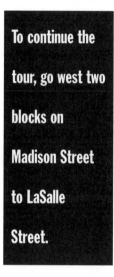

To continue the tour, go west two blocks on Madison Street to LaSalle Street.

"I NEVER SAW ANYTHING SO GRUESOME— EVEN IN BOMBED-OUT GERMANY"

June 5, 1946

The LaSalle Hotel was a Holabird & Root masterpiece; a spacious and comfortable hostelry opened to the public in 1909 at the northwest corner of Madison and LaSalle Streets. It was stated in the original prospectus that, "The Hotel LaSalle will be the largest, safest, and most modern hotel in America outside of New York City!" The LaSalle was built and owned by the Stevens family, who later built the Stevens Hotel (now the Conrad Hilton & Towers at Michigan Avenue and Balbo Drive). The owners and architects claimed that the structure was fireproof, which proved to be as exaggerated a claim as the arrogant boast of the White Star Line that the Titanic *was unsinkable. In 1936, a new ownership group modernized the building, but chose profits over safety. Fire concerns were ignored. The twenty-two-story LaSalle Hotel was a tinder box, and it only took a carelessly discarded cigarette to turn the building into a roaring inferno that claimed sixty-one unfortunate souls. Thirty years after the deadly fire, the mighty and glorious LaSalle Hotel was demolished. A functional office building at 2 North LaSalle Street stands in its place.*

On a dark and moonless June night in 1946, an astonishing tragedy jarred the complacency of a sleeping city. It had been forty-three years since the calamitous Iroquois Theater blaze, long enough for a new generation to forget how important safety precautions were in averting disasters in public buildings.

A few minutes past 12:30 A.M., when most of the 1,100 guests at the LaSalle Hotel had turned in for the night, George Le Vaque, night manager of the Silver Bar cocktail lounge off of the main lobby, heard the terrifying shout of "Fire!"

Le Vaque raced to the north side of the lobby, where he saw a sheet of flames erupting from the dumbwaiter. "I ran back and grabbed seltzer bottles to squirt out the fire, but they did no good," he said.

A lit cigarette, carelessly tossed into the pit of the Number Five elevator shaft, triggered the blaze. Within moments the fire roared out of control. Le Vaque called the fire department, but it was already too late. The whole ceiling was ablaze, and long tongues of flame extended from the north elevator to the mezzanine. The flames spread upward through the elevator shafts, reaching the seventh floor where they stopped. Deadly smoke poured into the corridors all the way up to the top floor.

Many of the LaSalle Hotel guests, thinking that the verbal warnings were a thoughtless prank, remained in their rooms, where they suffocated from the dense, toxic smoke.

As the fire spread, escape routes were cut off. Terrified and desperate guests threw hastily scrawled S O S notes to the street level, pleading for the help that would never come. Fire department ladders in those days only extended as far as the eighth floor.

Scantily attired guests in their nightclothes prepared to leap from the upper floors, heedless of the warnings of the firemen, who begged them to remain patient.

Luggage and personal belongings were hurled to the ground, crashing into the swarms of spectators, who were pushing and shoving past a police cordon on LaSalle Street for a better view. Moments later, several of the doomed guests trapped in the coffinlike darkness leapt out the windows to the pavement or fell upon the glass canopy on the third floor where they perished.

Air Force lieutenant Chandler Royal, who assisted in the rescue efforts, described the charred and gutted corridors of the hotel as being worse than bombed-out Germany. "So many blackened corpses in the halls and rooms . . . it was ghastly," he said in a quivering voice.

They were spectral reminders of the holocaust that pointed to the appalling lack of safety measures. The owners of the LaSalle exhibited a shocking disregard for repeated warnings. As early as 1927, hotel proprietors were told to limit the number of combustible draperies. Worse, there were no printed instructions in the guestrooms advising patrons what do in the event of fire.

Avery Brundage, maven of the Olympics and proprietor of the LaSalle Hotel, who was acting on behalf of the parent company, refused to issue a statement. While the dead and dying were being laid out in the corridors of City Hall for purposes of identification, Brundage said he did not wish to be disturbed.

Turn right (north) on LaSalle Street and go north to Washington Boulevard.

THE LAWBREAKERS OF BOOTH ONE: "OLD MEN FROM ANOTHER TIME"
1970–1991

An unpleasant slice of Chicago political folklore vanished on July 15, 1991, when Nick Borovilos bid farewell to his patrons and padlocked the doors of Counselors Row, his legendary coffee shop at 102 North LaSalle Street, directly across the street from City Hall. Borovilos could no longer keep up with his rent payments after a busboy's careless mistake sent his most important customers—the politicians, lawyers, favor seekers, coat carriers, judges, payrollers, and bagmen—scurrying for cover. The Alonti Deli & Salad Bar rents space at that address these days, but the restaurant was nearly empty during a recent noontime visit. It was apparent that the pols preferred to nosh in less conspicuous places.

For twenty spasmodic years of political intrigue, infighting, and double-dealing within the gloomy marbled corridors of the "Hall," Counselors Row Restaurant was a refuge for the political parasites that exploited a system driven by influence peddling and bribery.

Associate judgeships were brokered to friends of the First Ward Democratic organization. Commercial properties were rezoned for the pleasure of city contractors and real estate developers with inside connections. Criminal trials were fixed. Liquor licenses were granted; deals were cut. It was the "system," and those who aspired to drink from the trough understood the rules of the game, as well as the appropriate time to pitch the deal, or fold.

An oil painting of the late Mayor Richard J. Daley hung prominently with the photos of lesser mayors—solemn reminders of the enduring strength of the big city machine, which even survived the jarring political vacuum that accompanied Daley's sudden death in 1976.

The restaurant afforded its well-heeled clientele of pinky-ring politicos and County Building toadies a quiet intimacy—and the chance to decide weighty affairs of state away from the prying eyes of the media and idealistic reformers pledging to overturn a system that had been nurtured, patted, and refined by the acknowledged experts of graft for 150 years.

Counselors Row was a dimly lit rendezvous for the vanguards of the "Machine," the aldermen and state pols perpetuating Daley's particular brand of political "clout." Located just a few feet from the entrance, "Booth One" was reserved for First Ward Alderman Fred Roti; State Senator John D'Arco Jr.; First Ward secretary Pat Marcy—all of whose offices were housed in the same building—and First Ward Committeeman John D'Arco Sr. It was their custom to gather here midday to review the most recent requests for favors.

On the heels of the successful "Operation Greylord" prosecution, which revealed a numbing pattern of Cook County judicial malfeasance and led to the indictment of eighty-four individuals and the conviction of fifteen Circuit Court judges, the FBI and federal prosecutors decided to expand the investigation in order to establish long-suspected links between organized crime figures and public officials.

In the spring of 1989, the FBI installed secret video surveillance inside Counselors Row. They trained the lens of the camera on Booth One, with the hope of gathering enough incriminating evidence to help federal prosecutors build upon Greylord. The camera had been in place for less than three months when a busboy accidentally discovered the device tucked behind an odd-looking small hole, triggering new scandals and a fresh debate over the public's "need to know" versus their right to privacy.

The outraged county politicians followed the path of the wires down into the basement of the skyscraper. Newspaper revelations forced shame-faced FBI agents to dismantle their command post in the eighth-floor offices of an investment firm, but the Feds by then had enough evidence to start to turn the wheels of justice despite this rather embarrassing faux pas.

The spying on Booth One was dubbed "Operation Gambat," for the gambling habits of attorney-turned-informant Robert J. Cooley. One of the things uncovered by the Feds was a scheme to bribe Judge Lawrence Passarella in order to secure an acquittal for one Michael Colella, who was accused of beating police officer Cathy Touhy with a metal pipe in 1984. Colella was defended by Cooley, the First Ward mouthpiece, who compromised his principles for a once-in-a-lifetime chance to become a "player." Not surprisingly, Colella was found innocent of the charges, but the residents of Cook County knew better. Wisely, they voted Passarella off the bench.

Pat Marcy and Fred Roti were accused of paying $75,000 in bribe money to Judge Thomas Maloney in return for a favorable ruling in a Chinatown criminal case. Applying phraseology suitable to the circumstances by which Marcy and Roti were trapped in the net, U.S. Attorney Fred Foreman accused the First Ward fixers of masterminding a "movable feast of corruption."

Alderman Roti's lawyer argued unconvincingly that his client was a politician from the "old school; brought up in the saloon-bred politics of past decades. It involves old men from another time."

With world-weary resignation, former U.S. Attorney Thomas P. Sullivan summed up Chicago politics thusly, "There seems to be in Chicago and the surrounding areas a pervasive, deep-seated lack of honesty at all levels of government and business. I do not know whether it is worse here than elsewhere, but I do know that public and private corruption is commonplace in our city."

When Fred Roti was convicted on racketeering, bribery, and extortion charges on January 15, 1993, he became the eighteenth Chicago alderman in twenty years sent into exile. Was it merely coincidental that these ignominious events of recent political First Ward corruption, when the featured item on the menu at Counselors Row was a five-dollar hamburger called the "Lawbreaker"?

Continue north on LaSalle Street to Lake Street. Turn right (east) and go to State Street. Turn right (south) on State Street and go two blocks to Washington Street.

THE LOTTERY
January 21, 1867

Nineteenth-century architect William W. Boyington, his reputation eclipsed by that of Louis Sullivan and Daniel Burnham in more recent years, is mostly forgotten today. His most notable commissions were swept away by the Chicago Fire, leaving only the Water Tower on North Michigan Avenue as representative of his contributions to pre-fire Chicago's skyline. In the last year of the Civil War, Boyington drew up the blueprints for Uranus D. Crosby's $600,000 Opera House, a theater and restaurant complex that defied the economies of scale. Before it was claimed in the unrelenting wall of flame that swept through the business district from the south on October 8, 1871, Crosby's Opera House was acknowledged to be the finest theater west of the Hudson River. It was located a few doors west of State on Washington Street—yet another example of the curse on Block 37. In 1920, at a cost of $3,175,750, the Ascher brothers management company erected the Loop Theater, a vaudeville and movie palace at 16–30 West Washington. The foundation was laid on the same ground once occupied by Crosby's. The Loop, one of twenty-three theater holdings in the list of Ascher enterprises, is remembered today as the Schuessler-Peterson boys' final destination that Sunday afternoon in 1955 when they were abducted and murdered (see Tour 4).

The Republican Party returned to Chicago to nominate General Ulysses S. Grant and his running mate from Indiana, Schuyler Colfax, as their standard-bearers in the presidential election of 1868. For the setting of their convention, they chose Crosby's Opera House, built with a "lavish disregard of business principles," according to one contemporary source.

Crosby expended his entire fortune building this limestone monument that elevated Chicago commerce and the arts to new heights. Kinsley's Restaurant occupied the ground-floor space with Root & Cady, a musical publishing firm. The W. W. Kimball Piano Company (the Kimball family lived in Gilded Age splendor on Prairie Avenue until the neighborhood went into decline) had its sales showroom adjacent to Kinsley's.

From the very beginning of its short, unhappy existence, Crosby's stood on the edge of disaster. The gala grand opening of the famous "temple of art" had to be postponed for five days because of the assassination of President Abraham Lincoln on April 15, 1865.

Nearly bankrupted by the venture, Uranus Crosby disposed of the theater's famous art collection—and most of the interior furnishings—in a gigantic public lottery held on January 21, 1867, a year before the GOP nominating convention. Lottery chances were sold for $5 a ticket. When the great day arrived, the Board of Trade men proclaimed

CROSBY'S OPERA HOUSE IN RUINS FOLLOWING THE CHICAGO FIRE.

a public holiday and closed the floor. A carnival-like atmosphere spread through the city. Who was this Crosby anyway? A swindler? A blackguard? A horse thief?

Promoters sold 210,000 chances, but Crosby held 25,000 of them. It took 113 spins of the lottery wheel before a winner was announced. Skeptics frowned on the tawdry spectacle, believing that Crosby had rigged the drawing to his favor.

The winner of the drawing, one Abraham Lee of Prairie du Rocher, Illinois, located 275 miles south of Chicago, sold the building back to Crosby for $200,000. Lee was a man of simple virtues. What did he know about promoting high art on the frontier?

Mr. Crosby shook hands with Mr. Lee and regrouped. He was a clever man with a fair amount of intelligence and wit and somehow he managed to pull together another $80,000 to refurbish the theater building in the months following the convention. His two-year renovation was completed on October 7, 1871—the day before the great Chicago Fire consumed the "palace of opera more gorgeous than anything in the West."

Continue south on State Street to Madison Street. Turn right (west) on Madison Street and go one block to Dearborn Street. Turn right (north) and go to Randolph Street. Turn left (west) and go one block to Clark Street.

THE BEER RIOT THAT MADE CHICAGO FAMOUS
April 21, 1855

The deadliest civil disorder of the antebellum period of Chicago history gave rise to the modern police department. The mechanisms of law enforcement in 1855 were woefully inadequate to cope with the rising tide of lawlessness in the burgeoning frontier city. A daytime constabulary and a nighttime watch of twenty-eight untrained men patrolling the city for twelve straight hours was all that stood between the citizenry of Chicago and the lawless elements. In times of social unrest, such as the saloon licensing agitation that contributed to Chicago's Lager Beer Riot of April 21, 1855, the mayor of Chicago looked to the standing militias and volunteer companies to restore and maintain order, and not to the undisciplined rowdies in civilian clothing masquerading as city police. Mayor Levi D. Boone and his administration addressed these inadequacies by unifying the two law enforcement agencies into a single police department to meet the real or imagined threat of drunken armed men fomenting violence against civilian authority in the public square. The "riot," such as it was, occurred in Market Square, the seat of local government, which stood opposite the original Sherman House Hotel and architect John Van Osdel's two-story City Hall at Clark and Randolph Streets. The Richard J. Daley Center, a steel and glass courthouse tower, now looms over that intersection.

On that quiet but eventful Sunday in April 1855, the good Doctor Curtis was preaching to his faithful parishioners. They had come to worship and pray at the First Presbyterian Church located in the Chicago "suburbs"—on Washington Street, between Dearborn and Clark Streets. This busy commercial thoroughfare, now in the heart of downtown Chicago, was then lined with churches, small cottages, and gardens.

Mayor Levi D. Boone, grandnephew of the frontiersman Daniel Boone and a city physician, was relaxing in his modest wood-frame residence at State Street near Madison Street, when the tranquillity of the early afternoon was shattered. A pushing, angry mob of German and Irish immigrants emerging from the taverns of North Wells and Clark Streets in the Eighth Ward had gathered in Ogden Park to protest the imprisonment of their friends, persons who had been locked in the Bridewell for violations of the hated Sunday closing laws.

Mayor Boone was a temperance fanatic and a know-nothing bigot. He had vowed to rid the city of the "rowdy Irish elements" and the "low Dutch," whose drinking habits and "continental Sundays" enflamed the Puritan sensibilities of the city merchants who had elected Boone to office with a mandate to close the saloons . . . one way or another.

Backed by strong editorial support in the staunchly Republican *Chicago Tribune,* Boone raised the saloon licensing fees to an unconscionable $300 a year and closed the tipping houses on Sunday. The reaction of the immigrants living north of the Chicago River and along Milwaukee Avenue was one of outrage.

Armed with fowling pieces, truncheons, hammers, meat cleavers, and their bare fists, two hundred ragged tradesmen (according to a contemporary account) stormed the Clark Street bridge and advanced on Captain Luther Nichols's police column, amassed around the courthouse in Market Square.

Bemused churchgoers in their Sunday finery poured out of their houses of worship to view the affray, confident in the belief that Nichols and his men would make short work of the German and Irish ruffians. As the mob approached the courthouse from the northeast, the crackle of gunfire sent men in silk top hats and women carrying their Sunday parasols scurrying for the safety of their homes. In the midst of the rising panic, the constables held their ground against scatter-shot gunfire and hand-to-hand combat with the attackers.

"There were many broken heads, many persons roughly handled, more arrests, and again the repulsed assailants retreated to the North Side," wrote one observer of the

L. D. Boone

DR. LEVI D. BOONE,
MAYOR OF CHICAGO IN
1855. BELOW, AN
ENGRAVING SHOWS THE
THE COOK COUNTY
COURTHOUSE AT
RANDOLPH AND CLARK,
SITE OF THE LAGER BEER
RIOT.

melee. Officer George W. Hunt lost an arm, but his attacker, a German named Peter Martens, was shot in the back as he turned and fled. Hunt was awarded a bronze star for gallantry and retired to civilian life with a comfortable political job, which he held for the next thirty-two years.

The following day Boone called out the militias and invoked marshal law, but Judge Henry Rucker freed the prisoners as a token of goodwill to help ease tensions. Fed up with Boone's restrictive policies, the voters of Chicago rejected a prohibition amendment two months later, and tossed the mayor out of office in the election of 1856. Boone lost to Thomas Dyer, an Irishman and a liberal-thinking Democrat, who celebrated his triumph with beer, whiskey, and a noisy victory parade through the streets of downtown—a parade that the *Tribune* glumly referred to as the "Dyer Procession."

Go west on Randolph Street to LaSalle Street, turn right (north), and go to Lake Street. Turn right (east) on Lake Street and go to State Street. Turn right again (south) and return to Randolph Street. Turn right (west) onto

THE FLAMES OF HELL: THE IROQUOIS THEATER FIRE
December 30, 1903

In the obstreperous heyday of vaudeville, the play was the thing. Neither acts of God nor man's folly could prevent the show from going on. The day after the Iroquois Theater fire, all thirty-five Chicago theaters were open for business, except those under the Will J. Davis–Harry J. Powers management. Near the entrance of the Garrick Theater, where attendance was large, a wealthy railroad tycoon reflected on the mindset of his fellow Chicagoans in 1903. "The fact is, the people of Chicago live at so rapid a pace that they don't take the time to reflect seriously on anything. Their lives move swiftly and their pleasures are taken at the same pace." Five hundred seventy-one lives were lost in the wall of flame that consumed the interior of the Iroquois Theater. Another 350 suffered serious injuries. The devastation at 77 West Randolph Street (now 24 West Randolph Street) the afternoon of December 30, 1903, has only one parallel in modern history, Vienna's Ring Theater fire claimed 875 people during the Feast of the Immaculate Conception on December 8, 1881. The arching façade of the Iroquois Theater (minus the Roman columns) was replicated in a later successor, the Oriental Theater, a luxurious 1920s vaudeville house and movie palace located on the ground floor of the Civic Tower Building. The colorless brown-brick skyscraper towering above the theater occupies the same space on Randolph

Street as the old Iroquois Theater. Next door, the fully restored Delaware Building (a Wheelock & Thomas commission erected in 1874) houses (sadly) a McDonald's restaurant. The Oriental was reduced to a shabby ruin by the late 1970s after years of neglect. For a time, a wholesale electronics dealer sold personal stereos and other audio equipment from a storefront partition that was once the theater lobby. When the shop closed in 1981, another relic of Chicago's show business heritage was presumed lost. Then came a remarkable resurrection. When the renovated Oriental opened for business in 1998 as the Ford Center, a live-performance theater, it inspired a chorus of praise from critics, not unlike the notices appearing in the morning papers following the gala opening night at the Iroquois many decades earlier.

> *"A playhouse so splendid in its every appointment, so beautiful in its every part, so magnificent and yet so comfortable. The enterprise which made the erection of the new theater possible has given Chicago playgoers a virtual temple of beauty—a place where the noblest and highest in dramatic art could fittingly find a worthy home."*
>
> Chicago Tribune, *November 24, 1903*

> *"The Iroquois Theater was a firetrap. The whole thing was a rush construction. It was beautiful but it was cheap. Everything but the structural members was of wood; the roller on the asbestos curtain, the pulleys—all a cheap compromise."*
>
> *William Clendenin,* Fireproof Magazine

From parquet to gallery, the Iroquois Theater echoed with the opening-night excitement of Chicago theatergoers. They had come to preview Mark Klaw and Abraham Erlanger's production of *Mr. Bluebeard*, a comic farce fresh from a successful run at London's Drury Lane. Eddie Foy starred as "Sister Anne," with Harry Gilfoil as "Mr. Bluebeard."

In the back of a lower box sat the beaming architect, Benjamin H. Marshall, who overcame considerable labor-union difficulty to turn the first spade of dirt on July 28, 1903. A new century's fascination with mass entertainment necessitated construction of a magnificent new palace. Marshall pledged to give the city a sensuous beauty in his innovative Iroquois Theater design. Four months later, with corner-cutting and breakneck speed, the doors of the majestic new theater were thrown open to the public.

Before the old year faded into memory, Marshall was in deep despair, and theater owner Will J. Davis was branded a villainous spendthrift and held accountable for the horror that occurred.

It was the week after Christmas, and the city was in a festive mood. Nearly two thousand patrons poured past the great gilded marble foyer of the Iroquois for an afternoon matinee of *Mr. Bluebeard* in the 6,300-square-foot auditorium. Women and children outnumbered the men. It was a Wednesday afternoon and a workday for most people.

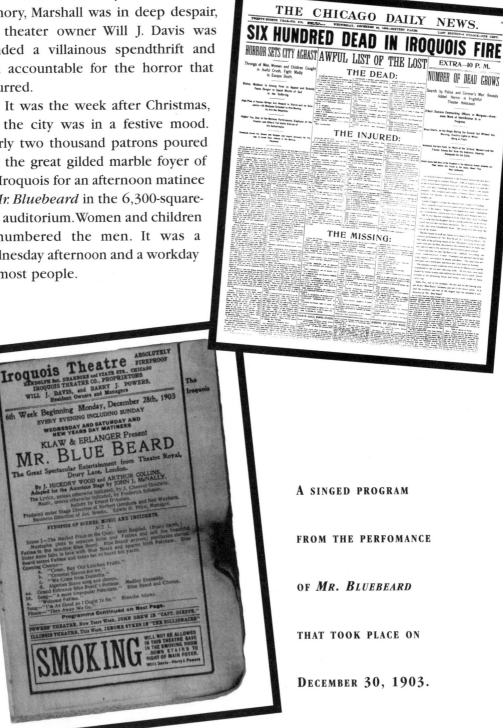

A SINGED PROGRAM

FROM THE PERFOMANCE

OF *MR. BLUEBEARD*

THAT TOOK PLACE ON

DECEMBER 30, 1903.

A few minutes past 3:00 P.M., during the "moonlight scene" of the second act, Eddie Foy noticed a spark descend from an overhead spotlight, then scraps of burning paper floated down upon the actors on-stage. A tongue of fire crept along the red-velvet curtain. There was a sudden gasp from the audience, but no immediate rush for the exits. A few even imagined that this was an elaborate trick, and part of the lavish stage spectacle they were watching.

"Now keep your seats, there is no danger!" cautioned the sprightly Foy, who weighed the dangers in his own mind, then darted off-stage to the safety of the alley after ordering the curtain lowered. The other players maintained remarkable composure until they, too, realized their dire predicament. Several chorus girls passed out, and had to be dragged off-stage. None of the 348 members of the cast and production crew were harmed.

Stagehands attempted to lower the supposedly "fireproof" asbestos curtain, which had been soaked in gasoline and ignited as a part of the routine city inspection prior to the grand opening. This time, however, the curtain failed the second and most important test of all. It stopped halfway down, fanning the flames outward into the auditorium. Screams of terror echoed through the theater, and then a deadly rush began for the Randolph Street exit.

Dr. F. C. Knight, who said he had a "premonition of disaster" during the first act, made up his mind to stand behind the rear railing of the parquet circle. Shielded from immediate danger, he attempted to stave off panic by warning people to remain calm and to please use the side exits. But it was to no avail.

Later, as police removed the charred, torn, and blistered remains from the theater, they discovered, to their horror and amazement, that a number of women were trampled and smothered in the crushing panic. One dead woman's face bore an unmistakable heel mark. In the upper galleries, bodies burned beyond recognition were stacked like cordwood, six deep. Men fell on their knees and prayed in the face of such frightening horror.

For nearly five hours, police, firemen, and newspaper sketch artists, who threw away their pencils and notebooks, carried out the dead. Even the archbishop of Chicago, pleading with the stricken and dying to place their trust in God, rolled up his sleeves to assist in the rescue effort.

At least 150 victims were piled high along the walls of the John R. Thompson restaurant, adjacent to the theater on the east end. Anxious relatives sifted through the remains searching for their lost loved ones.

Others were removed to police patrol wagons and ambulances and taken to the eighth floor of Marshall Field's department store on State Street. Jordan's, Buffon's and Rolston's downtown morgues were kept busy all through the night.

A narrow bridge one hundred feet above Dearborn Street made of scaffold planking, which connected the Iroquois Theater with the dental school of Northwestern University (replaced by a parking garage), allowed rescuers to reach the balcony exits. The first two survivors who emerged from the theater slipped and fell from the dangerously slippery boards, crashing to the alleyway below.

Under the pretense of humanitarianism, a ghoulish army of vagrants crept into the somber and darkened chamber to pick the pockets of the dead and dying.

The climax of the horror had been reached.

Someone had to answer for this awful affair. Powers and Davis were easy marks, if for no other reason than the fact that Will Davis had a history of managing firetrap theaters. Davis was in charge of operations when the Columbia at Dearborn and Monroe Streets burned to the ground in the fall of 1899.

Far from being an example of midwestern architectural genius, the Iroquois lacked the most basic elements of safety, which were already in place in the large New York theaters of the day—an adequate number of exits, doors that pushed outward, and an intake flue at the back of the stage to carry the flames upward. The presence of wood trim on everything and the cheap draperies guaranteed that this fire would not be contained.

In fact the whole thing smelled of cheapness, venality, and greed. Davis and Powers justly deserved public censure—and a long jail sentence—but their wealth and connections shielded them from punishment. Within months, the Iroquois charnel house reopened as the Colonial Theater, a few doors down the street from the Randolph Theater, managed by the Jones, Linnick, & Schaefer consortium.

To continue our tour, go west on Randolph Street to LaSalle Street. Turn right (north) and proceed to the Chicago River.

WHILE THE BAND PLAYED ON: THE EASTLAND DISASTER
July 24, 1915

It was to be the grandest, gala summer outing in the seven-year history of the Hawthorne Club, a social and fraternal organization formed for the enjoyment of the seven thousand employees at the Western Electric manufacturing plant located in West Suburban Cicero. The club sponsored dinners, amateur theatrical productions, adult education classes, and of course the festive picnic excursion to Michigan City, Indiana. The company spared no expenses, and the demand for tickets to the 1915 affair set a new record. The steamship Eastland, *with a notorious reputation as an unstable Great Lakes craft, was moored in its slip on the south side of the Chicago River between Clark and LaSalle Streets. When the last members of the Hawthorne Club were checked in, the gangplank was lifted, and the ship's master prepared to cast off. Then, at 7:40 A.M. on the morning of July 24, the worst maritime disaster in Chicago history struck.*

The July 1915 issue of Western Electric's company newspaper promised employees a rousing good time they would never soon forget. "There is no Jonah about this, but it will be a whale of a big success!"

The promoters of the event urged 100 percent participation in the fifth annual outing to Michigan City. They got that, and quite a few more.

The *Eastland,* a rusting Lake Michigan steamer owned by the St. Joseph–Chicago Steamship Company and launched at Port Huron in 1904, accommodated only 2,570 people. It was estimated that a crowd of 3,200, with women outnumbering men four to one, elbowed their way past navigation inspector Robert H. McCreary, whose counting device stopped working once the maximum capacity had been reached. On the east side of the river, the steamer *Theodore Roosevelt,* pressed into emergency duty, was taking on another load of Western Electric passengers and was set to sail half an hour after the *Eastland* cast off.

THE CAPSIZING OF THE *EASTLAND* WAS CHICAGO'S WORST NAUTICAL DISASTER.

The overflow crowd, attired in their finest summer clothing on a gray and drizzly Chicago morning, made their way to the port side of the steamer to wave handkerchiefs and banners at friends and well-wishers standing on the banks of the river just as Captain Harry Pedersen gave the order to sail. On the upper deck of the *Eastland,* a mandolin and fiddle orchestra played a lively ragtime tune. Spirits soared.

Up at the bow, the steam tug *Kenosha* sounded a merry "toot." The twin-screw propellers of the *Eastland* began to churn the water. Lines were cast off, and the *Eastland* inched away from the dock ever so slowly.

The ballast tanks of the ship were empty. The "stability line," which kept the Lake Michigan steamers upright, was only four inches deep. Government regulations called for a minimum depth of twenty inches. The crew and the owners of the steamship line were both negligent.

Freed from its mooring, the *Eastland* began to list to port, leaning toward the Reid, Murdoch & Company warehouse on the north side of the river. Crew members aboard the tugboat were still waiting for the tow line to be thrown when the *Eastland* dipped closer to the water.

The river was less than twenty feet deep, the shoreline even closer. Like a toy boat bobbing in a bathtub, the steamer flipped over on her port side trapping hundreds below the water line within plain sight of the dock and the safety it afforded. It was reported that a sea of bobbing heads cried out for help, while others slid helplessly down the side, and disappeared below the hull.

A human lifeline was formed on the steel shell of the *Eastland* as blowtorch operators attempted to open up an escape path from the interior. Captain Pedersen had to be physically restrained, because he did not wish to see his steamship mutilated. "My orders are to save lives, not be careful with the boat!" snapped one workman who heard the fists of desperate people pounding on metal from inside the ship. Forty people were eventually dragged through the hole and rescued.

From the Clark Street Bridge directly overhead, a wagon driver making his morning rounds tossed wooden chicken crates to be used as floatation devices to the helpless victims thrashing about in the water. (*Author's note:* That man was my grandfather, Richard Stone.)

The big downtown department stores sent wagons and trucks to ferry the injured and the dead to nearby hospitals and morgues. Large grappling hooks were used to pull the lifeless bodies from the water.

In all, 835 people perished in the polluted waters of the Chicago River that morning, including 22 entire families.

The Alfred P. Plamondon family was touched by the tragedy. Another chapter in that family's poignant saga was written that day. The Plamondons of Astor Street and North Park Avenue were Blue Book Chicago aristocrats, a prominent manufacturing family touched by the cruel hand of fate on three separate occasions within twelve years.

In 1903, Charlotte Plamondon was rescued from her private box as flames engulfed the Iroquois Theater. When the *Lusitania* was torpedoed by a German U-boat in the icy waters off the coast of Ireland in 1915, Mr. and Mrs. Charles Plamondon perished. Their remains were pulled from the ocean and returned to Chicago for burial.

E. K. Plamondon, a cousin of Charles Plamondon, his brother Ambrose, and their wives and children were all on board the *Eastland* that morning—one day after mourning the loss of the *Lusitania* victims at their double funeral. The family members aboard the *Eastland* were pulled from the river. They were shaken by the ordeal and in a state of collapse, but otherwise safe.

Befitting a disaster of such great magnitude, there were many human interest stories and compelling acts of singular heroism that would be retold for years to come. John V. Ebert, employed as a gauge manager aboard the *Eastland,* was also a *Titanic* survivor. He guided three dozen people imprisoned in the aft saloon of the *Eastland* to safety. Recalling the *Titanic,* Ebert said he was in the water forty-six hours before a German tramp steamer rescued him from a certain grave in the frigid seas of the North Atlantic. The *Titanic,* he said, hardened him to nautical tragedies.

The mystery of the *Eastland* was never completely resolved. There was no clear consensus concerning the root cause of the *Eastland*'s capsizing. Seven hundred lawsuits charging criminal negligence were filed, but almost all of them were thrown out by the judges of the Circuit Court of Appeals who held the owners of the steamship line blameless.

The *Eastland* was sold at a public auction to Edward A. Evers on December 15, 1915, and later transferred to the government where it was pressed into duty as the gunboat *USS Wilmette.* In 1946, the tragically cursed steamer was sold for scrap metal.

In 1988, the Illinois State Historical Society and the Mathematics and Science Academy placed a marker commemorating the sorrow and the tragedy of the *Eastland*'s capsizing in a sequestered spot along East Wacker Drive overlooking the Chicago River between Clark Street and LaSalle. On warm summer days, downtown office workers gather to eat lunch on the public bench, read a book, quietly reflect, or simply enjoy the ambiance of a tranquil and picturesque river setting that cloaks the memory of the horrendous catastrophe that occurred so long ago.

The Submarine at the Bottom of the River

S I D E T R I P

In a rather curious aside to this whole story, divers probing beneath the hull of the overturned cruise ship for bodies noticed a strange-looking object resting on the bottom of the riverbed. A large, circular craft was raised to the surface and from inside two skeletons were extracted. The metal object was the lost experimental submarine, Fool Killer, *designed by Lodner Darvontis Phillips (1825–1869) of Michigan City, Indiana. The underwater boat was sold to Chicagoan William Nissen in 1890. It sunk to the river's bottom during a test run, stranding poor Nissen and his hysterical dog. The ill-fated sub was exhibited to the public at 200 South State Street in 1916.*

Turn right (east) on Wacker Drive and take Wacker Drive to Clark Street.

DEATH OF THE SCHEMER
April 4, 1927

Across the street from the plaque commemorating the Eastland *disaster at the southwest corner of Clark Street and Wacker Drive opposite the new R. R. Donnelley building, gangster Vincent "Schemer" Drucci was shot to death by a Chicago cop while scuffling for control of a loose gun inside a moving police flivver. His gaudy funeral procession attracted thousands of downtown office workers who turned out to witness the $40,000 cortege as it wound its way south on Wells Street, then west to Mount Carmel Cemetery in Hillside. Chicago*

Police had a difficult time restraining the pushing, jeering crowd who strained for a glimpse of the celebrity gangsters who had come to pay their final respects. The crime bosses of Chicago were bigger stars than the movie cowboy Tom Mix and his horse, Tony.

Above the din of a crowded and noisy courtroom filled with the press and grieving relatives of North Side crime boss Vincent "Schemer" Drucci, Detective Sergeant Daniel F. Healy told a coroner's jury that he shot and killed the gangster in self-defense. "I felt I had to kill him, or he would kill me," explained the thirty-one-year-old officer, who had received a letter containing a death threat the day after the incident.

Though Sicilian by birth, Drucci had renounced his ethnic loyalties and sided with Dion O'Banion's Irish mob. It was his special dislike of the West Side Genna family that drove him into the arms of the hated North Side gang.

It was the eve of the city mayoral election, and the customary order went out to the police radio cars from Commissioner Morgan Collins to arrest all gangsters on sight. While making the rounds of the North Side, Healy and his squad spotted Drucci, who packed a "heater" as a force of habit.

Feeling harassed and put out by the police intrusion, Drucci chided Healy for being a "kid copper," spicing his opinions with more threatening epitaphs, as the police flivver crossed the Clark Street Bridge and moved south toward the detective headquarters on LaSalle Street. With the Schemer were two lesser known gunsels named Albert Singel and Henry Finkelstein.

"Shut yer yap and sit back!" warned Healy, but Drucci wasn't listening.

Suddenly Drucci made a lunge at Healy, whose gun was pressed squarely into the gangster's rib cage. "I'll take you, tools and all!" Drucci threatened.

Thrown off balance, Healy managed to pry loose Drucci's clenched hand from the barrel of his service revolver. With his left hand freed, the detective fired four shots point blank. Schemer was dead in an instant, and not even Al Capone could be blamed this time.

The family spent $30,000 on funeral flowers. One of the wreaths was fashioned into a broken wheel, symbolizing a family's grief for a young man who had taken a wrong turn in life. It was a lavish, star-studded event to say the least. When the spectators lining the sidewalks spotted George "Bugs" Moran, John "Dingbat" O'Berta, "Polack Joe" Saltis, Julian "Potatoes" Kaufmann, and other gangland luminaries trailing behind in their respective cars, an enormous cheer went up. You would have thought that the Cubs and White Sox were playing in the World Series.

Fistfight at State & Lake Street, c. 1861

SIDETRIP

According to reporter Norman Mark, Chicago's boisterous, larger-than-life, Civil War–era mayor, John Wentworth, slugged it out with Allan Pinkerton, founder of the famous detective agency, at the corner of State and Lake Streets one languid afternoon in the early days of the Civil War.

Pinkerton, shorter and more agile, got the best of the gin-soaked Wentworth as the two combatants pounded away at each other in a senseless display of male ego.

For nearly four years, spanning Wentworth's two terms in office, the two ambitious rivals had been at odds over proper policing methods in Chicago. Because most right-thinking people mistrusted the woefully incompetent and undersized city police force, prosperous merchants and well-to-do residents were in the habit of hiring their own private police, supplied by G. T. Moore, Allan Pinkerton, and Cyrus Bradley, to safeguard their property from roughnecks.

Wentworth shrewdly recognized that a private police department undercut his political clout and compromised his administration and, therefore, was opposed to the Pinkertons.

Long John Wentworth, a strapping six-footer, had his own ideas about law enforcement. He did not believe a uniform was a necessary requirement, and he deeply resented the Irish presence. Wentworth, a force in city politics for decades, was also a champion bigot and an exponent of Nativist Protestantism, an anti-Catholic movement of the 1850s. Thus, when Pinkerton blocked his path on Lake Street's wooden plank walkway outside Potter Palmer's dry goods store at 112, 114, and 116 Lake Street, the mayor raised his fists and challenged the Scotsman to a fight.

When the governor of the state of Illinois dared to meddle in Chicago's affairs (which Wentworth viewed as entirely his own) by imposing a three-member civilian police commission to arbitrate disciplinary disputes and oversee fiscal responsibility, Long John was apoplectic. He fired the entire police department—the whole lot of them—on March 27, 1861, leaving the city totally without protection from midnight until 10:00 A.M. the following morning when the commission hastily convened to hire new recruits.

The night passed quietly. All of the crooks and ruffians must have been locked up for the night by prior arrangement.

To continue, turn right (south) on Clark Street to Lake Street. Turn left (east) on Lake Street and proceed to Michigan Avenue. Turn right (south) on Michigan Avenue and go to Randolph Street.

"PLAY HY SNYDER IN THE THIRD!"

June 9, 1930

With the murder of Chicago Tribune *reporter Alfred "Jake" Lingle, the "Front Pagers," who found a certain romantic appeal in the twilight world of gangsters, showgirls, bloody crime scenes, and sorrowful ballads sung by murderers on the scaffold, were given a cold, hard lesson in reality. At the very least, the wiseacres of Chicago's fourth estate were forced to reassess their job descriptions and ponder the hidden message of Lingle's rise and fall. And that message was, perhaps, to always look over your shoulder and take nothing for granted when venturing out to the racetrack. It is still possible to retrace Jake Lingle's final steps. It's only a short walk from where the old Sherman House hotel stood at Randolph and Clark to the Illinois Central (IC) railroad depot at Michigan Avenue and Randolph Street. The historic Hotel Sherman closed its doors in 1973. A financially troubled partnership fronted by a Teamster official linked to organized crime and Ben "King of the Janitors" Stein owned the shuttered building up until it was condemned in 1980. The Sherman came down without a whimper of protest from the preservationist community. In its place stands the James R. Thompson State of Illinois Building, a glass and iron monstrosity inspired by the German Bauhaus movement of the 1930s. We do not recommend that people who suffer from vertigo or are faint of heart attempt to ride the elevators in this building without a blindfold. The IC train access ramp, adjacent to the Chicago Cultural Center on the southwest corner of Michigan Avenue and Randolph Street, is now a busy underground METRA rush-hour stop for downtown commuters. Lingle planned to catch an afternoon race train to watch the nags run at Washington Park when his schedule was interrupted. He was shot in the back of the head about one hundred feet east of the stairwell coming off Randolph Street on June 9, 1930, without ever knowing what hit him, or finding out why.*

Alfred "Jake" Lingle was not the only reporter in town who cozied up to gangsters for a good story. That he was able to conceal his jaunty reputation as a horse-playing rake in tight with gangsters on both sides of town from his editor, Edward Scott Beck, at the somber, solidly conservative *Chicago Tribune* is what makes this story so fascinating.

The literary wags of the *Herald-Examiner,* the *Journal,* and even of the occasionally bombastic and highbrow *Daily News* were known to hoist a cocktail or two in the company of underworld bons vivants. Their livelihood and reputations often depended on the tidbits of useful information they pried loose from a hood cradling a highball. Such was not the case at the good, gray *Tribune,* where reporters were expected to maintain aristocratic detachment and conduct themselves with the same decorum as foreign correspondents covering the Hague tribunals.

Jake Lingle was personally acquainted with Al Capone—their friendship began in 1920. In fact, Lingle was friendly with just about every politician, gangster, footpad, and cop on the make, including the commissioner of police, William Russell, a boyhood chum from California Avenue and Jackson Boulevard, whom Lingle helped elevate to the superintendency in 1928.

Jake Lingle was hired as a *Tribune* copyboy in 1918, when the pressroom was still located at Madison and Dearborn Streets. He had no aptitude for writing, but it was his long list of contacts and that nickel in his pocket for a phone call to the city desk that made him indispensable to the editors and rewrite men.

The brash and cocky reporter cultivated acquaintances in the courts, the lockup, and the gin mills of the North and South Sides. Relying on the word of informants and the bonds of friendship, he became the city's cleverest police reporter, and one of its wealthiest, through shrewd manipulation of the stock market and investment in syndicate-owned gambling clubs like the Sheridan Wave up on the North Side.

Lingle lived like a sultan at the Stevens Hotel. He kept a secret bank account at the Lake Shore Trust and Savings totaling $63,900—not a bad haul for a $65-a-week reporter. When details of the secret bank account and his spendthrift lifestyle were bared, it caused major embarrassment and a tidal wave of unwanted publicity for the "World's Greatest Newspaper." The *Tribune* editorial board was forced to back down from its hasty decision to elevate Jake to heroic martyrdom.

The afternoon of June 9, 1930, found Lingle milling about the lobby of the Hotel Sherman, where he greeted friends and colleagues with a firm handshake and warm, engaging smile. Jake was a crowd-pleaser, and he was well liked. In another life, he would have made a great politician.

After a light lunch at the coffee shop in the hotel, he exited on the Clark Street side and headed east down Randolph, past Marshall Field's, and toward the IC station to catch a 1:30 train to Washington Park in Homewood. Lingle paused at the newsstand outside what was then the central library to purchase a *Racing Form* and a newspaper. After handing the newsboy his change, Jake puffed his cigar, adjusted his straw boater, and walked slowly toward the subway stairs, scanning the scratch sheet. Three men sitting in a parked roadster called out to him.

"Hey Jake! Don't forget to play Hy Snyder in the third!"

Lingle smiled and waved. "Got him!" he replied.

As he descended the stairs, two men brushed up alongside him. If he knew who these men were, he did not let on, nor did he appear to be overly concerned, according to eyewitnesses. Inside the tunnel under Michigan Avenue, one of the men paused to buy a paper. A moment later a shot rang out.

JAKE LINGLE:

A REPORTER'S

LOT WAS

NEVER A

HAPPY ONE.

With a bullet lodged in his head, Lingle fell to the pavement, facedown. A blond-haired man tossed aside the .38-caliber murder weapon and disappeared into the crowd. At least fourteen people (probably many more) eyeballed the killer, but they did nothing to stop him.

Weeks and then months passed before the police produced a suspect. The serial number on the murder weapon had been defaced, but ballistics expert Colonel Calvin Goddard traced the origin of the gun to the sporting goods store owned by Peter Von Frantzius at 608 Diversey Parkway. Records showed that the weapon had been sold to one Frankie Foster, a member of Bugs Moran's North Side mob. Foster fled to Los Angeles hours after the Lingle shooting, but was indicted in Cook County as an accessory before the fact to murder.

Foster, whose real name was Frank Citro, was extradited to Chicago and held in the county jail for four months, but the evidence was inconclusive and the charge against him was nol-prossed.

Then, as hopes for a quick solution waned, a new suspect turned up. Leo Vincent Brothers, a labor union slugger from St. Louis, was arrested in New York and indicted for the Lingle murder. Great rejoicing and a collective sigh of relief came from the *Tribune* editorial board, who expected justice to be served and the gangsters handed their comeuppance. Brothers was convicted and sentenced to fourteen years in prison on April 2, 1931.

"I can do that standing on my head!" Brothers quipped, lending credence to the theory that he had voluntarily taken the fall for Jack Zuta, a North Side racketeer who ran a string of whorehouses, but who was already dead by the time the trial wrapped up.

Of course, it has long been suspected that Al Capone also wanted that double-crossing reporter shoved aside. It seemed that everyone had a motive and the opportunity, but crime historians are in general agreement that Brothers took the rap and served his time for a substantial cash payoff. We'll never really know for sure. The secret died with Foster, who suffered a fatal heart attack in Studio City, Los Angeles, on April 22, 1967.

The murder of Alfred Lingle galvanized public opinion against the gangs of Chicago. The bell began to toll for Al Capone, who had finally gone too far.

Front Page Addresses

1. *The* Chicago Democrat, *the city's first newspaper, was published in a single-room, wooden-frame building at Clark Street and Wacker Drive beginning on November 26, 1833. John Calhoun was the founding editor, but frontier roughneck "Long John" Wentworth was the publisher in 1840, when the* Democrat *became Chicago's first daily paper. Despite the ravings of Wentworth, the* Democrat *was regarded as the most influential news and opinion sheet in the Midwest until the* Gem of the Prairie, *an eight-column, 21 x 18-inch journal of poetry, literature, and politics, was launched in 1844. The* Gem of the Prairie *had a short eight-year run before being absorbed by the* Tribune.

2. *The editorial offices of the old* Chicago Evening Post, *published continuously from 1889 to 1932, were located at 211 West Wacker Drive (overlooking the Chicago River between Franklin and Wells Streets), in an eighteen-story office tower once owned by insurance magnate Alfred MacArthur. Nowadays, Frank Laterza's custom tailor shop occupies the ground-floor office space next to the Roman columns flanking the main entrance. The* Chicago Daily Times, *the city's first tabloid newspaper accenting crime stories and celebrity gossip from 1929 through 1948, shared space with the* Post *in the same building.* Times *reporters cracked two of the city's most sensational crimes. In 1946, Lou Paris and Jim McGuire fingered William Heirens as Suzanne Degnan's murderer by communicating their suspicions to Captain Michael Ahern, commander of the Rogers Park Station. McGuire achieved even greater journalistic notoriety that same year by exposing the criminal conspiracy that imprisoned Joe Majczek for a murder he never committed. Billed as "Chicago's Picture Newspaper," the* Times *merged with the* Chicago Sun *in 1948, after Marshall Field III purchased the struggling tabloid. He rechristened it the* Sun-Times, *but with this corporate merger, an end chapter in print journalism in the Windy City was written. Over the next fifty years, the number of daily papers in Chicago dwindled from five, to four, then three, and finally two.*

3. *In the city room of the old* Chicago Daily News *at 15 North Wells Street (a few doors north of Madison Street on the east side of Wells Street), Carl Sandburg, Ben Hecht, Finley Peter Dunne, Eugene Field, Lloyd Lewis, and Henry Justin Smith spun stories, spouted poetry, and related tales of the city to their faithful afternoon readership. The* Daily News *was the "writer's paper," not highbrow and occasionally turgid as was the* Tribune *under the reign of the McCormicks, but a journal of literary wit, wisdom, and common sense for the average man.*

The News *was published from the four-story hole in the wall from 1875 until 1929. You'll find a Standard Parking Garage and assorted street-level fast-food and retail emporiums there now.*

4. *The* Chicago Inter-Ocean *is long forgotten, but in the waning years of the nineteenth century, the influential Republican newspaper espoused the gospel of free trade and the gold standard and promulgated notions of empire under publisher Herman Henry Kohlsaat, a supreme egotist and political bigwig who controlled city patronage for many years. The motto of this paper, "Republican in Everything, Independent in Nothing!" reflected a time long past when newspapers were advertisements for the two major political parties and a candidate's platform by which to shape public opinion. The* Inter-Ocean, *published from 1872 until 1914, was headquartered at 55–59 West Monroe Street (the southwest corner of Monroe and Dearborn Streets), a few doors down from the sixth-floor offices of the Chicago Crime Commission at 79 West Monroe. A Sharper Image store occupies the first level of the Xerox Center, a glass and aluminum office tower a la Mies van der Rohe, which is located on the former site of the* Inter-Ocean.

5. *Beginning in 1902, the William Randolph Hearst chain published the* Chicago American *for ten years inside a cramped office space at 215 West Madison Street. A decade later, the editorial offices were transferred to a ten-story rococo-style tower, a building originally owned by the Marshall Field estate (at Madison and Wacker Drive). Reporters called this place the "Madhouse on Madison Street." Mr. Hearst, visiting his Chicago operation for the first time, refused to step inside after catching a glimpse of the hideous-looking porcelain-tile façade. Turning his back, he directed his chauffeur to return him to the train station, vowing never to lay eyes on the Chicago plant again. Instead, the paper was delivered by private airplane every morning to his secluded mountaintop estate, San Simeon, in California.*

To continue our tour, go west on Randolph Street to State Street. Turn right (north) and go north on State Street to Lake Street. Turn right (east) on Lake Street and go to Wabash Avenue.

THE RUSH HOUR ELEVATED CRASH
February 4, 1977

Looking back on the worst elevated train accident in city history, one is immediately struck by the appearance of imminent danger at Wabash Avenue and Lake Street every time a Chicago Transit Authority (CTA) train noisily careens around the ninety-degree turn. Many years have passed since a northbound Lake–Dan Ryan train rear-ended a six-car Ravenswood train sending two passenger cars plunging to the street, twenty feet below the elevated platform, and left two other cars dangling over the edge of the track. The curve, however, is as treacherous as ever, despite the addition of guard barriers, which the CTA ordered installed only weeks after the collision. The shrill whine of metal wheels straining against the unbending rails is a familiar, but no less haunting reminder of the perils inherent in Chicago commuting when equipment fails or there is a moment of human error by a motorman.

It was 5:30 in the afternoon, the height of the late-afternoon rush hour. Two CTA trains moving in opposite directions seemed almost tragically destined to collide at one of the weakest and most vulnerable points in the entire transit system.

Eyewitnesses to the tragedy recalled seeing the cars tumble to the street as if in slow motion. The real irony lay in the fact that the northbound train (which had begun its journey from Ninety-fifth Street and the Dan Ryan Expressway on the South Side), was moving slowly and deliberately toward the curve. The Lake–Dan Ryan motorman did not appear to be exercising poor judgment, showing undue lack of concern, or driving the train at a breakneck speed.

When Stephen Martin, the thirty-four-year-old motorman, spotted the Ravenswood train coming into view at Lake and Wabash, he instinctively applied the brakes, attempting to avoid direct impact with the rear end of the Ravenswood train. Both lines shared the same track in what comprises "the Loop."

The braking action, unfortunately, triggered the deadly derailment, which sent two cars spilling over the tracks and onto the street below. Four pedestrians, who did not have time to react when the first CTA elevated car hurdled over the side and landed on the east side of Wabash Street, were crushed to death. Two other cars were precariously suspended between the platform and the street.

Spectators who were seated in the Lakeview Restaurant at 179 North Wabash believed that the twenty-two-ton train car was about to crash through the window and kill them all. Chicagoan Agnes McCormick, who was seated in the restaurant, described the horror of the crushed and mangled bodies underneath the car to a *Chicago Sun-Times* reporter. "Then I saw a whole line of people pinned under the car. The train had fallen flat on them."

The Chicago Fire Department rescue equipment arrived moments later. A ladder was placed against the side of the dangling fourth car. Injured passengers, their faces pressed against the windows, were pulled through broken windowpanes, and lowered to the street. During the next few hours, power saws and acetylene torches were applied to the metal in an effort to free trapped passengers. Hydraulic jacks were used to free persons pinned under the crushing weight of the stainless-steel car outside the restaurant.

Nine different Chicago hospitals received the injured victims of the crash. Eleven people were killed, and 163 were injured in the derailment.

By midnight, the dangling car was brought down to street level, and another car was loaded onto a flatbed truck and hauled away. Frazzled CTA officials tried meanwhile to piece together the chain of events that triggered so deadly a tragedy.

Inside the pilot car, investigators located four hand-rolled marijuana cigarettes in a shoulder bag bearing the name of motorman Stephen Martin. Eager to pin the blame on something or someone, the National Transportation Safety Board (NTSB) drug-tested the injured Martin, but the results were negative, and the motorman was cleared . . . more or less.

In their rush to judgment, it was determined that the fail-safe crash prevention system was in proper order and the fault lay with Martin, whom they accused of ignoring a flashing red warning signal. The crash may not have occurred at all, argued CTA officials, if Martin had come to a complete stop at the first red warning light, three hundred feet from the parked Ravenswood train.

There have been numerous accidents and fatalities involving buses and elevated train cars in Chicago over the years. On November 24, 1936, a CTA train stopped at the Granville Avenue station was rear-ended by a Chicago, North Shore, & Milwaukee Express train sharing the tracks of the Red Line. Ten people were killed and 234 injured.

By far, Chicago's worst transportation mishap involved a Green Hornet streetcar and a gasoline truck at Sixty-second and State Street on May 25, 1950. The South Side crash resulted in a fiery explosion that gutted four buildings, and incinerated thirty-three people (see Tour 8).

The Gold Coast and the Slum:

The Near North Side from the Chicago River to Division Street

In 1962, a world-weary Chicago police sergeant testifying before Senator John McClellan's permanent subcommittee on investigations reported that the Near North Side—Chicago's sparkling Gold Coast, encompassing Tiffany's, Rush Street, and a concentration of swank eateries—was the "bread-and-butter district" of the crime syndicate.

Inside the tawdry dives mentioned in the sergeant's account, a galaxy of B-girls hustled champagne cocktails and padded the drink tab for bleary-eyed revelers too stoned to sign their own names after a night of wild abandon at such places as the "Talk of the Town" at 1159 North Clark Street, the "Eros Lounge" at 816 North Wabash Avenue, and "Club 19" at 19 East Chestnut Street. The X-rated adventures that titillated visitors to Chicago in those steamy days have passed from the scene, because the "scene," as it existed in the 1950s and 1960s, is no longer.

Tactical officers from the East Chicago Avenue Police Station, once the clearinghouse for hookers and their sponsors, who stumbled past the front desk after the nightly roundup, will tell you that the biggest problem these days is not prostitution or B-girls, but the theft of cellular phones carelessly left behind on the front seats of parked cars.

My, how times change.

In the frontier days of Chicago, the waterway separating the North Side from downtown was clogged with canal barges, grain boats, and timber vessels. Grain elevators, the tallest man-made structures in the Midwest, rose on the north and south banks of the river.

In their landmark study of urban history, *Chicago: Growth of a Metropolis*, Harold Mayer and Richard Wade describe the lumberyards that spread across ten miles of choice river front. The Near North Side, the last parcel of city real estate to be developed for residential use, thrived as a commercial trading center for heavy

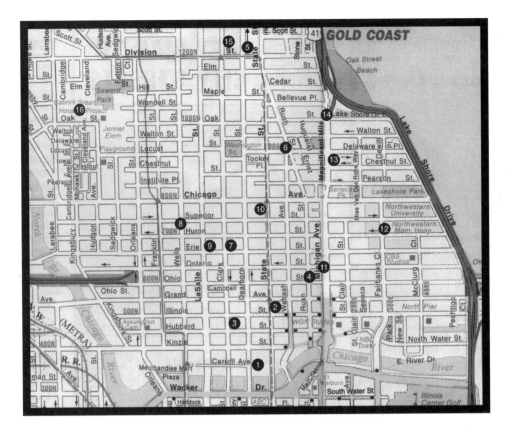

1. Marina City Towers.
2. Site of John Kinzie cabin, Wabash and Illinois.
3. Old Cook County Criminal Courts Building, Dearborn and Hubbard.
4. The Lenox House, where Jack McGurn was machine-gunned, Rush and Ontario.
5. Former Playboy Mansion, 1340 N. State Parkway.
6. The Maryland House Hotel, Rush and Delaware.
7. McGovern's Inn, now the Club Won Ton, Clark and Erie.
8. Sbarbaro's Funeral Home, now a townhouse at 708 N. Wells Street.
9. Bertucci's Restaurant, once the home of the Purolator Armored Car Company, LaSalle and Huron.
10. Holy Name Cathedral, and the former site of O'Banion's Flower Shop, State Street, between Chicago and Superior.
11. Former site of Celano's Tailor Shop, Michigan and Ontario.
12. The Chez Paree stood halfway up the block on Fairbanks, south of Huron.
13. John Hancock Center, where Lorraine Kowalski took the plunge, Michigan and Delaware.
14. The fashionable Drake Hotel, Oak and Michigan.
15. Dr. Cronin's office stood in the middle of the Sandburg Village on Clark, north of Division.
16. Death Corner in the heart of Cabrini Green at Cleveland and Oak.

THE NEAR NORTH SIDE

industry long before the Lake Michigan shallows were filled in near "Streeterville" (in the vicinity of Oak Street and Michigan Avenue).

Rough-hewn working men seeking relaxation, a glass of ale, a game of chance, and an escape from the drudgery of the pulp mills created their own diversions in Chicago's first red-light vice district—the "Sands," located near the *Chicago Tribune* building, which stands at 435 North Michigan Avenue. The grog shops, dens of ill-repute, and faro banks in the Sands were an irritant to the "better element" of Chicago society, but were tolerated as long as the patrons of these vile resorts did not cross the river and venture into the "respectable" neighborhoods south and west of downtown.

Chicago has had many vice districts that have thrived on the periphery of the central city. Crime and vice flourish in areas where there is minimal resistance—in neighborhoods with a high concentration of industry or near a transient, rooming-house population.

When efforts to close down the Sands failed in the courts, Mayor John Wentworth took it upon himself to end the menace through surreptitious means. Handbills advertising a horse race and cockfight were spread across the city, with the hope of luring the red-light trade away from the district. The ploy worked, and with spectacular flourish, Wentworth, backed by thirty city policemen carrying hooks and poles, pulled down the thirty Sand houses with brute force.

That district disappeared, but the Near North Side would never be completely liberated from the grip of vice and its illicit attractions.

In the late nineteenth century, just as the millionaires and philanthropists began moving into their spectacular limestone mansions lining Astor Street, State Street, and the east-west roads linked to Michigan Avenue (then known as Pine Street), an assortment of gambling dens, dipping houses, and bagnios sprouted up farther west. The North Side rialto district ran along Clark Street north from Division Street to the Chicago River. "Hot Stove" Jimmy Quinn, a minor player in Democratic politics at the time, controlled the district. It was said that Quinn would happily steal anything that wasn't nailed down, including a hot stove if it was there for the taking.

North Side gambling boss Mont Tennes was the leading purveyor of dice, cards, and off-track betting. Tennes flooded the Near North with an army of "hand-book" men clocking bets on the sly.

Buttressed by the Gold Coast mansions lying to the east and the wretched slum housing of "Little Hell" west of Orleans Street, Chicago's Near North neighborhoods were awash in gambling, dope, sex, sin, and sleaze. During the Prohibition era, the Near North was a bloody battleground for the control of bootleg-liquor distribution, pitting Dion O'Banion's outmaneuvered and vulnerable Irish mob against

Al Capone's army of gangsters headquartered in the South Side Levee.

No one was spared, not even the politicians, during the nearly fifteen years of unrelenting gangland warfare. Former alderman and Illinois State Representative Albert J. Prignano was "removed" from office—and the physical world—by blazing syndicate guns in December 1935. Prignano had defended the O'Banion interests, but when there were no more O'Banionites left alive to protect him, the Capone gang had the final word.

By the 1930s and 1940s, the action shifted to Wabash Avenue, Rush Street, State Street, Dearborn Street, and Clark Street north of the Chicago River up to Division Street; areas of the city well defined by a collection of low dives, transient hotels, escort agencies, and gaudy nightclubs catering to out-of-town convention-eers and slumming suburbanites with coins jingling in their pockets.

For a handsome "commission," Chicago cabbies delivered their customers to the front doorstep of the "French Casino," the "Talk of the Town Cocktail Lounge," or the "Nitelife"—a female-impersonator joint in the heart of "the Roaring 42," or "Honky Tonk U.S.A.," as it was otherwise known. There were dozens of such places, and when the "heat" was on during election time, the proprietors would simply close down for a while, change the name of the establishment if necessary, and re-open in due course.

Syndicate owned and syndicate maintained, the Forty-second Ward was an adult wonderland for nearly fifty years. Ross Prio, a mobster who lived in north-sub-urban Glenview far removed from the hustle and din of the all-night saloons, direct-ed vice activities with Jimmy "the Monk" Allegretti, his capable lieutenant, from the late 1940s up through the swinging 1960s.

Payoffs were funneled into the war chest of Captain Tommy Harrison, com-mander of the East Chicago Avenue Police Station, and his political sponsors, State Senator John "Botchy" Connors and his bagman, the fat-lipped Eddie Sturch. Those who followed Harrison into the district understood the game and abided by the rules.

In its heyday Rush Street was never more clean, and the after-hours attractions never more luminescent than in the golden age of Chicago's nightlife (the 1930s to the 1960s). The death knell for that time and place sounded with the arrival of tele-vision, changing attitudes about dressing up and going out for "a night on the town," and the sexual revolution, which rendered B-girls, hourly motels, and the "Monk" (Jimmy Allegretti) all but obsolete. And just as the mob abandoned Las Vegas in the 1980s for more fertile pastures in legitimate business, so, too, did they give up on Rush Street, and the glory days live on only in memory.

To understand Chicago and the world of Al Capone and his empire of crime, look no farther than the Gold Coast.

We will begin our tour of the Near North Side at Marina City, just north of the Chicago River at 300 North State Street.

MURDER INSIDE MARINA CITY
June 7, 1981

Almost as bizarre as the Picasso statue adorning the Richard J. Daley Plaza in downtown Chicago are the twin circular towers of Marina City designed by Bertrand Goldberg, a student of Mies van der Rohe. Radical for the times, the mixed-use apartment towers, constructed on the north bank of the Chicago River at 300 North State Street between 1959 and 1964, ushered in a residential real estate boom forever altering the appearance of the Near North neighborhood hugging the river. During the Depression, this area was a dingy, neglected warehouse district. Given the economic hardships, large-scale building projects ground to a halt and urban renewal did not resume until Mayor Daley's first term of office in the 1950s. Marina City represented a futuristic departure from traditional Greek Revival styles of architecture, and not all Chicagoans approved. Featuring twin movie theaters and a beautiful restaurant overlooking the river, Marina City was a civic achievement for architects and urban planners who wanted to free themselves from the shackles of rigid convention. But even these signature buildings of an extraordinary downtown skyline were not immune to tragedy.

On June 7, 1981, Chicago Police Deputy Superintendent James Riordan was fatally wounded inside the Captain's Table Dining Room while scuffling with an unruly patron. The entire city grieved for Riordan, who was eulogized by his peers as a "policeman's policeman." The Marina City eatery eventually closed, and the dining room remained empty for quite some time. The Smith & Wollensky Grill opened in April 1998, but the southwest corner of the restaurant complex remains boarded up, an eyesore reinforcing the notion that infamous crimes impart scars that never really heal.

For thirty-three years, Jim Riordan rode the political wave to wherever it happened to take him. Politics and policing are interchangeable in Chicago. Policing is politics, and politics is job security, a brokered promotion, and a comfortable retirement.

Riordan's elevation to the number two spot in the cadre began, as it did for many promising young line officers excluded from the promotional process, with the arrival of Orlando W. Wilson as the new Superintendent of Police in 1960. The Summerdale police scandal necessitated sweeping reforms, and the scholarly Wilson, coming from Berkeley, California, with fresh ideas, shook the system to its very roots.

Younger men, who had stagnated in the lower depths, were elevated to positions of responsibility, while the "political cops" were cast aside and uncooperative captains feeding on the spoils were reduced in rank.

During the 1968 Democratic National Convention riots, Riordan served as a field commander. His job strength, however, was not in riot control or suppressing civil disorder, but in administration. As Deputy Traffic Chief in the mid-1970s, he created a special unit to deal with truck drivers who abused the rules of the road. Two years later he was promoted to Deputy Chief of Patrol, where he earned the respect of the rank-and-file officers, who appreciated his candor and political independence.

Then he died as he lived—by the gun.

Riordan stopped by the Captain's Table for a quick bite around 9:00 P.M. He was officially off duty.

Seated near the bar, Riordan chatted with Alice and Martin O'Brien and another woman when a drunken and unruly patron attired in an urban cowboy getup accosted Riordan's dinner guests. Leon Washington had been bothering patrons all night. According to eyewitness accounts, the armed assailant pressed a gun—a Walther PPK .380-caliber, semiautomatic—against Alice O'Brien's head and clicked an empty chamber three times.

Excusing himself, Riordan rose from the table and forcibly removed the belligerent man from the dining area, trying to minimize the incident and maintain calm. Washington disappeared into the coatroom to "lock and load." In the corridor just outside the main restaurant, three shots rang out. The deputy superintendent, mortally wounded, collapsed into a shallow, decorative pool.

Washington dropped his weapon. "I'm okay. Don't worry man, I'm cool."

A restaurant patron stood between the shooter and his weapon until the police arrived minutes later. Riordan was rushed to Northwestern Memorial Hospital, where he died during surgery after receiving eighteen pints of blood and comforting words from Chicago Mayor Jane Byrne and Superintendent Richard Brzeczek.

Washington, a former Davenport, Iowa, police officer who ran an executive recruiting firm in Chicago, was described by Hazel Washington, his widowed mother, as a "good boy and a good son." The mother later sued the restaurant for serving alcohol to her son.

Remembered by friends and neighbors as a quiet and soft-spoken young man, as so many killers are before they erupt in a fit of unprompted rage, the accused was also a gun collector. His excuse: self-defense. He said he feared Riordan was going to shoot him in the hallway, so he let him have it first.

Washington said that he fired a warning shot before drilling Riordan three times, once in the chest and twice in the neck. "I shot him. I'm sorry. I'm guilty of involuntary manslaughter. Give me a break," he begged Judge Francis Mahon, who obliged Washington with a thirty-five-year prison sentence on December 3, 1981. The death penalty did not apply because Riordan was off duty at the time.

James Riordan is the highest-ranking Chicago police officer to be slain. The only other serious attempt made against a member of command personnel occurred on March 1, 1908, when Lazarus Averbuch, a Russian Jew newly arrived in the country, followed Police Commissioner George Shippy to his North Side residence. Averbuch attempted to slip a blank envelope into the chief's hand. Sensing imminent danger, Shippy, aided by his driver and his son, drew down his weapon and lunged at the assailant. Shippy, already infected by a deadly strain of syphilis that would later force his resignation, discharged five bullets into the man. Averbuch was subsequently identified as a member of an anti-Catholic religious sect, but his motive in the Shippy matter was unclear. Shippy's son Harry fired two additional shots into Averbuch for good measure. Afterward, city workers carted the body of the "anarchist" off for quick burial in a potter's field.

To continue our tour, go north on State to Illinois Street and right (east) on Illinois Street. Continue to Wabash Avenue. Wabash crosses over Illinois.

THE FATHER OF CHICAGO WAS ALSO A KILLER
Spring 1812

On April 29, 1891, a crew of workers digging the foundation of a new office building at the southwest corner of Cass Avenue (now Wabash Avenue) and Illinois Street unearthed a skeleton that would shed light on a mystery dating to the earliest days of frontier Chicago, when the marshy swampland and tall grass brushing up against Lake Michigan was known as Lee's Place. Employing very primitive forensic investigative techniques, medical examiners concluded that the remains were eighty to one hundred years old. Scholars from the Chicago Historical Society examining old property records concluded after much debate that the log cabin belonging to the Indian trader John Kinzie had stood at or near the construction site. They also concluded that the skeletal remains were those of Jean LaLime, a business rival Kinzie stabbed to death in 1812. The 1891 office building at 444 North Wabash is today a very old office and condominium building, housing the Jazz Record Mart on the ground floor.

A silversmith by trade, John Kinzie (1763–1828) established a successful commercial trading post in Michigan's St. Joseph River territory in the year 1795. A shrewd judge of land values, Kinzie purchased a large tract of property near the Maumee River in the Ohio Territory and bestowed instant wealth upon his family. In the prime of life, the adventurous Kinzie suddenly uprooted his family from their woodland setting and relocated to Chicago where he commenced trade with the natives.

It was the spring of 1804, and with his personal fortune Kinzie purchased the trading house belonging to French-Canadian trapper Jean LaLime, a transaction duly recorded in Detroit, the then seat of government for the Territory of Illinois.

Kinzie brokered his services to the military garrison at Fort Dearborn, acting as principal banker, sutler, financial adviser, and intermediary with the Potawatomi

JOHN KINZIE'S CABIN IN A PASTORAL SETTING. HE BURIED JEAN LALIME ON THE PROPERTY. WORKMEN DIGGING THE FOUNDATION OF THE BUILDING THAT IS NOW THE JAZZ RECORD MART UNEARTHED THE BODY EIGHTY YEARS AFTER THE MURDER.

Indians. Gradually he expanded his frontier empire into Milwaukee and Kankakee, journeying as far south as Sangamon County, in Illinois, to further build his wealth and reputation. The nineteenth-century historian A. T. Andreas had this to say about the ambitious Scotsman, "He [Kinzie] was beloved by the Indians and his influence over them was very great. The Canadian *voyageurs* in the service of Mr. Kinzie were about the only white men who had occasion to visit Chicago during those early years."

Andreas's flattering descriptions of "the Father of Chicago" skirt the truth. Kinzie peddled intoxicants to the Indians in defiance of a direct order from Captain John Whistler, commander of Fort Dearborn, who feared for the safety of his garrison and the lives of the civilians inside the stockade. Hot-tempered and easily provoked, John Kinzie was a formidable presence and a dangerous adversary. In 1810, after months of sniping with John Whistler, he prevailed upon the War Department to remove Whistler from his command. The War Department obliged.

In the spring of 1812, only a few months before the fateful encounter between the Miami Indians and the settlers and military personnel assigned to Fort Dearborn, Kinzie came to blows with LaLime, an educated man who served the army garrison as a language interpreter.

LaLime had bought out Du Sable's original claim for the sum of six thousand livres back in 1800. The original sale was witnessed by Kinzie, whose personal differences with the Frenchman exploded into a violent showdown outside the gates of the stockade.

On the evening in question, Kinzie left his cabin on the north side of the Chicago River to finalize a piece of business inside the gates of the fort, which was located at what is now the intersection of Michigan Avenue and Wacker Drive. His business complete, Kinzie was cautioned by Lieutenant Linai Helm to remain vigilant and cautious. LaLime was in a foul state of mind and had vowed to make short work of Kinzie.

Moments later, in the dark, LaLime accosted his business rival with a gun and knife. The two men grappled in the soft grass. An errant shot fired by LaLime grazed Kinzie's neck. While struggling to wrest the gun from his assailant, Kinzie managed to pry loose LaLime's dirk from his belt, and inflicted a fatal wound to his rival's side.

With blood pouring from a knife cut in his left hand, Kinzie retreated into the woods, where he prevailed upon friendly Indians to help him escape to Milwaukee. Kinzie knew that LaLime had many friends inside the fort, who would be likely to accuse Kinzie of being the aggressor.

Fearing the wrath of the settlers, Kinzie fled to Wisconsin, where he was sheltered by business acquaintances until a military tribunal, charged with assessing responsibility for the deadly affray, absolved him of wrongdoing.

The villagers accepted Kinzie's version of events, and the matter was forgotten until 1891, when the LaLime skeleton and scraps of wood—all that remained of the cheap pine casket built by Kinzie for the man who attacked him outside the fort—were found by workmen.

By this time John Kinzie occupied a place of honor in Graceland Cemetery on the North Side.

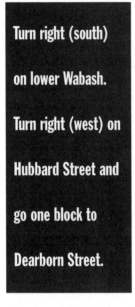

Turn right (south) on lower Wabash. Turn right (west) on Hubbard Street and go one block to Dearborn Street.

COURTROOMS TO CONDOS
1872–1929

Now Courthouse Place, condominiums managed by J. A. Friedman & Associates, the limestone Romanesque Revival building at 54 West Hubbard Street (on the northwest corner of Hubbard and Dearborn Streets) recalls the energy and vibrancy of an era of journalism and jurisprudence long past. Within the somber fortress of the Cook County Criminal Courts Building, the eloquence of famed defense attorney Clarence Darrow helped save the lives of "thrill killers" Richard Loeb and Nathan Leopold. This section of Hubbard Street has been appropriately designated by the City of Chicago as "Clarence Darrow Way." Directly in back of the courthouse stood the Cook County lockup and the gallows where the four convicted Haymarket men swung from ropes. Here, too, wife-murderer Carl Wanderer was coerced into crooning a sentimental ballad moments before dying by the nimble minds of the Chicago press corps, whose exploits were celebrated in Ben Hecht's stage play The Front Page. The Front Page *was set inside the Hubbard Street Criminal Courts Building. Here, convicted cop killer "Terrible" Tommy O'Connor pulled off the most daring escape in the annals of Chicago crime history. The jail, which housed O'Connor up until his fortuitous moment of escape, was torn down in 1936. In its place, directly across the alley from where Wanderer entertained the witnesses to his execution, stands the Chicago Fire Department Prevention Bureau. The iron bars guarding the windows of the courthouse facing the alleyway (and former prison courtyard) are solemn reminders of the wages of sin. In 1929, Cook County officials vacated the property in favor of a*

THE COOK COUNTY

COURTHOUSE AND JAIL

(REAR) AS IT APPEARED

IN AN 1884 WOODCUT

DRAWING, AND AS IT

APPEARS TODAY.

(Photo by Christina Carlson)

new and more spacious Criminal Courts Building located at Twenty-sixth and California on the city's West Side. Having outlived its usefulness as a court-house, the seven-story building was used first by the Works Progress Administration (WPA) during the Depression, then by the Board of Health and the Police Department, until 1986 when it was turned over to a private devel-opment group, who lovingly scrubbed the gray Bedford limestone façade and restored the entranceway. The richly detailed and polished cast-iron grillwork adorning the lobby stairs reminds visitors of how this stately building must have appeared to Ben Hecht and his rum-soaked colleagues of the Fourth Estate, who shared bawdy gallows humor amid the clacking of their Underwood typewriters, the pounding of the judge's gavel, and the groans of grim and anguished men awaiting the fateful drop.

North Market Hall, one of several open-air produce exchanges in the vicini-ty of the commercial thoroughfares of downtown Chicago, was built on this site in 1851. A three-story courthouse replaced Market Hall in 1874, but it was inad-equate for handling the growing volume of criminal cases in the expanding city. The problem was addressed in 1891 when architect Otto H. Matz designed a new Criminal Courts Building, which was completed within a year.

In these somber halls of justice, an extraordinary array of cunning villains and ne'er-do-wells, including the sausage vat murderer Adolph Luetgert (see Tour 4) whose uncaptioned portrait hangs on the lobby wall, stunned the courts and the packed galleries as the details of their infamy slowly emerged.

Every day was a new adventure. Each case was a revelation and lived on in the memories of the reporters whose writings echo this gloriously risqué past. Ben Hecht and Charley MacArthur understood the daily rhythm, the pathos, the occasional hilarity, and the unworldliness of the Criminal Courts Building. They wrote about those hectic days in clear, resonant tones that bristled with humor and a reporter's self-mocking irony.

In 1928, Hecht and MacArthur penned *The Front Page*, a breezy stage play based on the true-to-life escape of convicted cop killer "Terrible" Tommy O'Connor, who scaled a nine-foot wall and vanished forever . . . just four days before he was scheduled to swing from the rope.

In reality, O'Connor was a hardened criminal, a stickup man with an itchy trigger finger. He didn't care much for cops, and when they came to arrest him at his brother-in-law's home at 6415 South Washtenaw Avenue on March 23, 1921, Tommy was prepared. Cornered by five armed police officers, O'Connor burst through the rear screen door with his pistol blazing. He shot and killed Detective Sergeant Patrick "Paddy" O'Neill, then disappeared into the countryside.

O'Connor crept out of Chicago. He headed for Minneapolis, proud of the fact that he had outwitted the police. But trouble seemed to follow Tommy everywhere. Hearing that he had been arrested by the local police while attempting to rob a train porter, Detective Chief Michael Hughes rushed to Minnesota to escort O'Connor back to Chicago to stand trial for the murder of O'Neill.

Never had more effort been exerted to return a fugitive to justice than in the bloodstained manhunt for "Terrible" Tommy O'Connor, who continued to protest his guilt. "O'Neill was shot down by his own pals. A mistake of course, but they shot him," Tommy alibied. "And after that mistake they ran away and put the blame on me. Do you wonder why I ran away?"

The jury did not believe him. Convicted of first-degree murder on September 7, 1921, Tommy was ordered to die at the crack of dawn on December 15. Tempting fate and mocking death, O'Connor's friends and family put the word out on the street that that would never happen to their boy.

In cell number 427, O'Connor laughed and joked with four other convicts who kept his secret. Someone had smuggled Tommy a gun wrapped inside a sandwich.

On December 11, "Lucky" Tommy poked a nickel-plated revolver into guard David Straus's ribcage and demanded his keys. Nimble as a cat, O'Connor made his way through the cellblock and dashed down the freight elevator to ground level. He scaled a nine-foot wall and jumped inside a flivver on Illinois Street belonging to John Jensen, but the vehicle stalled. O'Connor darted out of the car and flagged down Harry J. Busch, who was to become one of Chicago's top-rated criminal defense attorneys in later years.

Busch drove O'Connor to Sedgwick Street and Chicago Avenue, then the car skidded across the slippery pavement into a curbstone. Cursing under his breath, the fugitive leapt out and commandeered another passing vehicle that took him to Larrabee and Hobbie Streets, where he disappeared.

Destiny had called, and Tommy had answered.

Rewards were posted. The cops had every expectation of success. "O'Connor will not be taken alive!" thundered Chief Hughes.

The police expanded their search across state lines, but it was all in vain. With each passing month, the trail grew colder and the actions of the police more desperate. The years rolled by. One by one, O'Connor's pursuers retired, then died. By the 1930s, the matter had been put to rest in the minds of the public. But the rotting wooden gallows remained in the basement of the courthouse until 1977 awaiting O'Connor's return, long after hanging was outlawed in Cook County.

Rumors circulated that O'Connor had fled to Ireland to take up the cause of Irish nationalism. Others believed that Tommy made it only as far as the South Side, where he lived out his remaining days in domestic bliss among friends and neighbors sworn to secrecy.

The Hecht and MacArthur play depicted O'Connor as the murderer Earl Williams, who escapes the long arm of the law with the help of the fictional reporter Hildy Johnson. Hecht based the character on the real-life exploits of John Hilding Johnson, a clever but cynically detached crime reporter covering the courthouse beat for the *Chicago Herald & Examiner.* The hit play was made into a Hollywood motion picture in 1931 starring Pat O'Brian and Adolphe Menjou.

The Chicago cops, outwitted and outrun, were no match for "Terrible" Tommy O'Connor or Ben Hecht's acid pen.

A Front Page Extra—Sheriff Peter Hoffman, Innkeeper of the County Jail

**S
I
D
E
T
R
I
P**

The Cook County Jail on Dearborn Street was termed the worst in the nation when the oafish Peter M. Hoffman was elected Cook County's thirty-fifth sheriff in April 1922. Running on a "reform" platform, Hoffman vowed to "throw the rascals out," so he could spend the next four years "cleaning up."

Behind the barred portals and stewing in the locked darkness of their cells sat the infamous Frankie Lake and his sidekick, Terry Druggan, Prohibition-era bootleggers in charge of the Valley Gang, West Side liquor distributors who were bigger crooks than Al Capone—at least during the early 1920s.

The jailed beer kings had just cut a deal with the supposedly unimpeachable Warden Wesley Westbrook, who was hired by the outgoing Charles Peters and given a slap on the back vote of confidence by the incoming Hoffman, himself a former grocery store clerk and county coroner.

Lake and Druggan agreed to pay Westbrook the "swag"—a $2,000 payoff hand-delivered by Twentieth Ward political boss Morris Eller on the first and sixteenth of the month. In return Westbrook granted the boys special considerations, including periodic furloughs from the Cook County Jail to attend to the business end of their bootlegging empire; clandestine visits from their flapper girlfriends; private rooms with their own baths; and deluxe accommodations by the kitchen staff.

When an inquiring newspaper reporter dropped by the jail one after-

noon to interview the gangsters, a secretary informed him they were not avail-able at the moment. "Mr. Druggan and Mr. Lake are out right now . . . an appointment downtown," she said pleasantly. "They'll return after dinner."

The scandal broke in September 1925. While Hecht and MacArthur furi-ously scribbled in their notepads (a gag writer could not have concocted such a far-fetched skit, even in his cups), Terry Druggan told an astonished federal grand jury just how accommodating Hoffman and Westbrook could be to a poor fella landing in the jug for no good reason.

> *Q: Now three times you were out visiting the dentist. What else did you do besides visit the dentist?*
>
> *Druggan: I used to walk. I used to walk from Grand Avenue east all the way around [sic] the lake every day to get my health back. I used to take them walks. Regularly, yes sir.*

The whole thing was a howling farce. Sheriff Hoffman and Warden Westbrook were charged with contempt of court, but they put their faith in the

NOTORIOUSLY CORRUPT

COOK COUNTY SHERIFF

PETER HOFFMAN WAS A

BLUSTERING OAF WHO

INSPIRED BEN HECHT TO

REINVENT HIM AS "PETER

HARTMANN" IN HIS

FAMOUS BROADWAY PLAY

THE FRONT PAGE.

(Courtesy of the Chicago Historical Society)

system to square things. Justice in Cook County is like Foxfire. Anything can happen.

Unamused, Federal Judge James Wilkerson sentenced the stumbling sheriff to serve thirty days in his own jail and ordered him to pay $2,500 in restitution. With a shrug of the shoulders Hoffman wondered aloud, "I don't know what all the fuss is about. I was only accommodatin' the boys." Hoffman passed away at age eighty-five on July 30, 1948.

Warden Westbrook, a former deputy superintendent of police, took the fall and received four months. His wife offered the opinion that he "must have been insane," as off to jail he marched.

> Go west on Hubbard Street to LaSalle Street. Turn north (right) and go to Ohio. Turn right (east) on Ohio. Turn left (north) on Rush and go one block to Ontario.

SORRY, WRONG NUMBER!
March 7, 1928

The Lenox Suites Hotel at 628 North Rush Street (southwest corner of Rush and Ontario Streets) is one of the oldest lodging houses in the Near North area. It is a not-so-small miracle that the Lenox has been so carefully preserved and maintained, while so many vintage buildings in this upscale neighborhood are thoughtlessly knocked down every year. Maybe it is because Houston's Restaurant (located inside the hotel) remains a popular watering hole for the after-five Michigan Avenue set, eager to soak up the glitz and glamour of the city's trendiest neighborhood. The yellow-brick hostelry has survived all these years despite an incident involving the murderous Gusenberg brothers who trained their machine guns on an occupied phone booth inside the first-floor smoke shop of the Lenox, then known as the McCormick Inn.

Al Capone was conveniently out of town, as was his custom when there was trouble brewing in the Windy City.

With Jake Guzik recovering from gallstones and Capone vacationing in the tropical heat of Florida, the organization was left in the capable hands of "Machine Gun" Jack McGurn. McGurn was a triggerman, failed prizefighter, and master strategist, who turned his attention to planting illegal slot machines in the cabarets and honky-tonks north of the Chicago River. McGurn's latest foray into

"Bugs" Moran's territory was based on the theory that the North Side gang was broken and spiritless following the deaths of Dion O'Banion, Hymie Weiss, and Vincent "Schemer" Drucci.

Jack McGurn was born in the Mulberry section of Italian New York. He adopted an Irish surname in order to break into the fight game, closed to Italians, Poles, and Jews during the formative years of this century. McGurn was a sucker for a right hook. He had a glass jaw and no heart, but with a machine gun in hand, the Irish gangsters gave pause. So, in a moment of pique, they decided to turn the tables and give him his just deserts using his weapon of choice.

Capone's top triggerman was seated inside the hotel smoke shop conversing with Joseph Eulo, owner of the McCormick Inn, and a companion named Nick Mastro, when he arose from the table and excused himself. "I gotta go make a phone call," he said.

Closing the door of the phone booth behind him, McGurn reached for some change in his pocket, when four men, one of them armed with a machine gun, the others with automatic pistols, dashed in from the street, firing a murderous volley at point-blank range. It is incredible and far-fetched to imagine *anyone* escaping such an onslaught, but McGurn sustained only minor bullet wounds to the shoulder and rib cage. He was dragged from the wreckage of the phone booth and taken in an ambulance to Alexian Brothers Hospital, at that time at Belden and Racine Avenues, alongside the wounded Mastro.

As to the identity of his assailants, McGurn told the cops to mind their own business. "I'll take care of the matter myself," he hissed.

And indeed he would. Less than a year later, Peter and Frank Gusenberg met death inside the infamous garage with five other unlucky Moran gangsters. Jack McGurn was a man true to his word.

Continue north on Rush Street until it intersects with State Street at Cedar Street. Go right (north) on State Parkway to 1340 North.

"IF YOU DON'T SWING, DON'T RING!"
January 13, 1975

Playboy *magazine was spawned in the sexually repressed climate of the 1950s by Hugh Marston Hefner, a product of Chicago's stodgy Bungalow Belt culture on the far Northwest Side of the city. The Catholic parish, the ward office, and the corner tavern on Friday nights represented important rites of passage for young men who were expected to live conventional, orderly lives within the harmony of marriage. Hefner, dreaming of a life of swinging sophistication away from the dull tedium of Northwest Side conformity, defied custom and sparked a social revolution. He published the first issue of* Playboy *from his apartment in January 1953. The magazine was a huge hit, and within a few years Hefner was living out his fantasies inside a French-inspired mansion built in 1899 by James Gamble Rogers for Dr. George Snow Isham. President Theodore Roosevelt and Admiral Robert Perry had been overnight guests at the manse in the early years of the century. Now, flash forward to the swinging 1960s, when an entirely different cast of characters enjoyed the mansion's amenities. Tony Curtis and Warren Beatty were among the Hollywood elite at the top of Hugh Hefner's guest list. Within this grand, seventy-two-room beaux-arts setting at 1340 North State Parkway (with the south annex at 1336 State), Hefner and a glamorous entourage of celebrities, starlets, Bunnies, Playmates, and fun-seekers cavorted in a wonderland of sexual unreality. Such goings-on stiffened the resolve of city politicians and U.S. Attorney James R. Thompson to expose the long-rumored love-ins, drug parties, and other assorted debaucheries to the world. Bobbie Arnstein, Hefner's trusted assistant for nearly fourteen years, became the unwitting pawn in this moral tug-of-war between the extremes of two divergent worlds. Her suicide in the timeworn Maryland Hotel at Rush Street and Delaware Place, just blocks south of the Mansion, climaxed a shameful episode in local jurisprudence.*

Two years after her graduation from Lake View High School on Chicago's North Side, Bobbie Arnstein went to work as a receptionist for *Playboy* magazine at their first corporate office at 232 East Ohio Street. It was 1960, and the dawn of the sexual revolution was at hand.

Hugh Hefner was formulating plans for the nation's first Playboy Club, which opened on February 29, 1960, in the former Colony Club, owned by Chicago Blackhawk magnate Arthur Wirtz, at 116 East Walton Street.

Arnstein, caught up in the social whirl with so many other young women who entered the Playboy orbit in the early years, looked forward to a secure and rewarding future working for the buoyant Hefner, who had asked her to consider an offer to become his private assistant.

Bobbie Arnstein was on a voyage of self-discovery, and she plunged into her career at a time when the Playboy phenomenon was spreading across international borders.

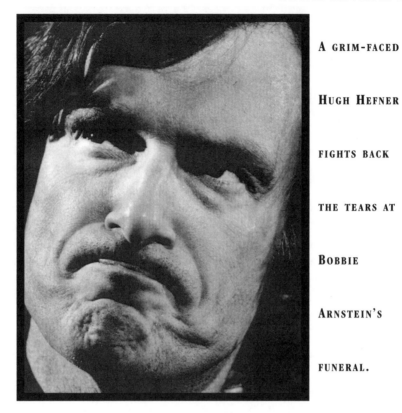

A GRIM-FACED

HUGH HEFNER

FIGHTS BACK

THE TEARS AT

BOBBIE

ARNSTEIN'S

FUNERAL.

In 1963, Arnstein's life took an abrupt U-turn when her fiancé Tom Lownes was killed in an automobile accident in Florida. Thereafter, Arnstein's life spiraled out of control and, at some point, she became involved in the drug culture.

Slipping into a depression she was powerless to overcome, Arnstein lapsed into a drug-induced coma about a year before her death. Left alone, the fragile and vulnerable young woman might have worked out her problems in due time. The government, however, initiated a malicious probe into Hugh Hefner's affairs, setting their sights on Bobbie Arnstein as the key to a successful grand jury prosecution of the Playboy founder. The scheme was engineered by the Drug Enforcement Agency, the U.S. Attorney, and the Cook County State's Attorney.

Arnstein was arrested by an agent of the DEA outside Hefner's gated mansion on March 21, 1974. A brass plate screwed into the front door bore the Latin inscription *"Si non oscillas, noli tintinnare,"* meaning: "If You Don't Swing, Don't Ring." The DEA agent decided to wait patiently on the sidewalk until Arnstein appeared.

Escorted to the Everett Dirksen Federal Building on South Dearborn Street, Arnstein was informed that she was under arrest for conspiring to distribute eight ounces of cocaine that she had allegedly brought back from Florida in 1971 in a shoulder bag. The government prosecutors pressured her to finger Hefner and other Playboy executives in a broader based pattern of conspiracy, but Arnstein refused to betray her boss, even if it meant prison.

For the next two years Arnstein's life was a living hell. She tried to emulate Hefner's freewheeling habits, picking up younger men she met in Rush Street bars and taking them back to her rooms for sexual adventures.

In the end, the court showed no mercy. Arnstein was found guilty on October 30, 1974, and given a fifteen-year conditional prison sentence. Then, Jim Thompson dropped a bombshell that sent her spinning over the edge. Summoning the anxious woman to his office, he informed her that there were rumors on the street that someone had put out a contract on her life. It is not exactly clear what Thompson hoped to achieve by conveying such disconcerting information to her at this time.

Free on bond pending appeal, Arnstein checked into Room 1716 of the Maryland Hotel at 2:44 in the morning under the name Roberta Hillman. The Maryland was a seedy dive swarming with mob-connected pimps and prostitutes who worked the infamous Cloister (later the Pago Pago Room), a hotel lounge controlled by Rush Street overseer Jimmy "the Monk" Allegretti. The hotel marked the end of the line for the downtrodden and the desperate.

Arnstein scrawled a suicide note on hotel stationery before ingesting tranquilizers, barbiturates, and sleeping pills. The hotel manager found her the next day.

The government's inquisition succeeded in driving an embittered Hugh Hefner out of Chicago forever.

Exonerated of wrongdoing by U.S. Attorney Sam Skinner on December 29, 1975, the Playboy founder exiled himself to Los Angeles and a freer moral climate. In August 1984, he donated the "big bunny hutch" on State Parkway to the School of the Art Institute, where Hefner had enrolled for a class in figure illustration back in 1946. The mansion served as a student dormitory until 1994, when the property was sold to condominium developers for redevelopment.

Go to the end of State Parkway at North Avenue and turn left (west). Continue to LaSalle Street. Turn left (south) and stay on LaSalle to Erie Street. Turn left (east) and go to Clark Street.

MAKING "WHOOPEE" AT MCGOVERN'S INN
1920s–1940s

To disgusted reformers, Republicans, and church deacons, the half-mile stretch of Clark Street immediately north of the Chicago River was infamously known as "Honky Tonk U.S.A." It was a dubious designation coined at the end of the 1940s by the late Herman Kogan, renowned journalist and author. For nearly half a century, the Talk of the Town, the Casino, the Gaiety, and other nightclubs opened in the North Side rialto district were the domain of gangsters, "21 Girls," hustlers, hookers, and neighborhood people looking for a few thrills in the pre-television era. There are few reminders of those times left today, and the Chicago outfit lost interest in the adjacent Rush Street area in the 1980s. The nightclubs of Honky Tonk U.S.A. have either been razed or converted to more utilitarian purposes. The modest green and gray four-story building at 661 West Erie Street (the northeast corner of Clark and Erie) has changed hands many times over the years. Today it is called Tonic. Undoubtedly, if Dion O'Banion and his North Side gang were alive today, they would remember it as McGovern Brothers' Inn, a place where they ate, drank, and plotted diabolical moves against Al Capone.

As a boy, Dion O'Banion fled from the home of his father, a plasterer, to take a job as a singing waiter at McGovern Brothers' Inn, where it is said he reduced grown men to tears with sentimental ballads of mother Ireland that stirred the heart. Afterward, the gimpy little hood, who nearly lost his leg in a streetcar accident when he was a mere lad, would pass the hat and pick their pockets without batting an eye.

Dion was an expert safecracker and hijacker who graduated from the Market Street Gang of toughs, who terrorized the neighbors at Chestnut and Orleans Streets, to the leadership of the Irish North Side mob.

O'Banion used McGovern's, a Prohibition speakeasy by 1921, as a blind for criminal operations. Here he was taught social refinements by Samuel "Nails"

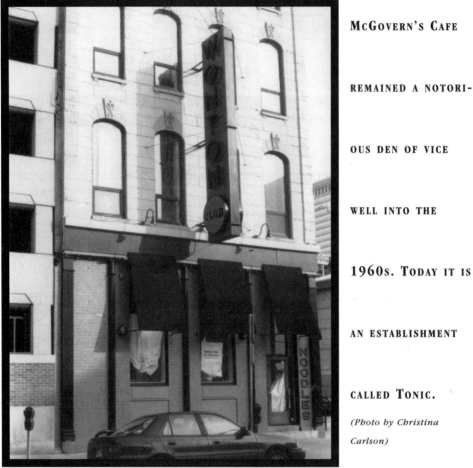

McGOVERN'S CAFE REMAINED A NOTORIOUS DEN OF VICE WELL INTO THE 1960s. TODAY IT IS AN ESTABLISHMENT CALLED TONIC.

(Photo by Christina Carlson)

Morton, another of McGovern's gangland aficionados, who showed O'Banion how to eat with a knife and fork and act like a gentleman. Morton was kicked in the head by his trusty steed while cantering about the Lincoln Park bridle path one Sunday morning in May 1923. Hearing this disconcerting news, O'Banion ordered Louis "Two Gun" Alterie to pump a bullet into the horse's head and carve him up for the dogs and cats.

McGovern's was a tough syndicate joint long before O'Banion and his gang arrived. The cabaret and resort was closed by an injunction obtained by the Committee of Fifteen in 1916 but, with so much at stake, such places rarely stay closed.

Renamed McGovern's Liberty Inn and Supper Club, the place continued to enjoy an infamous reputation well into the early 1960s as a "bump-and-grind" strip joint, where the only women passing through the doors were the "champagne solicitors" hiding their G-strings in their purses.

Champagne cocktails with one of the performers between sets ran upward of $10 in 1960.

A *Daily News* reporter, wandering into the Near North sin spot in 1962, reported seeing "a chubby waitress who wore only a loose vest above the waist—that's all—[it] jolts Liberty Inn customers when they get used to the darkness in the club." After this report was filed, the owners of the establishment were charged with serving a customer knockout drops and robbing him, an old Chicago trick practiced with greater success by Mickey Finn back in the 1910s.

"It even plays matinees and employs probably twenty-five peelers, and those are not its only distaff drawing cards," Jack Lait and Lee Mortimer said of the Liberty in *Chicago Confidential,* their epic tome of after-hours dissipation in the Windy City.

To continue our tour, turn right (south) on Clark Street and go to Ontario Street. Turn right (west) and continue to LaSalle Street. Turn right (north) and take LaSalle Street north to Chicago Avenue. Turn left (west) and go one block to Wells Street. Turn left (south) and go to 708 North Wells Street.

WHERE GANGLAND WENT TO MOURN
1920s

Gangster funerals were lavish affairs, and the John Sbarbaro Funeral Home at 708 North Wells Street, between Huron and Superior Streets, was the mortuary of choice for grieving wise guys and the women who loved them. Today the building is a residential apartment, nearly invisible amid the glittering tapestry of River North bistros and galleries.

John A. Sbarbaro was an anomaly of the gangland era. As an assistant state's attorney, he investigated a number of high-profile gangland slayings including the shooting of Dion O'Banion inside his State Street flower shop on November 9, 1924.

As a prominent North Side undertaker, whose Wells Street mortuary was a drop-off point for shipments of illegal liquor during Prohibition, Sbarbaro faithfully served the gangsters' interests both in life and in death.

Businessman Sbarbaro, satisfied that Dion's killers would never be found, drew up a contract with Viola O'Banion, the inconsolable young widow, who ordered a lavish funeral, the likes of which had not been seen in Chicago since the obsequies for Big Jim Colosimo in May 1920.

O'Banion's cortege was made up of 24 automobiles, loaded with flowers and trailed by 122 mourning vehicles. The casket cost $10,000. The Near North streets were choked with traffic for two miles, and a squad of motorcycle police cleared a path for the hearse of the slain gangster while a police band played a mournful refrain. The public was appalled by such gaudy excess, which would normally be reserved for the death of a cardinal or a mayor.

The roads pointing west from the Sbarbaro mortuary led to Mount Carmel Cemetery, where Vincent "Schemer" Drucci, another Moran gangster, was delivered in grand style on April 8, 1927. Thousands of downtown office workers and merrymakers lined the funeral procession's route. The largest floral display measured eight and a half feet high, and an American flag, recognizing Drucci's military service, draped the casket.

With flair and style, Sbarbaro delivered Hymie Weiss, Mike Merlo, and many other bootlegger big shots to their final resting places. He did not discriminate in

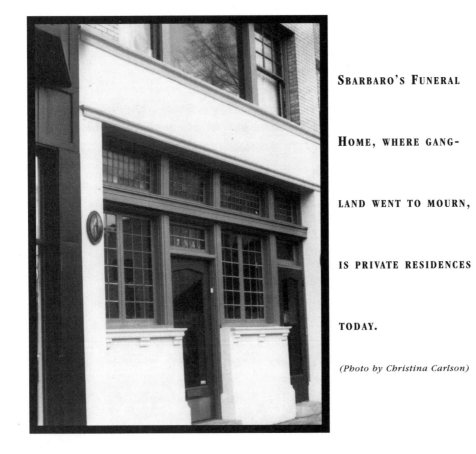

SBARBARO'S FUNERAL

HOME, WHERE GANG-

LAND WENT TO MOURN,

IS PRIVATE RESIDENCES

TODAY.

(Photo by Christina Carlson)

his choice of customers. He buried North Siders loyal to the O'Banion-Moran gang and Al Capone's allies in the Unione Sicilione. It did not matter to him at all, because as long as the hoods stumbled into the line of fire, Sbarbaro would be there waiting, sales contract in hand.

While en route to Mount Carmel, a funeral car in the Weiss procession reminded Chicago voters just who had choreographed this extravaganza: "Sbarbaro for Municipal Judge!"

On February 17, 1928, two years after his elevation to the bench, Sbarbaro's liquor warehouse in back of the funeral parlor was bombed. He attributed the cowardly act to the criminals he had sentenced to prison, but insiders knew better.

As a Superior Court judge in the 1940s, Sbarbaro was criticized for his friendship with crooked politicians and cops working the Forty-second Ward ("The Roaring 42") and the leniency he showed to syndicate criminals.

In 1946, the judge was named team president of the Chicago Stags, the newest entrant in the National Basketball League (forerunner of the NBA) and the lineal ancestor of Michael Jordan's Chicago Bulls.

Continue south on Wells Street to Erie Street. Turn left (east) and go one block to LaSalle Street. Turn left (north) and go one block to Huron Street.

BURIED LOOT IN THE BASEMENT
October 20, 1974

Purolator armored cars, once a familiar site along the bustling commercial thoroughfares of Downtown Chicago and the Near North, have disappeared, and the ignominy of that fateful night in October 1974 when the company was "relieved" of $4.3 million from its warehouse is largely forgotten by local residents. The former warehouse is a yellow-brick building standing on the southeast corner of LaSalle and Huron Streets that is today a Bertucci's Restaurant, where the denizens of the Gold Coast go to sip Chardonnay and feast on risotto.

In dollars and *sense* the Purolator burglary fell well short of the 1963 Great Train Robbery, when British thieves robbed an express train bound from Glasgow to London of $7 million. For sheer guile and raw nerve, however, Purolator stands alone in the annals of recorded crime.

Ralph Ronald Marrera was the "inside man" who assisted a gang of second-raters in pulling off the biggest cash heist in U.S. history; the theft of $4,374,398.96 from the Purolator Security Armored Express Company lying in the shadow of the Hancock Building and the Magnificent Mile.

Purolator was an inviting target, and Marrera, a disgruntled timecard employee who was paid a miserly $4.30 an hour to protect millions of dollars in cash and coin stored in the warehouse each night, was easily seduced by the promise of a pile of cash that he could use to finance a lavish Gold Coast lifestyle. It was all his for closing his eyes for just one lousy hour. Penny-pinching Purolator bean counters who offered substandard wages never bothered to check personal references before hiring new night watchmen. So they must share some of the responsibility for the chain of events that unfolded one night in the basement of Pasquale "Patsy" Marzano's Cicero home.

Under Patsy's guidance, Marrera, Jimmy "the Greek" Maniatis, Pete Gushi, Luigi "Lou" DiFonzo, and William "Tony" Marzano plotted the intricate details of the operation. The unlikely partners in crime believed they had all the angles covered.

Marzano was in debt up to his eyeballs, but with Marrera supplying the secret combination to the east and west vaults of the warehouse, his hopes soared. He believed he would soon be winging toward the Cayman Islands with more money in tow than Jackie Onassis had.

These men were strictly bench material; small-time neophytes from the suburbs and outlying neighborhoods of Chicago with a big plan but no connections, save Marrera. In hindsight, it was a lunatic stunt doomed to failure, but at the time, no one in the criminal underworld, where "big scores" are routinely discussed and analyzed, expected it or even saw it coming.

The Purolator heist went down on a Sunday night in October, a dull, listless evening. Marrera was working the overnight shift. He guarded $40 million in cash including the previous night's receipts from the Hawthorne Race Track in Cicero, home base of the Chicago mob. That evening, he was Purolator's first and only line of defense against the criminal intentions of evil-minded men.

At 1:11 in the morning, a time of night when bleary-eyed revelers are emptying out of the nearby Rush Street hot spots, a fire alarm sounded inside the Purolator vaults. By the time the fire engines pulled up at the curb, the acrid smell of smoke hung in the air.

Marrera defiantly blocked their path. "Nobody gets in! These are the orders!" Unamused at being rousted at this time of night for what could well be a wild-goose chase, the firemen indignantly brushed past him. Inside the vault they stumbled upon an odd but amazing sight. Someone had ignited the sacks of cur-

THE SCENE OF

THE PUROLATOR

HEIST IS WHERE

RESIDENTS OF

THE GOLD COAST

DINE THESE

DAYS.

THE SCENE OF THE PUROLATOR HEIST IS WHERE RESIDENTS OF THE GOLD COAST DINE THESE DAYS.

(Photo by Christina Carlson)

rency with gasoline-filled plastic bags, but the loss of oxygen once the vault doors had slammed shut extinguished the flames. Purolator was spared an estimated loss of $36 million, but spirits sank just as quickly as they had risen when it was determined that $4.3 million was missing.

Suspicion immediately fell upon the security guard, who enjoyed watching porno movies and late-night reruns while on duty. Marrera was the only Purolator employee to flunk his lie detector test, and only then did the company find out that he had also failed a similar test for Wells Fargo a few years earlier.

A task force involving agents of the FBI, Chicago police detectives, and the Illinois Bureau of Investigation (IBI) sprang into action.

The disconsolate Marrera was taken into protective custody on October 27 and shuttled to Cermak Hospital on Twenty-sixth Street after he failed twice to kill himself in a Rockford prison.

Patsy Marzano and his cousin Anthony were picked up in the Caymans as they prepared to depart for Costa Rica. A large chunk of the Purolator loot— $400,000—was recovered in Miami shortly thereafter. The case against the Marzano gang was building like an avalanche.

The high point of the investigation came less than a month later when a contingency of fourteen FBI agents and Chicago cops armed with sledgehammers and pickaxes stormed a red-brick bungalow at 2045 North Natchez Avenue on the Northwest Side. The Feds dug up $2.2 million buried in the musty basement under fresh cement. The bungalow, no different from tens of thousands of ordinary Chicago bungalows built between 1915 and 1935, was owned by Marrera's maternal grandmother, but was being used by the gang as a safe house.

Upon hearing the news, U.S. Attorney James R. Thompson was exultant. "As far as I'm able to tell, two point two million is the biggest recovery of stolen money in U.S. history." Smiling Jim preened for the cameras with the stacks of bills piled high in front of him. It was a career-building case that, following on the heels of a string of prosecutorial successes in the mid-1970s, vaulted Thompson into the governor's chair, which he would continue to occupy for a record four terms.

The case ended with $1.2 million still unaccounted for. It will probably never be found, but someone, somewhere, is living out Marzano's resort island fantasy. Maybe there is an outfit guy living the high life in the Caymans this very moment.

As for the Purolator burglars, who answered destiny's call but screwed it up at the eleventh hour because they flunked basic science, fate was not nearly so kind. Patsy Marzano was sentenced to twenty years in prison, but was paroled in 1983. His cousin Tony served his time alongside Watergate burglar E. Howard Hunt down in Florida. He published *The Big Steal,* a tell-all book about the caper, and enjoyed his ten minutes of fame.

Peter Gushi, who tried to drag the Chicago outfit into the case, entered the federal witness protection program after serving four years in a federal prison. DiFonzo was acquitted. As he walked out of the Dirksen Federal Building a free man, he spotted a Purolator truck and flipped the driver the bird, a symbolic gesture of contempt. Jimmy Maniatis served his term at the correctional center at Marion, Illinois, then drifted away.

Ralph Marrera simply cracked under the strain. He suffered a seizure and coma from sedatives administered by Cook County physicians at Cermak Hospital on the campus of the Criminal Courts Building at Twenty-sixth and California. His lawyers ingeniously convinced the court that he was a drooling imbecile who could not even remember his own name. Prosecutors were dubious, but Marrera was judged mentally incompetent in 1975 and ordered confined to a rest home.

In 1983, the government revisited the case. Judge John F. Grady of the U.S. District Court in Chicago, unamused by Marrera's soap-opera antics in the earlier trial, sentenced the former inside man to twenty years in the federal prison at Milan, Michigan.

The big score he daydreamed about in 1974 came late for the last of the jailed Purolator thieves. Paroled in 1989, Ralph Ronald Marrera was awarded a $650,000 settlement in his medical malpractice claim against Cook County.

To continue, go north on LaSalle Street to Chicago Avenue. Turn right (east) and go to State Street. Turn right (south). Holy Name Cathedral is in the first block on the east side of State Street.

"AT THE NAME OF JESUS EVERY KNEE SHOULD BEND IN HEAVEN AND ON EARTH"
November 10, 1924, and October 11, 1926

In the very presence of the house of God, there occurred two violent reenactments of earlier Prohibition gang wars. Dion O'Banion, boss of the North Side mob of hijackers and second-story men who graduated to the ranks of big-time bootleggers, was assassinated inside Schofield's Flower Shop on November 10, 1924. Schofield's, where O'Banion was manager, stood at 738 North State Street, directly across the street from the rectory of Holy Name Cathedral (situated between Chicago Avenue and Superior Street.). After the O'Banion murder, the owner kept the business going until his death in 1947. Schofield's son, Stephen, opened a second flower shop at 731 North Dearborn Street, but ran afoul of the law and was arrested in a gambling raid in December 1964.

On October 11, 1926, Earl "Hymie" Weiss, O'Banion's eventual successor as mob boss, was on his way back to the flower shop when a fusillade of bullets from the upper floors of a rooming house next door to Schofield's allowed him to take the proverbial shortcut to God. The Gothic post-fire limestone church across from the flower shop was erected in 1874. Generations of neighborhood residents have passed through its doors. The shots aimed at Weiss tore away portions of the inscription on the church cornerstone until all that remained was the cryptic wording ". . . every knee should . . . heaven on earth."

Tourists, who had never heard of the infamy of O'Banion and Weiss, gaped at the destruction for years, until the archdiocese of Chicago finally said enough is enough and obliterated the bullet holes and what was left of the biblical message. The rooming house at 740 North State Street that served as the assassin's lookout post was owned by Harry Stephen Keeler, a writer of crime thrillers. Schofield's Flower Shop and the other storefronts on the west side of the block were bulldozed in 1960. A parking lot hardly does justice to the memory of these famous events, but sadly, and regrettably, that is all that is left. Infamy, as we have seen so many times during our excursions, often contaminates a property for years, even decades into the future. However, the curious still flock to North State Street in tour buses, by car, and on foot. They view the flattened surface of the asphalt parking lot where the handicapped spaces are located (the proximate location of Schofield's) before crossing the street for a closer look at Holy Name. Visitors mill around in front of the famous cathedral for a few minutes, then depart, taking home a fleeting memory of wicked old Chicago.

Dion O'Banion was expecting company the morning of November 10, 1924. Mike Merlo, the president of the Unione Sicilione, had passed away quite unexpectedly, as the heads of this politically connected gangster fraternal society were wont to do, and O'Banion was applying the finishing touches to the funeral wreaths. The funeral was to be a lavish spectacle, drawing a large, but respectful, procession of ten thousand politicians, judges, cops, bankers, banana vendors, and flunkies. Merlo's friends had directed $25,000 worth of business to the Schofield flower shop in recent days.

O'Banion, in shirt sleeves with a pistol bulging from his vest holster, was trimming the chrysanthemums when he heard the gentle tinkle of the transom bell overhead. Three men, one of them dressed in a brown overcoat and matching fedora, walked to the rear of the store. Dion, a friendly and likable little Irishman with a noticeable limp, extended his hand in friendship to men he knew were his blood enemies. "Hello boys! You from Mike Merlo's?" he asked cheerfully.

Upstairs, Victor Young was attending to the company books. Bookkeeper Vincent Glavin was reviewing the bills and accounts receivable. At the first sound of gunfire, they raced down the stairs . . . and out the front door.

Mike Genna ("Il Diavolo, the Devil") clasped O'Banion's hand. Pleasantries were exchanged, and the porter William Crutchfield disappeared behind the curtain. Then Genna jerked the North Side gangster unexpectedly forward, throwing him off balance. Genna's two companions, believed to be the feared Mafia assassins John Scalise and Alberto Anselmi, pumped five shots into Dion's body, and added the *coup de grace*—a bullet in the mouth. The three men disappeared through the front door and into an awaiting Jewett sedan parked around the corner on Superior Street. O'Banion was sprawled on the floor, surrounded by flowerpots full of roses, his pruning shears lying nearby. By the time the cops arrived, the petals of the gentle flowers were covered with blood.

William F. Schofield, O'Banion's business partner, was attending to business at Mount Carmel Cemetery, but Crutchfield, the African-American handyman who swept up and looked after things for Dion, caught a glimpse of the killers and provided the only accurate descriptions to police.

The cops held out little hope of ever solving this murder. "O'Banion, above all things knew he was marked for death. He knew it," nodded Chicago police captain William "Shoes" Schoemaker, who had been following the bloody trail of dead bootleggers since the advent of Prohibition.

Though every effort was made on the dead O'Bannon's behalf, the Catholic church refused to allow a priest to preside over the memorial service. Because he had not been *convicted* of any of the twenty-five murders the police believed him responsible for and because his death was not a suicide, however, it was agreed that little Dion could be laid to rest in his $10,000 silver casket at Mount Carmel Cemetery, where he owned a large lot. Scalpers charged curiosity seekers a dollar a head for a space on the sidewalk from which to view the gaudy procession.

For nearly two years Earl "Hymie" Weiss, who assumed control of the North Side mob, stewed over the unfortunate death of his pal Dion O'Banion. His hatred for Al Capone grew and festered. Vengeance was uppermost in his mind and, to his way of thinking, the only appropriate way to settle old scores was for Capone to hand over Scalise and Anselmi, who were both incarcerated at the Stateville Penitentiary in Joliet on manslaughter charges. "I wouldn't do that to a yellow dog!" Capone snorted.

There was to be no peace in Chicago with so many hard feelings. Following the shootout at the Standard Oil Building (see Tour 1), the opposing forces agreed to a peace conference. But when Al Capone denied Weiss the courtesy of meting out punishment to O'Banion's killers, Weiss and George "Bugs" Moran led a hasty charge into the South Side badlands, intending to ambush Capone outside the Four Deuces at 2222 South Wabash. Capone miraculously escaped unhurt, but his driver, Tony Ross, died behind the wheel.

Weiss pulled another crazy stunt a week later, this time sealing his own fate. On September 20, 1926, a caravan of motor cars, each of them carrying a trio of machine gunners, drove slowly past Capone's Cicero headquarters at the Hawthorne Inn. Seated at a table in the crowded coffee shop, Capone was thrown to the floor by bodyguard Frank Rio when the first volley of shots were fired into the storefront by the passing motorcade. Thousands of bullets passed through the interior, but again, Al Capone escaped death. (For details of this event, see Tour 7.)

Fearless to the point of stupidity, Weiss maintained his high-profile lifestyle, goading Al Capone at every turn.

Hymie was an interested courtroom spectator at the murder trial of "Polack Joe" Saltis and his driver Frank "Lefty" Koncil the afternoon of October 11, 1926,

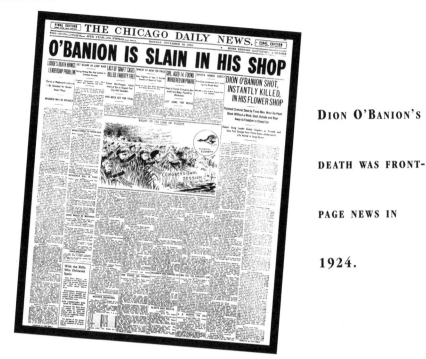

DION O'BANION'S

DEATH WAS FRONT-

PAGE NEWS IN

1924.

when he decided to take a break and return to his office above the flower shop. In the company of defense attorney William W. O'Brien; Benny Jacobs, a small-time bootlegger who worked for City Collector Morris Eller; driver Sam Pellar; and gunman Patrick Murray, the Weiss entourage drove back to Schofield's in two separate cars.

Waiting for them in a rented room at 740 North State Street were four machine gunners believed to be Frank Nitti, Scalise, Anselmi, and Frank Diamond. From their third-floor lair, they were afforded an excellent view of the street. There was a second gunman sequestered in a second-floor apartment around the corner at 1 West Superior (southwest corner of State and Superior), just in case the first crew missed the mark.

Hymie Weiss never had a chance. He was a sitting duck as soon as he alighted from his car on Superior Street, just south of the cathedral. He approached the flower shop with Murray at his side, oblivious to the dangers lurking all around him.

Then, there was the harsh and deadly roar of Tommy guns, as pedestrians scurried for cover.

Pat Murray died instantly. Weiss took ten bullets and was pronounced dead at Henrotin Hospital without ever regaining consciousness. In his pockets, police found $5,200 and a list of the jurors set to decide Joe Saltis's fate.

O'Brien, Pellar, and Jacobs suffered only minor injuries. They received emergency treatment from a neighborhood doctor.

The assassins bolted down the stairs, exited through the rear of the building, raced to Dearborn Street, then vanished into the crowd of pedestrians. A discarded machine gun was found in an alley off of Dearborn Street, but it did the police little good.

Chief Morgan Collins, a scrupulously honest administrator who was sincere in his desire to rescue Chicago from Al Capone and his legions, was bitterly resigned. "I don't want to encourage the business," he said. "But if somebody has to be killed, it's a good thing the gangsters are murdering themselves off. It saves trouble for the police."

The Magnificent Mile (Michigan Avenue from the Chicago River North to Oak Street)

Chicagoans at the end of the nineteenth century could not help but marvel at the city's stunning growth and remarkable triumphs. Few visionaries could foresee the coming importance of the Near North side, particularly that of Michigan Avenue, then a sparsely populated boulevard known as Pine Street. To the west, a collection of turreted mansions, smaller graystones, and balloon-frame post-fire shanties filled in the district. Then, with great ceremony, the Michigan Avenue Bridge opened in 1920. Later architects cut the ribbon of the Gothic Tribune Tower on July 6, 1925, welcoming visitors to Chicago's "Magnificent Mile," soon to become a destination point for tourists from around the world. Toxic memories of the Sands vice district, the antics of George Wellington Streeter (a squatter in a stovepipe hat who proclaimed himself the "Emperor" of the "Deestrict of Streeterville" after his houseboat ran aground in the Lake Michigan shallows at Chicago Avenue in 1886), and other untoward civic embarrassments from the distant past were wiped clean in the rush of urban development. Today, the Magnificent Mile rivals New York's Fifth Avenue for the luxury of its hotels and splendid appointments of its retail district, restaurants, and commercial buildings. Chicagoans are rightfully proud of this priceless treasure. There is no finer place to stroll on a warm spring day with the gentle breezes wafting off Lake Michigan and jazz ensembles serenading passersby outside of Water Tower Place.

To continue, proceed south on State to Ohio Street. Turn left (east) and proceed to Michigan Avenue. Turn left (north) and go north one block to Ontario Street.

"LITTLE AL" LISTENS IN
1959–1965

After 1957, FBI Director J. Edgar Hoover was finally forced to acknowledge the existence of a national network of organized crime stretching from New York City to Los Angeles. Meeting in secret at the estate of Joseph Barbara in Apalachin, New York, the "board of directors" of the national commission, the ruling body of organized crime, were rousted and sent running into the woods by local law enforcement. Spurred to action by the embarrassing disclosures in the national press, Director Hoover fashioned a Top Hoodlum Squad composed of teams of elite, incorruptible investigators. In Chicago, Hoover pressured Special Agents Ross Spencer, William Roemer, and their colleagues to install listening devices in known mob hangouts. Undercover electronic surveillance and a network of informants was the two-pronged strategy outlined by Hoover in the spring of 1959. A likely place to plant such a "bug" was an inconspicuous office building at 620 North Michigan Avenue housing the Black Orchid Nightclub and Celano's Custom Tailor Shop on the second floor. Sam Giancana had been making appearances here twice a week to meet and discuss business with the outfit heavies. It is highly unlikely that you will see gangsters passing through the portals these days. The Viacom Entertainment store and an Eddie Bauer anchor the newly built retail complex that now stands on Michigan Avenue between Ontario and Ohio Streets.

From the get-go it was a "black bag" job.

The word of caution imparted to Roemer, Special Agent in Charge Ralph Hill, Maz Rutland, and other bureau agents from Director Hoover was "Don't embarrass the bureau." It was plainly understood that if they were caught inside the tailor shop by a cop or a security guard after business hours, it was to go down as a "third-rate burglary" much like Watergate. Roemer, as honest and forthright as any agent who passed through the Chicago Bureau, nicknamed his pineapple-sized microphone "Little Al," after Al Capone. The mobsters who convened in the second-floor office of Celano's had code-named their meeting place "Schneider's," from the German word for a tailor shop.

It took eight Sundays and countless hours to string the wiring inside the tailor shop to make Little Al function. Remote monitoring was set up at FBI headquarters at 236 North Clark Street. (This was the original headquarters before the Bureau relocated to the Dirksen Federal Building at 219 South Dearborn in 1965.)

Little Al was inaugurated on July 29, 1959. In the days, months, and years to follow, the Chicago office learned the full extent of the mob's influence in politics, legitimate business, and crime operations. The subornation of Cook County judges, payoffs to cops, the fixing of political elections; and the other information flowing through Little Al and other remote monitoring devices provided a textbook of crime and malfeasance in the Windy City.

The issue of privacy is delicate and contentious, of course, and civil libertarians fought long and hard against electronic surveillance used as admissible evidence in court. By executive decree, President Lyndon Johnson ordered an end to the surreptitious bugging when Johnson learned that the Feds were listening in on his Lone Star State political cronies—otherwise known as the Texas Mafia.

Chez Paree, Mon Ami? 1930s–1940s

SIDETRIP

In Depression and war, the Chez Paree was the place to hobknob east of Michigan Avenue. Reservations were taken over the phone at DE-laware 3434, and the cover charge was a nominal two bucks for a lavish spectacle. The floorshow featured breathless chorus girls, baggy-pants Vaudeville comics, crooners, and swing bands set to entertain at 8:30, 12:00, and 2:00 A.M. on most nights. The Chez was most like the nightclubs of our popular imagination, depicted in grainy black-and-white 1930s gangster movies.

Men in tuxedos. Cigarette girls. Hollywood talent scouts. A chorus line. A full orchestra. Seated in the audience of five hundred on any given night was a phalanx of underworld big shots mingling with other Chez Paree patrons and sipping Lime Rickeys in the spacious comfort of the club. Chez Paree drew the biggest stars of motion pictures and radio, including ventriloquist Edgar Bergen, who in 1936 was awarded an exclusive three-year contract to perform at the Chez.

Legendary restaurateur Mike Fritzel opened his nightclub in the early 1930s with his business partner Joey Jacobson. Fritzel had operated many *downtown hot spots over the years, but none more famous than the Chez Paree, where, on opening night, the international con-man, society playboy, and supposed kidnap victim Jake "the Barber" Factor was "taken" for $40,000 in a rigged card game. Jacobson was smart enough to keep his lip buttoned and the gambling payoffs flowing into the political war chest of William J. "Botchy" Connors, ward committeeman, state senator, and protector of the Gold Coast rackets during the Depression and the war.*

Boss Connors functioned by and through Captain Thomas Harrison and the crooked cops headquartered at the Chicago Avenue police station. Similar arrangements existed in other wards of the city where gamblers, prostitutes, and their sponsors lurked in the shadows.

In 1950, after twenty uproarious years, the Fritzel-Jacobson tandem sold their interests. The Chez lingered a few more years, then closed, as all of the big-name nightclubs did sooner or later. The famous show spot was located at 610 North Fairbanks just north of Huron Street on the west side of the street. The Northwestern Memorial Hospital complex swallowed up the entire block, leaving no clues behind attesting to the gaiety and merriment of that lost era.

To continue our tour, proceed north on Michigan Avenue to the John Hancock Center located between Chestnut Street and Delaware Place.

JOHN HANCOCK DEATH LEAP
August 12, 1971

In this town, anything goes . . . and sometimes it goes out the window. In the wee small hours on the morning of August 12, 1971, a jilted and despondent woman plunged to her death from the dizzying heights of the ninetieth floor at the John Hancock Center at 875 North Michigan Avenue (between Chestnut Street and Delaware Place). Soaring to a height of 1,127 feet, the Skidmore, Owings & Merrill commission is the tallest office and apartment complex in the world. When the City News Bureau sent word of the apparent suicide over the wire, reporters from the major dailies scurried to the Chestnut Street side of the building to investigate. Experts agreed: It was impossible to take a flying leap from inside one of the residential units of "Big John." It couldn't be done, they said, but the proof was in the sidewalk, and onlookers with weak stomachs covered their eyes.

A widow at age twenty-nine, Lorraine Kowalski had been seeing Marshall Berlin, wealthy heir to the lithographing company founded by family patriarch I. S. Berlin, for over a year. Kowalski worked as a secretary at the RCA Corporation, and reasonably expected to tie the knot with the twice-divorced Berlin, who lived with his teenage son in the Hancock.

The vice-chairman of I. S. Berlin Press, a printing conglomerate with offices in Cleveland, New York, Los Angeles, Boston, Chicago, and Detroit, valued his bachelor lifestyle. Berlin, forty-five, had already left for a night on the town with another woman when Kowalski appeared at his apartment a few minutes past 8:00 P.M.

Kowalski's roommate Carol Thompson answered the door. She had been given a key to Berlin's bachelor pad earlier that afternoon, when the two friends agreed to rendezvous.

That evening, Kowalski and Thompson bar-hopped the nightclubs of the Near North—an area where Captain Clarence Braasch of the Chicago Police Department had systemized an elaborate extortion network of payoffs, shaking down the bar owners and making life miserable for the hookers, strippers, and hustlers until they anted up, thus perpetuating a wheel of vice and graft that had existed in the Chicago Avenue Police District since the early 1900s.

The women made the rounds of Sage's East, Alfie's, The Four Torches, and the Colony East; pick-up joints in the night where long-legged women in their knee-high boots and hot pants crossed their legs at strategic moments and sipped their Sloe Gin Fizzes suggestively. Shaggy-haired post-adolescents and Rush Street lounge lizards garbed in powder-blue leisure suits and white shoes played the waiting game. It was all about booze, one-night stands, Camaros, image, money, and dope.

Rush Street was awash in drugs and sex in the late 1960s and into the early 1970s. Everybody was looking for Mr. Right or the female equivalent of a good time, without strings attached. Disco, AIDS, Ronald Reagan, and changing societal attitudes toward public drinking and casual sex ended the dream. The party was canceled by 1984.

But while it lasted, Mr. Kelly's spelled big-time Las Vegas show-lounge entertainment for conventioneers, middle-aged suburbanites, and promgoers whooping it up on their first night out in the big city. Woody Allen, Mort Sahl, the mentalist Kreskin, the Original Jazz Band, Lenny Bruce, and Don Rickles were among the headliners.

The Happy Medium meant two things to music impresarios: red-hot jazz and 2:00 A.M. cocktails. The Tradewinds at 867 North Rush was a neighborhood bar owned by Artie Adler. His crumpled form was found stuffed in a sewer by sanitation inspectors on a routine tour at 1625 North Neva Street, two months after leaving his office on January 20, 1960, for a dinner engagement with his wife. The new owners of the Tradewinds changed the name of the club to the Living Room. Frank Sinatra and Liz Taylor were devotees when they were passing through town.

Life and death. Drugs and rock 'n' roll. The Lullaby of Rush Street.

Lorraine Kowalski heard the refrain at 3:30 in the morning, August, 12, 1971, as she staggered back to the Hancock incoherent, alone, and bleary-eyed from her night of adventure. Residents told police they heard Kowalski quarrel with her paramour. But Marshall Berlin went to great lengths to explain that she was despondent over the direction the relationship had taken. Carol Thompson said that her friend Lorraine was in her cups well before midnight.

With Kowalski's shrieking ringing in his ears, Marshall Berlin turned away and retreated to the privacy of his bathroom. When he returned a few minutes later, the bedroom window overlooking the street below was shattered into a thousand pieces, the woman's clothes scattered across the floor. The Lake Michigan winds wafted through the apartment. It was 4:10 in the morning. A hurried call was placed to the Chicago Avenue Police Station.

If Marshall Berlin's version of events are to be believed, Kowalski managed to crash through two quarter-inch-thick glass panels measuring fifty-four inches square on her own power. It was a very peculiar suicide. The building engineer told State's Attorney Edward V. Hanrahan that the glass was capable of withstanding 280 pounds per square foot before shattering. Kowalski weighed less than 130 pounds. A linebacker would have had trouble breaking through the unyielding glass.

Berlin refused to take a lie-detector test after being questioned at length by police. He would only say that Lorraine Kowalski muttered a threat to end her life moments before he retreated to the bathroom.

Structural tests were performed on a similar pane of glass by a Northbrook, Illinois, engineering company, but Hanrahan declined to press criminal charges against the wastrel Berlin. It didn't take the State's Attorney long to realize how few clues he really had to work with. If a crime was committed, there was no physical evidence, nor could it be proved beyond a reasonable doubt.

No further action would be taken. The first Hancock suicide investigation was officially closed.

Was it just a deadly mix of Rush Street, a woman's broken heart, and depression? We'll never know.

A $1.75 million damage suit was filed against the building management, but the matter was quietly settled out of court for $10,000 in 1975.

Continue north on Michigan Avenue to the corner of Michigan Avenue and Walton Drive.

"IT SURE 'COURAGED ME UP TO GO OUT AND TAKE THE DRAKE!"

July 30, 1925

Beckoning the world to its doors, the majestic Drake Hotel rises above the curving sweep of Lake Shore Drive at the foot of Michigan Avenue—anchoring the Magnificent Mile. The Drake is a fabulous hostelry; the grande dame of a lost age when personal service, small amenities, and an old and respected family name associated with the building of a great city during its formative years still counted for something. Architect Benjamin Marshall designed the Drake to the specifications set forth by John B. and Tracy Drake. The family crest "Aquila Non Capit Muscas" appears throughout the luxurious hallways and corridors. It means "An Eagle Does Not Catch Flies." The Drake has captivated guests from all around the world since its gala grand opening on New Year's Eve, 1920. A bartender in the Coq D'Or served the second legal drink in Chicago on December 6, 1933, following the repeal of Prohibition. The historic Drake is a signature Chicago hotel, as identifiable with Windy City comings and goings as New York's fabled Waldorf-Astoria; the patrician Mayflower in Washington, D.C.; or the Mark Hopkins, a San Francisco treat known simply as "the Mark." They are all white-glove hotels with "real" American-sounding names etched in the pages of history. If only these walls could speak to us now. They could tell stories of the famous and well-born, big-time plans and million-dollar deals gone astray, romance and tragedy, the pageant of life, and the spectacle of death.

Hotels have always held a special fascination for crooks. When asked why he decided to knock off the Pierre Hotel in New York to the tune of three million dollars, Bobby Comfort, the Big Apple's daring bandito, said, "It was perfect."

Joe Holmes, the "cursing Texan," was no criminal mastermind. On the very morning of the robbery, as he sloshed down a quart jug of Port wine in William Mullneschuck's third-floor flat at 4920 North Winthrop Avenue, Holmes had no idea he was on his way to commit a crime. (The gated three-story graystone on Winthrop Avenue is situated between Ainslie and Argyle Streets, a block east of Broadway in the Uptown neighborhood.) When it all went bad, Holmes blamed his misfortunes on the booze and bad company.

"Well, it sure 'couraged me up to go out and take the Drake," he guffawed to police. "I never had heard of it [the Drake] before."

A strange set of circumstances drew Joe Holmes into bad company. In the parlance of the road, Holmes, alias "Slim," or "Blackie," was a "traveling man." He had come from the hobo jungles west of New York City after his marriage broke up. When the drunken houri answering to the name of Mrs. "Blackie" Holmes came home with a young blade late one night, Joe took the rails and never looked back. He crisscrossed the country inside a series of boxcars, keeping a watchful eye out for the railroad brakeman and his wallet, which was usually empty. In Sweetwater, Texas, he met Ted "Tex" Court, a half-breed Cherokee who wrangled saddle horses on the K-K Ranch.

Ted Court and Joe Holmes reunited in Chicago some months later after Holmes took a job "no human being would hold" for the miserly sum of $1.60 a day. He was the key man at the State House, a vagrant hotel renting rooms by the hour in the South Loop, near the old Whiskey Row. It was forlorn, confining work, and Joe longed for the freedom of the open road. Before he could skip town, however, he ran into Court in a miserable dive at Harrison and State Streets—skid row.

The Cherokee Indian was "full of sociability" and coaxed Holmes into joining him up on the North Side, with his pals Jack Wilson and William J. Mullneschuck.

Wilson was another very sociable fellow. He had come from New York via New Orleans, where he made Ted Court's acquaintance in 1924. They spent their days and nights together rolling in their cups, grifting, singing songs of the road, and raisin' Cain.

Jack Wilson, alias "Jack Woods," worked as a busboy at the Edgewater Beach Hotel exactly a week before quitting in disgust. It was a long enough period of time to hook up with the resentful Eric Nelson, a waiter over at the Drake Hotel—"a place where the 'high hats' went to bunk out for the night."

It took the criminal daring of an "inside man" like Nelson to knit this band of road warriors and ne'er-do-wells together to stage a crazy stunt that they would not have even contemplated on their own volition.

Nelson was contemptuous of the society "swells" putting on inside the Drake's Silver Forest Room. Why should they have so much when he was so needy?

"We had our first talk about the robbery at Mullneschuck's room," Wilson recounted. "Nelson kept telling us, 'What's the use of working all the time, you never have anything. We might as well go out and get something big and have it over with.'"

In his disordered recollections, Wilson said that it was Nelson's idea to stick up the Drake, a big-time score worth between $20,000 and $30,000.

For the next few days, Nelson kept pushing his crazy scheme, but the other men registered little enthusiasm for the plan. Port wine, the kind brewed by the "Terrible" Gennas down on Taylor Street, fired them up and gave them courage.

"I didn't know until two o'clock in the afternoon when we started out where it was to be," Wilson said. "He told me as we were getting into the automobile that we were going to rob the Drake. I didn't pay much attention to him up to that time."

Eric Nelson, the Swedish waiter, boosted $15 from his parents' cupboard and the family Cadillac parked in the alley in back of their home at 4829 North Karlov Avenue. After picking up the hobo gang at the Winthrop Avenue address, Nelson took Lake Shore Drive down to Michigan Avenue, where he parked the car on Walton Drive. He handed Wilson a double-barreled shotgun wrapped in paper and hidden in a brown paper bag.

Brandishing revolvers, Mullneschuck, Nelson, Court, and Holmes burst through the hotel entrance on Walton Drive. There was a hushed silence among the guests and hotel personnel as the masked bandits raced through the lobby, momentarily confused by the layout of the sprawling building. Nelson covered the cashier working the cage, while Holmes raced among the hotel employees, relieving them of their watches and valuables.

Suddenly two shots rang out from behind the office door. Women screamed, and the men instinctively dove for cover. Panic ensued, as the amateur robbers screamed at the desk clerks.

The house detective had seriously wounded Ted Court, who staggered to the Oak Street entrance with two bullets in him. "When we came down to the sidewalk, Court sank down. None of the others tried to help Court so I had to drop him and get him into the automobile," Wilson said.

Patrick Hannigan of the Lincoln Park Police (an adjunct to the Chicago Police Department) administered the final blow. He pumped three more shots into "Tex" Court, who was lying prostrate under the hotel canopy.

Joe Holmes, meanwhile, found himself hopelessly trapped behind a locked door in the basement kitchen of the hotel after separating from the gang. He had shot and killed Frank Blair Rodkey, son of the Drake cashier, in the confusion, but had gotten lost in the maze of rooms trying to escape. With a quick eye and cool nerve, Lincoln Park police officer John Kelly grabbed Holmes in the darkness and wrestled him to the ground after his gun clicked empty.

"It was Court that Texas bad fellow that done it," Holmes stammered as he was dragged away to the lockup. "I just shot off a few doorknobs in trying to get out of that place!"

With a sack full of currency in hand, a sum fixed at nearly $10,000 by the Drake comptroller, the fleeing bandits who managed to escape the hail of gunfire coming from inside the hotel climbed into Nelson's Cadillac and raced north up Lake Shore Drive into Lincoln Park, where throngs of picnickers were enjoying the afternoon. Pursued by police, the bandit car crashed into another vehicle along a roadway bisecting the park, forcing the gang to split up.

Nelson commandeered a Yellow cab, but he could not shake off the relentless pursuit of the cops, who followed the taxi all the way north on Clark Street up to Winona Avenue, where the terrified driver collided with a trolley car.

Nelson fled the cab, losing his gun inside the cab in the process. Officers John Broecker and Charles Kiefer ran after Nelson, firing at the escaping robber. Broecker took the lead and caught Nelson in the basement stairway of 1454 West Foster Avenue, near Clark Street. Kiefer ran up from behind and with bland and disarming casualness, the cop drew a bead on Nelson as he grappled with Broecker in the stairwell. The bullet struck Nelson in the head and killed him instantly.

Back at the Winthrop Avenue address, Mullneschuck and Wilson held the cash, but a police bullet had grazed Wilson in the head. Dazed and bleeding, Wilson and his partner divvied up the stolen loot. "I got to get to a hospital fast," the wounded robber gasped.

Stashing his cut of the money in a satchel, Jack Wilson took a cab down to Cozzi's Restaurant at 1139 Taylor Street on the Near West Side. Frank Cozzi called for a doctor and agreed to hide the bills inside the restaurant until such time when his friend was bandaged up and ready to ride the rails. Cozzi and his brother Matthew later denied any dealings with Wilson. Said Frank Cozzi, "I did meet Wilson in the office of Dr. Chesrow and on the doctor's orders I drove him to the Jefferson Park Hospital. But I did not receive any money from him."

By virtue of his own stupidity, Wilson was in police custody less than two hours after checking into the Jefferson Park Hospital under his own name.

Tracy Drake, president of the family-owned hotel, announced a $5,000 reward for William Mullneschuck, the remaining fugitive. "We will never consider this case closed until Mullneschuck is caught. I hope to see a triple hanging," snorted the angry hotel executive.

Wanted posters were plastered in every police station house from Chicago all the way north to the Wisconsin border, and east to Indiana, but William Mullneschuck cleverly slipped through the dragnet. He was registered as a merchant seaman in the crew books of the Lake Carrier's Association, and may have easily shipped out on a lake steamer, free and unhindered.

There would be no triple hanging in Cook County. The last of the Drake holdup men was never again seen in these parts, and neither was the stolen Drake money.

The *Chicago Tribune* was outspoken in its condemnation of the lawless conditions that infected the city. Al Capone was only a small part of a larger problem. The Drake robbery was a spur-of-the-moment affair that underscored Chicago's vulnerability to independent triggermen acting outside the purview of organized crime. "It used to be a theory that so long as the gunmen, gangsters, sluggers, and tough citizens shot and slugged each other it was no damage to the community. There was one gone whenever one was murdered. We do not know how generally that theory is held today. We do know that there is general indifference to crimes of violence. Humanity will bring forth these perversions, but these men were the products of a society in collapse."

The captured bandits were examined by alienists (psychiatrists) before being arraigned on murder charges in Judge Jacob Hopkins's court. Aware of the damaging publicity surrounding this crime, Assistant State's Attorneys John Sbarbaro—gangland's favorite undertaker—and William McSwiggin—who would be target practice for the minions of gangland before another year would pass—promised a speedy and decisive trial.

There was little chance of reprieve for Woods and Holmes, the "two poor fools" who were adjudged sane by the Cook County courts and sentenced to die on the gallows in back of the Hubbard Street jail.

An impassioned plea to spare the lives of the befuddled killers by the ubiquitous Dr. Ben Reitman, social activist and director of Chicago's ignoble "Hobo College," sparked a wider debate on the merits of capital punishment for men whose sanity was in question. A chorus girl from a musical comedy, a stenographer from a Loop law firm, Reitman, and four other bleeding hearts maintained a curious candlelight vigil for the condemned men right up to the moment of execution at 9:44 A.M. on February 13, 1926.

Interviewed in his cell moments before taking the long walk, Woods expressed penitence. "It's a terrible thing to wait for—to be jerked to death. And all for what they say I did when I was ginned up and can't remember. Lay off that moonshine that's peddled nowadays," Woods cautioned the youth of Chicago. "We'd never done such a foolish thing if we had been sober."

Checking out of the Drake

**S
I
D
E
T
R
I
P**

Broken and defeated by the baseball establishment and bankrupted by a sport he dearly loved, the forgotten visionary who built Wrigley Field with his personal fortune died of a massive heart attack inside his Drake Hotel suite on October 2, 1938. "Lucky" Charlie Weeghman built a successful and highly profitable restaurant chain with ten Loop locations specializing in fast, "over-the-counter" service. Ray Kroc and Dave Thomas owe a debt of gratitude to Charles Weeghman, who invented the fast-food industry fifty years before Kroc got around to franchising his first McDonald's hamburger stand.

A millionaire before his thirtieth birthday, Weeghman siphoned off a significant portion of his restaurant fortune and plowed it into the Chicago Whales of the Federal League (an interloper challenging the hegemony of the National and American Leagues in the bitterly contentious baseball wars of 1914 and 1915). Weeghman traveled in fast circles, and he loved the Chicago nightlife. He was happiest sharing gossip in the company of show people, politicians, and gamblers. He sipped highballs and dined on filet with Mayor William Hale Thompson, and played the ponies with Mont Tennes inside one of his many North Side wire rooms.

Charles Henry Weeghman was a wide-eyed dreamer, but that was not such a bad thing if you had the talent, the money, and the energy to back it up. The Chicago Cubs might be playing in Toledo or Tacoma today if Fate had failed to unite the luckless baseball team with this imaginative Indiana-born hustler whose real-life exploits paralleled the Horatio Alger stories.

Through luck or sheer guile, Weeghman managed to play life's winning hand, except when it came to baseball, his one weakness. He spent $250,000 building a steel and concrete stadium at the intersection of Clark and Addison Streets on the North Side for his Whales, a team that ceased to exist after winning the Federal League championship in its second year. The Feds were ruthlessly squashed in a court of law by the baseball monopoly in the fall of 1915. Weeghman was allowed, however, to purchase the Chicago Cubs and move them into Weeghman Park in a less-than-generous settlement offer from the potentates of organized baseball. In 1918, Weeghman simply ran out of money and ideas after building a strong nucleus of talent for the incoming William Wrigley, who rechristened the tiny North Side baseball park in his own honor.

The chewing gum magnate reaped the harvest of Charlie Weeghman's sweat and toil with a National League pennant in 1918, by which time Lucky Charlie was struggling to prop up his business, which was in shambles fol-

lowing years of benign neglect. Two years later, the Weeghman restaurant chain was thrown into a receivership forcing its owner and proprietor to take to the road to reinvent fabulous new moneymaking schemes to bedazzle the public.

In the days of the Black Sox Scandal, "Unlucky" Charlie was spotted in a casino in Saratoga Springs, New York, throwing dice and playing his marker with denizens of the sporting fraternity who prowled the gaming tables prying loose information from the lips of the idle-rich sportsmen. In the 1930s, Weeghman was a familiar figure on Broadway. He squeezed out a living promoting Vaudeville acts, popcorn stands, and second-run theater before returning to Chicago to die a forgotten man's death in the Drake Hotel, just as the Cubs prepared to do battle with the New York Yankees in the 1938 World Series.

Follow the Inner Drive north to 1200 North Division Street. Turn left (west) on Division Street and continue to Clark Street.

WHERE IS DOCTOR CRONIN?
May 4, 1889

The long and bloody struggle to free Ireland from British rule was fought on many battlefields over the course of centuries. In the spring of 1889, the conflict washed up on the shores of Lake Michigan, exposing the vulnerabilities and ethnic prejudices of the Chicago Police Department and the deep infiltration of Irish radicals into municipal government. Little-remembered today, the sensational murder of Dr. Patrick Henry Cronin was labeled the "Crime of the (Nineteenth) Century," and a book by the same name appeared on the shelves within months of the first trial. By the time justice had run its full course nearly five years after the bloody deed had been committed, the Cronin case was being analogized to the Dreyfus Affaire in France. Irish nationalism was on trial in Chicago, not the cabal of killers who plotted the death of a highly regarded member of the medical profession. These men were heroes to a large segment of the Irish-American working class, and their crimes were justified in some quarters by prevailing Irish nationalist sentiment. The neighborhood where Cronin lived—and went to die—has undergone remarkable change in the last century. The Windsor Theater Building stood at 1225 North Clark Street, immediately north of Division Street across from the now pricey Sandburg Village condominium complex. Cronin maintained his North Side office here, and the *building survived until the mid-1960s when the Sandburg buildings were built. The naked body of the North Side physician was pulled from a catch basin nearly three weeks later on rural farmland at the southeast corner of Fifty-ninth Street (now Foster Avenue) and Evanston Avenue (now Broadway) in then suburban Lake View. The community was annexed to the city of Chicago that same year, and the pastoral countryside vanished quickly with the encroachment of road crews and real estate plungers waving fists full of dollars in the faces of Lake View farmers. No longer a rustic nineteenth-century pasture, the proximate location of the rural catch basin is the lot belonging to the Amoco gas station at Foster and Broadway; now a congested inner-city neighborhood on the far North Side of Chicago.*

Patrick Cronin, a well-to-do medical practitioner, was conferring with patients inside his office-flat at the Windsor Theater Building when a mysterious stranger suddenly appeared at the front door anxiously inquiring after the good doctor. "I want to see him on a life and death matter!" the stranger exclaimed. Unsure of what to do next, Mrs. Conklin, the landlady, summoned Dr. Cronin from the parlor.

"A workman has just been run over by one of our wagons at the Patrick O'Sullivan Ice Company, and is mangled across here, and here," the man said, pointing to his right thigh and abdomen.

"Then I'll come at once," Dr. Cronin assured him.

Cronin arranged his case of bandages and medical instruments and promptly left with the stranger. Frank Scanlan was the last man to see Cronin, and later remembered that he had reminded the doctor that he was expected at the Opera-House building later

DR. PATRICK

HENRY CRONIN,

MURDERED IN

THE NAME OF

IRISH NATION-

ALISM, MAY

1889.

DR. CRONIN'S

APARTMENT STOOD

ACROSS FROM WHAT

IS NOW SANDBURG

VILLAGE.

that evening to meet with the directors of the Celto-American Society, an Irish-American fraternal organization.

"I may get over in an hour, or it may be longer. I can't tell when," Cronin said anxiously, as he climbed into the rig.

The carriage, pulled by a white horse, sped north on Clark Street, toward the suburb of Lake View, and a prearranged rendezvous with death.

Dr. Patrick Cronin was an accomplished musician, a respected member of the medical community always welcome in the parlors of polite society, and a political moderate opposed to the militant faction within the secret, oath-bound society known as the Clan-Na-Gael (a forerunner of Sein Fein). This faction of the Clan plotted terrorist bombing campaigns against government targets in Great Britain. Cronin voiced strong opposition and was promptly expelled from the Clan in 1884 for treasonable actions.

Cronin had allegedly conspired with British agent Thomas Miller Beach (alias Henri LeCaron) to infiltrate and disrupt the secret society. Beach had freely circulated through Fenian camps in Canada and the United States on behalf of the British government. (Members of secret Irish and Irish-American societies committed to ending British rule in Ireland were called Fenians after a legendary band of warriors who defended Ireland in the second and third centuries A.D.) In 1866, Beach received word of a planned Fenian invasion of Canada and reported his suspicions to England, who repulsed the invaders at the border. Although there was not a kernel of truth to the accusation that Beach recruited Cronin into his intelligence-gathering mission, the seven-member executive board voted him guilty anyway, and set the punishment as death by execution. Dan Coughlin, a police detective from the East Chicago Avenue station drew the lot to carry out the death sentence.

On the morning of May 5, the Lake View Police Department found a blood-stained trunk in a grove of trees five hundred yards north of Sulzer Road (Montrose Avenue) and Evanston Avenue (Broadway) on the east side of the street. Hair particles believed to be those of Dr. Cronin's were closely examined.

Questioned by police, Patrick O'Sullivan denied summoning Cronin to his ice factory. There had been no accident on Saturday night that he was aware of.

The plot thickened.

"Dr. Cronin had a good many enemies—opponents is a better term," said Alexander Sullivan of the Irish-American League, arousing further suspicion. Following the discovery of the bloody trunk, Patrick Dinan, a livery man, told police that Officer Coughlin had arranged for him (Dinan) to rent a rig and a white horse through a third party. The horse and buggy were used to lure the doctor to a nonexistent appointment in a remote farmhouse out in the country.

"Where is Dr. Cronin?" a *Chicago Tribune* headline screamed.

The answer to the question on everyone's lips came on May 23, when three city sewer workers investigated a clogged catch basin three hundred yards from the Argyle Park Station of the Chicago & Evanston branch of the Chicago, Milwaukee & St. Paul Railroad (at what is now Foster Avenue and Broadway). They found a body, lying stark naked and floating in the tepid sewer water. The remains of the physician were easily identified and removed to the Lake View Morgue, where thousands of mourners dropped by to pay their respects.

The police investigation was led by Inspector Michael Schaak of the East Chicago Avenue District, who harbored deep ethnic hostility toward the immigrant Irish constituency who had settled among the Germans of the North Side. Schaak ruthlessly ordered the arrest and interrogation of three hundred suspects, among them the leaders of society and the commercial classes known to be sympathetic to the aims of the Fenian movement.

Piecing together the physical evidence of the crime—the trunk, clothing items found inside the remote cottage in Lake View where Cronin was murdered, and the blunt trauma to the head that induced death—a grand jury returned an indictment against the inner circle of Camp 20, the local chapter of Clan-Na-Gael: Dan Coughlin, O'Sullivan, Martin Burke, John Beggs, Patrick Cooney, Frank Woodruff, and John Kunze. Cooney, "the Fox," escaped to parts unknown. Burke, who had rented the murder cottage from Jonas Carlson, attempted to flee, but things quickly went wrong and he was arrested in Canada and extradited to the United States.

Amid charges of jury-packing and bribery against Clan-Na-Gael sympathizers in the judiciary, the first Cronin trial ended on December 16, 1889, with guilty verdicts returned against Coughlan, O'Sullivan, Kunze, and Burke and an acquittal for Beggs. The Cronin defendants were spared the rope.

Clarence Darrow, a rising star in city politics who served in the mayor's cabinet as corporation counsel, hailed the verdict as a victory for the common man. "The welfare of society is best served by preventing the wholesale execution of humans," he said.

Coughlan's appeal for a new trial was granted. The same testimony was repeated, but this time there was an entirely different outcome. The detective was acquitted on March 8, 1894. A large, enthusiastic crowd of supporters gathered inside the foyer of the courthouse on Dearborn to express support. Emerging

DR. CRONIN WAS FOUND IN THIS CATCH BASIN "OUT IN THE COUNTRY." AN AMOCO GAS STATION OCCUPIES THE SITE AT BROADWAY AND FOSTER AVENUES—NOW IN A CONGESTED CHICAGO NEIGHBORHOOD.

from chambers arm-in-arm with his wife, the former cop was greeted with a thunderous ovation: "Three cheers for Dan Coughlin!"

Women cried. Men threw their hats up in the air and rejoiced. In the Irish saloons of the North Side, pandemonium reigned.

There was little doubt of where the public's sympathy lay, despite a clear motive, intent, and resounding evidence of guilt. The verdict in the second Cronin trial was an unsatisfactory one for American justice, but Schaak's methods and an overzealous prosecution team touched raw nerves among the large Irish-Catholic population of Chicago, who united behind their moral convictions and a common cause. Logic was overruled by raw emotion, not unlike what was alleged in the political climate in America following the O. J. Simpson verdict a century later.

Later that day, floral wreaths were placed upon the grave sites of the deceased Clan-Na-Gael men bearing the inscription "Vindicated." O'Sullivan the ice man and Burke had both died in the Joliet prison hospital two years earlier. Dan Coughlin lived out his remaining days as a saloonkeeper in Chicago.

Continue west on Division to Larrabee Street. Turn left (south) and continue to Oak Street. Turn left (east) and go to Cleveland Avenue. Note: This intersection is in the middle of Chicago's most infamous housing proj-ect, Cabrini Green.

DEATH CORNER
1906–1912

Near the intersection of Milton Street (renamed Cleveland Avenue) and Oak Street, the Black Hand murdered dozens of people and waged a relentless campaign of extortion and terror over a period of six years. The victims were mostly recent arrivals from Italy who resided in the tiny ramshackle cottages of the Near North neighborhood known as "Little Hell" because of its poverty and propensity for violence. A vicious killer known only as the "Shotgun Man" was responsible for much of the Black Hand's seemingly random violence. This man of mystery wielded a sawed-off shotgun, which he employed with deadly efficiency. At the turn of the last century, Little Hell had been a mixed residential community of Swedes and Irish. The arrival of the Italians permanently drove the Swedes out of the neighborhood, but a cluster of Irish Americans chose to remain, among them the mother and father of Dion O'Banion. Cultural differences sharply divided communities such as Little Hell, and contributed to a pattern of ethnic and racial displacement that Chicago has never been able to overcome. With the Swedes gone, Little Hell evolved into an Italian ghetto until economic conditions worsened, and the neighborhood was abandoned. In 1941, the Works Progress Administration (WPA) began knocking down the dilapidated two- and three-story homes to make way for Cabrini Green, a sprawling low-income high-rise development managed by the Chicago Housing Authority. The houses surrounding Death Corner fell under the weight of the wrecker's ball, replaced by basketball courts and concrete-covered spaces.

I n 1890, a decade before the Black Hand thugs murdered with ruthless precision, the tenement area west of Orleans Street and south of Division was called "Smoky Hollow." In those days, "Fighting" Jimmy O'Neill, a swashbuckling bully possessing a manic energy and a vicious right hook, ruled an Irish gang engaged in petty theft and small-time crime. Smoky Hollow was a quiet, modest, and hardworking community, untroubled by serious crime except for occasional family squabbles and turf battles between rival Irish gangs. Farther west, "Little Sicily" took shape along Grand Avenue between Milwaukee Avenue and the Chicago River.

By 1900, the Swedes and Irish had already fled Smoky Hollow, and the needle trades these two immigrant groups had monopolized for decades were taken over by Italian women. Neighborhoods were halfway houses for immigrants, and the transition from one immigrant group to another was not unexpected. The arrival of the ominous Black Hand, however, was an unforeseen development that wreaked havoc on the poor, working-class Italians negotiating their way in Chicago. The police and members of the English-language press at the time were reluctant to believe that the Black Hand was a significant problem.

Black Hand terrorists armed with sawed-off shotguns mowed down seventeen victims during a fourteen-month period between January 1910 and March 1911. Seven of these unsolved killings occurred across the street from the dilapidated frame housing near the intersection known as "Death Corner," the intersection of Milton and Oak Streets. The Black Hand fiends who were responsible for this grisly reign of terror operated out of Frank Morici's saloon on the north side of Grand Avenue, east of Milwaukee, where old scores were settled and devilish new murder schemes hatched.

"The police, hampered at every turn by the silence of the Italian colony, are compelled to resign themselves . . . at present the police acknowledge the futility of further investigation," commented the *Chicago Tribune.*

Downplaying the seriousness of the situation, the cops from the West Chicago Avenue police station pegged the numerical size of the Black Hand at less than forty, but be they forty killers or forty thieves led by Ali Baba, they proved to be too much for the Chicago cops, who paid them grudging respect as an elusive and resourceful prey. Others simply denied the existence of the shadowy criminal conspiracy. The prejudices of the Anglo-Saxon opinion-makers failed to take into account the sense of helplessness and despair the fearful Italian immigrants experienced as they attempted to cope with the hardships of the slums in a dangerous and unpredictable new land. A "White Hand" society of neighborhood vigilantes was organized, but it was a largely symbolic and meaningless gesture.

The Black Hand had faded from view by 1920. The fragmented immigrant gangs regrouped under new leadership looking beyond the boundaries of the ghetto. Smoky Hollow became forever known as "Little Hell," then later in the century as the troubled Cabrini Green housing project where street-gang murder was the common denominator for impoverished African-Americans coping with the grind of slum living in plain sight of the Gold Coast.

North Side Pursuits:

Lincoln Park to Rogers Park

Nineteenth-century greed, bribery, and boodle nearly sabotaged an ambitious civic plan to beautify an uncultivated tract of land on the northern edge of the city that had existed as a cemetery since 1835. The land was a necklace of green parkways that in many ways mirrored New York's Central Park. The existence of the cemetery had effectively checked the downtown commercial district and the emerging residential streets of Chicago's Near North Side, stalling development north of Fullerton Avenue for many years.

Alderman Lawrence Proudfoot, largely forgotten by architectural historians, took his place on the City Council in 1865. The cemetery was a hot topic of discussion among the politicians, who had succeeded in removing and relocating many of the graves to other cemeteries in the anticipation of cashing in on the coming real estate frenzy. Proudfoot, a freshman alderman, had other ideas. It was his intention to reserve the sixty acres under contention for use as a public park for the benefit of all Chicagoans.

The Alderman took his proposal to Springfield after the City Council marshaled their forces and voted him down. The legislators, who stood in opposition to the political bigwigs of Chicago on principle, supported Proudfoot and established the North Park Commission on February 18, 1865, reserving a wide swath of lakefront property extending from the Oak Street Beach north to Montrose Avenue for open-air use. Playing one rapacious band of politicians against the other, the Chicago alderman, through clever manipulation, helped create Lincoln Park, which officially opened in 1868.

Proudfoot understood which way the political current of Chicago flowed and the shifty rivalries that existed between the downstate bosses and the gasbags of City Hall, whose historic misdeeds were given a unique sobriquet that sums up unchecked plunder and graft. Even today "boodle" remains part of the American vernacular.

North of Lincoln Park were the remote suburbs known as Lake View

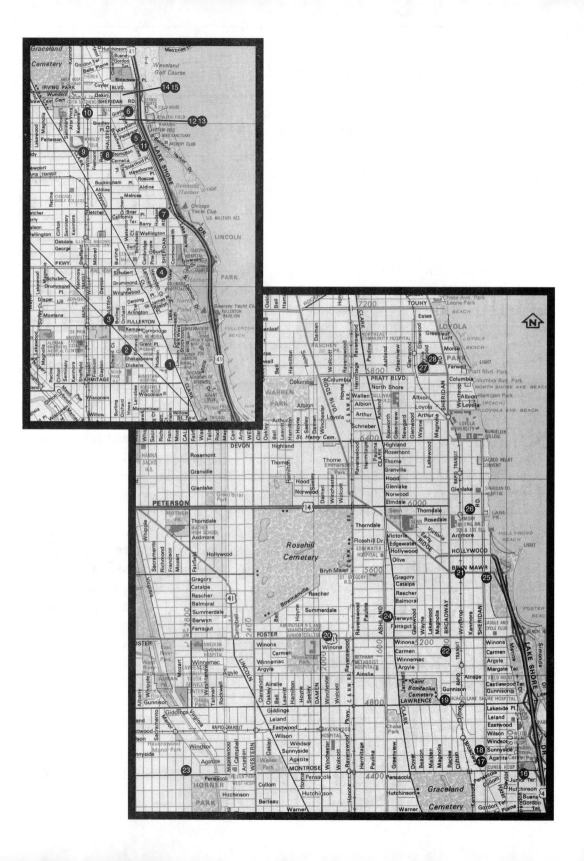

1. Site of the St. Valentine's Day Massacre, 2122 N. Clark Street, between Webster and Dickens.
2. Braithwaite Funeral Home, now a Mexican restaurant, at Webster and Lincoln.
3. The Biograph Theater on Lincoln Avenue, just north of Fullerton.
4. Diversey Avenue and Pine Grove, formerly the "New Commonwealth," where Joe E. Brown encountered "Machine Gun" Jack McGunn.
5. The Parliament Towers, where Evelyn Carey lived, located at the foot of Lake Shore Drive on Addison Street.
6. Manny Skar lived in the high-rise at Grace and Sheridan.
7. The stately Belmont Hotel, at Belmont and Sheridan, was the home of one of the Gennas.
8. John Dillinger slept here, in an unassuming two-flat at Brompton at Halsted.
9. Anna Sage maintained a bordello at 3500 Sheffield, a pop-fly from Wrigley Field.
10. The Carlos Hotel, on Sheffield between Grace and Sheridan, where Cub player Billy Jurges was shot.
11. The former residence of Dion O'Banion is an apartment house at Addison and Pine Grove.
12. The old Marigold Gardens stood at Broadway and Grace, where you see the IHOP restaurant; across the street, the "Wigwam" building.
13. The dingy Hotel Chateau, one of John Dillinger's crash pads, is located on Broadway north of Grace.
14. The Pine Crest Hotel, where the Navy WAVE was killed, still stands at Irving Park Road and Pine Grove Avenue.
15. Across the street and down the block, desperado Russell Gibson was killed in a shootout with the Feds.
16. At Clarendon and Junior Terrace, along the lakefront, John Dillinger and his party camped out in this courtyard apartment building.
17. The withered Sherone Apartments at Sheridan and Agatite, registered Verne Miller as a guest shortly before the G-men came after him.
18. The former McCready Funeral Home at Sunnyside and Sheridan is now a private residence.
19. The Green Mill nighclub still jumps at Broadway and Lawrence.
20. The art deco Summerdale police station is still in business at Damen and Winchester.
21. Underneath the elevated stop at Bryn Mawr and Broadway, Richard Morrison delivered Wesley's pizza to the Summerdale cops.
22. The "5100 Club," later a Western Tire & Auto store, stood at Carmen and Broadway, next to AON Corporation; it's a grocery store now.
23. Richard Morrison was arrested in an unassuming apartment building on Montrose, just south of California Avenue.
24. Gunman Gus Amadeo was shot down by Frank Pape in the middle of the intersection of Clark Street and Berwyn Avenue.
25. The luxurious Edgewater Beach, where ballplayer Eddie Waitkus was shot, was located in the 5300 block of Sheridan, south of Bryn Mawr; the Edgewater Apartments are there now.
26. William Heirens was convicted of murdering Suzanne Degnan, who was abducted from a residence at Kenmore and Thorndale that has since been torn down.
27. Heirens escaped into a building at Wayne and Farwell.
28. Heirens was finally subued and captured at Wayne and Morse.

THE NORTH SIDE

Township, incorporated in 1857 and bounded by Fullerton, Western, and Devon Avenues and the Lake Michigan shoreline. Lake View Township included the villages of Roseville, Bowmanville, Summerdale, Andersonville, Rose Hill, Gross Park, and Belle Plaine. It was annexed into the city of Chicago in 1889 and became known as the neighborhood of Lake View. Today there is Old Lake View and East Lake View, which includes New Town, Wrigleyville, Buena Park, and Uptown. The Lake View Township Town Hall was built in 1872 at the intersection of Addison and Halsted Streets, which is now the site of the "Town Hall" precinct station of the Chicago Police Department.

A visitor traveling northward beyond the boundaries of Lake View in the decade following the Civil War encountered only the occasional farmhouse and telegraph pole on what was mostly vacant land. Uptown, at the north end of Lake View, was sparsely populated and an ideal location for highwaymen and footpads to waylay the unsuspecting. The search for Dr. Patrick Cronin, the Irish nationalist who was abducted the same year Lake View was absorbed into Chicago, drove investigators deep into the country, where the body of the murdered physician was pulled from a catch basin at Foster and Broadway. (See Tour 2.)

By the turn of the last century, the quiet countrysides of Uptown, Edgewater, and Rogers Park were on their way to becoming high-density residential areas appealing to the rich and affluent. The immediate availability of land and the Northwestern Elevated Line, commencing service in 1900, sparked a nonstop commercial and residential building boom, converting cornfields into fields of cobblestone and asphalt.

Germans and Scandinavians formed densely populated ethnic pockets within this North Side milieu. However, because of the higher property values, and the dearth of factories and heavy industry to lure immigrant workers, the lakefront communities lying north of Lincoln Park and east of Ashland Avenue were mostly homogeneous settlements for families with Anglo-Saxon names.

The addition of hotels and high-rise apartments along the length of Sheridan Road, as well as the presence of Essanay Studios at 1345 West Argyle Street, sparked the development of Uptown as an entertainment and nightclub district, a district that coalesced near Broadway and Wilson Avenue well before World War I.

Gangsterism was the natural byproduct of such a district.

A highly mobile and transient stratum of the traveling vaudeville circuit rented apartments up and down the side streets in the lakefront neighborhoods. With so many song-and-dance men, chorus girls, comics, sixty-piece orchestras, theatrical agents, stagehands, and even no-name hacks coming and going at the same time, Uptown and Lake View were irresistible to the Chicago gang chieftains. By the 1930s, a conglomeration of peripatetic, skirt-chasing hoodlums passing through town on a whim, or looking for a place to crash for a week, a month, or even a year, found the surroundings highly suited to their immediate needs.

John Dillinger, Verne Miller, members of the Barker-Karpis mob, and many of their imitators drifted in and out of the North Side with reckless abandon. They appreciated the anonymity of apartment living, the casual lakefront lifestyle, and the chance to hide out in an agreeable setting, at least until the Feds were tipped and a squadron of G-men in Ford sedans sent them scurrying for cover and the next whistle stop.

The legendary Uptown nightclubs frequented by the gangsters also beckoned Chicagoans of more modest means from the outlying bungalow neighborhoods. The nightclubs promised much more than an escape from the drudgery of factory work and Depression hardship. The clubs spelled excitement, jazz, and a promise of romance (under the stars at the luxurious Aragon Ballroom near Lawrence and Broadway perhaps).

To satisfy the public's expectation of a roistering good time in a daring setting, the Prohibition mobs of the 1920s had to first engage in a long and protracted war. The battles were fought on many fronts spread across the landscape of Chicago. The striking climax to this fast-paced gangland narrative occurred in a small, out-of-the-way place at 2122 North Clark Street on a snowy Valentine's Day.

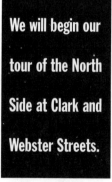

We will begin our tour of the North Side at Clark and Webster Streets.

A VALENTINE FOR BUGS
February 14, 1929

The garage where seven North Side gangsters were mowed down in a hail of machine-gun fire disappeared with little fanfare. The S. M. C. Cartage Company, which was housed in an innocuous single-story warehouse at 2122 North Clark Street sandwiched between two larger buildings that vanished with urban renewal, passed through the hands of several owners after its day of infamy. In 1945, Charles Werner opened an antique business, but later sold the property to land developers. The building was demolished in 1967, and 414 common house bricks forming the $7\frac{1}{2}$- by 11-foot high north wall were sold to an imaginative Canadian promoter named George Patey, who reconstructed the wall to exact specifications inside the Banjo Palace, a Vancouver nightclub. For the next thirty years, until he grew tired of maintaining his sideshow curiosity, Patey owned a relic of the past that the city of Chicago wanted noth-

ing more to do with. A tree-shaded park and asphalt parking lot adjacent to a senior citizens' high-rise stands on this "hallowed" gangster ground, which attracts thousands of tourists from all over the world each year.

Two other sites associated with the St. Valentine's Day Massacre are nearby. The apartment house once belonging to Mrs. Michael Doody at 2119 North Clark Street stands directly across the street from the former site of the garage. From the vantage point of the third-floor apartment facing the street, Al Capone's lookouts maintained a close vigil on the comings and goings of the Moran men. Today the lower level of the building is the Via Emile Italian Restaurant. A few doors to the north, at 2137 North Clark Street, Mrs. Minnie Arvidson's rooming house was identified by police detectives as another Massacre lookout. Both buildings date back to the turn of the century and are remarkably well preserved. Lost in their own thoughts, tourists allow their imaginations to wander back to that snowy Thursday morning in February 1929—the climax to a wild and decadent era that cemented Chicago's place as the nation's capital of crime.

This curious little rhyme appeared in the *Chicago Tribune* just six days after the St. Valentine's Day Massacre.

> *Five and twenty rum trucks come down the avenue;*
> *Champagne for the very rich,*
> *Hooch for me and you;*
> *Them that asks no questions, isn't told a lie;*
> *And watch the wall, my darling,*
> *While the gentlemen go by.*

Alas, that wall.

By 1929, most levelheaded Americans were fed up with Prohibition and had pronounced the "Noble Experiment" an ignoble failure. The country was awash in bootleg liquor. Placid city streets erupted into shooting galleries at a moment's notice, pitting one rum-running cartel against another in a desperate and vicious struggle to control the rackets and the corrupt politicians representing those interests. It was that way all over the country, but in Chicago the gangsters had taken matters to the next level.

Al Capone had become a civic and national embarrassment. His South Side gang had waged continuous warfare against rival bootlegging operations in every corner of the city. One by one, nine major South and West Side gangs (and lesser independents) fell into line through attrition or murder, leaving only the defiant

OUTSIDE THE S. M. C.
CARTAGE COMPANY, THE
REPORTERS GATHER
(ABOVE). THE GARAGE
DISAPPEARED IN 1967.
TREES GROW IN THIS
PUBLIC PARK—SAID TO
BE HAUNTED—ON THE
CURSED GANGSTER
GROUND.

(Bill Helmer collection; photo by Christina Carlson)

PETER & FRANK GUSENBERG (ABOVE).
THE CUTAWAY DRAWING SHOWS FRANK
BEING LOADED INTO THE AMBULANCE AND
THE POSITIONING OF THE EIGHT MORAN
GANGSTERS INSIDE THE S.M.C. CARTAGE
COMPANY MOMENTS BEFORE THE SHOOT-
ING STARTED. SOME OF CAPONE'S
"LOOKOUTS" WERE POSITIONED IN THE
UPPPER FLOORS OF THIS FORMER ROOM-
ING HOUSE (LEFT).

(Photo by Christina Carlson)

North Side conglomerate of George "Bugs" Moran standing in Capone's way.

The battle for Chicago was not only about liquor flowing into the Moran cabarets up and down the major thoroughfares north of Madison Street, but for control of the Cleaners and Dyers Union and the affiliated locals that Capone's sworn enemies had muscled in on earlier in the decade. It was also about political control of the Twentieth Ward and a dog-racing track in suburban Lyons, Illinois, which both Capone and Moran desired to add to their substantial holdings.

Bugs Moran's Irish-American gang had murdered every president of the Unione Sicilione to date: Tony Genna, "Samoots" Ammatuna, Tony Lombardo, and Al Capone's good friend Pasqualino Lolorodo, who was killed in the presence of his wife just two weeks before the massacre.

Al Capone had compelling motives and the necessary firepower to send Bugs off in grand style. Capone entrusted this delicate task to his favorite executioner, the boyish-looking failed prizefighter James Vincenzo DeMora (aka "Machine Gun" Jack McGurn). McGurn supervised every last detail of the slayings, down to the police car with its fake cops staging a phony raid as a means of catching the Moran men off guard.

On the morning of February 14, 1929, Al Capone was at his Palm Beach, Florida, estate entertaining boxer Jack Sharkey and Dade County Solicitor Robert Taylor. Whatever else can be said of "Scarface," the chubby gangster's timing was always impeccable.

In Chicago, temperatures fell into the single digits and snow was in the air. A black 1927 Cadillac touring car emerged from a rented garage in the back of 1722 North Wood Street and proceeded to the S. M. C. Cartage Company, a converted liquor depot and Moran gang "clubhouse," where five Moran men, a car

mechanic, and an optometrist thrilled to be welcomed into the company of mobsters were awaiting a truckload of Old Log Cabin hijacked from the Stockyards district a day earlier.

Two of the assassins were dressed as police officers. The other three wore long trench coats and fedoras. Tucked inside their coats were sawed-off shotguns and Thompson submachine guns, the newest and deadliest weapons of choice. The Cadillac eased alongside the curb a few minutes past 10:30 A.M.

At approximately 10:45 A.M., Mrs. Jeanette Landsman, hearing a deafening cacophony from the building next door, put down her iron and contacted the Thirty-sixth District police station on Hudson Avenue. There had been a shooting, she said. Minutes later, Sergeant Thomas J. Loftus and three members of the automobile detail burst into the warehouse, where they found a hysterical German Shepherd named Highball leashed to a truck, and six dead men sprawled on the floor. It was the bloodiest crime in the annals of gangland Chicago and was soon a headlining event all across the world.

There was one survivor. Clutching his stomach, hoodlum Frank Gusenberg crawled toward the door. "For God's sake, get me to a hospital," he gasped. Death reigned in that garage.

Gusenberg was removed to Alexian Brothers Hospital, where he died at 1:30 P.M. When asked who had fired on him, Gusenberg replied, "Nobody shot me." Bugs Moran, suddenly deprived of his livelihood but lucky to be alive, was blunt and to the point. "Only Al Capone kills like that," he said. With bootlegger Terry Druggan at his side, Moran had dropped in that morning for a cup of coffee to warm his bones, but he had had another appointment to keep and had left the building a few minutes ahead of the death squad's arrival.

Police canvassed Clark Street between Webster and Garfield (now Dickens) Avenues. In 1929, the area was a rooming-house district, and there were dozens of landlords and tenants to interview. Transients come and go, the cops were told, but Minnie Arvidson and Mrs. Michael Doody both reported that teams of suspicious men had recently rented rooms with a street view for $8 a day.

Jack McGurn was arrested at the Stevens Hotel by Lieutenant William Cusack of the Detective Bureau on February 27. Capone's top triggerman established a perfect "blonde" alibi—a showgirl named Louise Rolfe, who swore she had been at his side every day since January 31, when they registered at the hotel for a lengthy tryst. On the day of the Massacre, Rolfe explained, they had slept until 1:30 P.M.

The murder car, a smoldering wreck, was found in the rented Wood Street garage. The shooters had covered their tracks masterfully. The car had been set on fire with acetylene torches and chopped up with a hacksaw. Ownership of the

THE ST. VALENTINE'S DAY MASSACRE CORONER'S JURY IS SWORN IN (RIGHT). THE COPS FOUND THE REMAINS OF THE INCINERATED MASSACRE GETAWAY CAR—MADE UP TO LOOK LIKE A POLICE FLIVVER—DAYS LATER (BELOW).

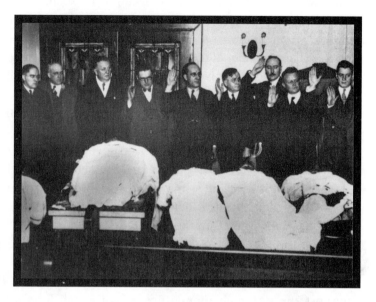

vehicle was traced to Cook County Commissioner Frank J. Wilson, who had sold the car to an auto dealership on Irving Park Road.

Fingerprints inside the garage were closely examined. Everyone knew this had to be the work of Al Capone, but substantiating such a charge was another matter. The sensational murder of seven gangsters inside a tiny North Side garage was never officially solved, though the January 1935 jailhouse confession of outlaw Byron Bolton must be given serious attention.

According to Bolton, an expert machine gunner in the U.S. Navy before turning to a life of crime and kidnapping, plans for the massacre were formulated at a conference of gangsters inside a resort owned by Fred Goetz on Cranberry Lake, six miles north of Couderay, Wisconsin, in October or November 1928. Present at this meeting were Al Capone, Gus Winkler, Goetz, Louis "Little New York" Campagna, Fred "Killer" Burke, and William Pacelli, a North Side politician who was later elected to the Illinois State Senate.

Bolton, arrested on January 10, 1935, at 3920 Pine Grove Avenue, fingered Claude "Screwy" Maddox, a Circus Gang alumnus; Murray "the Camel" Humphreys; and Gus Winkler as the shooters. They had lined the seven men up against the wall and opened fire with the full force of their Thompsons. Fred "Killer" Burke, a member of Egan's Rats, a St. Louis gang, and Fred Goetz were disguised as the police officers.

Informed of these developments, Chicago police captains John Stege and William Schoemaker, who were the most knowledgeable crime fighters in the city during the Prohibition era, believed Bolton. He went on to tell federal agents that Stege (later promoted to Chief of Detectives) was a dishonest cop on the payroll of the Capone mob who pulled down $5,000 a week. It was a bold accusation to make against a man with so sterling a reputation, but the charge was repeated by J. Edgar Hoover in one of his communiqués to his Chicago agents.

As to Bolton's inside knowledge of the planning and execution of the infamous St. Valentine's Day Massacre, most of the heads-up cops in the department agreed that there was probably a grain of truth to the story. Lieutenant Otto Erlanger of the Homicide Bureau said Bolton's story "was true in every word."

"The first suspect I sent for was Maddox," Schoemaker added. "I felt sure he was one of the executioners but I could not prove it. I had to let him go." Maddox was brought in for another round of questioning in January 1935 and was once again let go.

Gus Winkler was rewarded for his part in the massacre with an appointment from Capone to head his North Side gambling operations. Winkler bought a new Lincoln and rented a $325-a-month apartment on Lake Shore Drive.

Byron Bolton was being detained in St. Paul, Minnesota, for the ransom kidnapping of Edward G. Bremer when he made the startling confession. J. Edgar Hoover, director of the Bureau of Investigation (the FBI), weighed the evidence and then ordered an immediate investigation to determine if reporters from the *Chicago American* had planted a wiretap on the telephones inside the Chicago Bureau in order to scoop rival newspapers on the progress of the investigation. Hoover obsessed over this imagined breach of security. In recently declassified FBI documents dated January 23, 1935, the director ordered D. M. Ladd of the Chicago office to circulate a false rumor announcing the fictitious capture of outlaw Alvin "Creepy" Karpis. Hoover wanted to see if *Chicago American* reporters were listening in on bureau phone conversations, and if the paper would print the bogus story.

THIS MAP SHOWS THE SPHERES OF GANGLAND INFLUENCE IN THE CITY OF CHICAGO IN THE ROARING '20s.

"I told Mr. Ladd to keep me informed as to the results, and I suggested that the story be started that we have someone in custody. I stated that if we caught the *Chicago American* wire tappers tapping our wires, it was my intention to prosecute them," wrote Hoover.

No evidence of a wiretap was ever found.

Of all the combinations of gangster luminaries accused of complicity in the St. Valentine's Day Massacre at one time or another, Byron Bolton's version holds up. However, Director Hoover blandly dismissed the jailhouse confession with the lame excuse that the massacre was a "Chicago matter for the local police to resolve." If Hoover believed Bolton at all, he took no decisive actions in the matter, and the press gradually lost interest, and Bolton's story quietly died and was completely forgotten.

It must also be remembered that up until 1957, Director Hoover denied the existence of the Mafia.

Proceed south on Clark Street to Dickens Avenue and turn right (west). Go west to Lincoln Avenue. Turn right (north) on Lincoln Avenue to Webster Avenue.

THE DRAKE-BRAITHWAITE FUNERAL HOME
February 14, 1929

At 2221 North Lincoln Avenue (on the east side of the street) stands the building that was once the Drake-Braithwaite Funeral Home, where the six deceased Moran gangsters were transported. The funeral home now houses Burrito Joint #2. The gray-stone façade is immediately recognizable as a chapel and mortuary, even with the red and green awning covering the entrance.

Dr. Frederick M. Doyle of 2314 North Clark Street was summoned to the S. M. C. Cartage Company to examine the massacre victims and sign their death certificates. "All dead but one," he told Sergeant Loftus, who notified Cook County Coroner Herman Bundesen. After he conferred with Doyle, the coroner signaled Loftus to admit the throng of pushing and shoving press photographers, who quickly elbowed their way through the front doors to take shots for the morning papers.

Coroner Bundesen ordered the bullet-riddled remains of Peter Gusenberg, 40; mechanic John May, 35; Moran accountant and building manager Adam Heyer 40; Albert Weinshank, 26; Bugs Moran's brother-in-law Albert Kachellek (aka

BRAITHWAITE

FUNERAL HOME

ON LINCOLN

AVENUE IS NOW

A BURRITO

STAND.

(Photo by Christina Carlson)

James Clark); and Reinhardt Schwimmer, 29, a "retired" optometrist living off of his investments, removed to the Braithwaite Funeral Home. While the sweethearts and wives wept openly, all but Dr. Schwimmer's mother maintained a silent, unified front when asked about how these men earned their livelihoods. Mrs. Schwimmer, a sixty-year-old widow who financed her son's profligate lifestyle, said she had begged Reinhardt to steer clear of the gangsters. But he wouldn't listen, and ended up dead.

The doctor's wake was conducted with due solemnity at Drake-Braithwaite at 2:00 P.M. on Thursday, February 21.

The grieving widows of bigamist Frank Gusenberg appeared at their husband's wake, providing a moment of unintentional comic relief. The two women mourned the departed as much as it is possible to love a two-timing scoundrel whose saving grace was a fat bankroll.

Continue north on Lincoln Avenue to just past Fullerton Avenue.

THE LADY IN RED
July 22, 1934

Myths, lies, and legends surround the sensational shooting of Depression-era desperado John Herbert Dillinger in a narrow alley a few feet south of the Biograph Theater, at 2433 North Lincoln Avenue in the Fullerton-Lincoln-DePaul neighborhood. Rest assured, it is

Dillinger's remains at the Crown Hill Cemetery in Indianapolis and not some impostor hatched in the hyper-extended imaginations of conspiracy theorists. America's most famous twentieth-century bandit rests comfortably not far from the gravesites of three vice presidents and the famed Hoosier poet James Whitcomb Riley. There are many John Dillinger sites scattered across Chicago, but none more famous than the Biograph Theater, a quaint monument to the memory of an outlaw who in death became a folk hero. Tourists are often amused by the vintage 1930s marquee and the old-fashioned ticket booth as they retrace Dillinger's final steps from the neighborhood movie house to the alley. Once a year on the anniversary of the bank robber's death, the "John Dillinger Died for You Society" stages a grimly amusing testimonial to American pop culture's first antihero.

It was an extremely hot summer that Depression year of 1934, and like most Chicagoans toughing out the record-breaking 109 degree heat, John Dillinger decided to go to the movies for a little R & R, which meant relaxation and refrigeration on a steamy Sunday night.

In those days, movie theaters, icehouses, and the county morgue were about the only places where one could escape the blistering Chicago heat. It was Dillinger's great misfortune that on this particular night he would get to see his movie then end up on a slab in the Cook County morgue.

Melvin H. Purvis, the thirty-year-old Department of Justice agent, had been tracking John Dillinger's movements for weeks. Purvis was on the verge of losing his job unless he could convince J. Edgar Hoover that his errors of judgment, recklessness, and youthful exuberance did not add up to failure in so serious a matter. Earlier that year, Purvis dispatched a fleet of surveillance aircraft to northern Michigan in a costly but doomed effort to locate the bank robber and his gang.

Pressing on to Wisconsin, the federal agents cornered Dillinger a few weeks later at Emil Wanatka's Little Bohemia resort lodge, located in the woods thirteen miles outside of Mercer. Dillinger and his gang managed to evade a deadly trap. It was another humiliating setback for Purvis. The only "criminals" Purvis paraded before the reporters, following a furious gun battle waged against a nearly empty house, were three chalk-faced, frightened gangster molls—Helen Gillis, Marie Conforti, and Jean Crompton. Mr. Hoover was livid.

"Purvis merely gritted his teeth, intensified his watchfulness and kept working," the *Chicago Tribune* reported.

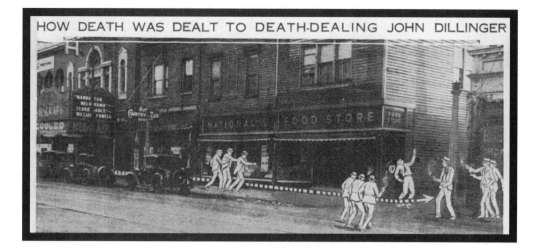

HOW DEATH WAS DEALT TO DEATH-DEALING JOHN DILLINGER

PHOTO-DIAGRAM OF JOHN DILLINGER AS HE IS AMBUSHED OUTSIDE THE BIOGRAPH THEATER (ABOVE). THE FOLLOWING MORNING, SIGHTSEERS GAWK AT THE POOLS OF BLOOD IN THE ALLEY WHILE THE COPS TRY TO MAINTAIN ORDER (BELOW).

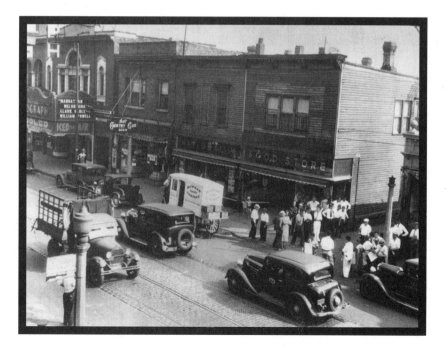

John Dillinger sidetracked to Minnesota, then retreated to Chicago, aware that Purvis and the full weight of the federal government were not far behind.

In mid-July, Purvis received a communication from Sergeant Martin Zarkovich of the notoriously corrupt East Chicago, Indiana, Police Department that Dillinger was living with Mrs. Anna Sage (née Anna Cumpanas), a Romanian national who ran a North Side prostitution ring. Until Mrs. Sage had been run out of East Chicago in 1927, Zarkovich had been shielding her operation for a percentage of the nightly take and an occasional sexual dalliance with Sage herself or one of the inmates of her resort. Sonny Sheetz, the crime boss of Lake County, Indiana, controlled Zarkovich.

Mrs. Sage agreed to betray Dillinger in return for a few quick bucks and the promise of leniency in her pending deportation case. If she took the government's guarantees at face value, she was naive and sadly misinformed. Sage would be shipped back to Europe along with a boatload of other "undesirables" on April 25, 1936, and would travel across Europe and the Middle East under assumed names until her death in 1947.

But on Sunday afternoon, July 22, Anna Sage tipped Purvis that Dillinger planned a movie outing in the company of Sage and his newest sweetheart, Polly Hamilton Keele, a working girl with a shady past. Long after this ordeal was over, Keele would marry a shoe salesman and settle into a life of mundane respectability.

But for the moment, neither the adventuresome Keele nor Anna Sage were sure which movie they would be seeing that night. The choice boiled down to *Little Miss Marker* at the Marbro Theater across town or *Manhattan Melodrama,* a "gang-and-gun" drama starring Clark Gable, William Powell, and Myrna Loy at the Biograph. The latter was more to Dillinger's taste.

"I felt that the clue I got early last evening to the effect that he would attend the picture show depicting the life of a man that ended in the electric chair would be a good one," Purvis recounted, with a mirthful twinge of self-satisfaction.

Purvis strategically positioned sixteen FBI agents up and down the block. At the last minute, he requested additional backup from the Sheffield Avenue precinct.

Sage advised Purvis that she would be wearing a red dress to the picture show. At approximately 8:30 P.M., Dillinger appeared at the box office with the two women. He was outfitted in appropriate summer attire—a white silk shirt, a straw boater, white canvas shoes, and gray trousers—and appeared completely at ease hiding out in plain view.

During the next two hours and four minutes, Agent Purvis, tense and nervous, paced the sidewalk outside the Biograph. Several times he entered the darkened theater, but he could not locate Dillinger. Just before 10:30 P.M., the house lights were raised and the crowd filed out in an orderly fashion through the doors and onto the street.

Melvin Purvis was standing in front of the Goetz Country Club, a saloon located just south of the theater when Dillinger and his lady friend emerged. Purvis fumbled with his cigar. It was the signal for the police and the G-men to move in.

"He gave me a piercing look," Purvis would later recall. "Just after he went by and was outside the building due south, a National Tea company store, I raised my hand and gave the prearranged signal."

Dillinger walked on. At the mouth of the alley, he suddenly whirled around and appeared to be reaching inside his coat pocket for a gun. He knew at that moment he was in a hell of a fix. "And that was when the shots that killed him were fired. Four altogether," Purvis said.

John Dillinger absorbed a bullet in the back of the neck and two in his left side fired by Agents Charles B. Winstead, Herman Hollis, and Clarence Burt,

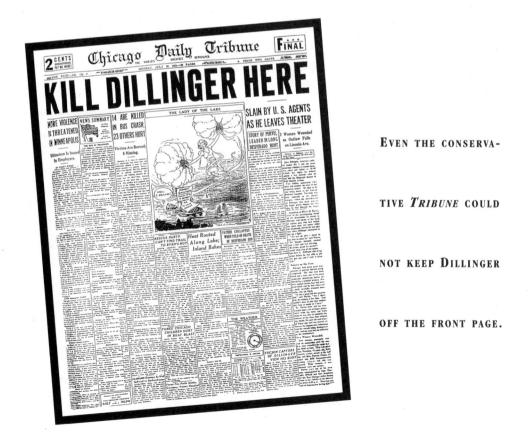

EVEN THE CONSERVATIVE *TRIBUNE* COULD NOT KEEP DILLINGER OFF THE FRONT PAGE.

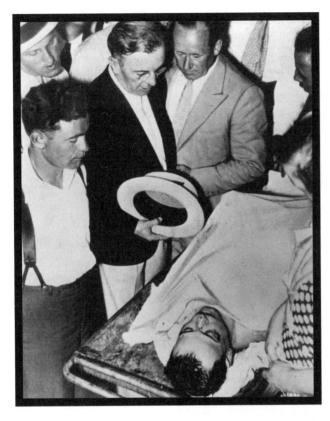

THE REAL JOHN DILLINGER—NOT AN IMPOSTOR BUT THE GENUINE ARTICLE—ON ICE AT THE MORGUE.

TO CAPITALIZE ON THEIR SON'S INFAMY, MEMBERS OF THE DILLINGER FAMILY AGREED TO APPEAR ON-STAGE AT THE BIOGRAPH IN A SLEAZY QUESTION AND ANSWER SESSION WITH THE PUBLIC.

according to FBI reports. Dillinger took three faltering steps, then collapsed onto the alley pavement.

It is rumored that Sergeant Zarkovich, a kinky cop working in a syndicate-controlled town, rifled through Dillinger's pockets and reportedly made off with the gun, a Colt .380 automatic. Zarkovich was assigned to keep watch on the Marbro Theater earlier that evening, but had raced over to the Biograph upon receiving confirmation of Dillinger's presence on Lincoln Avenue.

Others say with equal certainty that Purvis retrieved the weapon and passed it on to Mr. Hoover for safekeeping. It is believed that Dillinger's gun eventually found its way into the private collection of comedian Red Skelton. Hoover reveled in the company of celebrities and often bestowed souvenir gifts upon them.

There was no certainty at this point that the mortally wounded man was in fact the notorious John Dillinger. A crime writer out of Chicago asserts with deadpan seriousness that a Dillinger look-alike was set up to take the fall by Zarkovich, who hatched this fantastic plot with the help of attorney Louis Piquett and Anna Sage. Dillinger historians like William J. Helmer dismiss the "body double" angle as far-fetched, revisionist nonsense.

The body of the real John Dillinger was loaded onto a stretcher and placed on the floor of a Chicago patrol wagon for transport to Alexian Brothers Hospital. Meanwhile thousands of souvenir-hunting spectators eagerly pushed their way forward, hoping to dip their handkerchiefs and slips of paper in the pool of fresh blood. This was to become a Chicago crime scene tradition, repeated many more times before the ghoulish fad wore off. Others pried loose bullet fragments from a wooden light pole in the alley until the pole became so unsteady that it had to be taken down by city workers.

Moments before Dillinger reached the hospital, he was pronounced dead, and the patrol wagon was rerouted to the morgue where Coroner Frank J. Walsh conducted the inquest the following morning. "His identity was soon proven by prints of his fingers, although these had been futilely and clumsily disguised with acid, sandpaper, and surgery," commented the *Chicago Herald & Examiner.*

Sergeant Frank Reynolds of the Chicago Police Department instantly recognized Dillinger. He was so happy to see him lying in repose on the slab that he shook the corpse's hand.

John Dillinger's brief but spectacular flourish as a midwestern bank robber was over. He had paid his debt to society in blood. If he hadn't, surely the American public would have heard more of him in the intervening years.

Continue northwest on Lincoln Avenue to Sheffield Avenue. Turn right (north) and proceed to Diversey Parkway. Turn right (east) and continue to Pine Grove Avenue.

THE JOKER IS WILD
November 9, 1927

Diversey Parkway west of Sheridan Road is steeped in Prohibition gang lore. Peter von Frantzius supplied armaments to the bootleg gangs and was suspected of providing the submachine guns used by the Capone gang in the St. Valentine's Day Massacre. His sporting goods store, once the focus of numerous police inquiries, occupied a storefront in the Rienzi Hotel, a gang hangout. The Rienzi Plaza, a high-rise complex located at 600 West Diversey Parkway replaced the hotel. However, the former New Commonwealth Hotel can still be viewed at 2757 North Pine Grove Avenue (at Diversey). The New Commonwealth and other residential hotels just like it up and down the lakefront served a transient clientele of vaudevillians, nightclub chorines, and show people who appeared nightly at famous North Side cabarets like the Green Mill and the Marigold Gardens. Comedian Joe E. Lewis would never forget the New Commonwealth, the city of Chicago, or his near-fatal encounter with "Machine Gun" Jack McGurn. Years later his story was retold with touching poignancy in the 1957 motion picture The Joker Is Wild, *starring Frank Sinatra, Mitzi Gaynor, and Jeanne Crain.*

Born Joseph Klewan on New York's Lower East Side, Joe E. Lewis dazzled nightclub audiences at the Green Mill with his musical repertoire and clever comedic shtick. Lewis was pulling down $650 a week, a princely sum in those days, but the money, his newfound fame, and his friendship with the Capone gang overruled logic and common sense.

Lewis was a local celebrity, but he was not a big enough name to break a contract with a syndicate-run cabaret. On August 27, 1927, the owners of the New Rendez-Vous Cafe at Diversey Parkway and Broadway tendered Lewis a contract calling for $1,000 a week plus a cut of the gambling profits. Lewis had packed the Green Mill for a solid year, but he made it clear to manager Danny Cohen that he wasn't coming back.

A few weeks before his November 2 opening at the New Rendez-Vous,

Lewis ran into Jack McGurn on Diversey Parkway. The Capone gangster and professional killer urged the comedian to reconsider leaving the Green Mill. McGurn was friendly, but unpersuasive. Lewis, who had grown up with extortionists and thieves, told McGurn to take a hike.

"You'll never live to open!" Now McGurn wasn't being so friendly. His money and reputation were at stake. "Machine Gun" owned 25 percent of the Green Mill action.

It was rumored that Lewis was keeping company with one of Jack's girls—another reason to be circumspect. Lewis hired a bodyguard, but even a bodyguard had to sleep sometimes.

On October 30, the Chicago newspapers announced the grand opening of the New Rendez-Vous. And with it came more telephone threats to Lewis's room at the Commonwealth.

Joe went on as planned and for the next week the New Rendez-Vous was sold out every night. Then came the final warning, and with it a reprisal.

Lewis was asleep in his bed in Room 332 when he heard the rap on the door. In a fog, he admitted the three men who had come to kill him. No bullets were fired. The assailant, undoubtedly McGurn, slashed him from ear to ear, leaving Joe to die in his own blood. But Joe did not die. He clung tenaciously to life and hours later crawled to the elevator in the hall. A police wagon was summoned. Joe Lewis, still breathing but unconscious, was taken to Columbia Memorial Hospital.

A slow, painful recuperation followed. Lewis had to learn how to talk all over again, but he was back on-stage as a full-time comic less than eleven weeks later on January 28, 1928. Sophie Tucker, the "Last of the Red-Hot Mamas" gave up a $5,000 gig in order to be at the Club Rendez-Vous that night.

Al Capone, who knew Joe from his days down in the South Side Levee, where Lewis had made the big guy laugh, mollified Lewis's understandable anger. "Why didn't you come and see me, Joe?" he asked. "We could have avoided all this trouble."

Continue east on Diversey Parkway to Sheridan Road and go left (north) to Addison Street. Turn left (west) on Addison Street.

"26 SKIDOO": THE ESTELLE CAREY MURDER MYSTERY
February 2, 1943

There is still an elegance to the Parliament Towers apartment building at 510–534½ Addison Street, just a few yards west of Lake Shore Drive. The sagging structure has seen better days in a neighborhood that has undergone cycles of decay and urban renewal during the last fifty years. But in the 1940s, when this was one of the trendiest addresses along the Gold Coast, it took a fabulous income—a gangster's bankroll—to support Estelle Carey in her swank third-floor flat at 512 Addison Street.

Tall, voluptuous Estelle Evelyn Carey attained a certain gaudy eminence as the gangster "moll" of tough guy Nicky Dean. Her after-hours carrying on and her stubborn refusal to reveal the location of Dean's little "nest egg" while her sweetie was serving an eight-year prison sentence cost this former "26" girl her life.

Twenty-six was a syndicate dice game. Attractive young ladies like Carey passed the time of night hustling the patrons of Near North taverns to plunk down their dollar bills on a sucker's bet. Estelle Carey, a platinum blonde who dyed her hair jet black, was the queen of the dice girls who presided over the nightly snooker at the Colony Club, a Rush Street dive owned by syndicate heavies Nicky Dean, Henry "Sonny" Goldstone, and "Dago" Louis Mangano.

Nick Dean, whose real name was Circella, was convicted in New York in 1941 for his part in shaking down four of Hollywood's largest motion picture studios by threatening the industry with labor strikes. Dean's connections to the Chicago underworld dated back to the 1920s, when he guarded Al Capone.

Estelle Carey, the alluring siren whose address book listed the names of thirty past and present lovers, was paid $350 a week and 25 percent of the weekly take for managing the Colony Club and the Yacht Club in Dean's absence. She hobnobbed with New York gangsters linked to Joe Adonis and Frank Costello and charmed a young soldier into jumping the fence and going AWOL.

There was speculation that she was "holding out" on the mob. A million dollars of the racket-ridden movie union's wealth turned up missing during Dean's trial. Where was the pile? If Carey had any clue, she wasn't talking.

Estelle Carey was home alone the afternoon of February 2, 1943. Her room-mate was out for the day, so Carey decided to make a few phone calls. She was chatting on the phone with her cousin Phoebe when the doorbell rang. Phoebe remembered hearing Estelle's little dog yapping in the background, but Carey did not sound overly concerned. Ending the call, she rushed to the door to confront her killer.

The dice queen's death was hideous and appalling—the desperate act of a coward. Carey was bludgeoned with a rolling pin, which sparked rumors that the murderer was a vengeful wife. But vengeful wives are not in the habit of stabbing their victims with an ice pick, slamming an electric iron to their face and head, then setting their clothes on fire. The searing burns to Carey's legs and torso caused her death, not the brutal battering she had endured. The body was dis-covered by firemen a short time later.

Captain Bill Drury of the Town Hall station blamed Carey's underworld associates for the crime—whoever they were. "She's a good girl!" her widowed mother sobbed to reporters.

Dozens of underworld suspects were interrogated, and numerous finger-prints were lifted from the charnel house, but just whose prints they were was never determined. The press lost interest, and in time the matter was forgotten. Nicky Dean was deported to Argentina in 1955, and with his departure the last hope of solving this case ended.

Exiled to an orphanage by her widowed mother when she was an infant, Carey viewed life in its narrowest terms. Throughout her short, event-filled exis-tence, Estelle exploited her beauty and charm. She was one of the unfortunates who subscribed to Willard Motley's grim belief that one should always "live fast, die young, and have a good-looking corpse."

Turn back to Sheridan Road, and go north on Sheridan Road to Grace Street.

MR. FIX IT
September 10, 1965

Fifteen floors above Lake Shore Drive, Manny Skar's wife watched helplessly as her husband's killers fled west on Grace Street. She heard the shots and instinctively understood what had happened. Manny was a marked man, and his lifelong joy ride from Lawndale to a Gold Coast penthouse had reached a predictable end. When the cops arrived, the widow was hugging and kissing the deceased. Beatrice Skar was inconsolable. A two-way mirror mounted on a heavy wooden door protected Manny from mob rivals, but it couldn't save him in the streets. His success came at a terrible price. "Manny! Oh my baby Manny!" the widow cried. The Skars lived in one of Chicago's most exquisite locations, a classic and elegant high-rise located at 3800 North Lake Shore Drive (at the corner of Grace Street and Sheridan Road). Window air conditioners protrude from the walls. It's an old building with lots of history, and the view of Lake Michigan remains unobstructed.

It is that numbing, fearful certainty that the next breath you take may be your last that compels some men to live life fast, furious, and full of debt. Mandel Skar experienced both the best and worst of life in his short forty-two-year existence. Manny understood that there was no other way to go, because sooner or later it all catches up with you.

The late Virgil Peterson, the driving force behind the Chicago Crime Commission for nearly three decades, described Manny as a "flamboyant financier, bombastic manipulator, and business associate of big-time gangsters." Manny, all five foot five inches of him, ran with hoodlums and courted movie stars. When the neon lights of the Mannheim Road cabarets flickered on at dusk, the little *"ganef,"* who ran away from the Jewish West Side at age seventeen in order to avoid the draft, was in his element.

With microphone in hand and sweat pouring from his brow under the blazing spotlights of the Sahara Inn, Manny kissed the showgirls, introduced the talent, and wise-cracked with the wise guys he bummed around town with—Marshall Caifano, Rocco DeStefano, and Sam Giancana.

The Sahara Inn was a plush show spot located out on the Mannheim Road "strip" near O'Hare Airport. The luxurious hotel featured a torch-lighted swimming pool, a nightclub called The Club GiGi, and 267 guestrooms. Skar opened the Sahara Inn and a 150-room sister hotel at 4501 South Cicero Avenue in April 1962 with a $5.8 million line of credit from a savings and loan. The original beneficiary of the trust was Rocco DeStefano, a former associate of Al Capone. The mob, as one might expect, kept a watchful eye on their little "impresario," who once boasted to Lieutenant Joe Morris of the Chicago Police Internal Affairs Division that he could "fix just about anything."

The savings and loan foreclosed on Skar less than a year after the gala grand opening. Government attorneys accused Manny of diverting a substantial portion of the construction money into his own pockets. This, the mob did not want to

BEA & MANNY

SKAR IN HAPPIER

DAYS (RIGHT).

(Photo courtesy of Bea Skar & Gera-Lind Kolarik)

MANNY SKAR:

THE GOLD COAST

BECKONED

(BELOW).

hear, so Manny decided to lay low in Beverly Hills for a few months.

Gene Autry, the singing cowboy, bought Manny's $10.3 million operation in August 1963, but a black-powder bomb exploded in the parking lot five months later, knocking bandleader Fred Waring from the comfort of his bed. Singer Allen Jones checked out immediately, muttering to himself, "What a crazy place Chicago is."

Skar, meanwhile, continued to be hounded by creditors. Matters just got worse and worse. A Federal grand jury indicted him on income tax evasion in 1964.

A month before the tax trial was scheduled to open in October 1965, Manny suggested an afternoon on the town to his beloved Beatrice. The high-roller who borrowed millions to build nightclubs found it necessary to panhandle $100 from a North Side tavern owner in order to take his wife to a floorshow at the Scotch Mist, a hoodlum joint at 874 North Wabash Avenue. As they headed back home on Lake Shore Drive toward the Irving Park Road exit, Beatrice noticed a light-colored car driven by two dark-complected men. "Don't worry about it," Manny said with an air of unconcern.

Dropping his wife at the front door of the high-rise, Manny turned right on Grace, pulling into the courtyard parking area. Moments later the neighbors heard the unmistakable sound of an automobile backfiring. Beatrice Skar instantly knew that it wasn't firecrackers or a car's exhaust. It was much worse.

Two hundred people clustered around Manny's lifeless form, while the cops cordoned off the crime scene. In Manny's pockets, the cops found $32.18, all that was left of the hundred bucks from the tavern owner. Skar exited life as he lived it—in debt.

Bea Skar left Chicago and its unpleasantness behind not long afterward. She moved to Palm Springs, where, at last report, the gutsy widow had amassed a fortune in the corrugated packing business with her third husband.

Turn back south on Sheridan Road and proceed to Belmont Avenue.

THE ANGELO GENNA RESIDENCE
1925

Angelo Genna was the youngest of the six "terrible" Genna brothers and the first to die. He lived with his young bride, Lucille Spignola, in a spacious apartment on the upper floors of the Belmont Hotel at 3170 North Sheridan Road across the street from the residence of former Chicago Mayor William Hale Thompson. The Belmont

Hotel (on the southwest corner of Belmont Avenue and Sheridan Road) is an old and historic dwelling that has been converted to condominiums in recent years. It is one of the many jewels along Chicago's Lakefront.

The Genna brothers of Taylor Street manufactured a vile and potent blend of rotgut, which they peddled to the unsuspecting as the purest, highest quality liquor available in Chicago. Steeped in the Old World traditions of Sicily, where the peasants brewed their beverages at home, Angelo, Pete, Tony, Jim, Mike, and Sam Genna pressed into service hundreds of West Side Italian families to cook cheap, unrefined alcohol in their homes and backyards. The Genna brothers paid $15 a day and everyone came out ahead, especially the Gennas and the police officers assigned to duty at the Maxwell Street Station. The officers certainly enjoyed receiving two paychecks, one from the city and another from Angelo and his brothers.

The Gennas were wedded to their Old World customs, but were utterly ruthless when provoked. The brothers were blamed by the North Side mob for the murder of Dion O'Banion inside his flower shop. There would be no peace in gangland for the foreseeable future.

Angelo Genna succeeded Mike Merlo as head of the powerful Unione Sicilione, a Mafia fraternal society chartered in New York. Until Merlo was killed, Angelo's brother-in-law Harry Spignola was president of the local chapter of the society and the legal brain behind the Genna "alky-cooking" empire. O'Banion was preparing the floral arrangements for Merlo's funeral when Mike Genna and two friends assassinated the florist on November 1, 1924.

Swearing revenge, Earl "Hymie" Weiss directed forays deep into the Italian quarter. For months Weiss plotted the demise of the Gennas. Hearing that Angelo had moved into the Belmont Hotel in defiance of gangland edicts only deepened his sense of outrage.

Weiss bided his time as lesser gangsters on both sides were cut down in the line of fire. Finally, he could wait no longer. On May 25, 1925, Angelo Genna left Lucille at home and sped south and then west in his $6,000 roadster to close on a home he had just purchased in suburban Oak Park. Genna was motoring west on Ogden Avenue near Hudson Avenue when he was overtaken by a sedan containing Weiss, Vincent Drucci, and Peter Gusenberg. Unable to avoid the death trap, Genna slammed his car into a lamppost. Two shotgun volleys dispatched the arrogant Angelo to another world. Angelo Genna was buried in a casket that cost $1,000 more than what the widow O'Banion had paid to lay Dion to rest.

To continue the tour, turn right (west) on Belmont Avenue. Proceed to Halsted Street and turn right (north). Continue north to Brompton Avenue.

JOHN DILLINGER SLEPT HERE
March 3, 1934

Hours after John Dillinger escaped from Sheriff Lillian Holley's Crown Point, Indiana, jail with a hand-carved wooden pistol that had been smuggled into the jail and more guile and raw nerve than any hood alive, the fugitive hightailed it to Chicago where he hid out in a sec-ond-floor brick apartment house at 3512 North Halsted Street (at Brompton Avenue) in the block south of the Forty-second Precinct police station (Town Hall) at Addison and Halsted Streets. The apartment building's side entrance afforded Dillinger a perfect escape route just in case the Town Hall cops were tipped off.

Edward J. Kelly, mayor of Chicago during the Depression and the Second World War, was incensed when he was told that a female jailer's carelessness allowed John Dillinger to slip away. "I'm sick about it," he said. "It couldn't have happened in Chicago. Dillinger won't come here because he knows it's too hot for him."

Dillinger's wooden-gun farce pushed the limits of Kelly's patience. The fugitive crept back into Chicago that same day, driving Sheriff Holley's car directly to 3512 North Halsted, where Dillinger was provided a comfortable bed and a place to crash for the night in the second-floor apartment of Frances "Patsy" Frechette, sister of his favorite girlfriend, Evelyn "Billie" Frechette, a half-breed Menomonee Indian.

Louis Piquett, a former city prosecutor and North Side politician whom Dillinger insisted on calling "Pick-What," shared living quarters with Dillinger that night. The following morning, as police intensified the manhunt for America's most-wanted criminal, Billie Frechette dumped Sheriff Holley's car next to an apartment building at 1057 North Ardmore Avenue. The cops found the sheriff's .32-caliber pistol in the car, but no Dillinger. The chase was on.

Go north on Halsted Street to Addison Street. Turn left (west) and go to Sheffield Avenue. Turn left (south) on Sheffield Street and go one block to Cornelia Avenue.

ANNA SAGE'S "WRIGLEYVILLE" BORDELLO
1934

The tidy red-brick building with dainty white trim at 3504 North Sheffield Avenue (one block south of Wrigley Field) on the west side of the street is now in an upscale neighborhood that wasn't always quite so safe, or gentrified. Today, the Wrigleyville neighborhood is steeped in urban charm; a "happening" place for young singles. When baseball is in season, thousands of daydreaming Cubs fans pass by this anonymous building en route to a ballpark that transcends the game played on the field. In earlier years, when Hack Wilson—not Sammy Sosa—was belting home runs over the wall, Anna Sage created her own special "happenings" for a very different clientele shuffling in and out of her parlor at the Sheffield Hotel.

The Sheffield Hotel was the last active whorehouse owned by illegal Romanian immigrant Anna Sage, the madam who betrayed John Dillinger for $5,000 in cash and a false promise of sanctuary in the United States. Sage began her professional career in 1919 in East Chicago, a steel-mill town. Twice married, Sage drifted into Chicago, where she opened a string of cheap bordellos, managing at all times to keep one step ahead of the law. In June 1934, she closed the Sheffield property and moved into a building at 2420 North Halsted (which has since been demolished). There she provided Dillinger with a feather bed and a girl, Polly Hamilton, to share it. Hamilton, one of her working girls, comforted Dillinger while he recovered from his face-altering plastic surgery.

Turn around and head north on Sheffield Avenue past Addison Street. Proceed north past Grace Street.

SHE CALLED HER SHOT
July 6, 1932

Chicago Cubs shortstop Billy Jurges was living at the Carlos Hotel at 3834 Sheffield Avenue, between Grace and Byron Streets, when a tearful twenty-three-year-old divorcée named Violet Popovich Valli burst in on him in an unguarded moment with her gun blazing. The Carlos Hotel is now the Sheffield House; a small, out-of-the-way residential dwelling with a beautiful ornate façade exhibiting the original name in cut stone above the entranceway. With the passing of time, the Carlos Hotel declined with the surrounding neighborhood, offering rooms at affordable rates to transients. New ownership has improved the appearance of the once elegant address.

Violet Popovich worshiped Billy Jurges from the grandstand of Wrigley Field. When the games ended, the love-struck Chicago woman, who yearned for a show-business career, waited patiently outside the clubhouse for a glimpse of her idol. Sometimes Violet would tug on the sleeve of his coat, and once she managed to push her way past a throng of autograph seekers. Cubs management was alarmed by her persistence, but did nothing to discourage her vigil.

Popovich was ambitious, talented, and determined to make a name for herself, if only to win the affections of Billy. She sang and pranced her way into Earl Carroll's "Vanities" review, a traveling road show featuring scantily attired lovelies. Violet discovered how easy it often was to meet ballplayers in their familiar nightclub haunts, especially if you had a show-biz pedigree.

Popovich was formally introduced to Jurges at the end of the 1931 season by Cubs outfielder Hazen "KiKi" Cuyler, who himself was attracted to the young brunette dancer. But it was Jurges who remained Violet's ideal man. She even rented a room at the Carlos Hotel to be near him.

It is uncertain whether or not the popular Cubs shortstop had "jilted" Popovich, as she later told police. But in her own mind at least, she was seriously

THE CARLOS HOTEL,

WHERE A SMITTEN

WOMAN TRIED TO MUR-

DER CHICAGO CUBS STAR

BILLY JURGES.

(Photo by Christina Carlson)

involved with him when he seriously rebuffed her. At that moment, she decided that life was no longer worth the trouble.

Violet scrawled a suicide note to her ex-husband and tucked it inside her purse along with a cheap .25-caliber handgun. The note read, "To me life is not worth living, but why should I leave this earth alone?"

A resident of the Carlos Hotel who was passing by the girl's room heard her say to a friend, "If he denies this, I'll forgive him. Otherwise I'll give him the works!"

Jurges had been warned about Popovich being a dangerously unstable woman. He dismissed the advice, however, and admitted Violet to his room the morning of July 6, 1932, after receiving three frantic telephone calls from Popovich from the lobby begging him to admit her.

Shutting the door behind her, Popovich displayed the weapon and threatened to kill herself. Then she fired three shots at Jurges, sending one bullet through his hand and another into his side. The Cubs shortstop lunged at Popovich and managed to disarm her before another shot could be fired.

After she had been disarmed and subdued, Jurges was taken to Illinois Masonic Hospital where his wounds were treated. Popovich was booked on a charge of assault to kill, but Jurges refused to prosecute the matter for personal reasons. He requested that gangland's favorite undertaker, Judge John Sbarbaro, withdraw the charges. The grateful Popovich burst into tears. "I owe it to my self-respect to consider the entire affair a thing of the past," she said, and was never heard from again.

Billy Jurges was sidelined for the remainder of the 1932 season, missing out on the thrills of a pennant. The Cubs went to the World Series that year, and Jurges was replaced by former Yankee Mark Koenig who was awarded a miserly half-share of the bonus money by Cubs management.

This led to some intense bench jockeying between Babe Ruth's Yankees and the Cubs ballplayers. In the third game of the World Series, Ruth responded to the merciless bench jockeying coming from the home team's third-base dugout by "calling his shot." Ruth drilled a home run over the centerfield wall of Wrigley Field in the exact spot he had pointed to only a moment earlier. The demoralized Cubs lost the game, and the World Series in four games.

It can be reasonably argued that this tragic turn of events would have never happened if only Billy Jurges had kept his door locked for the night.

Return to Addison Street and turn left (east). Proceed east on Addison Street and turn left (north) on Pine Grove Avenue.

AT HOME WITH DION O'BANION
1924

At the time of his death on November 1, 1924, family man and North Side rackets boss Dion O'Banion lived in a very opulent and handsome-looking graystone mid-rise apartment building at 3608 Pine Grove Avenue (on the northwest corner of Addison Street and Pine Grove Avenue). Although O'Banion owned another residence at 6081 North Ridge Avenue, he preferred the amenities of lakefront living.

Dion O'Banion married Viola Kaniff on February 5, 1921. She was just eighteen and he a seasoned pro of twenty-nine when they met at a Christmas dance.

At O'Banion's funeral just three years later in Sbarbaro's mortuary, Viola recalled her husband's endearing ways as the procession of mourners filed by his casket and a heart-shaped floral wreath decorated with two thousand American Beauty roses. The simple inscription read: "Husband."

"Oh, he was all I have in the world. He was not a man to run around nights, only to take me to the show. And never one of these men with women calling him up. He was home-loving, wanting his friends about him, and never leaving without telling me where he was going."

In quiet times, Dion loved to tinker with the crystals and wires inside his radio set. He stroked the keys of a $14,000 player piano after dinner. "And such a pride in his furniture, wanting only the finest," Viola sobbed. "Pretty lights and deep, comfortable chairs." O'Banion spared no expense. "He didn't like vulgar ostentation," she added. "He had one car. It was a little sedan he bought for my use."

The grief-stricken widow said she had no idea what to do next. Viola could hardly think, but she vowed eternal devotion to Dion's sacred memory.

Within the next four years, however, Mrs. O'Banion was married two more times, first in secret to Frank Frak, and then to a wealthy real estate developer named Oswald Turner. Her doomed marriage to Frak was annulled by the church without protest or comment from the husband.

"I am only twenty-four," she explained to reporters. "I know Dean [as Dion was sometimes known] would not want me to live alone."

Or without funds.

Continue on Pine Grove to Grace Street. Turn left (west) on Grace Street and go to Broadway.

"LOVE ME OR LEAVE ME," THE MARIGOLD GARDENS
1920s

The Broadway nightclub district, like so many other entertainment districts crowding the thoroughfares of Chicago in a time far removed, was doomed by the advent of television and changing public tastes. The Marigold Gardens, located at the intersection of Broadway and Grace, was the North Side's premier show spot during the World War I era. Now it is largely forgotten. A nondescript International House of Pancakes and a parking lot replaced the cabaret long ago. One by one the famous Chicago nightclubs disappeared, and along with them a star-studded era of floorshows and vaudeville matinees featuring pie-in-the-face comedians, cabaret torch singers, big bands, and magicians. They all disappeared—with a flick of the television channel.

Before World War I, Chicago's sizable German-American community dined in comparative luxury at the Bismarck Gardens. Wartime anti-German fervor and the advent of Prohibition forced a change in ownership.

The continental dining room, with its seventy-five-piece orchestra, was originally owned by the Eitel brothers, but they sold the place to Henry van Horne, who capitalized on the dry laws by turning it into a first-class speakeasy, which he named the Marigold Gardens.

Van Horne (known around town simply as Henry Horn) was a flamboyant show-business promoter who operated a number of North Side nightspots in the 1920s, including the New Rendez-Vous, where Joe E. Lewis was working the night he fell victim to "Machine Gun" Jack McGurn's slashing blade.

In its heyday, around 1919, the Marigold Gardens was a sprawling complex of indoor and outdoor dance floors, terraces, and dining facilities. Forty chorus girls danced across the stage each night to a packed house of table-hopping swells, gangsters, and nouveaux riche. Table d'hôte, served between the hours of six and nine each evening, cost a hungry patron only $2.00.

An air of intrigue and danger hung over the place, but much the same could also be said of the Green Mill Gardens, just blocks north of the Marigold in the

Uptown neighborhood, and Colosimo's place down in the Levee. The so-called "decent element," which railed against sin and vulgarity on Sunday, joined in on the decadent fun on Fridays. And so it went, year after year, in good times and in bad.

Henry's principal showstopper in those days was Ruth Etting, a torch singer from Nebraska. Etting danced in Florenz Ziegfeld's *Follies* after she became a "protégé" of the famous musical producer Paul Ash, who helped launch her career as a solo performer.

When she wasn't in New York or on a national tour with the *Follies,* Etting baby sat van Horne's little boy, Rudy, between sets.

Chicago's "Singing Sweetheart" was only eighteen when she married Moe "the Gimp" Snyder, an unpleasant little gunman and labor racketeer with a low boiling point and a propensity for violence. When he failed to see eye to eye with café management, Snyder, acting as Ruth's personal manager, would resolve disputes with threats and a quick right hook. For a while the intimidation factor helped boost Etting's singing career and her bookings. With the money from her hit records, the couple purchased a Beverly Hills mansion.

Snyder was a Chicago thug and insanely jealous. He never fit into the Hollywood scene, where he made enemies right and left. Once, when he discovered that his wife was romantically linked to a composer named Merle Alderman, Snyder drilled the songsmith with his automatic. The "Gimp" was lucky that Alderman survived—extremely lucky. Moe was locked in the Los Angeles County Jail for a year, giving him plenty of time to sort things out. True, he did lose the love of his life, who filed for divorce that same year, but he had a boatload of stories to bring back to the lunchtime crowd at Fritzels' Restaurant in downtown Chicago, where with a wave of his cigar and a sip of gin, he held court for many years to come.

In 1955, *Love Me or Leave Me* debuted on the big screen with Jimmy Cagney, perfectly cast as the snarling Moe Snyder, and Doris Day as the delicate chanteuse Ruth Etting.

Meanwhile, Rudy Horn, Henry Horn's son, ran away from home at the age of twelve to become a chorus boy in *Fine and Dandy, Hellzapoppin',* and *Broadway Nights.* He said he owed it all to his sometime baby sitter Ruth Etting, who encouraged him to remain versatile and true to the calling.

Rudy never forgot Ruthie. He was her greatest fan and would call her long-distance every year on her birthday until she was well into her eighties and long forgotten by her public.

THE WIGWAM, 3751 NORTH BROADWAY
1920s–1930s

The Wigwam, named for its triangular shape when viewed from above, is directly across the street from the IHOP restaurant that intrudes upon the space of the fabled Marigold Gardens.

This rather gloomy-looking red-brick structure with its many retail storefronts and maze of upper-story apartments was once the Marigold Hotel and, for a brief period of time, the headquarters of the O'Banion-Drucci-Moran mob. The Club Southern was a street-level nightclub, a bucket of blood popular with a fast-moving clientele. Members of the John Dillinger gang and their girlfriends were frequent patrons.

> Turn right
>
> (north) on
>
> Broadway and
>
> proceed one
>
> block to East
>
> Sheridan Road.

HOTEL CHATEAU, 3838 NORTH BROADWAY
1930s

Up the street from the Wigwam, on the west side of Broadway, stands the Hotel Chateau, a sagging dowager whose youth and beauty faded long ago. Members of the Dillinger gang often rendezvoused inside an apartment belonging to John "Red" Hamilton's girlfriend, Pat Cherrington, and her sister, Opal Long, a brassy, heavyset woman who kept company with Russell Clark, a member of the Dillinger gang. When Cherrington received word that Hamilton had been killed outside St. Paul, Minnesota, the hysterical woman nearly tore the hotel apart. Dillinger, it is said, forwarded an envelope full of cash to ease her suffering. The gangsters' molls, along with another woman named Jean Helen Burke, were arrested by federal agents at the Chateau on June 2, 1934.

Turn right (east) on East Sheridan Road and go to Pine Grove Avenue. Turn left (north) on Pine Grove Avenue and go to 3941 North Pine Grove Avenue.

"FOR HEAVEN'S SAKE, CATCH ME BEFORE I KILL MORE!"
December 10, 1945

The case of the infamous "Lipstick Killer" intrigues armchair crime buffs even now, more than half a century after the Chicago Police fingered University of Chicago student William Heirens for the murder of Navy Wave Frances Brown on the sixth floor of the Pine Crest Apartments at 3941 North Pine Grove Avenue (just south of Irving Park Road on the east side of the street). Heirens, some believe, was a convenient scapegoat who was easily framed by overzealous Chicago Police trapped in the crossfire of divided public opinion concerning their inability to end a serious post-war crime wave that hit Chicago in the winter months of 1945.

Chicago is a city that beckons both fortune hunters and simple folk of good will and lofty ambitions to its shores. The city on the prairie (aka "The City on the Make") has always been a powerful magnet luring young daydreamers filled with wanderlust from rural farming communities scattered across the greater Midwest.

Frances Brown, a pretty, bright-eyed brunette, was a homespun girl who moved to Chicago in 1934 from Richmond, Indiana, along with her brother and mother. She attended business school, worked hard, and eventually landed an office job with the A. B. Dick Company. When the war came, she enlisted in the WAVES and put her office skills to good use as a telegrapher. She spent three years in the service, then returned to her old job after the Japanese surrendered in August 1945.

Brown was home alone the evening of December 10, 1945, preparing for the next workday. Viola Butler, Frances's roommate of three years, was spending her Sunday night at a friend's house. It was somewhat curious that Butler did not return home. Had she done so, the killer might not have had such an easy time of it when he slipped in through the bathroom window between 3:00 and 4:00 the next morning.

A neighbor heard gunshots, and the night clerk later told police that he

THE PINE CREST APARTMENTS,

WHERE NAVY WAVE FRANCES

BROWN WAS BRUTALLY MUR-

DERED IN DECEMBER 1945.

(Photo by Christina Carlson)

observed a man in his thirties come down the elevator and disappear into the night. The description of the suspect hardly fit that of seventeen-year-old William George Heirens.

A maid discovered the body of Miss Brown the following morning, along with an odd, maniacal message scrawled in lipstick on the living room wall, which read, "For heaven's sake, catch me before I kill more. I cannot control myself." Whoever butchered Frances Brown with a knife and left the cryptic message also felt compelled to wipe up the bloody mess with a towel.

This was the second sensational murder of a single woman in less than six months. Josephine Ross, a mother of three, was stabbed to death in her apartment at 4108 North Kenmore Avenue on June 3, leading police to the obvious conclusion that the "Lipstick Killer" was also responsible for her death.

Detective John Sullivan, a seasoned Chicago police investigator who was always willing to cooperate with the press, theorized that the killer was a woman. "It would be out of the ordinary for a man to pick up a piece of lipstick and write a message with it," he said. "It was a feminine thing to try to wipe up the blood."

Leon York, the famous Chicago graphologist who was called upon to examine Bruno Richard Hauptmann's handwriting when he was on trial for the 1932 abduction-murder of Charles Augustus Lindbergh Jr., strongly disagreed with Sullivan's opinions. "He is a gourmet," York said of the killer. "This affects his sex instincts. I would describe him as a scrubby, fat type lacking in refinement."

Others believed a sleazy crime reporter scribbled the message on the wall for a cheap headline and a front-page "exclusive" for the afternoon newspaper.

Then, less than a month later, the Brown murder was temporarily forgotten when seven-year-old Suzanne Degnan was abducted from her second-floor bedroom at 5943 North Kenmore Avenue and murdered. The sensational manhunt for the fiend ended on June 26 when Heirens was arrested on a burglary charge and a confession was pried out of him.

Handwriting experts who later compared the ransom note allegedly written by Heirens to the family of the little girl with the curious lipstick message on the wall in Room 611 found no connection. This opinion was affirmed by Charles Wilson, head of the Chicago Police crime detection laboratory.

What the cops did find in Heirens's room at Gates Hall on the University of Chicago campus, however, were personal items belonging to the victims. A preponderance of circumstantial evidence and the probability that he was threatened to within an inch of his life until he confessed sent Heirens to prison for life.

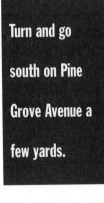

Turn and go south on Pine Grove Avenue a few yards.

"I'LL DIE BEFORE I SURRENDER!"
January 8, 1935

The spacious courtyard apartments across the street and down the block from the Pine Crest Hotel, where Frances Brown was slain in 1945, provide an interesting backdrop to one of the most frenzied police shootouts in Chicago gangland history. Russell "Roy Slim" Gibson, wanted in connection with the abduction of wealthy St. Paul, Minnesota, banker Edward George Bremer a year earlier, was holed up with members of the Barker-Karpis gang inside 3922 North Pine Grove Avenue (one block south of Irving Park Road on the west side of the street). Gibson chose death rather than surrendering to federal agents.

The Feds were closing in fast. One by one, Melvin Purvis and his men were making short work of the Ma Barker–Alvin "Creepy" Karpis gang. "Ma" and her four sons were seasoned bank robbers, but they attracted little attention outside their home state of Missouri until they branched out into kidnapping. Crisscrossing the upper Midwest in the darkest days of the Depression, the Barker brothers and Alvin Karpis inspired fear and terror. Linked to the big-city criminal organizations by blood, they were not lovable, fearless, or popular folk heroes.

From time to time, the Barker-Karpis gang passed through Chicago to transact business with the Capones, or take a few days off and enjoy the city's considerable attractions.

Melvin Purvis, with his ear to the ground, received reliable information that Russell Gibson, William Harrison of St. Louis, and their traveling party were relaxing in an apartment on Pine Grove Avenue up on the North Side. Thirty federal agents were dispatched to the address on January 8, and they covered every door and window of the large, rambling apartment house with automatic weapons.

On cue, one of Purvis's men rang the doorbell inside the vestibule. There was no response.

Moments later, Gibson rushed out of the rear entrance firing at the agents with a high-powered pistol similar to a machine gun. When his gun jammed, the agents riddled his body until he collapsed to the pavement. At that moment, a contingent of angry police officers arrived on the scene. They were indignant at Purvis for not being told of the stakeout in advance.

Gibson was rushed to the American Hospital with bullets in his liver and right lung. While he writhed in agony on the operating table, the federal men pumped him for information. Gibson was told he had one chance in 20,000 to live, and he might as well come clean. Frowning at the coppers, the bank robber looked away. Hours later Gibson was wheeled off to the morgue.

Just eight days later, Ma and Freddie Barker were killed in a Florida shootout.

Go south on Pine Grove Avenue to Sheridan Road. Turn right (west) and proceed to Clarendon Avenue. Turn right (north) on Clarendon Avenue and proceed to Junior Terrace.

JOHN DILLINGER'S HIDEOUT
Fall 1933

The courtyard apartment building at 4310 North Clarendon Avenue (facing east at Junior Terrace) is a remarkably well-preserved example of prairie-style architecture. There is an obvious pride in ownership. Perhaps the residents sense that the building is historically important, if for no other reason than that the building served as a hideout for the Dillinger gang and their girlfriends in the fall of 1933.

John Dillinger never lingered in one place too long. Home was a place to crash for the night: a bed, a bottle of booze, and a babe in his arms. That was the life he had become accustomed to, and the accomplices who followed Dillinger from place to place trusted his instincts.

In the fall of 1933, the Dillinger gang rented a stately six-room apartment with a veranda on the third floor at 4310 North Clarendon Avenue. The veranda is still visible from the street, and we can only imagine what words passed between the hoodlums and their molls as they gazed out at the city lying before them. Dillinger, Harry Pierpont, and Harry's mistress, Mary Kinder, were joined by Billie Frechette in early November.

Neighbors recalled that the Dillinger gang kept to themselves and were "good neighbors." At least that's the story they related to police who raided the building on November 15, 1933. A day earlier, Dillinger visited the offices of Dr. Charles H. Eye at 4175 West Irving Park Road on the city's Northwest Side. The fugitive had contracted a case of ringworm during his recent prison stay, and was seeking a cure for the malady.

The police laid a trap while Dillinger was being attended to in the examination room. Noting the presence of police flivvers outside his office, Doctor Eye warned his patient. Dillinger flew out of the office and into Billie Frechette's stolen roadster. The couple simply outran the slower cop cars and lost their pursuers at Elston Avenue, less than a mile east.

That night, Deputy Chief of Detectives William V. Blaul raided the Clarendon Avenue apartment, but Dillinger and his gang were gone, and the department suffered another blow to its sagging reputation.

Continue north on Clarendon Avenue to Montrose Avenue. Turn left (west) and go to Sheridan Road. Turn right (north) on Sheridan Road.

SHOOTOUT IN UPTOWN
November 1, 1933

The Sherone Apartment Hotel at 4423 North Sheridan Road (at Agatite Street) has seen better days. Viewing the classic ornamentation silhouetted against the upward rush of red brick, one senses a certain loss of dignity. Like other residential and commercial sections of Uptown, this building suffers from urban decay and neglect. When it was an apartment hotel catering to its well-heeled Uptown neighbors, and when its street-level retail addresses were not defaced by the ugly collage of discount stores that are there now, the Sherone was the place to go, especially if you were young, carefree, and enjoying the nightlife and the irresistible lullaby of Broadway.

Verne C. Miller was a desperate little gunman who enjoyed an international reputation for mayhem and violence. Born in the jumpin' flats of Huron, South Dakota, Miller grew up to become sheriff of that whistle-stop burg before he turned bad. At the height of the Depression, after he exchanged his tin star for a machine gun, Miller rode with a gang of marauding gunslingers from the Southwest, the ranks of which included Harvey Bailey and George "Machine Gun" Kelly.

At various times in his criminal career Miller performed services for the Purple Gang of Detroit and Al Capone's homegrown bootlegging operations in suburban Melrose Park. Miller drifted into town, stayed pretty much to himself, and moved on. Verne Miller was as dangerous and unpredictable as the times he lived in, but he lacked the cachet of fame and glamour that accompanied fellow outlaw John Dillinger. Miller just killed for the sake of killing and offered no explanation or apology.

Miller was one of a trio of machine gunners who raked the entranceway of Union Station in Kansas City, Missouri, in a bold attempt to spring bank robber Frank "Jelly" Nash from his FBI captors. The "Kansas City Massacre" claimed the lives of Nash and four agents on June 17, 1933.

Fresh from these adventures, Miller retreated to his old haunts in Chicago and was holed up with a girlfriend named Bobbie Williams at the Sherone

GUNMAN VERNE

MILLER SHOT HIS WAY

TO FREEDOM AFTER

BEING CORNERED

INSIDE THE SHERONE

HOTEL.

(Photo by author)

Apartments when an informant tipped off the FBI that he was in town and up to no good.

Seven federal men were spread across the perimeter of the hotel and strategically positioned in the lobby awaiting a prearranged sign—the informant was supposed to drop his keys to the floor when he spotted Miller coming down from the upper floors.

At 9:00 P.M., the blond-haired, blue-eyed gunman with the bushy mustache and flashy clothes appeared in the lobby. But once the keys clattered to the floor, Miller's gun blazed. He smelled a trap and was ready for it.

He bolted through the entranceway leading to Galt Avenue (now Agatite

Avenue) and raced east down the block. The bullets were whizzing by him, but none found their mark. When an FBI agent let loose with his machine gun, it marked the first time that a representative from law enforcement used the deadly weapon in the streets of Chicago.

Miller leapt into a late-model coupe driven by his girlfriend and sped off, first to Clarendon Avenue, then south to Montrose, west to Vista Terrace (now Dayton Street), then south again. The pursuit ended on Montrose where the car stalled after one of the tires blew out. By the time the agents caught up with the car, Miller and his lady friend were long gone.

Neither the Chicago Police nor Melvin Purvis and his men managed to catch up with Verne Miller, who fled to the East Coast, then retraced his steps back to the Midwest. Miller was murdered by either Abner "Longy" Zwillman, a mobster who controlled statewide gambling operations in New Jersey, or former associates in Detroit's Purple Gang four weeks later on November 28.

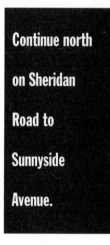

Continue north on Sheridan Road to Sunnyside Avenue.

JOHN DILLINGER'S DEATH SLEEP: THE MCCREADY FUNERAL HOME
July 24, 1934

The former McCready Funeral Home at 4508 North Sheridan Road, a few doors north of Sunnyside Avenue on the west side of the street, is a private residence nestled among a row of low-income SRO's (single-room occupancy buildings) and other residential buildings in a section of Uptown caught in the grind of gangs, drugs, and street crime. The cream-colored building is well maintained and easily identifiable as a funeral home. The letter M carved into an upper-story turret is a reminder of past times.

John Dillinger was not officially waked in Chicago. His body was removed to Indiana by his grief-stricken father, John Wilson Dillinger, three days after the shots were fired at the Biograph Theater.

Before the Dillingers arrived in Chicago, the lifeless remains of John Dillinger were placed in a wicker basket and shipped to the McCready Funeral Home. According to biographer G. Russell Girardin, thousands of curiosity seekers lined Sheridan Road for a final glimpse of the remains but were turned away.

The weather-beaten old man who was Dillinger's father, defeated by time

THE REMAINS OF JOHN DILLINGER WERE STORED OVERNIGHT AT THE MCCREADY FUNERAL HOME AT 4506 (NOW 4508) NORTH BROADWAY, BUT CURIOUS NEIGHBORS WERE NOT DISSUADED FROM CATCHING A GLIMPSE.

DILLINGER IS

TRANSPORTED IN

A WICKER CASKET

TO THE MCCREADY

FUNERAL HOME.

and circumstances, said he wouldn't want to see a dog shot down like that. Then, gazing at the corpse for the first time, the father exclaimed "My boy! My boy!" The elder Dillinger promised his boy a Christian burial and thanked the people of Chicago "for being so kind."

Continue north on Sheridan Road to Lawrence Avenue. Turn left (west) and proceed to Broadway. Turn right (north) on Broadway.

THE GOLDEN AGE OF THE GREEN MILL

The storefront show lounge at 4802 North Broadway (on the northwest corner of Broadway and Lawrence in Uptown) is Chicago's oldest nightclub, offering continuous entertainment since 1907. Known for its jazz, gin, and world-famous poetry slams, the Green Mill preserves Chicago's fading show-business heritage and the bitter legacy of "Machine Gun" Jack McGurn.

In Chicago in 1927, the Green Mill Gardens was the "jumping-est" joint on the North Side. Thirsty jazz aficionados flocked to the Uptown nightclub to savor this evolving musical art form born in the deep South, but nurtured in Chicago in the years following World War I. The jazz set ignored Prohibition and secreted their bootleg whiskey in the hollows of walking canes and concealed hip flasks in deep coat pockets.

The Green Mill was a place to escape for a nightcap following an evening of romance under the twinkling starlit ceiling of the Aragon Ballroom (a block away at 1106 West Lawrence Avenue).

In the mid-1920s, after Henry van Horne relinquished his interest in the place, the three Chamales brothers leased the club to the Al Capone mob. Although it seems unlikely that Capone would have wanted to risk his personal safety straying so far north into the heart of enemy territory, he seemed to enjoy the charms of the dimly lit cabaret. The Green Mill helped launch the careers of torch singer Helen Morgan, Anita O'Day, Billie Holiday, many jazz combos, and a procession of vaudevillians, both great and small, who dropped by to jam, or just to relax between sets.

The Green Mill opened in 1907 as Pop Morse's Roadhouse. From the very beginning, the club was a favorite rendezvous for show-business folks. "Bronco Billy" Anderson, the star of dozens of western silents filmed at George Spoor's

A REAL WINDMILL ONCE SAT HIGH ATOP THE GREEN MILL GARDENS NIGHTCLUB. IN 1919, WHEN THIS ADVERTISEMENT APPEARED, THE CLUB FEATURED A 10,000-SQUARE-FOOT DANCE FLOOR.

IT IS LESS THAN HALF THAT SIZE TODAY. THE FAMOUS GREEN MILL ONCE OCCUPIED THIS ENTIRE BUILDING. NOW IT IS A SMALL STOREFRONT, BUT ONE THAT CONTINUES TO LURE JAZZ AFICIONADOS FROM ALL OVER THE CITY.

(Photo by author)

ONCE A POPULAR NIGHTSPOT KNOWN AS THE "5100 CLUB," THIS BUILDING AT

5100 BROADWAY BECAME AN AUTO PARTS STORE TARGETED BY BURGLAR RICHARD

MORRISON, THEN IN RECENT YEARS A COLLECTION OF NONDESCRIPT STOREFRONTS.

(Photo by author)

Essanay Studios at 1345 West Argyle Street before 1920, often rode his horse to Pop Morse's. The proprietor installed a hitching post that Anderson would share with Wallace Beery and William S. Hart. Years later, when comedian Danny Thomas played the "5100 Club" at 5100 North Broadway, three blocks north of the Mill, he would drop in from time to time.

Around 1910, the Chamales brothers bought the club from the original owners. They placed a kitschy green windmill on the roof above the spacious beer garden, beckoning the flotsam and jetsam of late-night Chicago to its doors.

Mary Louise "Texas" Guinan, the darling of the New York "Gay White Way," strutted and pranced across the Green Mill stage until a 1930 shooting inside the club outraged the censors, who closed down her racy act.

However, it is the legend of Jack McGurn, mastermind of the St. Valentine's Day Massacre, that attracts the curiosity seekers, who inevitably ask the bartender to tell them "the real story" as they sip Manhattans in the cozy comfort of the green-plush upholstered booths.

McGurn managed the club for Capone. He acted as the booking agent for the mob and collected 25 percent of the weekly take, which is why he was so enraged when Joe E. Lewis broke his contract at the Mill.

Lewis survived McGurn's switchblade attack, and eventually returned to the Green Mill, as everyone who wishes to experience America's Jazz Age inside this charming little bistro does sooner or later.

Continue north on Broadway to Foster Avenue. Turn left (west) on Foster Avenue and go to Winchester Avenue.

THE BABBLING BURGLAR
January 1960

A chance encounter between a brainy twenty-three-year-old sneak thief named Richard Morrison and a ham-fisted cop from the Summerdale Police District set in motion a historic chain of events that forever changed the face of law enforcement in Chicago. The devastating scandal involved eight cops/burglars, whose sins rocked the Chicago Police Department to its bare roots. The reforms initiated in the wake of Summerdale permanently ended the miasmatic nineteenth-century method of police administration that traded on the favors of politicians and organized crime, and the willingness of the public to tolerate rampant abuse of the "system"—so long as that same public was not inconvenienced by an unexpected appearance in traffic court or a burdensome fine. Collecting a sawbuck from motorists during routine traffic stops, expecting presents from retail merchants at Christmastime, etc., was all fine and dandy. It was the price Chicagoans paid for "efficient" law enforcement not so long ago. Cops knocking off stores in Morrison's company were quite another matter, however. The Summerdale Police Scandal, presaging Watergate by more than a decade, was much more than a "third-rate burglary."

Should you care to explore the Summerdale "heritage trail" on your own, the tour begins outside the Twentieth District police station at 1940 West Foster, a cracker-box-sized Art Deco building where the cops/burglars planned their jobs and split up the loot. The embarrassing Summerdale name was quietly dropped after the scandal died down, but the cramped stationhouse situated between Damen and Winchester Avenues lives on, despite recent austerity cutbacks that closed several other outmoded city precinct houses. The tour winds past Wesley's, the former pizza joint at 1116 West Bryn Mawr Avenue, located underneath the Chicago Transit Authority (CTA) elevated stop. Morrison caddied late-night snacks to the boys in blue at Summerdale while working as Wesley's delivery driver and loading unpaid parking tickets in his glove compartment. The pizza restaurant is gone, replaced by Sunflower Fashions, an unpretentious little apparel store in Edgewater's down-and-out commercial strip. The once-a-week burglary ring hit dozens of stores in Andersonville, other parts of Edgewater, and Uptown, none more famous than the Western Tire and

Auto Store at 5100 North Broadway, a favorite burglary target and a building with quite a history of its own. The tire dealer was the first of ten major heists in which the uniformed police were active participants. This historic Uptown building at 5100 was once the "5100 Club," a North Side hot spot. Now an Asian grocery store, the former Western Tire and Auto Store, in a very real sense, changed the course of modern policing. Morrison lived in a red-brick, three-story courtyard apartment building at 4332 North Sacramento Avenue, just south of Montrose Avenue and before Cullom Avenue, in the Albany Park neighborhood. His arrest inside the apartment building on July 30, 1959, ended a chain of events that began with a chance encounter outside a North Side liquor store nearly a year earlier.

In the darkened doorway of a liquor store on Berwyn Avenue east of Broadway, Officer Frank Faraci of the Summerdale station stumbled into an old acquaintance. "Well if it isn't the little burglar Richie Morrison," he sneered. The smell of liquor on Faraci's breath was unmistakable. Morrison nervously asked how things were going. He was never very comfortable in the presence of no-good cops.

"Well, they would be a little better if you would cut us guys in on some of your jobs," Faraci suggested. "You know Al Karras and some of the other fellows, and they'll go along with the show. A set of golf clubs might be nice . . . for starters. After all, we like nice things too."

The police officers of the Fortieth District knew Morrison from the neighborhood and by his kinky reputation. Some of them had attended classes with Morrison at Senn High School. Now they demanded free pizzas from him, which he happily delivered direct to the station.

Richie completed his apprenticeship as a sneak thief by posing as a buyer of industrial safes and vaults in order to familiarize himself with the location of tumblers, the thickness of steel, and the vulnerabilities of strongboxes. With manila rope, purchased in 10,000-foot lengths, he fashioned ladders to help him gain after-hours entry through the roof ventilation systems and skylights of dozens of stores.

He never used the same equipment twice, and to taunt the cops, he always left his burglary tools at the scene of the crime. Morrison boasted that he had committed 150 burglaries in six months and had stolen loot worth $100,000.

On July 31, 1958, pressured about the golf clubs, Morrison slipped into Evanston to loot a parked automobile on Forest Avenue, a quiet side street off of busy Sheridan Road. There had been a rash of automobile thefts in Evanston, and Morrison was strongly suspected. His reputation was known far and wide. The suburban cops planned a stakeout after hearing that the thief was coming to town. A set of borrowed golf clubs was positioned in an open station wagon.

Morrison was a good wheelman and managed to avoid a deadly trap. Crouching down low in his car, he spun his Cadillac in the other direction as a thousand bullets pierced trees, parked cars, and the sidewalk curbing. He ditched the Cadillac on Sheridan Road and retreated back into Chicago's North Side, rattled, but unhurt.

The Evanston cops ransacked his apartment on Lakewood Avenue in the Rogers Park neighborhood, but the resourceful Morrison had already flown the coop. Eventually located after nearly being lost, the glib little thief was arrested, cuffed, and returned to Evanston.

Deciding he needed money and police "clout" to defend himself in the auto looting case, Morrison agreed to commit burglaries for Faraci, Karras, and six others assigned to the midnight to 8:00 A.M. watch at Summerdale.

The Summerdale gang sprang into action in the early morning hours of October 1, 1958, when four squad cars were deployed in the vicinity of the Western Tire and Auto Store. It was shortly before 3:00 A.M. Morrison and his sidekick, Robert Crilly, were told to keep the cash as a reward. Television sets, shotguns, tools, tires, radios—all of it ordered in advance by the Summerdale cops—were piled high at the delivery platform door for pickup.

"I told [Patrolman] Allan Brinn on the three-wheeler to stay off Carmen and if a police car came we would know it was not them and we could duck in some gangway," Morrison would later testify. "We were loading up our car for the third time, and a three-wheeler came down Carmen. We dropped the shotguns we were carrying and ran into a gangway where we had put the back seat of the car to make room for more merchandise. But it was Brinn."

This was to be the first of ten major retail burglaries in which uniformed police officers were active participants. The following week, Morrison opened up the Edmund J. Self Custom Furniture Store at 6322 North Broadway, just south of Devon Avenue. (A parking lot for several fast-food emporiums is there now.) Lighting a cigarette, Morrison leaned against the wall and chuckled to himself as the greedy cops helped themselves to a marble tabletop, bolts of draperies, and the display furnishings. After all, they liked nice things too.

It went on like this for the next nine months until Richie Morrison was collared inside his flat at 4332 North Sacramento Avenue by Chicago burglary dicks Jim McGuire, Howard Rothgery, Pat Driscoll, and James Heard after a short strug-

(Photo courtesy of the Chicago Historical Society)

gle. The little thief fumbled with his gun, but he wasn't much of a triggerman and was easily disarmed by the veteran detectives.

For the moment he was silent, which was unusual for the nervous and high-strung thief who is remembered as a nonstop talker. Thus, the full story of Morrison's connivance with the Summerdale cops unraveled very slowly.

The Morrison case came up for a hearing in Branch 44 of Felony Court at Twenty-sixth and California on October 10, 1959. Richie counted on his friends in Summerdale to pull him out of the fire, but their loyalty extended only as far as the jailhouse door. Unable to work a deal with Judge Charles Doherty for a reduced sentence, Morrison made his disclosures to the public defender, Gerald Getty, instead.

Assistant State's Attorney Jim Daugherty promptly notified Paul Newey, Chief Investigator under State's Attorney Benjamin S. Adamowski, the unofficial head of the city's Republicans and an outspoken critic of Mayor Richard J. Daley. Adamowski had personal designs on the mayor's chair since breaking party ranks and joining the Republicans in 1956.

Newey was less concerned about the political machinations. He was a work-aday law enforcement pro, a soft-spoken intellectual who was interested in ferreting out wrongdoing, even if it threatened to rock the political establishment.

Having moved into the witness quarters of the Cook County Jail complete with a free TV, quality food, and special treatment, Morrison was brought before

Adamowski and his team of investigators. There Morrison spun a fantastic tale of police crookedness that extended from the North Side of Chicago up to Evanston. Single-handedly, this glib thief brought down the ruling cadre of two police departments and helped initiate sweeping internal reform, ending a mind-set that essentially said to new police recruits that graft is good as long as you can get away with it.

While Morrison enjoyed the pleasant surroundings of the Cook County jail and a nonstop stream of friends and well-wishers—one of them smuggled in a bottle of whiskey concealed inside a birthday cake—the Chicago cops-turned-burglars were rousted from their beds in the wretched cold of a January night by a team of investigators handpicked by Newey and beyond reproach.

Art Bilek, sent in by Newey to arrest Peter Beeftink, one of the accused cops/burglars, at his North Side apartment, vividly recalls Beeftink's pathetic (but clever) plea to "take it all . . . take it all away, but please leave that easy chair over in the corner. It was a gift to my wife, and she loves it so." Bilek refused, and ordered the chair impounded. Examining the item later, Bilek found the incriminating hand-stitching that confirmed that the purloined furniture had come from E. J. Self's store on Broadway. Beeftink understood that the chair was the only piece of marked merchandise in the entire lot.

CHIEF OF POLICE

TIMOTHY O'CONNOR

(LEFT) ABOUT TO TAKE

THE FALL FOR THE

SUMMERDALE SCANDAL,

WHILE A PEEVISH MAYOR

RICHARD J. DALEY

(RIGHT) PLAYS HIS HAND.

(Courtesy of the Chicago Historical Society)

Faraci and company were hauled down to the posh Union League Club, where they were thoroughly interrogated by Adamowski, and his assistants Frank Ferlic and Paul Newey.

Finishing his all-night vigil inside a coffee shop on Jackson Boulevard, Walter Spirko broke the front-page exclusive in the pages of the *Sun-Times* the morning of January 15, 1960. Less than a week later, Police Commissioner Timothy O'Connor resigned as the scandal rocked the city and threatened to undermine Mayor Daley's administration. That same day, Daley appointed a committee of experts to select an impartial outsider; a man with impeccable credentials, to guide the Chicago Police Department through an arduous reform period and save Daley's administration further embarrassment.

Dean Orlando West Wilson of the University of California Criminology Department was hired on February 22, 1960, and handed a blank check to initiate an internal housecleaning that weeded out the "political cops" and instituted internal controls that would ensure no repeat of Summerdale.

All eight accused police officers were found guilty in a 1961 jury trial. Peter Beeftink and Henry Mulea were ordered to pay modest fines. Pat Groark, the son of a Chicago police captain, accepted his sentence and served his time. Five other cops fought their convictions all the way to the United States Supreme Court. The high court refused to hear the case after the Illinois Supreme Court upheld their convictions on January 22, 1965. The doors of the penitentiary swung open.

Richard Morrison, forever immortalized by the Chicago press corps as the "Babbling Burglar," was shotgunned outside the Criminal Courts Building on March 20, 1963, while exposing secrets about mob-friendly doctors who were conveniently forgetting to tell police about the gunshot wounds they were treating.

His spirits broken, his right arm mangled, and his number invalidated in the old hometown, the diminutive burglar was dropped off at the Illinois-Indiana state line and told to scram. Morrison shifted his base of operation to Fort Lauderdale, Florida. At last report, he was working as a police photographer. He has not been seen nor heard from for more than thirty years.

Turn back east on Foster Avenue to Clark Street. Turn left (north) on Clark Street and go two blocks to Berwyn Avenue.

LIGHTS OUT FOR A COP KILLER
October 29, 1954

An eerie replay of the John Dillinger shooting unfolded at the intersection of Berwyn and Clark Street twenty years after the Depression-era holdup man was gunned down outside the Biograph Theater a few miles to the south. Under nearly identical circumstances, a woman (she wasn't wearing red, unfortunately) tipped police of a planned rendezvous with cop killer Agostino "Gus" Amadeo two blocks south of the Calo Theater (still standing, but now the home of the Griffin theatrical company) located in the center of the North Side Swedish neighborhood known as Andersonville. Led by Lieutenant Frank Pape, one of the department's most feared gunslingers who was in line to become chief of police following the Summerdale scandal revelations, the police set an intricate trap.

Frank Pape was the real-life inspiration for Lieutenant Frank Ballinger, a hard-boiled cop portrayed by Lee Marvin in the 1950s anthology series *M-Squad*.

Pape was the genuine article, who insisted that he never intended to kill anyone who didn't deserve to die. Pape never kept a running tally; he is exceptionally modest about the number of notches in his gun handle, but it is safe to say that at least nine felons were dispatched to local cemeteries by this pugnacious Irish-German cop from Bucktown, who stirred up so much controversy while heading the day-to-day caseload of the Chicago Police Department's robbery unit back in the 1950s.

In the secretive oath-bound brotherhood known as police work, nothing arouses more intense passion than when one of their own falls in the line of duty. And so it was the night of October 21, 1954, when Detective Charles P. Annerino, one of Pape's guys, was shot through the heart by twenty-six-year-old Gus Amadeo, a recent escapee from the Cook County Jail.

Amadeo was the focus of a citywide manhunt. Shrugging off all of the press attention, he hid in plain sight at home in Ravenswood, his old neighborhood.

Annerino and his partner, William Murphy, were making the rounds of the local taverns, rousting thieves, junkies, and second-story men, when by chance and poor timing they spotted Gus seated inside the dingy Circle Lounge at 1756 Lawrence Avenue. The tavern had a notorious reputation. In Chicago there are neighborhood cop bars, and then there are the crook bars. Circle Lounge was one of the crook bars.

A brief and violent struggle followed. Murphy grabbed at Amadeo's gun, but it discharged right into Annerino's chest. Breaking loose, the killer eluded two hundred cops who searched from house to house over the next couple of hours. His discarded jacket was found by the Northwestern Railroad viaduct, but there was no trace of Amadeo. The dragnet was a disappointing failure.

Frank Pape had no remorse for crooks and cop killers and was impatient with alibiing defense attorneys and bleeding hearts. He lost one partner in June 1945, during a shootout on the sidewalk at Clark and Hubbard Streets, and never forgot what it was like to watch a pal die. His partner made it a practice to fire a warning shot over a fleeing suspect's head. Pape would never make that mistake again.

The robbery detail traced Amadeo's movements to a West Side restaurant owned by Fred Del Genio, whose sister Dolores Del Genio Marcus had dated the killer. Pape installed a listening device inside the grill, picking up loose information that Amadeo was hiding out on the North Side and needed a car and some personal items.

Pape pressured the sister-in-law to cooperate with the police or he would make it hot for Fred, who had experienced some recent trouble with the law.

Dorothy nervously agreed to a meeting with Amadeo near Wrigley Field. An ambush was arranged. Parked in a 1951 Dodge, the young woman sat directly in the line of fire. Shooters were positioned on the rooftops and in the alleys, but Amadeo failed to keep his date.

The trap was rescheduled for the following night. Gus Amadeo said he was going to take in an early movie at the Calo Theater at 5404 Clark Street, and agreed to meet Dorothy in her car parked near the Swanson Drug Store (now the Landmark of Andersonville, a new business incubator), two blocks south on Clark Street at Berwyn Avenue at 7:30 P.M.

Pape concealed his men in panel trucks, taxicabs, parked cars, and second-story apartments up and down Clark Street. The cops were cleverly disguised in the shabby attire of day laborers and taxi drivers. There were cops hidden everywhere. The detail easily tripled the size of the Dillinger squad.

The fugitive wore hunting clothing with a cap pulled down low over his forehead, but Pape recognized him from inside the drugstore. "Gus, stop right there!" Pape yelled, but Amadeo turned, raced across the street, and blindly fired two shots. Pistols, machine guns, and shotguns erupted from every corner. Gus

Amadeo crumpled and fell to the pavement, a showy sendoff for a graceless little thug.

A bystander was shot in the side, but no one paid much attention, not in the swarming throng of three thousand pedestrians who pushed and shoved their way forward. Recalling John Dillinger's moment of death, several spectators instinctively dipped their handkerchiefs in the pool of blood forming around the corpse.

A worthless souvenir as it turned out. Gus Amadeo was a nobody and quickly forgotten, but his death earned Lieutenant Pape a departmental commendation and the ninth and final notch on his gun handle.

Frank Pape was promoted to captain five years later and assigned to the South Side Englewood District. He aroused deep enmity within Chicago's African-American community a few years later when one of his raiding parties entered the residence of one James Monroe in the mistaken belief that this man was a murder suspect. Pape was accused of racism and brutality, charges he hotly denied well into his advancing years. When *Time* magazine published an unflattering account of the Monroe case, Pape sued for damages and lost. The case went all the way to the Supreme Court.

Police reporters and columnists reveled in the exploits of this cop they called "The Fearless Man." Pape was colorful and highly opinionated. As to recent claims that Frank Pape holds the unofficial city record for most confirmed "kills" in the line of duty, sadly, for so-called "street cops" and other admirers within the law enforcement community who remember when a gun was still a cop's most trusted friend, the historical record proves otherwise.

Sylvester "Two Gun Pete" Washington, a trigger-happy legend of Chicago law enforcement, mowed down twelve people between 1931 and 1948 patrolling the South Side community surrounding Fifty-fifth and State Streets.

After each successful kill, "Two Gun" added another notch to the wooden handle of his trusty Magnum .357.

Continue up Clark Street to Bryn Mawr Avenue. Turn right (east) and go to Sheridan Road.

THE NATURAL
June 14, 1949

Hell hath no fury like a ballplayer's jilted girl-friend. In 1949, Eddie Waitkus of the Philadelphia Phillies learned the painful truth about the inherent dangers involved when lust overrules logic and you join a strange young woman in her hotel room for an after-hours tête-à-tête. The bizarre shooting of Eddie Waitkus occurred inside the Edgewater Beach Hotel, 5349 North Sheridan Road. The hotel was closed in 1967 and demolished two years later. The Edgewater Beach Apartments, located at the foot of Lake Shore Drive on the southeast corner of Sheridan Road and Bryn Mawr Avenue, are a final reminder of elegant 1940s hotel living.

One of the last vestiges of an era defined by grace and style vanished with the swing of the wrecker's ball when the lovely old Edgewater Beach Hotel, once one of the most fashionable addresses along Chicago's North Shore, came tumbling down in 1969.

The yellow-stuccoed Edgewater Beach, with its elegantly appointed Marine Room overlooking one thousand yards of Lake Michigan beachfront property, was designed by Benjamin Marshall of the firm of Marshall & Fox and opened in 1916 for the comfort and enjoyment of the leisure class. Wealthy North Shore socialites quickly signed lease agreements for the Edgewater Beach Apartments in the residential annex at 5555 North Sheridan Road once their availability was announced.

In depression and war, prom-goers fox-trotted and waltzed the biggest night of their young lives away to the arrangements of Glenn Miller, Wayne King, and Guy Lombardo in an unforgettable, romantic setting.

Ruth Steinhagen, a tall, willowy nineteen-year-old brunette, also daydreamed about moonlit beaches, soft summer nights, and a leisurely stroll down the Marine walk with the object of her heart's desire—former Chicago Cubs first baseman Eddie Waitkus. Steinhagen fell in love with Waitkus in 1946, two years before he was traded to the Philadelphia Phillies for Dutch Leonard.

Ruthie went to work as a typist for a Michigan Avenue insurance company, but she kept the torch burning for Eddie, worshiping him from a private "altar" in her rooming-house bedroom at 1950 Lincoln Avenue.

When the Phils lost, as they so often did in those days, she wrote in her diary, "I bet it's none of Eddie's fault . . . I'll be glad when you're dead, you rascal you." Steinhagen also professed love for actor Alan Ladd, and Cubs outfielder Harry "Peanuts" Lowrey.

Alarmed, her parents sent her to a psychiatrist, but she defied them and moved out of the house. Her obsessions deepened. Waitkus wore number 36. Ruth bought all the hit records from 1936. Eddie was born in Cambridge, Massachusetts. Ruthie began eating Boston baked beans. At night she studied

Lithuanian, which of course was Eddie's ancestral tongue.

Pooling her entire life savings of $80, Steinhagen purchased a .22-caliber rifle at a pawnshop. She attended the Cubs-Phillies game with a girlfriend that afternoon, and cheered her idol as he scored two runs in a 9-2 Philadelphia victory. "I'm sure I can't have Eddie Waitkus, and if I can't have him, nobody will!" she confided to her companion.

She then checked into the Edgewater Beach Hotel where the Phillies were staying, and plotted her next move.

After downing two whiskey sours and a daiquiri, Ruthie penned a mash note and handed it to a bellboy. "We're not acquainted but I have something of importance to speak to you about. My name is Ruth Ann Burns and I'm in Room 1297-A. Please, come soon. I won't take up much of your time. I promise." The mysterious Miss Burns said she was from the old hometown. "Hmm . . . what could this mean?" Waitkus's curiosity, and testosterone, peaked.

Sometimes it is difficult for visiting ballplayers with time on their hands to remain cooped up in their room with so many admiring females milling around hotel lobbies, temptation being what it is.

At around 11:20 P.M., Waitkus rapped on the door and introduced himself. As Eddie sat down, Ruthie reached inside the closet for her rifle. "I have a surprise for you," she smiled. "For two years you've been bothering me and now you're going to die." She backed him up against the window, and then shot him at close range. The bullet passed through his chest and lung, lodging in his back, near his spine. "Baby, what's this all about?" Waitkus gasped as he crawled toward the door.

Steinhagen leaned over Waitkus and whispered, "You like that, don't you?" She composed herself and called the front desk. Minutes later a house detective found the troubled girl sitting on a bench next to the elevator. Eddie was rushed to the hospital, confused but still alive. Steinhagen was booked on an assault charge with intent to murder.

Five operations were needed to restore Eddie to good health. But he was back on the field in 1950 and named Comeback Player of the Year, helping the Phillies win their first pennant since 1915.

Waitkus lingered in the big leagues until 1955, putting up solid offensive numbers for Philadelphia and Baltimore.

Ruthie Steinhagen was committed to the Kankakee State Hospital. In her delirium, all she could talk about was Eddie Waitkus, whose strange encounter with the crazy woman formed the inspiration for the character of Roy Hobbs in Bernard Malamud's novel, *The Natural.*

Turn north on Sheridan Road and go to Hollywood Avenue. Turn left (west) and go one block to Kenmore Avenue. Turn right (north) and proceed to Thorndale Avenue.

"A BOLD, BRAZEN CRIME!"
January 6, 1946

When the question of paroling William George Heirens arises, as it does every few years, there is a consensus among police and older Chicagoans who remember the abduction-murder of seven-year-old Suzanne Degnan that a monster in human form should remain caged. Heirens is now in his sixties. He has spent more time behind bars than any living prisoner in the state of Illinois. By all accounts he is a cooperative model inmate, and his supporters will say that the articulate, highly educated "lifer" no longer poses a threat to society. The weight of circumstantial evidence convicted Heirens, though students of criminal justice who have reviewed the essential details of this case concede that police tactics were outrageously brutal, high-handed, and simply wouldn't hold up under the scrutiny of civil libertarians in more enlightened times. For now, there is little hope for the convicted man despite evidence of mounting public support and the publication of Dolores Kennedy's sympathetic account, titled William Heirens: His Day in Court. *The memory of the trail of bloody remains scattered through the streets and sewers of Edgewater's Winthrop-Kenmore corridor on the far North Side is overwhelming, and bears mute testament to the weight of this crime upon the Degnan family and the community. The James Degnan residence, occupying the first floor of a spacious two-story yellow-brick mansion at 5943 North Kenmore Avenue (one block east of Sheridan Road on the northeast corner at Thorndale and Kenmore Avenues) is gone. The original structures in this neighborhood were single-family houses and small apartment buildings, typically with four and six units. Beginning in the 1920s, many of the private residences on Winthrop and Kenmore were razed in favor of the common-corridor apartment houses that seemed to sprout overnight. The Degnan home was one of the casualties. A "four plus one" residential apartment building stands on the site now. It is understandable why the family and succeeding families could not live in a place so tainted by the heinous murder. William Heirens was apprehended outside a two-story gray-stone walkup at 1320 West Farwell Avenue, after he attempted to burglarize a third-floor apartment located just around the corner at 6928 North Wayne Avenue in the East Rogers Park neighborhood. That building is still standing, a stately six-story building with Corinthian columns flanking the front entrance. It is now a senior citizens' home. It is located a few doors south of the intersection of Wayne and Morse Avenues.*

James Degnan and his family moved from the East Coast into a fashionable Edgewater apartment house in February 1945. Degnan, a successful but nonetheless relatively poor man employed by the Office of Price Administration (OPA), always made sure that his little girl Suzanne was escorted to and from her classes at Sacred Heart Academy, 6250 North Sheridan Road.

There was considerable talk going around that Chicago was an unsafe place to live. The post-war world was full of uncertainty, and desperate men were committing vicious and depraved acts of violence against society.

The newspapers had reported a dangerous upsurge in serious street crime and noted with frustration that there was not enough money budgeted to hire additional police officers to counter the threat. In the densely populated Summerdale district where the Degnan family resided, only six patrolmen were making the rounds of the neighborhood between midnight and 8:00 A.M., when the tragedy occurred. Feeling the political heat, Mayor Edward Kelly pressed four thousand Democratic precinct workers into duty as part-time police officers, but it was too little, and way too late for the grieving family.

Jim Degnan and his wife Helen slept in a bedroom adjoining Suzanne's. On the raw, winter evening of January 6, 1946, the family retired at the appointed hour. The night passed uneventfully, though Mrs. Degnan did hear the child say, "I don't want to get up now." The parents assumed that Suzanne was talking in her sleep. They didn't look in on her until 7:30 the next morning. The window was wide open; their little girl had been taken away. A hastily scrawled ransom note written on standard 8½-by-11-inch paper and demanding $20,000 in fives and tens was left behind.

Police deduced that the kidnapper had used a ladder to scale the eight feet from the ground to the bedroom. The ladder was found nearby. It was an eerie, near identical reenactment of the abduction of Charles Lindbergh's infant son nearly fourteen years earlier in Hopewell, New Jersey.

"No one in our family has any enemies we know of, and we have no money," Degnan sighed. He earned $2,500 a year in salary from the OPA. The police believed that someone who was angry with the OPA might have plotted the crime, or a professional. The FBI was summoned to shed light on the mystery.

Before the police or the Feds could launch a full-scale investigation, the severed head of Suzanne Degnan was pulled from underneath a manhole cover in an alley behind 5860–5900 Kenmore Avenue. The search was over with the grisly discovery, but the nightmare had just begun. Over the next few hours, body parts kept turning up at various locations along Kenmore Avenue.

Captain John L. Sullivan of the Summerdale Station, where the abduction was first reported, called it a "bold and brazen crime."

Suspicion immediately fell upon two janitors, Hector Verburgh and Desere Smet, who attended the furnaces at 5901 North Kenmore (this building is still standing), where the victim's bones were found. Verburgh and Smet were seized and tortured beyond human endurance. In the notorious "blue

INNOCENT OR GUILTY?

AFTER FIFTY-THREE

YEARS, THE QUESTION OF

WILLIAM HEIRENS'S

GUILT IS STILL DEBATED.

room," where round-the-clock interrogations produced results, suspects were routinely hung by their heels, beaten to insensibility with telephone books, and forced to endure the dreaded "Third-Degree Sweat." (*Author's note:* The practice was bitterly denounced by the criminal defense bar for many years. The picturesque and occasionally bombastic attorney Robert Emmet Cantwell outshone even courtroom tactician Clarence Darrow in his condemnation of the unconstitutional extortion of confessions by the police.) Verburgh was eventually awarded a $15,000 settlement in his lawsuit against seventeen of the so-called "toughest cops in Chicago" who attempted to pry a false confession from him.

The Chicago Police were utterly ruthless in those days, and with the tide of public opinion turned squarely against them for failing to halt the intolerable post-war crime wave, the brass was all the more determined to clear this mystery up as quickly as possible.

The city breathed easier, for the moment at least, when the police pinned the crime on seventeen-year-old William George Heirens, a University of Chicago student arrested on June 26 outside the apartment building at 1320 West Farwell. The police received a tip that an intruder had broken into Joanne Pera's apartment in the Wayne Manor Apartments at 6928 North Wayne around the corner. Shots were fired at William Owen and Tiffin P. Constant, the responding police officers who chased Heirens down the block. The sneak thief raced up the stairs to the apartment of Mrs. Frances Willett at 1320 West Farwell. Out of breath and exhausted from his adventure, Heirens asked for a glass of water. He collapsed into a chair while Mrs. Willett, noting a police buildup on the street, called the station from another room.

Heirens, meanwhile, threw himself on Officer Constant from the second-floor porch as the police closed in. Heirens was subdued by Sergeant Abner Cunningham, an off-duty Chicago cop who was walking his dog when he noticed the commotion. Cunningham crashed three flowerpots onto the young man's head from the second-floor porch, rendering Heirens unconscious.

Heirens was taken to Edgewater Hospital to recover from his wounds. From there he underwent a four-day grilling at the Bridewell Hospital at the Cook County Jail where doctors administered a spinal tap and injected sodium Pentothal. During that time, Heirens blamed the killings on a George Murman (or murder man), a character that police and psychiatrists believed Heirens invented in his delusional state. Heirens would later say that he confessed to murder on July 30 to save his life.

At Gates Hall, Heirens's residence at the University of Chicago, police found personal items belonging to Frances Brown and Josephine Ross; circumstantial evidence, but compelling nonetheless. Latent fingerprints lifted from the various crime scenes and a pair of binoculars with scrawled initials matching the handwriting on the ransom note implicated him in the murders. William Heirens was convicted and sentenced to three consecutive life terms.

Betty Degnan Finn, who was ten years old when her sister died, has successfully lobbied the parole board to keep him behind bars. Meanwhile, Heirens's friends and supporters keep pressing the state for a new trial, arguing that he was framed by the Chicago Police and the state's attorney's office.

The Land *Approaching* O'Hare:

Chicago's Northwest Side

An exploration of working-class Chicago, that world apart from the Gold Coast and Lincoln Park, begins at the foot of Milwaukee Avenue. Milwaukee Avenue was once an Indian trail, but by 1849 it had already been converted into a plank road.

Today, Milwaukee Avenue runs in an almost straight line northwest from downtown past some of Chicago's most colorful and historically significant ethnic neighborhoods.

The West Town neighborhood, where "Machine Gun" Jack McGurn was mowed down on the seventh anniversary of the St. Valentine's Day Massacre, was at one time the hub of Chicago's Polish-American settlement; and the triangle formed by the intersections of Milwaukee Avenue, Ashland Avenue, and Division Street was its living, breathing heart. Up and down lower Milwaukee Avenue, a colorful pastiche of late nineteenth and early twentieth century commercial buildings stands as a not-so-silent testament to the generations of Poles, Italians, Germans, and Slavs who passed through this neighborhood on their way to the suburbs. Today, the area is largely Hispanic.

It was in Wicker Park, an old and storied neighborhood, where novelist and poet Nelson Algren penned "City on the Make," his lyric tribute to the junkies, poolroom hustlers, and flimflam artists of his youth. Algren lived among them and made sense of their world, translating the deliberate pace of life lived along these poor side streets crowding up against Milwaukee Avenue for the rest of the world. Today the area is rapidly becoming gentrified. Real estate values are soaring as stockbrokers, financial planners, and other young urban professionals move in and "re-hab" the old buildings.

Nelson Algren. If he is remembered at all by today's high-powered urban upper class, it may be through a commemorative street sign. As it happens, Algren Street in Wicker Park is near the exact spot where the crazed gunman Richard Carpenter shot it out with the cops in a real-life echo of Humphrey Bogart's *The Desperate Hours.*

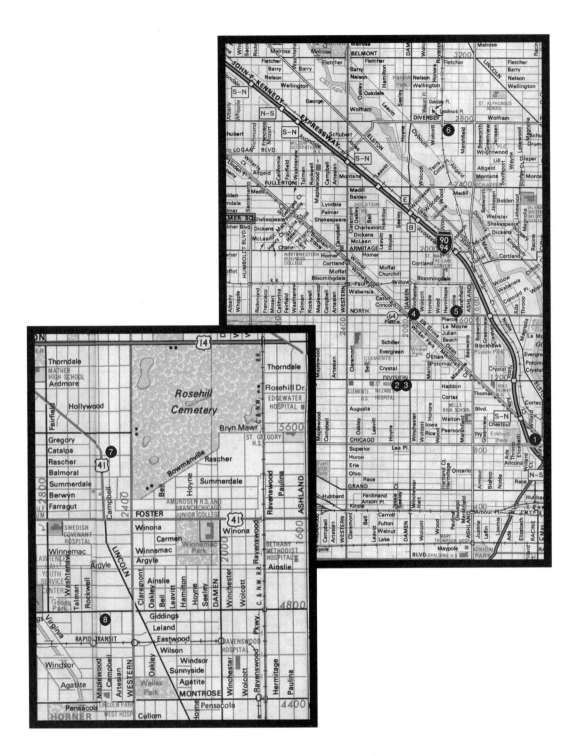

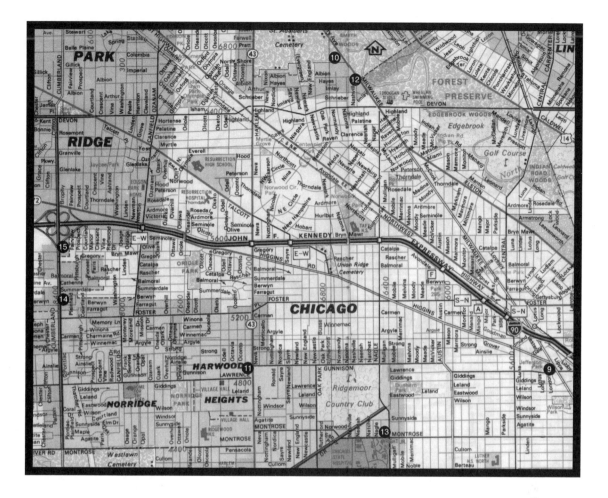

1. Jack McGurn killed at 805 N. Milwaukee Avenue (near May and Chicago).

2. The former site of the Biltmore Theater, an empty lot at 2046 Damen Avenue, south of Division.

3. Richard Carpenter was trapped here: Potomac Street, between Hoyne and Damen.

4. Patsy Lolordo killed in his home, 1914 W. North Avenue, east of Milwaukee Avenue.

5. Circus Gang headquartered at 1651 North Avenue.

6. Luetgert Sausage Vat Murders: 1700 block of Diversey, east of the Kennedy Expressway.

7. Mark Thanosauraus hit, corner of Campbell and Catalpa.

8. The "Ragged Stranger" murder at 4732 Cambell Avenue in Lincoln Square.

9. The Schuessler-Peterson boys disappeared from this intersection at Milwaukee and Lawrence.

10. Former site of the Lone Tree Inn just over the Niles border at Ebinger Street.

11. Meo's Norwood House is now a Polish restaurant at Harlen Avenue and Lawrence.

12. The former "sin strip" at Milwaukee Avenue and Albion is a shabby little strip mall and not much to look at these days.

13. An empty lot at Montrose and Narragansett next to the McDonald's marks the site of the old "Wagon Wheel" floating crap game.

14. John Wayne Gacy resided on Summerdale, a few doors east of Cumberland Avenue.

15. O.J. Simpson checked into the O'Hare Plaza—now the Wyndham Garden—at Cumberland and the Kennedy Expressway.

The Prohibition-era taverns on the first floors of the two-flats in Bucktown, Wicker Park, Shakespeare, and points farther west that were serviced by the "Circus Gang" may now be seen as casualties of the modern age—conversions to art galleries, fern bars, and quaint Mediterranean restaurants. The transformation of the greater Northwest Side is nearly complete.

Milwaukee Avenue takes a while to navigate. It is two lanes of stop-and-go automobile traffic walled in by pedestrians and old buildings. But with patience and imagination, one can observe the patterns of immigrant migration away from the central city while driving northward ever so slowly along this clogged thoroughfare.

The Milwaukee Avenue landscape changes dramatically in Portage Park, Jefferson Park, and Norwood Park. Here, a dozen or so miles north and west of the Chicago Loop, we find newer residential neighborhoods, early suburbs carved out of farmland during the land boom of the 1920s that were soon swallowed by the city.

We are now entering the nearly crime-free zones of the city, which urban sophisticates along the Lakefront derisively refer to as "The Land *Approaching* O'Hare," as opposed to "The Land *Beyond* O'Hare," which connotes (with not-so-mirthful sarcasm) bedroom suburbs, philistinism, Republicans, and strip malls. The "invisible wall" dividing the two widely disparate classes of Chicagoans is Ashland Avenue.

For travelers coming in and out of the "world's busiest airport," and for the great majority of Gold Coast and Near North inhabitants, the only encounter they will have with the far Northwest Side of Chicago is the traffic gridlock on I-94, also called the Kennedy Expressway, as it inches maddeningly toward downtown. Whether or not the travelers bound for their Michigan Avenue and Lincoln Park destinations realize it or not, they are passing through John Wayne Gacy's neighborhood, and John Wayne Gacy is a name they most assuredly recognize.

Jammed into the farthest part of the city's northwest quadrant are a great number of firefighters, police officers, and city workers hemmed in by tough residency requirements. Sturdy bungalow construction. Safe streets. Trimmed parkways. The far Northwest Side is an anomaly in the grand scheme of Chicago living.

There is history here, some good and some bad, if one looks closely amid the usually peaceful backdrop of Little League games and Weber grills in the backyards. It is a part of Chicago largely ignored by the pundits and chroniclers. As to culture and art, maybe the only thing lacking west of the Ashland Avenue "wall" is a Nelson Algren to bring forth the story. Or perhaps another exit ramp off of the Kennedy would suffice.

The Near Northwest Side: West of Ashland, East of Cicero, North of Grand

We will begin our tour at the intersection of Milwaukee Avenue and Chicago Avenue. Turn north on Milwaukee and 805 North Milwaukee is right there.

THINGS COULD BE WORSE . . .

February 15, 1936

When asked by the Chicago Police what he did for a living, "Machine Gun" Jack McGurn's brother Anthony Gebardi bluntly replied that Jack was a golf pro at the Maywood Country Club and a real straight shooter—which was no wild-eyed exaggeration. The manager of the west-suburban course vigorously denied McGurn had ever worked there, but admitted that Jack was a better than average duffer on the links. On his best day, he shot a 70—a bit of macabre humor, since McGurn's golf score matched the number assigned to him in the Cook County Morgue, where he ended up exactly seven years and one day after the St. Valentine's Day Massacre, which he masterminded. McGurn was an avid sportsman. In addition to golf, he enjoyed bowling, and he was in the middle of his third frame at the Avenue Recreation Parlor at 805 North Milwaukee Avenue the night of February 15, 1936, when five gunmen shot him dead on the varnished hardwood floor. The shooters left behind a comic Valentine. The ancient three-story building remains intact; it is nestled within the colorful West Town neighborhood where Chicago Avenue intersects with Milwaukee Avenue and May Street near the Kennedy Expressway. The bowling alleys and pool hall are gone. The interior space is occupied by the American Office Furniture Company.

While not completely out of favor with the Capone mob, Jack McGurn had recently fallen on hard times and was shuffling around the city doing odd jobs here and there to sustain his gangster lifestyle. In the years following the St. Valentine's Day Massacre, McGurn had purchased a new home in the comfort and safety of suburban Oak Park at 1224 North Kenilworth Avenue, where he lived with his beloved "Blonde Alibi," Louise Rolfe.

Lately, McGurn had been involved in bookmaking and was rumored to have taken part in the murder of New York rackets boss "Dutch" Schultz at the Palace Chop House in Newark, New Jersey. What else is there for an unemployed assassin to do when there is a monthly mortgage to pay, a demanding golddigger for a wife, and no work to be found in the old hometown?

McGurn might have been pondering the cruel hand that fate had dealt him the night of February 15 when he rolled into the Avenue Recreation Parlor at 12:50 A.M. with two companions. He had risen from bed less than two hours earlier after attending the wake of a friend.

The second-floor alleys were busy this time of night. Twenty bowlers and owner William Aloiso were otherwise engaged when three armed men posing as stickup men threw the place into an uproar. While these three pretended to rob the establishment, two other men believed to be the two companions who had accompanied McGurn to the bowling alley shot and killed him. The murderers then grabbed the score sheet bearing their names and raced out the door. Seventeen of the twenty bowlers fled in terror after the shots rang out.

Eight feet from the body, the cops found a Valentine's Day greeting (one of several sent to McGurn in recent days), which read:

> *You've lost your job, you've lost your dough—*
> *Your jewels and cars and costly houses—*
> *But things could still be worse you know—*
> *At least you haven't lost your trousas!*

In McGurn's pockets, the police found $3.85, further evidence that his financial situation had changed dramatically since 1929.

No one who was inside the premises that night had a clue as to the identity of the killers. Or if they did, they weren't talking. Interviewed at her home, the "Blonde Alibi," tense, pale, and suffering nervous exhaustion, said she never found out what Jack did for a living, and wondered aloud why anybody would want to kill so sweet and dear a man.

McGurn's former friends from the Chicago mob conducted a secret wake at an undertaking parlor at 624 North Western Avenue. One by one, through a rear door sheltered by darkness, "the boys" filed past to mourn their pal in the customary manner. "Tough" Tony Capezio, an alumnus of the old Circus Gang of killers frequently employed by McGurn, had come to pay his respects. When asked what he was up to, Capezio feigned ignorance. "Who did you say? McGurn? I don't know the party!"

JACK MCGURN:

SCRATCH GOLFER

AND DEADLY

TRIGGERMAN.

Wicker Park

Continue up Milwaukee Avenue to Division Street and turn left (west). Go west on Division Street to Damen Avenue. Turn right (north) and go two blocks to Potomac Avenue. Turn left (west) on Potomac Avenue.

MANHUNT!
August 15–18, 1955

Chicago police detective William Murphy escaped death by a narrow margin when he stood toe-to-toe with fugitive gunman Gus Amadeo inside the Circle Lounge on October 21, 1954. (See Tour 3.) Counting himself among the fortunate, Murphy was burned on the hand by a powder blast from Amadeo's gun. Lying on the floor of the dingy North Side tavern was Murphy's partner, Detective Charles Annerino, slain by Amadeo. Having put this unhappy affair out of his mind, Detective Murphy showed no fear when he stared into the barrel of a gun belonging to an even more desperate fiend—the quick-triggered holdup man Richard Carpenter, whose thrill-packed capture at 2042 Potomac Avenue in the Wicker Park neighborhood ended Chicago's greatest manhunt since the G-men drilled John Dillinger outside the Biograph Theater. Carpenter was hiding out inside the Biltmore Theater at 2046 West Division Street (just west of Damen Avenue) when he was spotted by an off-duty cop taking in a movie with his wife. Neighborhood theaters provided the perfect cover for generations of hoods, some luckier and more resourceful than others. The Biltmore, unlike the restored Biograph or the Calo performance theater up on North Clark Street, was torn down. An empty lot strewn with weeds, rubble, and other assorted debris marks the spot where Carpenter shot it out with Officer Clarence Kerr before fleeing into the quiet residential side streets off of Division Street. Carpenter holed up in a gray-stone walkup at 2042 Potomac Avenue, on the north side of the street between Hoyne Avenue and Damen Avenue, one block south of Evergreen Avenue. Wicker Park is an old, gentrified neighborhood, celebrated in the writings of its most famous resident, author, poet, and cynic Nelson Algren, who wrote about the junkies, gamblers, and girls of the night inhabiting Division Street, west of Milwaukee Avenue. It's not that way now. Rising property values and a generation of "re-habbers" and investment sharpers drove the poor, unwashed denizens of Algren's nether-world out of Wicker Park in the 1980s and 1990s. You're more likely to find stockbrokers walking their Pomeranians these days, than anyone resembling Nelson Algren's fictional Man with the Golden Arm.

Richard Carpenter was busted by the cops in 1950 after shooting and injuring his mother. Mary Carpenter deeply loved her only son and wished him no harm. What would happen to him if he went to prison? Booked on an assault charge, Richard was released by the courts after his mother declined to press charges. "It was an accident," she said, but in the back of her mind she wondered what brand of mischief her incorrigible twenty-year-old son would do next to disturb the tranquillity of their little home at 757 North Schiller Street.

The boy was a bad seed—a mature and dangerous criminal by age twenty-five and a death-row inmate three years later.

Lieutenant Frank Pape and his crack-shot robbery dicks had been chasing Carpenter for weeks. He was a prime suspect in 150 tavern robberies committed in a two-year period by a lone gunman in his early twenties. In 1951 Carpenter was sentenced to a year in the Cook County Jail for carrying a concealed weapon. Burglary, armed robbery, and purse snatching were his criminal specialties. Carpenter dreamed of being a big-timer, another Clyde Barrow or John Dillinger, when in fact he was nothing more than a witless gunsel lacking brains and imagination.

It was a few minutes before 8:00 P.M. Detective William Murphy, a thirty-four-year-old father of two who had abandoned his dream of joining the priesthood to become a cop, was on his way to work when he spotted Carpenter seated on board his CTA subway train.

Rumbling past trees and tenements on its way north into the Loop, the train pulled into the Roosevelt Road station, one block south of police headquarters. Murphy followed Carpenter off the train and approached him. Flashing a badge and a recent photo from detective headquarters, Murphy inquired in a matter-of-fact tone, "Is this you?"

Richard Carpenter instinctively produced a gun and fired five shots in quick succession. Two of them struck Murphy in the chest and shoulder.

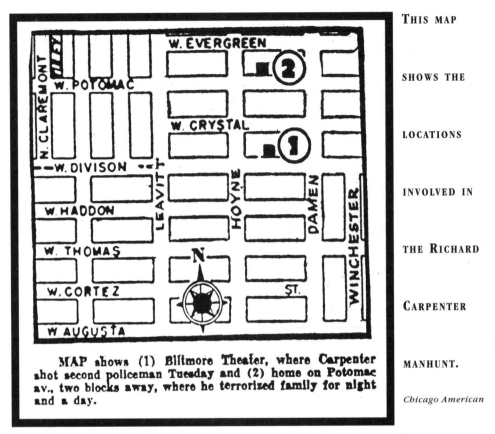

THIS MAP SHOWS THE LOCATIONS INVOLVED IN THE RICHARD CARPENTER MANHUNT.

MAP shows (1) Biltmore Theater, where Carpenter shot second policeman Tuesday and (2) home on Potomac av., two blocks away, where he terrorized family for night and a day.

Chicago American

Racing up the subway stairs to street level, the gunman commandeered a vehicle belonging to Charles A. Koerper, a retired Commonwealth Edison employee. He ordered the man at the point of a loaded gun to drive to Madison and Dearborn Streets. "Look straight ahead! Don't make a bad move!" The driver nervously complied.

At detective headquarters the following morning, Koerper examined hundreds of police mug shots before identifying Carpenter. "That's him. I'm sure of it," he said. Latent fingerprints lifted from Koerper's automobile matched Carpenter's. The chase was on.

Sixty police squads were mobilized with a standing order: "Shoot to kill." The whole city was aroused. One of Pape's guys had gone down. And because he had committed the unpardonable sin of shooting a cop, everyone knew that it would only be a matter of time before the killer was brought in—dead or alive.

For the next thirty-six hours, Carpenter camped out inside movie theaters. The darkened movie houses offered a temporary safe haven.

Carpenter was seated inside the Biltmore Theater, catching a few Z's during a double-feature showing of *We're No Angels* and *Soldiers of Fortune,* when Clarence Kerr, an off-duty cop from the Hudson Avenue station, recognized Carpenter as he sat alone in the rear of the auditorium during the intermission. Showing his badge, Kerr unholstered his weapon and closed in on the suspect. "Police. Hold it right there!" Hearing these familiar words, Carpenter whirled around and fired three rapid shots, striking Kerr in the chest.

Seriously wounded, the police officer was taken to St. Mary of Nazareth Hospital, where he staged a near-miraculous recovery. Clarence Kerr rose to the rank of captain before retiring from the department.

The shooting of a second officer intensified the search. "Not a policeman in the city could be expected to give Carpenter more than a split second chance to give up," recalled one reporter.

Grazed by a bullet from Kerr's gun, Carpenter burst out of the theater's side entrance and fled into the neighborhood, pausing in front of a two-story apartment house belonging to truck driver Leonard Powell and his wife, Stella, at 2040 Potomac Avenue. The porch light was on, and Powell was latching his screen door. Carpenter was desperate. Panic was beginning to erode his confidence.

"When I barged in their apartment the Powells were scared," Carpenter told police following his capture. "I boasted to them about other shootings. I just said I'd shot others because I wanted to keep them scared and impressed that they should be afraid of me."

Carpenter terrorized the Powell family for nearly twenty-four hours. To throw the police off the trail and alleviate a neighbor's suspicion, Carpenter sent Powell to work the next morning. Once again it looked like the cop killer was going to walk away scot-free.

That night, however, 250 Chicago cops combing a one-square mile of the Northwest Side neighborhood closed in. Police hurled canisters of tear gas into the Potomac Avenue address, ordering Carpenter to surrender. Spotlights were trained on the second-floor apartment. Inside the police could see the shadowy figure moving from room to room in desperate panic. When he refused an order to surrender, the cops opened up on the building with machine guns and rifles while thousands of spectators gathered in the streets below to watch the duel.

Carpenter jumped through the Powells' rear window and across a narrow area separating the 2040 address from the 2042 building. As police marksmen trained their sites on this address, Carpenter yelled out, "Don't shoot! Please don't shoot!" Bleeding from his wounds and minus a shirt, he surrendered to police in the hallway outside Stanley Sciblo's apartment at 2042 Potomac.

Carpenter was treated for his wounds at the Bridewell Hospital, then booked on a charge of murder.

Richard Carpenter went to trial in November 1955. After a week of deliberation, a jury convicted him of murdering Detective Murphy. Carpenter was sentenced to death by Judge Gibson Gorman.

For the next twenty-two months, Carpenter languished inside the jail without uttering a word to anyone. Finally breaking his silence, Carpenter expressed no remorse for what he had done, just snarling anger. He said he did not believe in God, and issued a warning from the grave. "After I'm dead I'm coming back and kill more coppers!"

Carpenter was executed on schedule at the Cook County Jail on December 19, 1958. Bitterly defiant right up to the end, Richard Carpenter was the first person to be electrocuted in Illinois since Emmanuel Scott on March 19, 1953.

Chicago Crime Facts

The first execution in Cook County took place on July 10, 1840, when John Stone was hanged in Chicago for the rape-murder of Lucretia Thompson, a farmer's wife. Afterward, Stone's corpse was delivered to Dr. Levi D. Boone for dissection. Boone later became mayor of Chicago (1855). Between 1840 and 1958, the year that Carpenter was put to death, there were 165 executions in Cook County. In the 1930s, 61 men died in the electric chair, making the 1930s the peak decade for capital punishment in the state of Illinois. From 1930 through 1960, there were 88 executions in Illinois. Of these, 79 occurred between 1930 to 1949. The state of Illinois did away with the gibbet and the rope in 1928, adopting the more efficient, and presumably more humane, electric chair.

Return to Damen Avenue and continue north. Turn right (east) on North Avenue at the intersection of Damen Avenue, Milwaukee Avenue, and North Avenue. 1921 West North Avenue is on the south side of the street.

A TOAST BEFORE DYING
January 8, 1929

Pasqualino "Patsy" Lolordo agreed to take on the unenviable task of holding together the fractious and bitterly divided Union Sicilione following the daylight murder of Antonio Lombardo at Dearborn and Madison Streets in 1928. Lolordo, a quiet man, gentle and refined, who respected the ancient customs of his homeland, lived with his thirty-two-year-old wife in a red-brick two-flat at 1921 West North Avenue (a block east of Milwaukee Avenue on the south side of the street). Down the street at 1914 West North Avenue was a satellite organization he controlled known as the Italian-American Citizens' Club. The former Lolordo residence still stands, but the neighborhood is now a lower- to middle-income Hispanic enclave rapidly undergoing the process of gentrification.

I n the kitchen of her home, Aliena Lolordo prepared a hasty lunch for her husband and some unexpected visitors. She had become accustomed to strange men coming into her home at all hours. Some of them she recognized by sight, others she did not know at all. Her husband was an important man in Italian-American civic life and such intrusions were expected.

The three strangers rapped on the door a few minutes past three o'clock in the afternoon, and were escorted into Patsy Lolordo's sitting room to discuss private business. Lolordo closed the door separating the two rooms, and Aliena went about her cooking and ironing, taking no notice.

Her husband spoke with the men for about an hour. They drank and joked and talked. Aliena could hear the tinkle of glasses as toasts were offered.

There was nothing unusual about any of this until she heard shots fired, eleven in all, in rapid succession. Throwing open the door, Aliena brushed past the gunmen to attend to her fallen husband, who had sustained gunshot wounds to the head, neck, and shoulders. A few minutes later, after the three men had

A TOAST BEFORE DYING: THE HALF-FILLED WINE BOTTLES ARE STILL VISIBLE ON THE TABLE, HOURS AFTER PATSY LOLORDO WAS GUNNED DOWN BY JOE AIELLO INSIDE LOLORDO'S NORTH AVENUE APARTMENT.

A PILLOW WAS PLACED UNDER PATSY LOLORDO'S HEAD AS A TOKEN OF RESPECT BY JOE AIELLO.

exited the premises, Aliena's sister-in-law Anna Lolordo arrived at the home, and immediately called the Hochspier's Mortuary at 2410 West North Avenue to attend to the body while she comforted the widow.

Later that night, Aliena identified Joseph Aiello from a book of police mug shots as one of the killers. Comforted by City Sealer Daniel Serritella, a longtime Capone ally, she said that this was the man who shook her husband's hand in friendship seconds before shooting him. Aiello, one of seven brothers, ran a small independent bootlegging operation on the North Side. Bitter and angry at being snubbed by the Unione Sicilione, which did not appoint him to the directorship, Aiello joined forces with the O'Banion-Weiss-Moran gang.

Crossing Al Capone in so shocking a manner was a reckless and foolhardy act. Joe Aiello, marked for death, was machine-gunned to death outside his West Side home at 4518 West End Avenue just as soon as Capone discovered his hiding place.

Continue east on North Avenue.

A CIRCUS WITHOUT THE CLOWNS
1920s

Three blocks east of the Lolordo home at 1651 West North Avenue (at Paulina Avenue on the south side of the street) the Inside Art Company occupies the shell of the old Circus Cafe, the stronghold of the Circus Gang, who supplied muscle and firepower to Al Capone during the waning years of Prohibition.

Things were quiet at 1651 West North Avenue around Valentine's Day, 1929. The Circus Gang, headed by Claude Maddox (aka John Edward "Screwy" Moore) and "Tough" Tony Capezio, a graduate of the St. Louis badlands, went into hiding when their principal members became the focus of a police manhunt. The cops had good reason to believe that the Circus Gang had supplied the armaments, the manpower, and even the police car driven by Jack McGurn for the St. Valentine's Day Massacre. Judge John H. Lyle, upon receiving word that Maddox assisted in the planning of the massacre, issued warrants for a police raid on the café. The warrants disappeared and were never served.

"Screwy" Moore's gang had a long and prosperous affiliation with the South Side Capones. Moore oversaw bootleg operations on the Northwest Side, pushing Al Capone's slop into Wicker Park and Lincoln Park taverns in open defiance of the farcical peace treaty with the O'Banion-Weiss-Moran mob, which ceded the territory north of Madison Street to "Bugs" Moran.

The Circus Gang waged a relentless campaign of terror and extortion against tavern owners who refused to buy the Capone beer, or who had made other arrangements. On April 30, 1929, just two months after going into self-imposed hiding, members of the Circus Gang signaled their return by exploding three incendiary devices outside street-level saloons owned by Polish-Americans at 1101 Noble Street, 1533 Wabansia Avenue, and 1801 West North Avenue.

In each of the buildings, immigrant families with very young children asleep in their beds on the upper floors were hurled to the floor by the force of the blast. Luckily no one was killed, but in this high-stakes booze war respect for human life was nonexistent.

Turn and go back to Damen Avenue. Proceed north to Diversey Parkway. Turn right (east). The Luetgert factory/residence was on the southwest corner of Hermitage Avenue and Diversey Parkway, just before Paulina Street.

THE SAUSAGE VAT MURDER
May 1, 1897

It was a ghastly business, having to sift through the dregs of the acid used to dissolve the human remains of Louisa Becknese Luetgert, the second wife of Adolph L. Luetgert, proprietor of the A. L. Luetgert Sausage and Packing Company. Being a cop in Chicago in 1897 was not always about collecting bribe money from brothel keepers, slopping up free beer, running errands for the alderman, or arresting foreign-born "anarchists" to please Inspector Michael Schaak of the North Division. Sometimes the job required real detective work, and the nauseating duty of locating fragments of human bone from a slimy quagmire. The Chicago Police Department performed admirably in this one instance because of the determination of Captain Herman Schuettler, an honest but occasionally brutal detective who raised the torture techniques of the "third-degree sweat" to an art form. Schuettler cracked the "Sausage Vat Murder" in a Northwest Side neighborhood that bears little resemblance to what it was in 1897. Luetgert's five-story factory and private residence adjoined the Chicago and Northwestern Railroad embankment at the southwest corner of Hermitage Avenue and Diversey

LOUISA LUETGERT MET AN

UNFORTUNATE AND GRISLY

END AT THE HANDS OF

HER HUSBAND.

Parkway (east of Damen Avenue and west of Paulina Street). The factory burned down in 1902, and Hermitage Avenue is no longer a through street. The proximate location of the factory is difficult to determine, but journalist Pat Butler, an expert on the case, believes that a portion of the concrete foundation and brick wall was still visible as recently as 1988. It is likely that Luetgert's building stood opposite the three-story frame home adjacent to the railroad viaduct on the south side of Diversey in the 1700 block. It was haunted, some say, by the nocturnal wanderings of Louisa Luetgert through the empty hallways. The neighborhood isn't much to look at either. Empty lots, grimy factories, and a gated community of new townhomes to the immediate west pockmark a sparse urban landscape nowadays, but on a moonlit night it still might be possible to observe Louisa, with her blonde hair wrapped tightly in a bun and her long skirts swishing along the pavement. Outside, we might even detect the faint echo of a cruel chant of the neighborhood waifs as they rolled their hoop down the street singing:

> *Old man Luetgert made sausage out of his wife*
> *He turned on the steam; his wife began to scream—*
> *There'll be a hot time in the old town tonight!*

On the third day of his wife's disappearance, old man Luetgert assured his worried in-laws that Louisa, a diminutive woman who weighed only a hundred pounds, had gone to visit an aunt in Kenosha, Wisconsin, and there was no cause for alarm. Suspicious and deeply worried by Adolph's air of unconcern, Dietrich Becknese, the younger brother of Louisa Luetgert, reported the matter to detectives at the Sheffield Avenue police station, who began a discreet inquiry.

The police, as it turned out, had had their eye on Luetgert for some time. He was a bellicose man with a violent temper, and the neighbors told of hearing many late-night quarrels. Luetgert was also a womanizer, and he had brought scandal upon his poor wife. His dalliance with Mary Siemering, Louisa's niece who worked as a household servant, had further strained the troubled marriage, and caused the tongues of the neighborhood gossips to wag.

Wilhelm Fulpeck, a hostler employed by Luetgert, recalled seeing Louisa disappear into the factory around 10:30 P.M. on the night of May 1, never to return.

A chain of circumstantial evidence connected the Northwest Side sausage king to the fiendish murder. As Captain Schuettler's men poked around inside a twelve-foot-long, five-foot-high vat in the basement, where the large furnaces used for smoking the meat were located, they found two gold rings in the debris, one of them bearing the initials "L. L." In addition, smoke of a mysterious origin was observed pouring out of the smokestack the night of May 1.

"All the appliances for the disposition of a body are at hand," the *Chicago Tribune* reported. "Furnaces, machine knives for cutting meat, large vats, immense sewage systems, all offer a ready means of secreting all evidence of the dead." Bloodstains were found on the bedroom door inside the factory, and skull fragments were extracted from the smoke shaft. It was a remarkable piece of forensic work, given the primitiveness of detection methods at the time.

Adolph Luetgert, protesting his guilt, was arrested by Officers Qualey and Dean of the Sheffield Station on May 7, and transferred on a Chicago streetcar to a dank cell inside the East Chicago Avenue police station.

Schuettler theorized that Luetgert strangled his wife, boiled her in acid, then disposed of her in the smoke shaft. The factory had been closed for ten weeks during a reorganization, but in a very suspicious move, Luetgert had ordered 378 pounds of crude potash and fifty pounds of arsenic the day before Louisa's disappearance.

There were no witnesses to the crime, but the circumstantial evidence was overwhelming. Adolph Luetgert, who had come to Chicago from Germany to

ADOLPH LUETGERT, THE

NORTHWEST SIDE SAUSAGE

KING (RIGHT). A NEWSPAPER

SKETCH SHOWS THE LUETGERT

FACTORY AT HERMITAGE AND

DIVERSEY (BELOW).

become the sausage baron of the North Side, was indicted for murder on June 7, 1897. Luetgert's first trial ended in a hung jury on October 21 after the jurymen failed to agree on a suitable punishment. Eight favored imposing the death penalty, and three argued for life imprisonment. Only one member of the jury believed Luetgert innocent of the crime.

A second trial with a change of venue to Judge Joseph Gary's courtroom was ordered. The craggy white-haired jurist who presided over the Haymarket trial allowed the prosecution wide latitude. The court held that it was not necessary that the body of the murdered woman be produced, an extraordinary legal precedent. "Nor is it necessary that every circumstance in a circumstantial case should be established," Gary added, sealing the fate of the accused.

The verdict was anticlimactic. On February 9, 1898, Luetgert was convicted. He was sentenced to life in prison at the Joliet Penitentiary, where it is whispered the ghost of his dead wife haunted his waking hours. Pale and anxious, Luetgert babbled incoherently to his jailers that Louisa would come back . . . some day. Luetgert died in 1900, still wrapped in denial.

Defense attorney Lawrence Harmon believed his client was telling the truth. Harmon spent $2,000 of his own money and devoted the rest of his life to finding Louisa before being committed to an asylum, stark-raving mad.

LUETGERT IN THE NET

Sausagemaker Charged with the Murder of His Wife.

EVIDENCE OF CRIME

Blood Stains on the Door of His Private Room.

FIND RINGS IN A VAT

Witnesses Testify Concerning the Man's Suspicious Actions.

Web of Proof Slowly but Surely Surrounding the Husband of the Missing Woman.

Adolph L. Luetgert, was arrested yesterday afternoon at 1:30 o'clock on a charge of murder.

His wife has been missing since May 1, and the police have secured a chain of circumstantial evidence that points directly to him as her murderer.

The scene of the supposed murder was the large sausage factory at the corner of Hermitage avenue and Diversey street,

THE *CHICAGO*

TRIBUNE UPDATES

ITS READERS ON

THE LUETGERT

CASE.

(*Chicago Tribune*)

Lincoln Square

To continue, turn

around and take

Diversey Parkway to

Western Avenue.

Proceed north to

Lawrence Avenue. Turn

left (west) two blocks

to Campbell Avenue.

Turn south on

Campbell Avenue.

THE CASE OF THE RAGGED STRANGER: A DUEL IN THE DARK
June 21, 1920

The former residence of Carl and Ruth Wanderer is located at 4732 North Campbell Avenue in the Lincoln Square neighborhood, one-half block south of Lawrence Avenue, and two blocks west of Western Avenue. The white, two-story duplex has been significantly remodeled since 1920. New siding has been added, and the number on the house is not visible. The oversight is probably intentional. The narrow gangway leading into the yard, where Ruth perished at the hands of the "Ragged Stranger" is protected with a high wooden gate.

Echoes of the near-perfect crime involving a decorated war hero, his comely young bride, her unborn child, and a shambling skid-row bum with no name tugged at the public conscience long after the noose was tightened around the neck of the convicted killer.

The case of the "Ragged Stranger" has been recounted time and again in books and detective magazines, and even in a Hollywood movie based on the recollections of the famous Chicago detective who helped crack the case.

Carl Otto Wanderer's inner rage toward his unsuspecting wife grew slowly over a two-year period. Wanderer may have even consciously loved nineteen-year-old Ruth Johnson when the young couple tied the knot on October 1, 1919, but love died in that little flat on Campbell Avenue where he was forced to share living space with a nagging mother-in-law who hoped that one day he could finally get on his feet and buy his own house.

Wanderer, a thirty-two-year-old German-American butcher, spent many sleepless nights pondering his options. He had a new sweetheart to think of—a chubby sixteen-year-old typist named Julia Schmitt whom he squired around the midway of the Riverview Amusement Park when Ruth was otherwise engaged. And then, shortly before Christmas, Ruth joyfully announced she was pregnant. Carl Wanderer accepted the news with dismay, but kept his feelings to himself and bided his time.

On June 21, 1920, Ruth and Carl attended an evening performance of *The Sea Wolf,* a rousing adventure playing at the Pershing Theater at Lincoln and Western Avenues. As they strolled home on this warm and pleasant June night discussing the movie, the baby, and their mounting financial woes, Wanderer claimed to have spotted a sinister-looking figure lurking in the shadows of the doorway of Zindt's Drug Store on Lawrence Avenue. According to Wanderer, the man crushed out a cigarette and followed the couple home, keeping a respectful distance.

"Ruth went up ahead of me when we reached the house," Wanderer would later relate to the cops. "She opened the outer door and I heard her fumbling with the keys to the inner door of the hall. I asked her, 'Can't you open it, honey?'"

Ruth chuckled and reached for the little ribbon dangling from the overhead light.

The "Ragged Stranger" emerged from the darkness, his gun trained on Ruth. "Don't turn on the light! Throw up your hands!" Without waiting for her reply, he fired two shots into the woman. "The baby," Ruth Wanderer gasped as she collapsed to the floor, her life ebbing away.

Carl jerked out his gun, a .45-caliber army revolver, and fired back at the "Ragged Stranger." When the smoke cleared, Ruth and the stranger lay dead. By now the neighbors were awakened by the ruckus. They helped carry the lifeless girl into the waiting arms of her mother.

Detective Sergeant John Norton of the homicide squad arrived minutes later. Norton, a strapping investigator who had been shot four times in a celebrated police career that dated back to 1891, was a plainclothes man almost from the moment he joined the force. Norton demanded a fast answer to the obvious question of why Wanderer happened to be carrying a gun at that fortuitous moment.

Carl was on the ball with an equally quick answer. He explained that he worked in his father's butcher shop at 2711 North Western, and was taking necessary precautions following a robbery attempt on his birthday. A business card from a traveling circus was found on the body of the dead man. There were no other identifiers. A fingerprint check turned up nothing. At the inquest that followed a few hours later at Ravenswood Hospital, Wanderer embellished the story even more. This same man, he said, had flirted with Ruth only a few nights earlier, and she had come home and reported this news to Carl in a near panic. She was terrified that the stranger was laying a trap.

The morning papers told of Wanderer's gallantry and reviewed his exemplary military record. During the Great War, he was a lieutenant in the seventeeth machine gun battalion. Before that he fought the Mexican outlaw Pancho Villa in the wide-open spaces of Columbus, New Mexico. For the moment, Carl Wanderer was accorded hero status in a cynical post-war world craving new celebrities and overnight heroes who defended the honor of their women.

Detective Norton, with a little help from legendary crime reporter Harry Romanoff and his editor on the city desk of the *Chicago Herald-Examiner,* Walter Howey, poked holes in the theories concerning the thorny mystery.

Howey and Norton could not understand why a ragged stranger who could barely afford a cup of coffee would want to own such an expensive sidearm. If robbery were the motive, wouldn't it have been a whole lot easier to pawn the gun? Wanderer's weapon and the gun that the stranger carried were identical military-issue service revolvers. With the serial numbers in hand, a telegram was sent to the Colt firearms company.

Ownership of one of the weapons was traced to Peter Hoffman, a telephone repairman who purchased it at the Von Lengerke & Antoine Sporting Goods store in Chicago. Hoffman passed it on to his brother-in-law, Fred Wanderer, who, by no small coincidence, was Carl's cousin.

The motive for the killing was easily established when Romanoff and Summerdale Police Lieutenant Mike Loftus went to interview Mrs. Johnson, Ruth's mother. While Loftus engaged the woman in conversation, thus diverting her attention, Romanoff rifled through Wanderer's belongings in the bedroom and found incriminating photos of Wanderer and fragments of a letter to a young woman named Julia Schmitt. When Julia was found, the girlfriend unraveled Wanderer's presumably airtight story. It was more than enough evidence to pry a confession out of him. Wanderer told the cops that in the confusion, he fired the shots at Ruth, not the robber.

The "Ragged Stranger" was Al Watson (another account lists his real name as Bernard T. Ryan), a vagrant and a drifter who got by living in a fifty-cent flophouse on Madison Street, Chicago's skid row. Watson had agreed to stage a phony holdup for the promise of $5 down and $5 on delivery. The trusting fool did as he was told. In death, Watson was honored by the saloon proprietor where the deal was struck with a headstone bearing the simple inscription "The Ragged Stranger."

Carl Wanderer was twice indicted and twice convicted. After his first trial, his sentence was twenty years, which so outraged Howey that he used the editorial might of his afternoon paper to keep the story alive and demand a new trial.

Public outrage over the verdict resulted in a second trial and a death sentence for Wanderer, who was interviewed by scores of "alienists" and prison doctors who determined that he was in his right mind when he planned his wife's murder. He admitted that he had grown tired of marriage and longed to return to army life.

Wanderer was denied an eleventh-hour pardon by Governor Len Small, who was in the habit of pardoning every big-shot gangster who came before the parole board if it pleased his corrupt political sponsors in City Hall. This time he refused to listen to any more nonsense coming from the bleeding hearts that he believed had delayed justice for months.

Wanderer was marched to the gallows at the old Criminal Courts Building at Dearborn and Hubbard on September 30, 1921, by Cook County Sheriff Charles West Peters.

Ben Hecht and Charley MacArthur, the *Front Page* literary wags of a colorful and outlandish era of journalism who were covering the hanging for their respective newspapers, persuaded Wanderer to croon a rendition of "Old Pal, Why Don't You Answer Me?" moments before the drop. He sang it with a "lugubrious but steady tenor," commented a reporter from the *Chicago Post*.

"Have you anything else you wish to say?" asked Peters, when the song had ended.

"Christ have mercy on my . . ."

Carl Wanderer never finished the sentence.

In a more sober era, civil libertarians would be aghast at such politically incorrect mirth. But MacArthur, Romanoff, and Sheriff Peters, who rubbed elbows with the denizens of the underworld every day of their roguish careers, were charmed by Wanderer's maudlin display, which lent dignity to what otherwise might have been a dull gathering. "Romy," MacArthur sighed, "that sonofabitch would have been a hell of a song plugger."

Return to
Lawrence Avenue
and turn left
(north) on
Western Avenue.
Proceed north to
Catalpa Avenue
(north of Foster
Avenue across
from Rosehill
Cemetery). Turn
left (west) on
Catalpa Avenue
and go two
blocks to
Campbell Avenue.

STOOL PIGEONS DIE
July 21, 1977

The crime scene is located at the intersection of Campbell and Catalpa, two blocks west of Western Avenue and one block east of Lincoln Avenue on the city's Northwest Side.

Nobody in his right mind kills a cop. Not in this town. Not in "Clout City," where every syndicate hood north and south of Madison Street respects the physical prowess and mental toughness of the "thin blue line." Chicago's cops are tough, raw-boned Irish, Polish, German, and Italian sons of the working class who gravitated out of bungalow-belt neighborhoods and into law enforcement.

The code of the police officer, however, does not extend to respecting or honoring crooked cops who become stool pigeons.

Mark Thanasouras was considered a rising star in a new era of professionalism. When Superintendent O. W. Wilson reorganized the Chicago Police Department in the wake of the Summerdale Scandal of 1960, he immediately promoted younger, college-educated men presumably free of political drag and mob ties. Thanasouras, who came on the job in 1956, made sergeant just five years later, and lieutenant four months after that. He was named commander of the Austin District on the crime-ridden West Side on April 5, 1966.

Thanasouras was one of Wilson's boys, a ramrod disciplinarian who ran his district like a boot-camp drill sergeant. These attributes served him well on the force but alienated the community and local businessmen. Tavern owners doing business in Austin kept their mouths shut and their wallets open as Thanasouras and eleven other crooked Austin policemen collected $275,000 in protection money "helping" the bars avoid fines and harassment for supposed violations of the liquor laws.

Chicago Tribune columnist Bob Wiedrich exposed Thanasouras as a grafter in 1968. It took the department five years to confirm these charges, by which time the district was awash in corruption, narcotics trafficking, and racial discord.

Thanasouras was finally relieved of his command in 1973, and sentenced to three and a half years at Terminal Island Prison by Federal Judge William J. Bauer, after copping a surprise guilty plea. The captain's life behind bars turned out to be a living hell. Threatened by members of the Black Panther Party, who circulated jailhouse rumors that Thanasouras was a brutal racist guilty of extreme measures in the aftermath of the 1968 West Side riots following the assassination of Dr. Martin Luther King, the ex-cop agreed to cut a deal with the government. He promised to talk about police and mob corruption in return for a shortened sentence.

After eighteen months in the jug, Thanasouras was back on the streets, working the overnight shift as a bartender at the L & L Club No. 2 in North Suburban Lake Bluff. It wasn't much of a job, but it was a second chance.

In court, Thanasouras supplied damaging testimony that resulted in the indictments of four Austin watch commanders. He was preparing to tell even more, but he was accosted at five in the morning on July 21, 1977, in a quiet residential section of the Northwest Side by a man wielding a twelve-gauge shotgun.

It was Thanasouras's custom to drop in on a woman with whom he had been keeping company, who lived in one of the spacious courtyard apartments adjacent to the intersection of Campbell and Catalpa. The shooter was observed conversing with Thanasouras by one of the neighbors seconds before blasting holes in his victim. The lone assassin, who apparently had followed Thanasouras for several days and was familiar with his daily routines, disappeared down a nearby gangway. His motive and identity were never determined, but former U.S. Attorney Sam Skinner, as well as every lifelong Chicagoan who understood the mindset of cops and the underworld code, were in general agreement.

"Any time you associate with people with organized crime ties you run the risk that your former friends will become your enemies. And this certainly appears to be an organized crime hit." Skinner said nothing about the strong possibility that the assassin might have worn a star and carried standard police issue at one time or another.

Far Northwest Side, West of Cicero Avenue, and North to O'Hare Airport

To continue the tour, go back south to Foster Avenue. Turn right (west) on Foster and proceed to Milwaukee Avenue. Turn left (south) on Milwaukee Avenue and go to Lawrence Avenue. Turn left (east) on Lawrence Avenue and on your left you will see the Copernicus Center, formerly the Gateway Theater.

THE CRIME THAT SHOCKED CHICAGO

October 16, 1955

The botched murder investigation of three young boys who were abducted from a Northwest Side street corner in the fall of 1955 pointed to the absolute necessity of adopting a concept known as Metropolitan policing to eliminate turf battles and jurisdictional rivalries existing between rival law enforcement agencies. Nearly forty-five years after the triple homicide of Anton and John Schuessler and their friend Robert Peterson, law enforcement is still comprised of 135 autonomous suburban policing agencies scattered across Cook County and the Chicago Police Department, any grouping of which can be at loggerheads during sensitive criminal inquiries. The Schuessler-Peterson slayings underscored the need for more efficient policing, and awakened a quiet, virtually crime-free community on the far Northwest Side of the city to the ever present dangers. Robert Peterson lived at 5519 West Farragut Avenue; the Schuessler brothers lived at 5711 North Mango Avenue in a bungalow neighborhood of Chicago not normally associated with violent crime. All three boys attended Farnsworth grammar school (5414 North Linder Avenue) at the time of their disappearance, a disappearance that vexed criminal investigators for forty years until a suspect was finally identified and a conviction secured.

On a crisp Sunday afternoon in the fall of 1955, three Northwest Side boys, with their parents' consent, agreed to head downtown, bum around State Street, and catch a matinee performance of *The African Lion*, a Walt Disney picture playing at the Loop Theater.

It was an adolescent rite of passage and a sign of maturity for a young man to journey into the heart of the big city with his buddies from the remote neighborhoods of the Northwest and Southwest Sides. In the 1950s, parents who trusted their children's better judgment never gave the matter a second thought.

With $4 in loose change jingling in their pockets, John and Anton Schuessler and Bobby Peterson ventured into the Loop without parental supervision for the first time in their lives. Peterson's mother personally selected the movie they would see that afternoon.

Around 6:00 P.M., long after the matinee at the Loop Theater ended, the boys were spotted in the lobby of the Garland Building at 111 North Wabash. Peterson's eye doctor maintained an office in the building, but it seems rather odd that a thirteen-year-old boy would want to see his optometrist on a Sunday afternoon.

Many years later, Chicago police detective John Sarnowski pushed a theory that Peterson and his friends were attempting to rendezvous with an older boy named John Wayne Gacy, who often "cruised" the Garland Building lobby, a 1950s hangout for gays, prostitutes, and hustlers. Peterson's signature on the lobby registry the afternoon of October 16, 1955, suggests that he had some purpose for being in the building. The theory that it was to meet with Gacy, who lived only a few blocks away from the Schuessler brothers at 4505 North Marmora Avenue, may or may not have merit.

Maybe the boys just wanted to use the washroom. Peterson and his companions dashed up to the ninth floor but came right back down again. They lingered inside the Garland Building for less than five minutes before returning to the Northwest Side.

Around 7:45 P.M. that same evening, the three wandered into the Monte Cristo Bowling Alley at 3326 West Montrose Avenue. The ten-pin parlor, located at the southeast corner of Milwaukee Avenue, was a neighborhood place to meet and drink. The proprietor told police he observed a "fifty-ish" looking man showing "an abnormal interest" in several younger boys who were bowling. It is doubtful that he made contact with the Schuesslers.

After leaving the Monte Cristo, the trio walked over to a bowling alley at 3550 West Montrose Avenue, but the disappointed boys were turned away because a league had rented all of the available lanes for the evening.

Out of money, but not quite ready to pack it in for the evening, the three youths reportedly thumbed a ride at the busy intersection of Lawrence and Milwaukee Avenue kitty-corner from the Hoyne Bank in Jefferson Park, about a half-mile north of the bowling alley. It was 9:05 P.M., and their parents were starting to get worried.

That was the last time anyone saw them alive.

The boys' naked and bound bodies were discovered two days later in a shallow ditch about one hundred feet east of the Des Plaines River. A passing salesman, who had stopped to eat his lunch in a picnic grove at Robinson's Woods Forest Preserve south of Lawrence Avenue on River Road (near suburban Schiller Park), telephoned police.

Coroner Walter McCarron disclosed that the cause of death was "asphyxiation by suffocation." The youngsters had been dead for thirty-six hours.

Peterson had been struck repeatedly and strangled with a rope or a necktie. The killer used one-inch adhesive tape to cover the eyes of all three victims. The boys had been dragged or thrown from a vehicle. Their clothes were never found.

Overcome by grief, Anton Schuessler Sr. issued a statement. "When you get to the point that children cannot go to the movies in the afternoon and get home safely, something is wrong with this country."

Lieutenant James McMahon of the Chicago Police said that he had never before seen such horror grip the city of Chicago as did in the wake of these killings. The world these people knew was changing rapidly.

Police officers from the Jefferson Park station conducted a door-to-door neighborhood interrogation, while search teams combed the Robinson's Woods underbrush for clues and items of clothing. The murderer or murderers had gone to great lengths to remove fingerprints and obliterate possible clues.

Solving this crime was beyond the abilities of the various city and suburban police departments who descended on the murder site like a swarm of locusts. While the city mourned, the police tripped and stumbled under the leadership of Cook County Sheriff Joseph D. Lohman, a University of Chicago egghead who offered $2,500 from his personal savings for information leading to an arrest. Lohman was desperate, and the newspapers exacerbated mounting public frustration by sensationalizing the case. The *Chicago Daily News* hired a team of divers to scour the murky depths of the Des Plaines River for clues, but they came up empty.

Meanwhile, an honor guard of Boy Scouts carried the tiny coffins from St. Tarcissus Roman Catholic Church at 4844 North Milwaukee Avenue to a hearse bound for St. Joseph Cemetery. The church was filled to capacity with 1,200 mourners.

"God has permitted sin, evil, and suffering because He knows He can bring good from the suffering," Reverend Raymond G. Carey reminded the congregation. Outside, another 3,500 people stood silently as the solemn Requiem Mass concluded. The burial of the three boys was the first sign that an age of innocence had passed.

With no statute of limitations on homicide, the case remained officially open, but as the years passed, the hope of finally bringing closure to the families faded. At best, the Schuessler-Peterson murders provided parents with an apocryphal lesson and a cautionary tale to relate to a generation of baby-boom children about the perils of conversing with strangers in cars.

For four decades the murderer remained undetected and free to kill again. Then in an unexpected turn of events, a paid government informant named William Wemette accused Kenneth Hansen of the crime during a police investigation into the 1977 disappearance of Deerfield, Illinois, candy heiress Helen Vorhees Brach.

In 1955, Hansen, then twenty-two, worked as a stable hand for Silas Jayne, a millionaire horseman from Kane County. Violent and unpredictable from birth and a street brawler, Jayne was involved in all kinds of skullduggery during his rise to power and acquisition of fabulous riches through shady manipulations of the horse breeding industry. He went to prison in 1973 for the ambush murder of his half brother George, culminating a lethal family feud that spanned the decades. Kane County residents, accustomed to the Wild West antics of these two, characterized the warring brothers as the "Jayne Gang."

Prosecutors from the Cook County State's Attorney's office showed jurors how Hansen lured the boys into his car on a pretext. They retraced the path of the killer in chilling detail, as he drove to Silas Jayne's Idle Hour Stables in the 8600 block of Higgins Road to show off Jayne's prized mares.

According to the testimony of other young men who were told these stories by the boastful Hansen, he molested and killed the Schuessler brothers and Bobby Peterson one by one. Fearing the indiscretion of his employee would ruin him, Jayne torched his stable in order to obliterate crime scene evidence. Hansen's brother allegedly dumped the bodies in the woods. After matters had quieted down, Jayne filed a bogus insurance claim on the ruined property.

Breaking a forty-year silence, Kenneth Hansen's victims came out of the woodwork recalling promises of jobs made to scores of young boys in return for sexual favors. He bought their silence with threats. Failure to comply meant that they would "end up just like that Peterson boy."

Silas Jayne had departed the world in 1987, taking secrets of the Schuessler-Peterson murders, horse swindles, Helen Brach, insurance scams, and untold frauds with him to the grave.

Minus physical evidence and eyewitnesses to corroborate the prosecution team's allegations against Hansen, a Cook County Criminal Court jury nevertheless convicted the sixty-two-year-old sexual deviate in September 1995, after deliberating less than two hours.

Places to Eat, Drink, and Gamble with "da Mob"

1. *Opened as a roadhouse by Carl Bromberger in 1921, the Lone Tree Inn (now Irene's Restaurant & Lounge) at 6873 North Milwaukee Avenue straddles the Chicago-Niles border (opposite St. Adalbert's Cemetery, south of Ebinger Street). During Al Capone's infrequent forays into the North Suburban roadhouse district during the 1920s beer wars it was simply, "Al's place." Capone sat at the end of the Lone Tree bar with a ham sandwich and a glass of lager firmly clutched in his beefy right hand. His torpedoes stood guard outside while the "Big Fella" plotted the takeover of the Northwest corridor, where Roger Touhy and his brothers peddled a high-quality blend of intoxicants to the barkeeps up and down Milwaukee Avenue. Capone dispatched Murray Humphreys out to Niles to discuss a "merger" with the five "Terrible Touhys," but Roger gave him a straight-up answer. "Tell that sonofabitch we don't want anything to with anybody like him!" John Touhy paid the price for Roger's snarling insult—with his life. Syndicate bullets cut him down inside the Lone Tree in 1927. The bloodstained wood-plank flooring was hard to clean. With a shrug of his shoulders, owner Bob Freebus just left it there, figuring it added notoriety and a touch of class to the place.*

2. *Meo's Norwood House, 4750 North Harlem Avenue (at Lawrence Avenue in Harwood Heights), was a favorite meeting place for the crime syndicate elite during Friday afternoon get-togethers in the 1950s and 1960s. During Tony Accardo's 1960 income tax evasion trial, the Chicago "Godfather" conferred with his defense attorneys over highballs in the restaurant lounge. Antoinette Giancana remembered Sunday afternoon dinners with her dad, Sam Giancana, as her "reward for being good for a week or two at the boarding school." The Meo brothers noon-time fashion show in the "Westwood Room" on January 26, 1968, lured all of the outfit bigwigs for a private showing—Jackie "the Lackey" Cerone, Felix "Milwaukee Phil" Alderisio, Joey Aiuppa, Paul "the Waiter" Ricca, and Lenny "Needles" Gianola. Brittle Virgil Peterson, the racket-busting Executive Director of the Chicago Crime Commission, took down the names and license plate numbers, forcing the hoods to run for cover. Where were the Chicago cops? The restaurant has been substantially remodeled and is now the Old Warsaw, serving up a sumptuous Polish-American buffet. It is very popular with the*

large Polish immigrant population who poured into the greater Northwest Side during the Solidarity uprising in the early 1980s.

3. *In the 1950s and 1960s, the Riviera Lounge at 6540 North Milwaukee Avenue and the Guys & Dolls Tavern, two doors north at 6544 Milwaukee on the Niles-Chicago boundary line, were big-time hood joints featuring girls, booze, and slot machines in the back room installed by mob kingpin Eddie "Dutch" Vogel. The Cook County Sheriff's Police raided these places so many times, they lost count. In August 1959, an exotic dancer named Theresa "Debby" Scavo was murdered inside the Riviera by Carl Ingo, one of Rocco "the Parrot" Potenza's bouncers. Potenza, the owner of the dive, was an alumnus of Sam Giancana's "42 Gang." Debby Scavo's husband, Phillip, and his brother Ronald were whacked by the mob outside their bungalow at 7851 Elmgrove Drive in Elmwood Park on April 26, 1962. It was not the first time, nor would it be the last, that a husband and wife "rolled the bones" with the Chicago outfit and lost. Looking for some action? You won't find it at 6540 North Milwaukee these days. This is now the address of the local headquarters of the American Aid Society. The General Tire Company, a few doors south of Albion Avenue in this same little acre of Northwest Side immorality, replaced Guys & Dolls long ago.*

4. *The old Wagon Wheel gambling operation (a floating crap game that moved from place to place, always one step ahead of the law) was a thorn in the side of the Chicago Crime Commission for many years. The Cook County Sheriff's Police turned a blind eye as far back as 1947, when Virgil Peterson drafted a letter to Sheriff Elmer Walsh advising him that card and dice games and roulette were running wide open at 4416 Narragansett Avenue (on the southwest corner of Montrose Avenue and Narragansett Avenue). That was also the case at 6416 Gunnison Street, an alternate location set up on the Harwood Heights–Chicago boundary line by Sam Giancana, who reported $98,258.10 in personal income from the Wagon Wheel operation during a three year period, 1947–1950. In 1961, when the Wagon Wheel was running full tilt, Virgil Peterson fired off three letters to Sheriff Frank Sain alerting him to the presence of illegal gambling in his jurisdiction. They were all ignored. The syndicate dives are, of course, gone. The Narragansett address is now a parking lot for customers of Jay's, a fast-food drive-up. The Gunnison location, in back of Elliot's Dairy, was also paved over.*

To continue the tour, turn around and go west on Lawrence Avenue to Mulligan Avenue. Turn right (north) on Mulligan Avenue and go one block to Gunnison Avenue. At Harlem Avenue, turn left (south) and go one block to Lawrence. Turn west on Lawrence Avenue and continue west to Cumberland Avenue. Turn right (north) and go to Summerdale Avenue in Norwood Park Township. Turn right (east) on Summerdale Avenue.

NO TEARS FOR THE CLOWN
December 23, 1978

Hours before he was scheduled to die by lethal injection at the Stateville Correctional Center on May 9, 1994, John Wayne Gacy feasted on a shrimp dinner, smoked his last cigar, and showed little remorse or pity for the thirty-three young men he murdered in a killing spree that lasted from 1975 to 1978. As Gacy prepared for the inevitable, the families of the victims spoke out. "I should be the one to pull the switch," said Richard Szyc, who lost a son to Gacy in 1977. Few people shed a tear for the "Killer Clown." Some even bought $10 T-shirts bearing the inscription, "No Tears for the Clown." Assembled outside the prison walls, the emotionally scarred families sang a chorus of "Na-Na, Hey-Hey, Good-Bye," when word of his execution was sent down from Illinois Department of Corrections officials. The people who wanted to see Gacy executed outnumbered the anti–death-penalty protesters 3-1. John Gacy's former neighborhood in Norwood Park Township has returned to normalcy. The ranch house at 8213 West Summerdale Avenue, which yielded terrible secrets on the night before Christmas Eve, was torn down by the city in April 1979. A new home—with a different address—stands on the former crime site, amid three-flats and post–World War II housing stock. It is located south of the I-90 Tollway between Courtland and Plainfield, one block east of Cumberland Avenue. In this quiet Chicago community bordering the vast suburban sprawl surrounding O'Hare Airport, local residents do not dwell on the macabre aspects of the case, or debate the whys and the wherefores. The national horror story is finally over, and they desperately wish for life to move on.

John Gacy's second mother-in-law remembered the terrible odors that wafted through the house. "There was an awful funny smell all the time," she said, "like dead rats. We complained about the smell but he said it was standing water in the crawl space."

The crawl space. It was only eighteen inches high.

Underneath the floorboards of Gacy's living room, police located the remains of twenty-nine young men buried under two feet of lime. The twice-divorced building contractor, who dabbled in local politics, shook the hand of First Lady Rosalynn Carter, and entertained the kiddies on the weekend in his clown suit, freely confessed his crimes. He sent the police down to the junction of the Kankakee and Des Plaines River in Will County searching for more decomposed remains.

"He's giving all kinds of statements saying there's a body here, a body there, a body in the lake or lagoon, a body buried," Cook County Sheriff Richard Elrod said, vowing to drag the waterways and dismantle the entire house.

What sort of man commits such heinous crimes? Acquaintances remembered "good neighbor" Gacy as a personable, outgoing man who maintained his property. A manicured lawn and painted eaves, leaf-raking in the fall, a plowed sidewalk in winter, and a cheerful countenance invite peer acceptance in the highly insular Northwest Side neighborhoods, which fan out toward O'Hare Airport from the central city. These are truly the "suburbs within the city."

For a long time, Gacy was a part of that world. He offered employment to young men he met in the neighborhood, and paid them well for after-school jobs. He volunteered his time to charity outings and delighted the neighbor's kids at afternoon birthday parties. While in college, he had majored in psychology.

The other Gacy was a sexual predator maneuvering on the slippery lower edge of society. He was arrested on a charge of sodomy in 1968, after luring a teenage boy into his home in Waterloo, Iowa, while his first wife was away. He was sentenced to ten years in the Anamosa Men's Reformatory, only to be paroled two years later.

Gacy ended his parole back in Chicago in 1971, but there were more complaints about his deviant behavior and whisperings of a sex and drug ring that he organized. He was often spotted cruising Washington Park, the famous "Bughouse Square" at Clark and Walton Streets opposite the Newberry Library on the city's Near North Side, once famous for radicals, deep thinkers, and stump speakers.

John Gacy managed to slip past the watchdogs of the justice system. He kept up appearances and cleverly maintained a double life invisible to everyone except his second wife, Carole Hoff, who recalled her husband's fascination with homosexual pornography and his dysfunctionalism in the marital bed.

Gacy always maintained that he was a bisexual who gravitated into the construction business because of the availability of young men. He started P. D. M. Construction out of his house in 1975.

Using his experience as a clown and magician to his advantage, Gacy tricked unsuspecting men into participating in his handcuff game. After applying the shackles, he approached them from behind with a rope or a two-by-four in hand. The sadistic rituals culminating in murder went on for nearly three years. Seventeen-year-old John Butkovich was the first victim. He disappeared on July 29, 1975. Robert Piest, the end chapter of this saga of slaughter, was last seen inside the Nisson Pharmacy at 1920 West Touhy Avenue. Gacy had agreed to do some remodeling work at the drugstore.

On December 11, 1978, fifteen-year-old Bobby Piest told his mother that he was going over to Summerdale Avenue to see about a part-time job. Des Plaines police detectives, acting on a mother's suspicions, visited the home two days later. After a judge reviewed the criminal record, a search warrant was secured. Workers armed with jackhammers, crowbars, and handsaws began tearing up the floorboards the following day. Their nightmare was only beginning.

O. J. Checks Out, June 13, 1994

S I D E T R I P

Before his fateful flight to Chicago on June 12, 1994, O. J. Simpson was yesterday's pop-culture icon; a face on a football trading card, a bit player in a series of witless B-grade comedies—in short, a washed-up ex-jock resting on past laurels.

It is safe to say that O. J. Simpson would have drifted into permanent obscurity, remembered by a handful of autograph chasers at sports memorabilia shows and admirers from his football days until former wife Nicole Brown Simpson and her close friend Ronald Goldman were found murdered. The dual murders were a cause célèbre, a sickening media orgy feeding the insatiable curiosity of supermarket-tabloid readers.

By the time the Simpson case had mercifully run its course, it was called the "crime of the century." For sheer exploitative value, it perhaps is the crime of the millennium.

It is a pointless exercise to weigh O. J. Simpson's guilt or innocence. The much discussed, over-analyzed murder case is clouded by the racial divisions in American society, and only Simpson can answer that question to God.

The facts by now are well established. At 6:15 on the morning of June 13, Simpson was safely ensconced inside his room at the O'Hare Plaza, a 243-room airport hotel immediately south of the Kennedy Expressway at 5615 North Cumberland Avenue. The O'Hare Plaza, now under new management, is situated just about a mile north of John Wayne Gacy's former residence. The high-rise hostelry is visible to Kennedy motorists trapped in the eastbound lanes of the expressway just past the Cumberland exit.

Simpson was scheduled to play a round of golf with a select group of Hertz Rent-a-Car clients that afternoon. He was unwinding in Room 915, and perhaps even practicing his putting when the phone rang. A Los Angeles police detective relayed the sad news that Nicole and Goldman were found dead. According to the investigator, Simpson never asked how Nicole had been killed, or whether her death had been an accident. He expressed the usual platitudes and inquired into the well-being of the children.

Curious perhaps, but people react in different ways to horribly shocking news that deadens the senses.

Simpson telephoned his criminal defense attorney Howard Weitzman and told him to be at the Los Angeles airport when he returned home.

Late that evening, O. J. was winging his way back to California, where the feeding frenzy was about to kick into high gear.

Meanwhile, back in Chicago, the O'Hare Plaza was preparing to close its doors. Later that year, on September 10, thirty-six items from Room 915 were sold in a private auction to souvenir hounds. The organizers of the event were probably disappointed. Only $2,117.50 was collected for the entire lot.

A bound Gideon Bible was sold for $120. A water glass was purchased for $60. Simpson claimed that he had cut his hand on a glass moments after hearing the news about Nicole, which undoubtedly triggered the imagination of the proud owner of this artifact.

"I was in the bathroom, and I just kind of went bonkers for a little bit," O. J. later explained.

The hotel once known as the O'Hare Plaza had already changed hands. It has undergone several major renovations during the course of its existence. In the 1980s, the name on the marquee was the Rodeway Inn until the chain pulled up stakes. The O'Hare Plaza promoters closed the place in the summer of 1994, around the time police investigators were sifting the hotel parking lot for murder clues.

Five years later, the Wyndham Garden is still in business. The orange neon sign fronting the expressway beckons O'Hare passengers to its door. Why go all the way downtown? The airport location is ideal if one's plans are about to unexpectedly change or if the weary traveler is summoned back to the home office.

To continue the tour, return to Cumberland Avenue and proceed north to Touhy Avenue. Turn left (west) and go to Mount Prospect Road.

FLIGHT 191
May 26, 1979

The crash of an American Airlines DC-10 moments after takeoff from O'Hare International Airport on Saturday, May 26, 1979, remains the worst civil aviation disaster in the nation's history. All 272 passengers and crew died on impact, easily surpassing the jetliner accident occurring on September 1, 1961, when a loose tail bolt was responsible for the crash of a TWA Constellation, claiming the lives of 78 passengers in a field near south suburban Clarendon Hills. Flight 191 crashed in a grassy area used by the Chicago Police Department canine unit near Mount Prospect Road and Touhy Avenue in Des Plaines, south of the I-90 Tollway, which connects Chicago to Madison, Wisconsin. The impact site was once a small commercial airport before it became a graveyard.

Flight 191. It is a story of an aeronautical disaster of epic proportions. Those who witnessed the plane's gradual ascent from the O'Hare runway and the sudden cartwheels that began six hundred feet up in the air, analogized the doomed aircraft to a toy plane spinning out of control.

Five seconds after takeoff, the number one engine separated from the left wing, forcing the craft to bank sharply to the left until it was nearly perpendicular to the ground. The low-flying plane was unable to right itself, silently plunging toward the open field adjacent to a trailer park. Then, there was a tremendous explosion and a mushroom cloud of black smoke. The wreckage of the McDonnell-Douglas DC-10 was barely recognizable to emergency rescue personnel sent to the crash site. White stakes were driven into the ground, and a photo was taken each time a body was located.

On board the ill-fated flight bound for Los Angeles were many publishing executives, editors, and marketers en route to the annual American Booksellers Association convention. Sheldon Wax, vice president and managing editor of *Playboy* magazine, was flying to LA with his wife, Judith, journalist, poet, pundit, and author.

The DC-10 was designed to fly safely, even with one of its three engines out of commission. It was a puzzle to the National Transportation Safety Board why the jetliner spun helplessly out of control. Most often, human error is the contributing factor.

After months of analysis, the NTSB concluded that faulty maintenance procedures were to blame. Two months earlier, a crack was created in the support pylon by mechanics who had removed the General Electric–built engine for routine maintenance. The crack severed electric and hydraulic lines in the wing.

Subsequent NTSB inspections revealed manufacturers' defects in twenty other DC-10s belonging to domestic carriers.

North by Northwest:

Kenilworth to Barrington

For many years it was generally acknowledged by urban dwellers that the pastoral farm communities and distant suburbs linked by the railroads to the central city held the key to a safer, more healthful lifestyle for children and an escape from crime.

Chicago's northern bedroom suburbs, fanning westward from Sheridan Road and the elegant mansions of verdant, secluded Kenilworth, have for the most part fulfilled the American dream for the post–World War II generation, but at the price of congestion, unchecked sprawl, and the occasional headline murder that lingers long in the memory. When a crime occurs, it is often a crime of such magnitude that it befuddles local law enforcement for years to come. There are at present 135 autonomous suburban police departments across Cook County. Advocates of metropolitan policing say that the system is unwieldy, outmoded, and compromised by political intrigues at the highest levels. The answer, they say, is to consolidate resources into a single countywide agency with the capability and sophistication to attack the problem of crime head-on and provide closure to the most baffling and infamous crimes of recent years. Taking into consideration "turf" issues and the agenda of the local politicians, the dream of metropolitan policing may remain just that—a dream.

We will begin our suburban explorations on the North Shore, moving west from the affluent community of Kenilworth.

Kenilworth

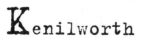

Kenilworth, one of Chicago's wealthiest suburbs, is nestled between Wilmette and Winnetka along the magnificent shoreline of Lake Michigan. The average family income, according to the latest available census figures, is $166,536 per household. Single-family homes are valued between $329,000 and $3 million.

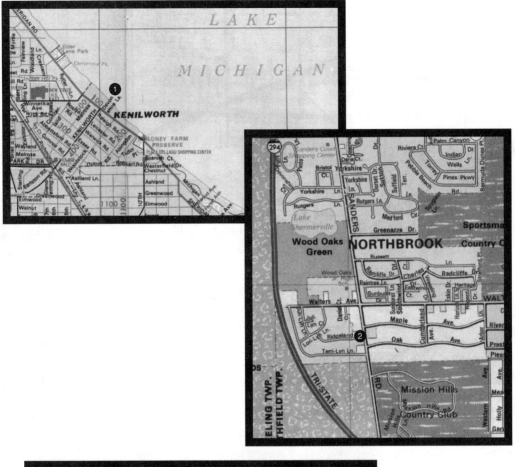

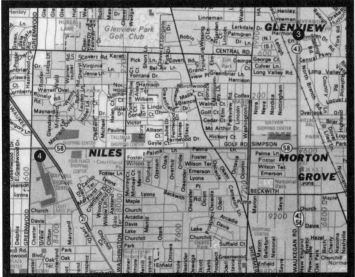

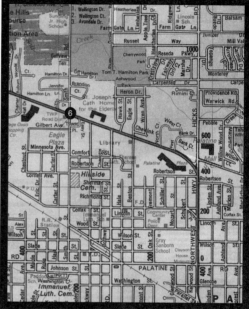

1. Valerie Percy murder, Devonshire Lane, Kenilworth.
2. Werner Hartmann murder on Ridgeland in Northbrook.
3. Townhouse fire at Carriage Lane, Glenview.
4. Scene of Terrence Zilligen murder, Sears Roebuck store at Milwaukee and Golf, Golf Mill shopping center in Niles.
5. Dorfman shooting, Lincolnwood Hyatt Hotel, Touhy and Lincoln in Lincolnwood.
6. Brown's Chicken and Pasta murders, Smith and Northwest Highway, Palatine.

THE NORTHWEST SUBURBS

In 1994 there was only one violent crime reported for the entire year. It has often been said that a policeman's lot is never a happy one; but a drive through posh Kenilworth offers convincing proof that the old bromide may not necessarily be true in this serene setting where street crime is almost nonexistent.

To begin the tour, take Sheridan Road north to Devonshire Lane. Turn right on Devonshire Lane.

TRAGEDY IN THE NIGHT
September 18, 1966

Nestled in a wooded setting high on the bluffs overlooking Lake Michigan, Kenilworth is the jewel of Chicago's North Shore, home to the titans of industry, finance, and philanthropy. Since its incorporation as a village in February 1896, there have been only two murders in this staid community of just over 2,400 residents. When Diane B. Davis, a victim of domestic violence, was found slain in her Mediterranean-style home on Oxford Road in 1991, it instantly brought to mind the horrific murder of twenty-one-year-old Valerie Jeanne Percy. Valerie was the daughter of Senator Charles Percy, and the Percy family lived less than half a mile away from the Davis house in a secluded villa off Sheridan Road at 40 Devonshire Lane. The Percys called their Tudor mansion "Windward." What happened here remains one of the most baffling murder mysteries in the annals of Cook County crime, and it is all the more shocking because of the apparent lack of motive. Whoever invaded the Percy home that night must have planned the deed very carefully. The fiend did not leave a single, tangible clue in his wake. Coming on the heels of the murders of eight student nurses, the killer sent a chilling warning to a frightened city that nothing in life can be taken for granted, least of all our sense of security and well-being.

Charles Percy's inspiring rags-to-riches climb provided American youth with a blueprint for success in cynical times. The tragedy that befell him and his family at the hour of his greatest triumph underscored the fragility of the American dream he had clung to during the darkest hours of the Depression.

At the age of five, young Percy began selling magazine subscriptions. While attending New Trier High School, he worked four jobs simultaneously to help his mother put food on the table. The Percys lived in posh Wilmette, but there was uncertainty day to day regarding his father's job. Even to this day, not everyone listing a North Shore address can afford private tennis lessons and membership in a local country club.

Chuck Percy would not begin to enjoy these rich men's trappings until much later in life, not until after he was named president of Bell & Howell on January 12, 1949. Through vigor, ambition, and a slavish devotion to the work ethic, Percy had worked himself up from the status of a lowly $12-a-week office clerk to the head of one of the nation's most influential manufacturers of photographic equipment.

In the spring of 1966, Percy resigned his post as chairman of the board in order to campaign for a U.S. Senate seat against Democrat Paul Douglas, a grizzled New Dealer getting on in years. Chuck Percy was still very much a political novice. He had chaired the 1960 Republican National Convention and had feverishly raised funds in Illinois for the party stalwarts, but he had never held an elective office. The party looked upon him with favor, however: a handsome young candidate with sterling credentials and a reserved disposition to parade before middle America—at last, a Republican with the Kennedy mystique from the wealthy Chicago suburbs.

That summer at the annual Bell & Howell company picnic, Percy, his sleeves rolled up, moved easily among his friends and well-wishers pressing the flesh. He had the look of a winner. Then tragedy struck.

The murder of Valerie Percy occurred in the heat of a political race where everything hung in the balance. What, if any, connection existed between the rough-and-tumble world of Chicago politics (for it is here, and not downstate Illinois, where the real turf battles are fought) and the tragedy that befell this close-knit family will never be known.

What is known and generally accepted as fact, is that Valerie Percy, a recent graduate of Cornell University, said goodnight to her dinner guests and retired for the evening shortly after 10:00 P.M. on Saturday, September 18, 1966. Her father returned home to Devonshire Lane around midnight. Candidate Percy had just spoken to a gathering at the Germania Club and decided to unwind in front of the television before going to bed.

Hours later (between 4:00 and 5:00 A.M.), the killer, armed with a flashlight, a club, and a two-edged knife, broke into the seventeen-room mansion through a glass-paneled door in the downstairs music room. Valerie's stepmother, Loraine Percy (Charles's second wife) was partially awakened by the sound of breaking glass. Convinced it was just one of her stepdaughters moving about, she gave it no more thought.

The intruder rushed up the carpeted stairs, moved past two other bed-rooms, and entered Valerie's room. "The killer knew what he wanted to do," said one investigator. "It looks like he was going after one person." But why? The unan-swered question haunts the Percy file to this very day.

The next sounds Loraine Percy heard were groans coming from down the hall. This time she raced into the hall. When she opened the door to Valerie's bed-room, a silhouetted male figure crouching over the bed shined a flashlight directly into Loraine's eyes, temporarily blinding her. The man rushed past her and was gone into the night just as the burglar alarms sounded.

Mrs. Percy drew a mental picture of a man who stood five feet eight inches high and was of medium build and weight, but she could not supply Kenilworth Police Chief Robert M. Daley with any substantive details that might shed light on the identity of the killer.

There were no clues in the bedroom. Fingerprints were lifted from the downstairs entranceways, and nearly one hundred people were questioned. The police were hoping that someone would have noticed unusual activity in the neighborhood, but Kenilworth is very quiet at that hour and no one report-ed any strange occurrences.

There were no jilted boyfriends to question, no political enemies that Percy knew of, just the numbing certainty in the minds of police that the trail was cold as soon as the murderer escaped from the house.

The next afternoon, Cook County Board President Seymour Simon received five threatening phone calls at his office including an anonymous mes-sage that he "would get the same thing the Percy girl got" if he wasn't careful. Simon, a former Chicago alderman and seasoned politician, dismissed the calls as the work of a crackpot, but questions remained. Did Percy's high visibility mark his daughter for death? The mystery will never be solved without a suspect and a motive.

For a moment in 1973, police believed they had stumbled upon a solid lead when an Iowa convict named Francis Leroy Hohimer fingered two members of his own gang, cat burglars Norman Jackson and Frederick J. Malchow, who were active along the Chicago North Shore in the 1960s. Jackson jumped off a build-ing. Then Malchow died in a 1967 jailbreak from the Norristown, Pennsylvania, prison, and a once promising clue held no special significance.

Charles Percy defeated Paul Douglas in the fall election, and served three unblemished terms in the U.S. Senate (1966–1984). He chaired the powerful Senate Foreign Relations Committee, a political plum awarded to the consum-mate Washington insider. Percy, a noncontroversial, monotone figure through much of his professional life, became the ultimate "Beltway" insider in later years.

In honor of the young woman lost to her family in the prime of life, Senator Jay Rockefeller and his wife, the former Sharon Percy of Kenilworth, named their daughter Valerie.

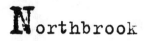orthbrook

Well-to-do Northbrook is located twenty-five miles north of Chicago's Loop and is bordered on three sides by acres of forest preserve and lagoons. The land was ceded to the U.S. government by the indigenous Potawatomi tribe in 1829 and was dedicated as Shermer Station in 1885. The name was officially changed to the Township of Northbrook in 1923. An ordinance banning all outhouses passed three years later.

Needless to say, the pace of life in this quiet community of thirty-one thousand upper-income souls is slower. Not much of consequence happens to upset the suburban routine, but when it does . . .

Now, drive north on Sheridan Road, and follow the twisting highway until you reach Willow Road in Winnetka. Turn left, and proceed west to Sanders Road in Northbrook where you will turn right (north). Continue past Techny Road to Ridgeland Lane. Turn left (west).

THE BLACK WIDOW
June 8–9, 1982

As murder-for-hire schemes go, this one had all the elements of a late-night Alfred Hitchcock thriller with the added ingredient of illicit sex. The cuckolded murder victim married a former "exotic dancer." He moved her into his Northbrook home, where they lived under the same roof with his ex-wife. Wife number two had married him for his money, but she quickly decided he was worth much more to her dead than alive and plotted his death to cash in on a life insurance policy. The sordid murder of wealthy businessman Werner Joseph Hartmann inside his mansion at 4125 Ridgeland Lane in Northbrook is an eerie but fascinating hybrid of the films Double Indemnity *and* Psycho. *The intriguing aspects of this case have recently been depicted on* American Justice *for the Arts & Entertainment network. Surrounded by one-story homes on a quiet side street off Sanders Road (a half mile east of*

Milwaukee Avenue), the Hartmann estate has been substantially remodeled since the 1982 murder. The beige stucco mansion at 4125 Ridgeland Lane bears no resemblance to the four-bedroom home that stood on this site in 1982. Properties become poisoned by heinous crimes, and the memory of these past misdeeds sometimes must be erased in order for there to be peace.

Hartmann was a self-made millionaire who had emigrated to the United States from Mannheim, Germany, in 1968. Business associates remembered him as one of the "smoothest-talking" salesmen they had ever had an occasion to meet. Hartmann married Vasiliki Cruse in 1964, and divorced her thirteen years later. He kept his ex-wife on the payroll long after the ink had dried on the divorce decree.

Bewitched by a head-turning young stripper he met at the Smoker's Lounge near his Franklin Park stereo shop, Werner Hartmann courted and wed the woman the following year. "I married you for the money," cautioned the second Mrs. Hartmann, a gold digger who dropped out of high school at age fifteen to become a dance instructor.

To keep pace with the insatiable demands of his young wife, it became necessary for Werner Hartmann to borrow against his flourishing car-stereo business. He lavished her with jewels, furs, a $100,000 Rolls-Royce, a silver Mercedes-Benz convertible with the vanity plate "Debra 2," a Lincoln Continental, and other riches.

The neighbors thought the Hartmanns extravagant; but nouveaux riches in Northbrook are not an uncommon sight. Werner and Debby kept to themselves, and soon they were taken for granted. Behind closed doors, however, the marriage was less than idyllic. Flaunting the trappings of wealth with a mix of sexual intrigue, Debby Hartmann began a three-year affair with tennis pro John Scott Korabik, who worked in a gun shop. Werner Hartmann prized his beautiful young wife, and made certain "accommodations" to keep the marriage going. According to a family attorney, Hartmann voluntarily surrendered the marital bed to Korabik. One night when he had had enough, Hartmann fired shots from his derringer into the $100,000 Rolls as Debra spun out of the driveway. Debby claimed she was hospitalized several times following beatings inflicted by her abusive husband.

In September 1981, Debra Hartmann was driving the Rolls through the Near North Side nightclub district when an empty champagne bottle, carelessly tossed from inside the car, struck a pedestrian. When the cops pulled Hartmann and her five passengers over, they discovered a concealed Beretta handgun. One of the passengers was a convicted drug mover, free on bail. Cocaine fueled a less than zero lifestyle.

With Hartmann's fortune within her grasp, but goaded to madness by the fear that he would soon divorce and disinherit her for violating the sanctity of their marriage, Debra and her lover, John Korabik, plotted Hartmann's death. Hours before he was slain, Hartmann confided his suspicions to his lawyer. He said he wanted a divorce and that he would probably have to leave the country to get away from the diabolical pair.

Life seemed to be imitating art when Werner Hartmann stepped out of his shower and stood toe to toe with a killer who had been lurking in the shadows of the empty house. In Hitchcock's *Psycho,* Norman Bates slashes Janet Leigh's character while the water cascades across her body. Hartmann was drilled outside the shower stall by fifteen bullets fired from a .380 automatic pistol.

From the severe powder burns evident on the body, it was clear to police that the killer stood only twelve inches away from the victim when the shots were fired.

The gunman picked up the spent shell casings from the floor and disappeared. There was no evidence of forced entry or a struggle, and a burglar alarm connected to the Northbrook police station had not gone off. It had to be an inside job.

Debra Hartmann and her fourteen-year-old stepdaughter, Eva, met Hartmann's ex-wife for dinner at the Snuggery Saloon in Schaumburg. At 4:20 the following morning, Debra and Eva returned home alone. Eva discovered the bullet-riddled body in the second-floor dressing room, and together they drove to the police station to report the crime rather than step over the body to reach the telephone.

Bold and quick-witted, the grieving widow showed the world a grim face and a stoic demeanor. She told the cops that it had to be suicide. "Like everyone else in the family sometimes I'm fine, sometimes I'm not," she said. "Like I will be doing something and on the desk I see something in Werner's handwriting and I just break down."

Debra Hartmann promised her late husband a grand sendoff. No expense would be spared. "He's going to go in style," she said. "We picked the most expensive plot in the cemetery and we'll have limos and everything for the funeral."

She could certainly afford it. The insurance money was what the fast-living playgirl and her tennis-pro boyfriend were after all along, and Debra Hartmann was a perfect actress. She dumped the boyfriend in 1983, cashed in the insurance policies totaling $589,000, and moved to 14966 Walnut Drive in an unincorporated area near Deerfield a year later. The "perfect" crime was complete.

The police investigation languished for the next five years until Special Agent James DeLorto of the Bureau of Alcohol, Tobacco, and Firearms began to unravel the mystery. DeLorto filed an affidavit in federal court implicating Debra Hartmann, her lover, John Korabik, and a jailbird named Kenneth Kaenel in a far-reaching murder conspiracy aimed at defrauding the insurance companies.

Kaenel had written a series of letters to Hartmann and Korabik from his jail cell in Springfield, Missouri, urging them to retain a unified front. Kaenel eventually cooperated with federal authorities. He accused Korabik of offering him a $50,000 bribe to kill Hartmann in 1982, but said that he turned the offer down cold.

Kaenel's letters never reached Debby. Instead, they were delivered to the FBI.

No one was officially charged with committing the actual murder, but Hartmann and her two confederates were convicted of multiple mail and wire fraud in December 1989. Described by prosecutors as the "Black Widow," "a beguiling charmer," and a "narcissistic parasite" who "lived for parties and money," the Hawaiian-born Hartmann was eventually sentenced to twenty-two years in prison. Co-conspirators Kaenel and Korabik received twenty years and sixteen years, respectively.

Addressing the judge in his chambers, Hartmann played upon the sympathies of the court in an attempt to cast herself as a battered and misunderstood wife without a motive.

"I did not want my husband dead," she went to great pains to explain. "It's true we had our moments when he hit me, but I felt if we would have had a separation, if we had gone for some counseling, things would have worked themselves out."

Glenview

The Village of Glenview was incorporated in 1899, four years after local residents voted to change the name from Oak Glen to Glenview.

To continue the tour, return to Sanders Road and go south to Willow Road. Turn left (east) and continue to Waukegan Road. Turn right (south) and continue past Glenview Road to Palmgren Drive. Turn left (east) into the Carriage Hill development. Carriage Hill Drive is in the center of the development.

FOREVER AMBER
April 9, 1965

Lovely Linda Darnell, star of stage and screen and one of Hollywood's reigning beauties, died in a tragic house fire on April 9, 1965. Darnell had just completed work on her forty-sixth film, Black Spurs, *and was enjoying a respite at her former secretary's secluded town home in a wooded subdivision of Glenview when plumes of smoke wafted up to the second-floor bedrooms and awakened the slumbering occupants. The actress might have escaped if she had only had the presence of mind to crawl through an open upstairs window instead of racing downstairs and directly into the roaring inferno. The two-story Colonial town home at 675 South Carriage Hill Drive was rebuilt not long after the fire, and is situated in the middle of the gated 1950s Carriage Hill development on Waukegan Road between Golf and Glenview at Palmgren Drive.*

At the height of her career, Linda Darnell confided to a press agent that the life of a glamour queen was not all that exciting or rewarding. "I never got the things most girls do," she said. "I never attended a high school dance, never took a spin in a cut-down jalopy. I worked. Now when I meet boys my own age, I feel too old to find them interesting."

Driven to despair trying to please her stage-struck mother and deprived of the normal childhood accoutrements, Monetta Eloyse Darnell began carving out a show-biz career when she was eleven years old and a department store model in Dallas.

Talent scout Ivan Kahn discovered her a few months shy of her fourteenth birthday. With Pearl Darnell's blessing, the breathless young starlet who sang, played the piano, and studied ballet was on her way to Hollywood for a screen test. It was 1938, but the big studios did not want to take a chance defying the Hays Code and moral censors by signing an underage minor. A year later, Darryl

F. Zanuck put the auburn-haired charmer under contract after she claimed first prize in the *Gateway to Hollywood* radio-show contest.

Her first starring role was in Elsa Maxwell's *Hotel for Women,* one of two motion pictures she made for Zanuck in 1939. A versatile actress, she would be remembered more for her million-dollar legs and love affairs with Howard Hughes and director Joseph Mankiewicz than the dramatic ability she exhibited in her most famous film, *Forever Amber.* Darnell was also an accomplished visual artist, and was once approached by a Chicago art gallery to show a collection of her work.

Twice married and divorced, Linda Darnell kept busy through the 1940s and 1950s grinding out action and adventure films like *Blood and Sand* and *The Mask of Zorro.* She was a dependable, hardworking performer whose personal life was in shambles following an adulterous love affair with Mankiewicz, who directed her in *A Letter to Three Wives.* Mankiewicz said that Darnell was "a marvelous girl with very terrifying personal problems."

In the 1950s, the Hollywood movie offers dwindled, as so often happens to thirty-plus actresses. To resuscitate her sagging career, Darnell toured the dinner theater circuit and made occasional television appearances. She last appeared before Chicago audiences in *Love Out of Town,* at the Pheasant Run Playhouse in St. Charles in October 1964.

The following Easter, Darnell decided to unwind and take a few weeks off from her busy performance schedule at the Glenview residence belonging to her former secretary Jeanne Curtis. Resolved to unburden herself from mounting financial worries, a bout of depression, and the director's tight production schedule for *Black Spurs,* Darnell seemed to enjoy camping out in Chicago's Northern Suburbs before the unexpected hand of tragedy struck.

The two women were sorting out tax records when Darnell paused to scan the *TV Guide.* She noticed that one of her early films was set to air on the late show. Giddy as a schoolgirl, she coaxed Jeanne and her daughter Patty to share a Hollywood memory or two over coffee before retiring for the evening.

The movie was *Star Dust,* Linda Darnell's semiautobiographical picture for Twentieth Century Fox, which was completed in 1940.

The sudden, devastating fire broke out just before dawn when everyone was asleep on the second floor. Awakened by Patty's frightened screams, Jeanne Curtis raced around in the darkness as the heat and smoke filled the upstairs hallway.

Curtis and her daughter managed to escape the danger by crawling through an open window and onto the safety of an overhanging ledge. Patty and Jeanne jumped to safety, but Linda was trapped inside the house.

The savage flames and searing heat destroyed the first-floor living quarters, burning them beyond recognition. The cause of the fire was never determined.

Disoriented and confused, Darnell wandered into the path of the fire, perhaps in the mistaken belief that Patty was trapped downstairs, or perhaps desiring to retrieve some personal item. Days after the deadly fire, there were whispers that the actress's deep depression drove a subconscious suicide attempt. Family members vigorously denied the allegation.

Linda Darnell sustained burns over 80 percent of her face and body. She was pulled from the charred embers in a state of collapse, but clinging precariously to life.

Rushed to Skokie Valley Community Hospital on Golf Road, where an emergency tracheotomy was performed, Darnell was transferred a few hours later to the Samuel L. Koch Burn Clinic at Cook County Hospital. Several of the nation's top specialists labored valiantly through the morning hours to save the life of the famous actress, but death came at 2:25 P.M. on the afternoon of April 10.

Pheasant Run producer Carl Stohn noted with grim irony that for all of man's stunning scientific and Space Age achievements, careless accidents more often than not reap the greatest toll in human life. "It is indeed a tragedy that in this day and age when we're getting ready to fly to the moon someone still can be killed in something as mundane as a fire in their home."

Niles

Just over the Chicago border on the far north end of Milwaukee Avenue lies the curious little suburb of Niles, a blue-collar bedroom community with an interesting and checkered past. The Village politicians are not sure just how the town happened to come by its name, except to say that in the year 1899, President John Huntington and his fellow board members petitioned for its incorporation as Niles, Illinois.

In the 1920s and 1930s, Niles was a notorious "roadhouse" district. Gangsters spilling over from Chicago battled Roger Touhy for control of beer distribution, and shootings, while not on the grand scale of Chicago, were not uncommon. In 1923, the Sheriff's Police, a fledgling, one-year-old agency, established a command post on the northern end of Cook County in a functional three-story limestone building lying just north of Dempster Street at 8970 North Milwaukee Avenue in Niles. Syndicate hoodlums, prostitutes, strippers, and the riffraff hauled out of the old Blue Dolphin Motel and show lounge, a notorious den of vice lying just north of the Golf Mill shopping center on Milwaukee

Avenue near Greenwood, were processed in and out of the sheriff's station up until the 1980s, when public pressure closed the Dolphin. The Cook County sheriff's headquarters closed in 1984. The famous "cop shop," where many three-round fistfights were fought on the second floor, curse words spoken, and sad excuses invented, is now the Niles Historical Museum.

To continue the tour, go south on Waukegan Road to Golf Road. Turn right (west) and proceed to Milwaukee Avenue and the Golf Mill Shopping Center.

THE SEARS ROEBUCK HEIST
March 14, 1964

The busy Golf Mill Shopping Center at 9440 North Milwaukee Avenue (the intersection of Milwaukee and Golf Road in Niles) is one of the oldest suburban shopping plazas in Northeast Illinois. In the 1960s, it was famous for the Las Vegas–caliber entertainment headlining at Mill Run, the legendary show lounge and auditorium located in the north end of the vast parking lot fronting Golf Road. The escalating salaries of the performers and the unreasonable demands of their agents drove Mill Run out of existence in the early 1980s. In the waning years of the nightclub era, the theater lent class and a touch of elegance to the otherwise dull strip mall surroundings. Today Mill Run is nearly forgotten, swallowed up by suburban sprawl.

The vintage outdoor shopping plaza of the 1950s has undergone similar drastic changes. It is now a bland indoor mall resembling a thousand other colorless malls with common-sounding names like Southgate, Westgate, and Northgate, visible from the major interchanges that slice across the American suburbs. They'll tell you it was a necessary change that allowed the good burghers of the Village of Niles to keep pace with the times. But don't believe it. The old Golf Mill, with its quaint mill pond and live performance theater, had a certain charismatic charm that is missing today.

The Sears Roebuck store, where TV salesman Terrence Zilligen lost his life trying to be a hero before God and company, still anchors Golf Mill, but it bears little resemblance to the cozy family store peddling flannel shirts, work shoes, Hillman's groceries, and Kenmore refrigerators to the parents of the post–World War II baby boom. The fiercely antiunion retailer replaced the fixtures, the interior decor, and the exterior façades, and in a painful cost-cutting move eliminated much of its dedicated staff of full-time sales employees in the name of efficiency and reduced overhead.

Why wasn't anyone prosecuted for the Terry Zilligen murder when the identity of the killers was so agonizingly clear to five eyewitnesses?

All of the witnesses brought into the Niles police station for the "show-up" alleged that Paul "Peanuts" Panczko was one of the three men involved in a fatal altercation with TV salesman Zilligen as the gang of armed robbers attempted to flee moments after snatching $32,000 in checks and $20,000 in cold cash from the second-floor cashier's cage.

Niles Police Chief Clarence Emrikson told reporters that the men wore clear plastic face masks. While one bandit vaulted into the cage, the other two held three customers at bay with loaded pistols. Panczko was easily identified by the size and "redness of his neck, general build, and peculiar shuffle."

Moments before the Brink's armored car arrived to pick up the day's receipts, the robbery was complete. The perpetrators raced three hundred yards down the main aisle toward the north end of the store, through the furniture department where Terry Zilligen, the father of three whose wife was expecting a fourth child, stood in their path.

The salesman was shot in the head when a bullet discharged during the scuffle with the robber carrying the sack of money.

"Peanuts" Panczko was the youngest member of the thieving Panczko brothers' gang of jewel robbers and second-story men. Paul and his brothers would steal anything not nailed down, including an unattended earthmover from a road grade (and they did) if there was a percentage in it. They were notorious throughout the 1940s, 1950s, and 1960s.

Before he entered the federal government's Witness Protection Program in 1986, Panczko had dedicated his life to crime. Lacking the color and flamboyance of his older brother Joseph "Pops" Panczko, who depicted himself as a "teef who steals tings," Peanuts compensated with a fertile imagination and a criminal cunning that Pops lacked.

The younger Panczko surrounded himself with a gang of hijackers and professional thieves who skirted the edges of 1960s Chicago organized crime: Guy "Lover Boy" Mendola, Pat Schang, Joey D'Argento, Mike LaJoy, Frank DeLegge, and Gerald Tomasczek. The Chicago Police Department's Criminal Investigations Unit (CIU), led by William Hanhardt, chased this crew for years, according them a grudging respect as elusive yet worthy adversaries.

If a tractor-trailer of razor blades disappeared from a storage yard late one night, Hanhardt and his elite squad of burglary dicks would roust Panczko's crew from their known haunts. It was academic. When a big score went down in the Windy City, it was likely the Panczko gang had something to do with it. Think of them as the midwestern chapter of *Good Fellas*.

The Sears Roebuck job, however, was a miserable botch. No one, least of all the Panczkos, expected a salesman whose family subsisted on the meager commissions the giant retailer paid its workforce to intervene in a holdup planned down to the last detail.

Schang, LaJoy, Mendola, D'Argento, and Panczko were fingered for the Sears holdup. Mendola allegedly waited in the getaway car, a late-model red Pontiac, while his confederates affixed a pair of handcuffs to the handles of the store's door. The car sped off down Greenwood Avenue headed toward Park Ridge. After hearing what had happened, Guy Mendola panicked. The men inside the car quarreled and cursed one another, as hoods are known to do when there is an unexpected setback. The car was abandoned in the parking lot of Lutheran General Hospital where, ironically, Zilligen passed away. The case was far from over, however.

Considered weak, and suspected of ratting on his pals to the government, Guy Mendola expired from a shotgun blast fired at point-blank range inside his garage at 1554 North Forty-third Avenue in Stone Park the evening of August 31, 1964.

Joey D'Argento was brought in for questioning, but the interrogation was fumbled by Richard Cain, the mob-friendly chief investigator for the Cook County Sheriff's Police. (See Tour 6.)

Peanuts Panczko was arrested by Sergeant James "Packy" Walsh of the Cook County Sheriff's Police not long after the robbery and murder, but he was never convicted of the Zilligen slaying. It is one of those senseless crimes that occasionally fall through the cracks, but that does not ease the sorrow of the victim's family.

For years afterward, the Chicago retailer made it a special point during employee orientation sessions to advise sales floor personnel not to get involved in potentially lethal altercations. The insurance risks and the risks to human life were far too great.

Lincolnwood

Improvements in public transportation sparked the rapid growth of the "close-in" suburbs of Lincolnwood, known for many years as Tessville, and Skokie, a rural farming district called Niles Center in the days when Roger Touhy and his gang controlled the roadhouses and bootlegging operations in the Northern Suburbs. The addition of the Skokie Valley route of the North Shore line in 1926 confirmed the importance of these sleepy little towns and contributed to an upsurge in population. Lincolnwood is now a commuter suburb of 11,500 residents located 42.00 degrees north of the equator and eleven miles from downtown.

To continue, take Milwaukee Avenue south to Touhy Avenue. Turn left (east) on Touhy Avenue and, crossing over the Edens expressway, proceed to Lincoln Avenue.

DEATH IN TEAMSTER TOWN
January 20, 1983

From the bloody labor wars early in the twentieth century through modern times, syndicate goons in silk shirts and pin-striped suits have been a malevolent, corrupting force in organized labor. In recent years, several influential Teamster locals in Chicago have been placed in trusteeships by the federal government, the books audited and seized, and the mob-affiliated bosses shown the door. In a 1988 anti-racketeering suit, the U.S. Justice Department said the International Brotherhood of Teamsters (IBT) was under the thumb of organized crime. And yet one is left with the overwhelming sense that the rank-and-file Teamster views these men as martyrs to the cause, in the mistaken belief that management concessions are more easily obtained by syndicate muscle than through the proper channels of the collective bargaining process. The meddlesome and corrupting influence of the Chicago outfit and its satellite mobs in Kansas City and Milwaukee nearly bled dry the Teamsters Union's Central States Pension Fund in the 1970s and 1980s, sparking labor unrest and the assassination of Allen M. Dorfman, a millionaire insurance executive and pal of Jimmy Hoffa. Dorfman had been convicted of taking $55,000 in kickbacks to secure a $1.5 million loan from the Fund in 1972, and was about to be sentenced anew on bribery and conspiracy charges when two assassins emptied five slugs from a .22-caliber pistol into the back of his head in the parking lot outside the Hyatt Lincolnwood Hotel at 4500 Touhy Avenue (the corner of Lincoln Avenue and Touhy Avenue). The Hyatt Hotel, easily identified by its familiar purple-brick exterior, is now *the Radisson Lincolnwood. Tessy's, the hotel restaurant where Dorfman and bail bondsman Irwin S. Weiner were headed for lunch when the shooting occurred, is now T. J. Peppercorn's.*

War hero Allen Dorfman was earning $4,000 a year as a physical education teacher at the University of Illinois in 1948. Five years later, he was well on his way to becoming a millionaire thanks to his father's friendship with the powerful Teamster boss James Riddle Hoffa.

Allen Dorfman's father, Paul "Red" Dorfman, was a former professional boxer and an associate of Tony Accardo, whom he addressed by his first name. For many years, Allen's father ruled the Chicago Waste Handler's Union. It didn't much matter to union members that Red Dorfman had never worked a day of his life as a trash hauler.

In the rough-and-tumble world of union politics, Red Dorfman was a brute who pounded the chairman of the waste handlers' employers' association to insensibility one night, using a set of brass knuckles concealed in a glove. The victim of this assault wisely refused to prosecute.

Dorfman's son, a university graduate with a refined manner and a businessman's polite demeanor, formed the Union Casualty Insurance Company (later, the Amalgamated Insurance Agency) in 1950. Allen and his family were awarded a contract to handle the insurance affairs of the Central States Pension Fund because of Red's long-standing ties to Hoffa, receiving $3 million in commissions and service fees over the next eight years.

In 1964, a San Francisco jury acquitted father and son of strong-arming a California financier in an attempt to recover $100,000 from a failed investment. But Allen Dorfman's troubles were far from over. Several years later, after Hoffa went to prison, Dorfman narrowly escaped death when two masked gunmen fired four shotgun blasts at him as he pulled out of the driveway of his home at 1001 Hoffman Lane in the tiny suburb of Riverwoods, which is sandwiched between Northbrook and Wheeling in Lake County.

Under constant scrutiny by congressional committees (father and son once took the Fifth Amendment 135 times), federal authorities, and insurance licensing agencies in a number of states in which Union Casualty operated, Dorfman openly flaunted his friendships with mobsters. His name was linked to a shady land-development project in Los Angeles, which was bankrolled by $12 million in unpaid loans from the Central States Pension Fund. In Denver, the Villa National Bank borrowed $200,000 from the fund.

Dorfman's mishandling of union money and the attendant publicity surrounding fraudulent pension loans invited governmental intervention. In 1977, the Pension Fund trustees relinquished control to an independent management firm.

The bell was already tolling for Allen M. Dorfman. In a dramatic criminal trial underscoring the union's deep and pervasive ties to organized crime, Dorfman, Teamster President Roy Williams, and Chicago mob boss Joey "the Clown" Lombardo were found guilty of attempting to bribe Nevada Senator Howard Cannon to delay passage of a trucking deregulation bill. Facing a fifty-five-year prison term, fines totaling $29,000, and a second criminal trial charging him with extortion in connection with the bombing of a home belonging to Lake Forest builder Robert Kendler, Dorfman weighed his options, not the least of which was full cooperation with the government. The inner circle of the Teamsters was unfazed, according to F. C. Duke Zeller, a union advisor and author of *Devil's Pact.* "Dorfman ain't long for this world," confided Jackie Presser, who was elected president of the Teamsters in 1983. "It's just a question of time. The word's out that he is going to talk and make a deal with the government. I say good riddance."

It was shortly before 1:00 P.M. on the afternoon of January 20, 1983. Dorfman and Weiner, a local bondsman with crime syndicate ties who founded three firms using Teamster Pension Fund monies, had just pulled into the parking lot of the Lincolnwood Hyatt after Weiner had withdrawn $7,500 from the First National Bank of Lincolnwood for partial repayment of a personal loan.

It was a brisk, clear afternoon. Weiner was walking directly in front of Dorfman, about three feet ahead, when two armed assailants crept up from behind and announced a holdup. Less than seventy-five feet from the restaurant and in plain sight of four witnesses, a bearded gunman wearing a ski cap pumped five slugs into the back of Dorfman's head, while the sixty-five-year-old Weiner, still recovering from a heart attack, froze in his tracks.

The assassins dashed to an escape car, a green Dodge Polara according to witnesses, and sped south down Lincoln Avenue toward the city leaving Dorfman on the ground, his camel's hair coat saturated with blood.

The weapons and discarded license plates were located several days later in a Northwest Side Dumpster. The identity of the assassins remained a puzzle, but the burglar Joseph "Pops" Panczko believed he had a clue. In a 1989 interview with Art Petacque of the *Chicago Sun-Times,* Panczko revealed that a low-level syndicate fence named Ray Spencer fired the fatal shots. Panczko said he bought the killer breakfast the morning of the shooting at a busy coffee shop located at Dempster and Harlem Avenue.

The statute of limitations had already run out on Spencer. He died in Florida in 1984.

The motive, as everyone suspected, was mounting syndicate paranoia that Dorfman was about to spill mob secrets. "It's part and parcel of life in the United States that association with the Cosa Nostra often leads to a sudden death," commented FBI Special Agent Edward D. Hegarty.

Palatine

Palatine is a middle-income bedroom suburb miles from the mean streets of Chicago, northwest of O'Hare Airport. Palatine shed its small-town image after World War II, when the municipality grew from two thousand inhabitants to a sprawling suburb in excess of thirty-nine thousand.

To continue the tour, take Touhy Avenue west to Northwest Highway. Turn right (northwest) and continue through Palatine to Smith Road.

THE PALATINE MURDERS
January 8–9, 1993

The Palatine Police Department has ninety-two employees, sixty-nine of whom are sworn officers. The department bears the ultimate responsibility for protecting a community whose motto, "A Real Home Town," speaks to an idealized version of this country that no longer seems to exist. This sense of domestic tranquillity was permanently shattered when the owners and five employees of a Brown's Chicken and Pasta Restaurant on Northwest Highway (Route 14) and Smith Road were executed gangland style. The crime was a shocking one; there had not been a murder within the Village limits in the prior four years. At issue from the very beginning was the inability of a multi-jurisdictional police task force to identify, arrest, and prosecute the perpetrators responsible for this outrage. The murders would bitterly divide the community, local law enforcement, and the families of the victims for years to come. An independent panel chaired by the Better Government Association and the Chicago Crime Commission concluded that inefficiency and police "turf battles" had clouded the investigation all along.

The crime remains unsolved, and the restaurant never reopened. The building was retrofitted and reopened as Signature dry cleaners, but within a few years that business was gone too. Today, virtually unrecognizable in the noisy commotion of Northwest Highway, the former Brown's restaurant remained for a long time an empty shell. A "For Lease" sign posted in the parking lot was recently removed and a new fast-food establishment opened.

Seven murder victims were carted through the green door of the small family-owned franchise in the early morning hours of January 9, 1993.

A Palatine patrol officer made the grisly discovery at 3:11 A.M.; two hours after a concerned parent telephoned a Palatine police dispatcher, frantic that her son had not returned home from his job. It will undoubtedly remain one of the most terrible shocks the officer will ever experience.

A patrol car responding to the dispatcher's call arrived at the Brown's Chicken and Pasta Restaurant at 1:04 A.M. It was a cold and snowy January evening. On nights such as this, it is hellish to be a cop, making the rounds in the neon gallery of deserted suburban strip malls.

The responding officer conducted an external search of the premises, but the interior of the fast-food eatery was dark. There was no sign of activity, and presumably no cause for concern. The night crew had all gone home hours ago, or so it appeared.

Across the street, the Palatine cop observed a man and a woman pulling into the strip mall. Crossing the side road feeding into Northwest Highway, the officer pulled up alongside the vehicle. "I'm the one who called the police," the anxious woman told the cop. "My son has not come home." The police officer suggested that maybe the young man went out after work with his friends. Acknowledging the possibility, the parents of Michael Castro drove off, and the Palatine cop continued his rounds through the sleepy bedroom community.

Meanwhile, inside the restaurant, their son lay dead on the floor.

Among the seven people who were shot to death inside two walk-in coolers in the kitchen area of the back of the building were the owners, Richard and Lynn Ehlenfeldt. They had bought their slice of the American dream just seven months after Richard lost an executive job with Group W Cable as a result of corporate restructuring. Unbeknownst at the time to these unfortunate people, they were about to fall prey to the nightmare of modern life—cruel and cunning criminal mayhem foisted on the unsuspecting—that seems to occur in America with numbing regularity.

In police parlance a case like this was called a "heater"—a high-profile, make-or-break murder mystery the CBS Evening News would cover in prime time. With the nation's eyes focused squarely on Chicago, it was imperative for the image and reputation of local law enforcement that the crime be solved. The first step was to try to piece together the chain of events, and that presented the first serious challenge.

In their final report, the FBI concluded that little planning and coordination occurred prior to the time that the killers entered the store, presumably to rob the cashier just before closing time. The shootings may have occurred as an after-thought to the robbery because the .38-caliber bullets extracted from the victims came from only one gun. In all, twenty-one shots were fired. The brass shell cas-ings, which might have shed light on where the ammunition was purchased, were missing. The shooter or shooters retrieved them prior to exiting the restaurant.

If robbery was the only motive, why was it that the thieves walked away with only a portion of the loot—about $1,200? Left untouched in the bottom compartment of the safe was $300 in small denominations. Investigators were puzzled as to why this money was left behind.

As they exited the restaurant, the killers opened the wall panel box and flicked off the switches, cutting off all electrical power. The kitchen wall clock stopped cold at exactly 9:48 P.M. Police estimate that the killers entered the store and ordered their chicken dinners shortly after 9:00 P.M.

Palatine Police Lieutenant Bob Haas was on duty at the station when the fateful radio call came in asking for an ambulance to be dispatched to Smith Road and Northwest Highway. He alerted Deputy Chief Jack McGregor, who placed a call to Chief Jerry Bratcher at his home to advise him of what had gone down. Bratcher, a political wheel-horse with outside business interests, arrived at the Brown's restaurant ten minutes later.

Then, about an hour later, Chief Bratcher called in a second agency, the Northern Illinois Police Crime Laboratory, for assistance, when it became appar-ent that this was a crime in desperate need of highly technical resources. There was only one problem. The NIPCL was formed by Bratcher and his friends and colleagues from adjoining suburbs. The Village had a "relationship" with the NIPCL, and contributed $50,000 a year toward its upkeep. According to the Better Government Association, "The lab, the site where all evidence, fingerprints and blood samples were processed, had applied for—and failed to receive—accreditation several times."

Scientists and technicians from the Crime Lab jointly began the analysis of the restaurant and parking lot. By daylight, a phalanx of investigators was swarm-ing over the site. A formal, investigative task force involving FBI personnel, the Illinois State Police, the Cook County Sheriff's Police, and ten suburban depart-ments was organized by Bratcher two days later.

Task force members searched the Dumpsters, and the parking lot was combed for clues. The interior and exterior of the restaurant were videotaped, and food containers were analyzed. It seems evident that the crime scene was contaminated, and any potential clues like the tire prints of exiting vehicles from the parking lot were inadvertently trampled underfoot by state's attorneys and officers from the various agencies converging on the scene. The investigation may well have been blown in these first few critical hours; reminiscent of the way Sheriff Lohman's ace detectives botched the Schuessler-Peterson and Grimes murder sites back in the 1950s.

Three days later Bratcher made a request for the FBI's Investigative Support Unit responsible for tracking down serial killers. The specially trained unit flew in from Quantico, Virginia, but they were unable to develop a solid profile of a suspect because they theorized that there was more than one killer involved.

A stopped clock, a collection of bullet fragments, and a half-empty safe were the most tangible clues pointing to the robbery and homicide. But these clues alone did not reveal the identity of the individuals who killed the Ehlenfeldts, their cook, Guadalupe Maldonado, Thomas Mennes, Marcus Nellsen, and the two teenage cashiers Michael Castro and Rico Solis.

From the very beginning there was a dearth of suspects to question. Those responsible for this atrocity had covered their tracks well—either through accident or subterfuge. "Our assumption is, it was a robbery that went bad," Chief Bratcher theorized on the one-year anniversary of the murders.

In the next twelve months, investigators received more than three thousand calls coming into a special hot line. They checked out more than one thousand leads with negligible results. Two hundred fingerprints were collected at the Brown's restaurant and sent to police departments in Milwaukee, Indianapolis, and Chicago for computerized matching, but no matches were found. James F. Bell was one of the outside experts brought in to coordinate the Brown's task force. Bell, an FBI agent experienced in major case management, specializes in tracking down serial killers. He worked on the Ted Bundy case and the still unsolved Green River killings in the Pacific Northwest.

The regional task force was eventually whittled down to seven investigators assisted by two civilians, and the number of incoming phone calls dwindled to nothing. In desperation, a $120,000 cash reward was offered to the public for information that might lead to the killer.

Eight weeks after the massacre, the search for additional evidence at the crime scene was called off. Nothing more could be found inside the establishment. Meanwhile, Chief Bratcher clung to the theory that it was a robbery gone bad.

From the very beginning the investigation into the Palatine killings was marred by internal disputes—turf issues between rival police agencies—and a lack of central authority and coordination. There were persistent complaints that the more seasoned homicide investigators were not being allowed to properly effectuate, that is follow up on crucial leads that might shed light on a possible suspect.

Commenting on the efficacy of Jerry Bratcher and his team of suburban "super sleuths" charged with unraveling the mystery, the Better Government Association bitterly noted: "Bratcher's troops were like the Argentine Army generals with chests full of medals who had never seen combat and suddenly the Falklands, and it all began to crumble against the battle-tested British. What would he do? He had told everyone over and over again how great he was. How would they handle this?"

"People have to check their egos at the door," countered Palatine Police Sergeant John Koziol at one point. "That's the nature of the job."

The most troubling aspect to the investigation goes well beyond ego massaging and turf management. There were persistent complaints of poor leadership and lack of direction within the task force itself and, even worse, the controversy surrounding "Lead 80"—the confession of Reynaldo Aviles, a member of the PR Stones street gang, who was found dead in his cell at the Cook County Jail in May 1993 while awaiting trial. His death was officially classified as a suicide by the Cook County medical examiner, but twenty-two abrasions found on the body and a head laceration suggested that he met with foul play—punishment for being a snitch.

Aviles was a suspected gangbanger, drug dealer, and gun buyer who allegedly ingested a fatal dose of asthma medicine that he had received from correctional officers. Knowledgeable insiders maintain that it is virtually impossible to commit suicide inside a Cook County Jail cell, and Aviles's death had more to do with ratting on another gang member than fatally ingesting a prescription. The Aviles confession became known as "Lead 80," and for a brief moment there was finally a glimmer of hope.

The task force concluded that "Lead 80" had no particular significance, but acknowledged that the massacre probably had something to do with gang recognition. The robbery might have gone bad when the gunmen recognized one of the store employees through a street gang affiliation.

Brown's chairman and CEO, Frank Portillo, drafted a letter to Bratcher asking him to analyze the residue of cottonseed oil and flour found inside the restaurant. Portillo, a compassionate and deeply involved community leader, reasoned that it was highly probable that this material would have been inadvertently transferred into a getaway car by the killers. Brown's is the only major chicken franchise in the area that prepares its food with cottonseed oil.

The ingredient is used by all of Brown's short-order cooks, and the filmy substance adheres to the walls and floors. Because it did not occur to the task force investigators to seek possible clues within the oily residue at the time, Portillo asked Bratcher to have the laboratory technicians check for the presence of this material in an impounded vehicle allegedly driven by the killers.

Frank Portillo had other pressing concerns about the tenor and conduct of the investigation. No one within the top levels of the suburban task force seemed to be very interested in finding out who had been coming and going from the restaurant in the days and weeks leading up to the murders. There were at least seventeen outside vendors and employees who had access to the front and rear areas of the dining establishment during that time. No one was asking the hard questions except Portillo, but his amateur sleuthing was callously and thoughtlessly shoved aside by the task force pros.

If police had obtained such a list from Portillo in the early stages of the investigation, they might have saved themselves the added effort of eliminating work-

LOCATION OF THE BROWN'S CHICKEN AND PASTA MURDERS. THE BUILDING STOOD EMPTY FOR A LONG TIME, THEN REOPENED AS A HOT DOG STAND.

ers' fingerprints from those who realistically might have been regarded as suspects.

"All I want is for the various law enforcement agencies to work together harmoniously to effect a final resolution and let the chips fall where they may," pleaded the embattled Portillo. Portillo has since rededicated his life to awakening the citizens of Chicago to deadly crime conditions, holding the politicians accountable for the larger failures of the criminal justice system. Combating voter apathy, Portillo purchased time on a Chicago radio station to advocate for legislator accountability in his "Citizens' Lobby." From the seeds of this tragedy, the Brown's chairman has stirred the conscience of the community.

On the third anniversary of the Palatine murders, Chief Bratcher called a press conference to release new details to the media. Bratcher surmised that the killer must have stood between six feet and six feet six inches tall based on footprints left behind. The weapon was a .38-caliber or .357-caliber revolver and was the only one employed by the shooter.

The execution-style murders of seven employees of the Brown's Chicken and Pasta Restaurant on Northwest Highway is no closer to being solved today than it was more than six years ago.

"This case has been screwed up since the beginning," commented Larry Schreiner, a contributing columnist for the *Daily Herald,* a Northwest Suburban newspaper. "Authorities are no closer to solving the case today than they were at the beginning. They can say what they want, but that is the truth."

Barrington

Baby Face Nelson put Barrington on the map. Before that time, the old settlers spun tales of earlier Indian days. The Potawatomi and Mascouten tribes roamed the woods in this area until they were forced from their lands in 1833, when the native peoples inhabiting the Chicago region were forcibly relocated to the Plains states. Yankee settlers from Vermont, upstate New York, and Great Barrington, Massachusetts, in Berkshire County, founded the farming community around the present-day intersection of Sutton Road and Route 68 (Dundee Road) and named it Miller's Grove. At the suggestion of Cook County Sheriff Isaac Cook, Miller's Grove was renamed Barrington Station in 1850. Four years later engineer Robert Campbell created a plat, and laid out an eighty-acre town. Things remained pretty quiet until caravans of Depression outlaws began to trundle past the sleepy village en route to their hideouts in southern Wisconsin.

Continue north-west on Northwest Highway to Barrington. Cross Route 59 and on the left is Langendorf Park.

THE CUTEST LITTLE BABY FACE
November 27, 1934

Illinois Route 14 (Northwest Highway) twists and turns from its southernmost point at Milwaukee Avenue in the Jefferson Park neighborhood of Chicago, past the site of the Brown's Chicken murders, all the way northward to the Wisconsin border and points beyond. In the 1930s, caravans of slow-moving automobiles toiled their way northward past rolling farms and cornfields toward the picnic groves, orchards, and waterways of the Chain of Lakes in Illinois and Lake Geneva, Wisconsin. Motels, filling stations, and roadside diners punctuated the rolling countryside. During the "Public Enemy" era, the winding two-lane highway bisecting the Northwest Suburbs provided a convenient escape route to the northern woods and access to the resort lodges for gun-toting fugitives like John Dillinger and "Baby Face" Nelson.

Nelson was a Chicago car thief, bootlegger, and gunman possessed of a fiendish temper and a willingness to shoot on sight. He met his own demise in Barrington, where he engaged FBI agents in a violent showdown on November 27, 1934, that left two federal men dead. A bronze plaque, placed inside Langendorf Park by the Current and Former FBI Employees of the Chicago Field Office and the FBI National Academy, pays homage to the memory of Inspector Samuel Cowley and Special Agent Herman Hollis, who made the mistake of trying to capture Baby Face Nelson on that autumn afternoon so long ago. The pitched gun battle between a crazed killer vowing never to be taken alive and the FBI agents blocking his path was fought alongside a road grade near the Langendorf Park driveway fronting Route 14 on the south side of the road. Langendorf Park is centrally located just west of Route 59 (Hough Street) in Barrington, but a Burger King and a McDonald's flanking the driveway have swallowed up and digested the actual location of the shooting long ago. The Jeep-Eagle dealership across the street and the rows of uninspired strip malls up and down Northwest Highway contribute to a suburban sprawl that obscures the memory of a pleasant little country town made infamous by Baby Face Nelson.

Born Lester Joseph Gillis in Chicago on December 6, 1908, and raised in a three-story flat at 944 North California Avenue by Belgian immigrants, the professional killer later known as "Baby Face" Nelson was a picked-on child, whose simmering hatred for the police and individuals in positions of authority was nurtured by the petty slights of older, tougher boys who mocked his diminutive stature.

Standing only five feet four inches, Gillis compensated for his physical limitations with a murderous temper and a willingness to employ a switchblade or a gun without hesitation or remorse for the intended victim.

During Prohibition, Gillis performed special favors for the Al Capone gang, and was particularly useful as a "slugger" during times of labor unrest. An expert thief and second-story man, Gillis, who by this time had adopted the name "George Nelson" after a prizefighter he admired, was stealing cars and robbing jewelry stores.

Nelson struck out on his own in 1931 but was arrested on a bank robbery charge and sentenced to a stretch in the Stateville Penitentiary at Joliet. He escaped on February 17, 1932, and embarked on a cross-country crime spree that placed him high on the FBI's "A" list of public enemies.

It was notoriety that the short-fused Gillis craved. Each time he spotted his name in the newspaper, the pint-sized outlaw was inspired to commit even more brazen crimes with his henchmen, John Paul Chase, a former San Francisco bootlegger, and Tommy Carroll, an ex-boxer recruited into the gang because of his skill with a machine gun.

Early in 1934, Nelson wormed his way inside the John Dillinger gang, following Dillinger's escape from the Crown Point, Indiana, jail and his subsequent flight from justice. Understandably wary of Nelson's manic aggression and his shoot-to-kill attitude, the Dillinger gang took him into their inner circle as they traversed the Twin Cities, Iowa, and Wisconsin robbing banks with willful abandon.

Following a robbery in Mason City, Iowa, in March 1934, the gang was forced to split up. Separating from Dillinger, Nelson disappeared into the swampy marshlands of Iron County, Wisconsin, north of Park Falls. On April 22, he shot down Special Agent W. Carter Baum outside Koerner's resort near Spider Lake, sparking a manhunt. Scores of federal agents and woodsmen volunteers led by Melvin Purvis combed the backwoods, but the city boy from Chicago outsmarted them all. He hid inside an old Indian cabin in the Lac du Flambeau region, then retreated to Chicago in Baum's automobile with his wife, Helen Warzanski Gillis, at his side.

For much of that summer, Nelson laid low. He was hiding out in California when he received word of John Dillinger's demise at the Biograph Theater in Chicago. Nelson smirked. He deeply resented that the bounty on Dillinger's head was higher than that on his own. The berserk killer interpreted this as a slap in the face and an insult to his good name and reputation.

"Don't these lawmen know they are dealing with the most dangerous man in America?" he snorted. "They should want to pay top dollar to get the most dangerous man in the country, don't you think?"

The hunt for Baby Face Nelson abruptly ended in Barrington on November 27, 1934. Special Agent Herman Hollis and Inspector Samuel Cowley received a tip that Nelson, his wife, and John Paul Chase were scouting the Illinois-Wisconsin border country for a place to hole up for the winter. FBI agents laid a trap at Hobart Hermanson's Lake Corso Hotel in Lake Geneva, but they failed to identify Nelson's car, a mistake that cost the Bureau two of its most capable agents.

With Nelson behind the wheel, the traveling party headed toward Chicago when they were spotted outside the resort town of Fox River Grove by Agents William Ryan and Thomas McDade. The FBI men pursued Nelson's sedan down Route 14, but bullets tore through the radiator, disabling the government car.

John Paul Chase felt the noose tightening. He smelled a federal trap.

"Johnny old pal," Nelson sneered, "I'm going to get me them two guys!"

Interviewed by federal agents weeks later, Chase recounted those next few moments. "I told him he was a fuckin' fool. Our cue was to scram. 'Listen Les,' I said, 'we got a clear road ahead. Let's take a chance on living a couple of more months.'"

Moments later, a second federal car, a 1934 blue Hudson sedan driven by Herman Hollis and Samuel Cowley, approached them from the southwest.

According to Chase, the wife was "game" for anything Nelson wanted to do, but this time she had reservations and begged her husband to retain his composure. For Nelson, that was, of course, impossible.

Turning their car around, the agents pursued Nelson's V-8 Ford, trading shots with the fugitive killer as they raced down the dusty highway.

His fuel pump shattered by FBI bullets, Nelson crashed his car in the ditch and prepared to shoot it out with the G-men who took positions behind their Hudson automobile and a telegraph pole.

"Les and I each grabbed a machine gun and jumped out of the car,"

Chase recalled. "He yelled to Helen to lie flat in a ditch or she'd get her head blowed off."

Helen Gillis, a former Woolworth's cashier lured into the gangster life by Nelson when she was only eighteen, took cover behind a clump of trees across the road from Frances Kramer's filling station. Seconds ticked off the clock as Nelson weighed his options. Suddenly he climbed onto the road and walked directly into the line of Cowley's machine-gun fire. "I'm going down there to get those sons of bitches!" he snorted.

The slugs of the G-men (seventeen in all) tore into Nelson who kept on coming and coming, uttering curse words and goading the Feds to fight like men.

Hollis was killed instantly. Cowley died of his wounds at Sherman Hospital in Elgin. But with a burst of superhuman energy, the nearly indestructible Nelson managed to stagger back to his car on his feet.

When the smoke cleared, Nelson attempted to climb behind the wheel of the federal car, but he was groaning in pain and weak from a loss of blood. Helen gently laid her husband into the back seat of Cowley's Hudson.

After speeding away from the scene of the Barrington shootout, the bandits evaded a police dragnet. By now, the Chicago Police had been alerted to the fatal affray in Barrington.

At a safe house in Niles Center (now the Village of Skokie), Helen Gillis, aided and abetted by a Catholic priest, applied cotton balls to her husband's wounds to stop the bleeding, but Nelson was beyond help.

At her arraignment, Nelson's widow described his final moments. "After a while Les said, 'It's getting dark, Helen. Say good-bye to mother.' He mentioned all the family—his brother and sisters and their children then he came to our own children. He couldn't hold back the tears when his tortured lips formed their names. He cried."

Baby Face Nelson died in her arms seconds later with a smile on his face. The naked corpse was wrapped in a blanket and left in a ditch near Long Avenue and Niles Center Road not far from the entrance of St. Peter's Cemetery.

"During the ride I sat in the back seat with him, holding him up as if he were alive," the platinum blonde told the cops. "We put him down comfortably on the grass by the road after I got the blanket. I couldn't get it out of my head how Les had always hated the cold, so I tucked it around him."

The stolen car was abandoned at Winnetka Avenue near the Skokie Valley route of the Chicago, North Shore, and Milwaukee Railroad.

For the next twenty-four hours, Helen Gillis waited patiently for a printed notification in the newspapers that her Baby Face had been found. When there was no word, the anxious widow placed an anonymous call to the undertaker.

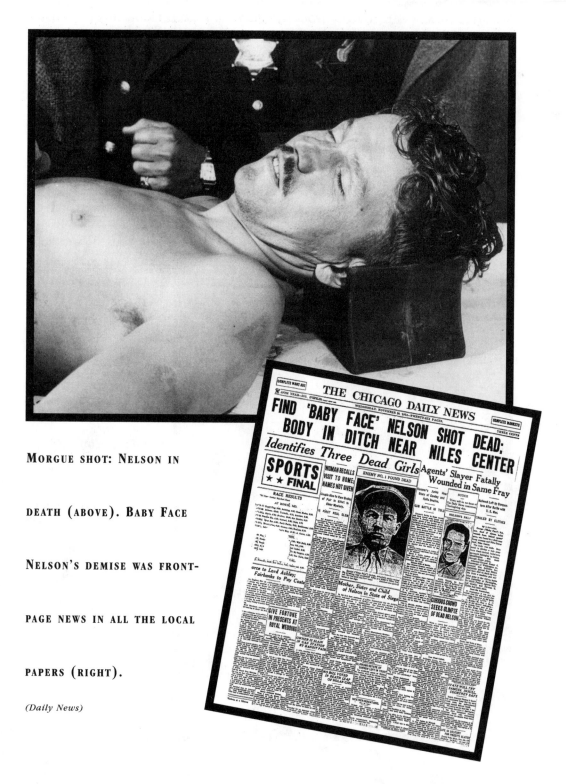

MORGUE SHOT: NELSON IN

DEATH (ABOVE). BABY FACE

NELSON'S DEMISE WAS FRONT-

PAGE NEWS IN ALL THE LOCAL

PAPERS (RIGHT).

(Daily News)

The body was recovered from the ditch and taken to Bradley & Haben's undertaking parlor at 8057 Niles Center Road in Skokie, where the remains were identified through fingerprint analysis. When the G-men were done, family members were notified and the remains of Baby Face Nelson, "Public Enemy #1," were taken back to Chicago.

There was a ten-minute wake for Nelson at the undertaking parlor at 1845 N. Hermitage Avenue. Family members consoled Nelson's widowed mother, Mary Gillis, who had taught French to high school students in her younger years. She remembered him as a "clever boy," at least up until the fourth grade. Lester Gillis was buried at St. Joseph's Cemetery in West Suburban River Grove.

Helen Gillis, weighing only ninety-four pounds soaking wet, voluntarily surrendered to police on Thanksgiving Day. The widow served a year in the women's

MELVIN PURVIS AND

J. EDGAR HOOVER.

THE HANDSHAKE WAS

PURELY FOR THE

SAKE OF PUBLICITY.

penitentiary at Milan, Michigan, for harboring the fugitive John Dillinger in Wisconsin, then disappeared from the public spotlight.

John Paul Chase was grabbed outside a fish hatchery in Mount Shasta, California, on December 27, 1934. Chase was tried and convicted for the murder of Agent Cowley. He died in federal custody years later.

From Washington, FBI Director J. Edgar Hoover praised the efforts of the slain agents and offered employment to Mrs. Baum and Mrs. Cowley, but he was in a jealous stew, resentful over the spate of publicity Melvin Purvis was receiving from the newspapers and the airwaves. When Purvis told reporters that he had taken a solemn vow to avenge the death of his friend Cowley, it was the last straw. Director Hoover removed him from the Public Enemies file.

In 1960, the dauntless G-man who spearheaded the Public Enemy's field investigations in the 1930s committed suicide at his home in Florence, South Carolina, using the gun given him by fellow FBI agents at his retirement party.

The pistol that John Dillinger carried the night he died was by this time in the hands of comedian Red Skelton—a gift from J. Edgar Hoover.

West Side Stories

With its many residential neighborhoods moving outward from the central city, the West Side mirrors the remarkable growth of Chicago from its earliest days as a frontier garrison to the imposing industrial metropolis it soon became. The history of the West Side for the most part is the history of the plain people, the poor and the downtrodden, and the despairing from other lands seeking to negotiate a better way of life in the crowded tenements lying west of Halsted Street.

Chicago was incorporated in 1837. During the peak years of growth before and after the Civil War, many second-generation Germans, Irish, Scandinavians, and Yankee settlers from Bluegrass country and the mid-South settled the Near West Side.

Ashland Boulevard, one of the city's most stylish residential addresses in the mid-nineteenth century, was part of Chicago's "West Division," as this side of town was commonly known in the pre-fire period. This was where Mayor Carter Henry Harrison groomed his son to become his eventual successor.

But as the great industrial boom took root on the West Side, a landscape of smokestacks, foundries, and rolling mills hastened the departure of the "old settlers" of Harrison's generation. By the time of the Great Chicago Fire, which began in a hay barn in Conley's Patch, one of the poorest working-class neighborhoods of the Near West Side, the powerful mobilizing forces of ethnic dispersal and resettlement were already taking shape.

Much of the land lying to the immediate west afforded people of modest means the chance to start over. Beginning in the 1880s, waves of immigrant Italians, Russian Jews, Poles, and Greeks escaping the pogroms, poverty, and political oppression of their homelands settled the Near West Side, in the vicinity of the present-day University of Illinois campus and Cook County Hospital complex.

Bohemians, Lithuanians, Germans, and Slovaks filled in the Lower West Side of Chicago, adjoining Eighteenth and Twenty-sixth Streets in Pilsen. When the sprawling Cook County Jail complex was opened at Twenty-sixth and

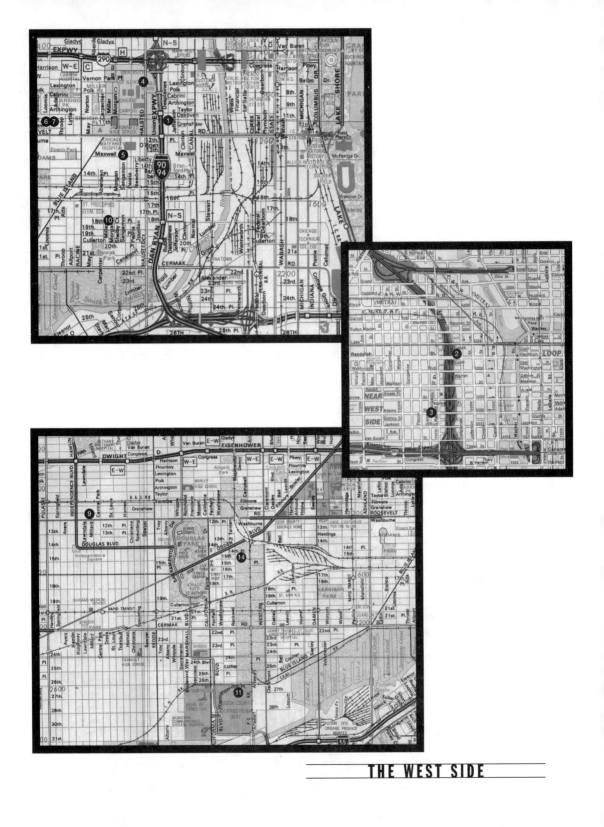

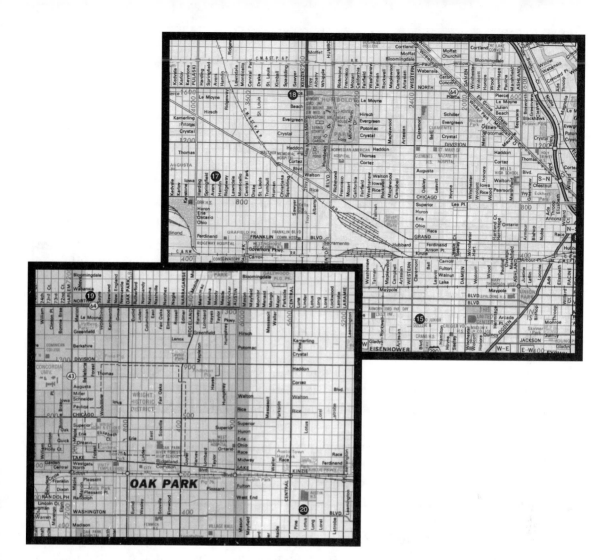

1. DeKoven and Jefferson, starting point of the Chicago Fire.
2. Haymarket Riot, DesPlaines Street between Lake and Randolph.
3. The West Side Levee, Halsted Street between Lake and Jackson Boulevard.
4. Hull House, Polk and Halsted.
5. Maxwell Street police station, Maxwell and Morgan.
6. Former site of Genna warehouse, 1022 W. Taylor.
7. Deadman's Tree, Loomis and Taylor.
8. Former location of Rosa's Snack Shop, where Richard Cain was killed, Grand and May.
9. Site of murder of Ben Lewis, Roosevelt Road and Central Park Avenue.
10. Clem Graver abducted at Eighteenth Place and Morgan Street.
11. Cook County Criminal Courts Building, Twenty-sixth and California.
12. Former site of Carter Harrison mansion, Ashland Avenue between Monroe and Harrison.
13. (Not shown on this map) Former home of Carter Harrison at Clark and Harrison.
14. Site of murder of Edward O'Hare, Ogden Avenue between Talman and Rockwell.
15. Monroe Street and Western Avenue: the Black Panther raid.
16. House of Weird Death: the Wynekoop murder, Monroe Street near Homan Avenue.
17. Lady of Angels Parish, Iowa and Avers.
18. Charles Gross murder, Kedzie and North.
19. Former Sam DeStefano residence, Sayre and Wabansia.
20. 125 Lotus, near West End; Roger Touhy slain on the front porch.

California in 1929, it created jobs for the immigrants of Pilsen through the political "clout" of one Anton Cermak, who at that time controlled the Cook County Board.

By 1920, it was estimated that two hundred thousand people lived in the Greek Delta, Taylor Street, Roosevelt Road, the Valley, Pilsen, and points west. Their lot was not a happy one, because the prairie utopia they dreamt of in the old country never came to pass in the murky depths of the ghetto. Terrorized by the Black Hand extortionists, the colony of Italians living along Taylor Street and Grand Avenue coped as best they could with the deadly menace of crime and murder. The Jews living in cold water flats and Civil War–era housing off of Roosevelt Road, Maxwell Street, and Douglas Park were menaced by other immigrant groups and subjected to ethnic and religious intolerance. To survive in such dangerous and unpredictable environments, the immigrants organized gangs for the purposes of self-protection and defense of the neighborhood.

The youthful gangs spawned on the West Side early in the century would, in more recent times, evolve into the nucleus of modern organized crime we know today. A generation of Al Capone's successors climbed the economic ladder of opportunity through intimidation, fear, and adroit maneuvering within the system. Later they followed the money and moved into the suburbs.

The gangs of the West Side are today mostly black and caught up in the entanglements of drugs, high unemployment, and zero opportunity. The West Side Vice Lords and their satellite gangs were founded at the Illinois State Training School for Boys in St. Charles in the 1950s. They are today the largest and most imposing of the criminal cartels, casting a long and dangerous shadow over the West Side.

The African-American presence on the West Side was negligible before World War I, but their numbers became appreciable by 1960; the intervening years were the years of the "Great Migration" from the Jim Crow South. Gradually, the Jews of Lawndale and Douglas abandoned their communities and the greater West Side.

A period of economic stagnancy and infrastructure decay set in—a pattern that was nearly impossible to reverse as the West Side became almost exclusively black. However, in recent years, portions of the West Side have benefited from ambitious urban renewal projects. There are hopeful signs that the economic recovery of these historic neighborhoods will continue as we enter the new millennium.

We will start our tour at the Chicago Fire Academy at 558 West DeKoven Street. DeKoven Street is just south of Taylor Street and east of Jefferson Street.

THE COW KICKED OVER THE LANTERN, OR DID SHE? THE GREAT CHICAGO FIRE
October 8–10, 1871

A long and blighting drought preceded the Great Chicago Fire of 1871, a tragedy of nature that virtually destroyed our robust midwestern metropolis from the southern edge of Twelfth Street up to Fullerton Avenue on the North Side. The dispirited fire department fought the blaze valiantly but could not check the steady advance of the flames as they swept northward from the wooden shanties and dirt streets surrounding the Conley's Patch neighborhood, where Patrick and Catherine O'Leary lived, into the warehouses and lumber mills of the industrial section. From fireplug to fireplug, Fire Marshal Robert A. Williams's poorly equipped and undermanned forces retreated, moving only when their hair was scorched and their faces blackened by the soot and cinders. At the Van Buren Street Bridge, a desperate stand was made by one fire company that turned and ran only after the engine was surrounded by flames. It is hard for us to imagine what the Chicago Fire must have really been like. So much has been written over the years, to the point where fact, fiction, and folklore have converged. There is general agreement that the conflagration had its origins inside a hay barn owned by Patrick O'Leary at 137 DeKoven Street, where Jefferson Street intersects. For many years it was accepted as fact that an ornery milk cow tipped over a kerosene lantern, igniting the blaze that was to destroy the city. The O'Learys, an Irish immigrant family struggling against long odds, were thought to be asleep inside their abode until the frightened shouts of the neighbors awakened them. After many years of debate, analysis, and reinterpretation, historians have concluded that so simple an act could not possibly precipitate so calamitous an event. The following account presents new evidence suggesting that the O'Learys were celebrating the arrival of friends and neighbors from the old country, who had come to Chicago to stake a claim on the West Side, when a carelessly discarded ash altered the course of history. The O'Leary's frame house was razed in the 1870s. A three-story stone mansion built for a family of affluent means went up on the site with a commemorative marker added by the Chicago Historical Society in 1881. Years, then decades, passed. The resi-

dential area was gradually abandoned after a second devastating fire swept through the Patch in 1874. Warehouses and industrial plants altered the appearance of the neighborhood until only the decaying 1881 residence, its chipped masonry caked with soot and grime, remained. The building survived until 1956, when the property was cleared by a three-year redevelopment plan launched by Mayor Richard J. Daley. In 1959, the $2 million Chicago Fire Academy, with a comprehensive training and recruitment center, opened at 558 West DeKoven Street (just south of Taylor Street). A sculpture of a golden flame designed by Chicagoan Egon Weiner and dedicated on September 15, 1971, faces Jefferson Street. It marks the exact location of the O'Leary barn.

In the dry, arid summer of 1871, business opportunities in the bustling lakeside metropolis of Chicago appeared limitless. Chicago was on the move, and eager real estate brokers were busy plotting new residential subdivisions well beyond the borders of downtown.

Commenting on the prospects of the coming year, a civic booster noted in September 1871, "A few years ago the curious traveler from the East, who wished to see the young giant of the West and examine its marvelous growth, approached the city over a flat plain, bare and dreary but with a few miserable farmhouses." The traveler, he continued, "went back to the East and said of Chicago, 'It is a marvelous city but I wouldn't want to live there. It has no suburbs. It is a city dropped down from the bare plain.' But all this has altered . . . the traveler is treated with a pleasant and often beautiful transition from the flat uninhabited prairie to the thickly built city."

Chicago had grown with reckless, and often unwise, abandon. New residential dwellings sprouted up overnight in the three principal geographic divisions of the city—the older, more established West Division, where the greater majority of working-class people lived; the developing South Division, with its many furniture factories, planing mills, and stockyards; and the up-and-coming North Division, populated by some of the city's wealthiest entrepreneurs, society dandies, and land barons. The three divisions sparred in civic rivalry to lure eastern investment capital.

Evidence of a speculative frenzy in land acquisition was the sale of vacant land below Twelfth Street (Roosevelt Road in later years) owned by former Mayor William B. Ogden that was valued at $150 an acre in 1858 and sold for $1,500 an acre in September 1871—just before the great firestorm roared

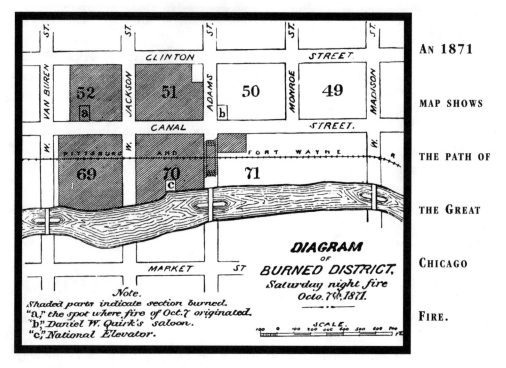

AN 1871

MAP SHOWS

THE PATH OF

THE GREAT

CHICAGO

FIRE.

through the city. The few remaining private residences downtown were gradually retreating before the advancing trade.

There was, however, an ominous flip side to these economic boom times. Chicago was a city encased in a wooden tinderbox. In the rush to build and build to meet a growing demand for cheap housing, local contractors ignored the omnipresent fire threat and constructed miles and miles of squat frame dwellings with tarpaper roofs for the working poor, separated in their misery by only a few feet.

Unusually heavy winds fanned the flames of a series of devastating late summer fires that the undermanned and dispirited Chicago Fire Department seemed almost powerless to stop. The accidental upsetting of a kerosene lamp in a hay barn belonging to former Eighth Ward Alderman James Hildreth destroyed his property on September 10, 1871. It was a portent of the evil that would descend upon Chicago less than thirty days later; an evil that was foretold by visiting lecturer George Francis Train, who issued a dire prophecy to his audience at Farwell Hall at Madison and Clark Streets the evening of October 7, 1871.

"This is the last public address," warned Train, "that will be delivered within these walls! A terrible calamity is impending over the city of Chicago! More I cannot say; more I dare not utter!" The *Chicago Times* ridiculed Train as the "Prince of the Blatherskites" until his horrifying vision of the Windy City's Armageddon came true less than twenty-four hours later.

For many decades historians and authors refused to accept at face value contemporary newspaper accounts, which traced the beginnings of the Great Chicago Fire of October 8, 1871, to a ramshackle hay barn owned by Patrick and Catherine O'Leary at 137 DeKoven Street (now 558 DeKoven Street) in the impoverished Irish quarter of the West Division. The colorful, but unproven, fable that O'Leary's agitated milk cow kicked over a kerosene lamp was given original credence by contemporary journalists filled with the anti-Irish prejudices that were very common in those times.

Survivors and their descendants offer a slightly different version of the story, however. According to Philip Michael Kane, whose father Michael was inside the O'Leary barn that fateful night, carelessly discarded ashes from a clay pipe set the hay ablaze.

"My father told us as kids that on the night of the fire the O'Learys had a party at their home," the eighty-seven-year-old Kane related in a 1961 interview. "They had about sixteen people there. The party was honoring several newcomers who were just off the boat from Ireland."

Pat McLaughlin dusted off his fiddle. The hay was pushed back to the rear of the barn to make room for the partygoers to dance. Kane continued with his

POST-OFFICE AND CUSTOM-HOUSE.   WHERE THE FIRE BEGAN

WOODCUT DRAWINGS ILLUSTRATE THE DEVASTATION OF THE CHICAGO FIRE.

long-forgotten narrative. "So there was laughing, singing and dancing the jig, along with a bit of whiskey drinking."

The reporters sent out to investigate the root causes of the fire were shocked to discover that the wretched living quarters in which the O'Leary woman sheltered her brood had miraculously survived the fire, while magnificent limestone structures like the *Chicago Tribune* building (supposedly fireproof) were vanquished within moments of coming into contact with the flames.

The *Chicago Times* was unrelenting in its scorn for Mrs. O'Leary and the squalid conditions it found along DeKoven Street.

O'Leary, only thirty-five years old at the time, was described as a "hag" and a "crone" who relied on the charity of the public rolls to scrape by. Scorned and publicly humiliated by her neighbors, Mrs. O'Leary was forced to seek refuge in a rundown section of Wallace Street, in the Town of Lake (later incorporated into Chicago). There, one of her two sons, Con "Puggy" O'Leary, murdered a woman and maimed his own sister following a long night of drinking. Another prodigal son, James O'Leary, became the gambling and crime boss of the Stockyards District when Al Capone was still in diapers. O'Leary's deluxe gambling emporium at 4183 South Halsted Street offered the finest amenities—a Turkish bath, billiards, upstairs gambling, a saloon, and outsized steaks and chops for the western drovers bringing their cattle to market.

The Chicago Fire probably did begin in the hay barn just as the contemporary newspaper reports describe. Further evidence reveals that young O'Leary and several mischievous companions were shooting dice in the hayloft when Louis Cohn overturned the kerosene lamp. The lads were busily engaged in such mischief while the old folks danced to the fiddler's tune immediately below them.

The offending cow disappeared during the fire but was later recovered by Mrs. O'Leary who, by this time, had become the neighborhood pariah. Two weeks later, the animal was sold to a German man named Schick who owned a shop at Fifteenth and Morgan Street. A cow named "Dudley," who was reputed to be the sister of Mrs. O'Leary's cow, was owned by "Paddy" Sexton of 28 Waller Street until the animal's death was dutifully reported by the Chicago press in September 1890.

Whatever the circumstances of the true origins of the fire and the final fate of the O'Leary bovine, the devastation of the wooden city was perfect and complete. The fire struck in the late evening hours of Sunday, October 8, 1871, and it burned out of control until Monday at midnight. The flames cut a swath across an area measuring four miles in length and two-thirds of a mile in width. Some 17,450 structures of wood and stone were obliterated; $190 million worth of

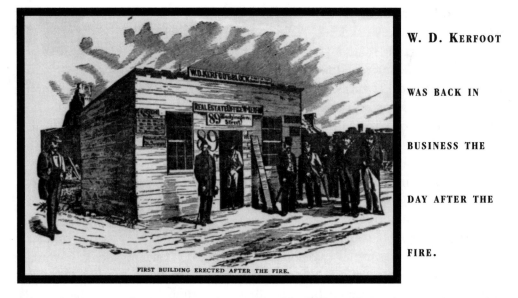

FIRST BUILDING ERECTED AFTER THE FIRE.

W. D. KERFOOT

WAS BACK IN

BUSINESS THE

DAY AFTER THE

FIRE.

property destroyed; 98,000 people rendered homeless; and at least 120 (possibly as many as 300) perished in the flames or disappeared.

The fire spared nothing, including Conley's Patch on Wells Street (Fifth Avenue), a seedbed of crime. The major north-south streets of Wells, Franklin, and lower LaSalle were dissolute vice districts plagued by soaring crime rates before the fire.

"There were low ranges of dirty buildings, dirty men slouching on the walk and slatternly women lounging out of the windows," the *Chicago Inter-Ocean* reported in June 1872 when the rebuilding progressed at breakneck speed. "Wells Street was a street fallen out of Hogarth—of as bad repute as any in the city."

When the ordeal finally ended on Tuesday the tenth, the city of promise— the beacon of light on the solitary, windswept prairie—and even its sordid dens of iniquity, whose passing would not be mourned, were transformed into a mass of charred and blackened ruins.

The indomitable "I Will" spirit of Chicago was born that night, evidenced by Realtor W. D. Kerfoot's wooden sign, which he bravely posted outside his wrecked office. "All gone but wife, children, and energy," it read, which about summed up the plight of most Chicagoans. The sign was immortalized by a photographer who roamed the fire district in search of interesting material, and was mounted above the fireplace in Kerfoot's private residence for many years to come.

Out of the seeds of gloom, tragedy, and desperation that were the Chicago Fire came a spectacular triumph; an architectural miracle—echoing the words of Daniel Burnham who, with other men of his generation, was inspired to soar with eagles on the wings of opportunity.

"Make no little plans," Burnham said, "for they have no magic to stir men's blood."

On the twentieth anniversary of the Chicago Fire, the *Chicago Tribune* rejoiced in the belief that ". . . the great fire was a blessing to Chicago stimulating her to energetic expansion that would otherwise have been impossible, calling her new blood to flow through our commercial arteries, attracting enterprising men from all parts of the earth and awakening the people of other lands to the facts of our existence."

To continue our tour, go north on Jefferson Street to Lake Street. Turn left (west) and go one block to Des Plaines Street. Turn left (south) and go one block to Randolph Street.

THE HAYMARKET SQUARE RIOT
May 4, 1886

The novelist Edna Ferber remembered Haymarket Square west of Des Plaines Street on Randolph Street as an incredible "tangle of horses, carts and men." Once a flourishing center of commerce where rural farmers came to exchange produce for cash (one of five such public squares in the central city), Haymarket Square provided the backdrop for a pivotal event in local labor history that had worldwide repercussions. Chicago has changed a great deal since 1886, but several fine examples of industrial architecture dating back to that time line the north side of Randolph Street at Halsted. The area, however, is rapidly undergoing loft conversions and other forms of urban gentrification. In the quiet of late afternoon with so many joggers out and about, it is hard to imagine how the clatter of iron-wheeled horse wagons negotiating the uneven cobblestone must have sounded. This is an old and historic area, and a powerful sense of past events reverberates in its broken sidewalks and timeworn buildings. The Twenty-second District Police Station, housing Captain Ward's detail of bluecoats, stood until 1950 on the west side of Des Plaines Street (at Waldo, now Court Place), between Washington Boulevard and Randolph Street. In its place we find a parking lot, separating the Chicago Kidney Center and the factory building housing the Catholic Charities of Chicago. It is believed that the fateful bomb that claimed the lives of seven police officers was thrown from the vestibule of the Crane Brothers Plumbing factory occupying the northeast corner at Randolph and Des Plaines. Samuel Fielden, one of the indicted "coconspirators," was perched atop a dray parked six feet north of the cobblestone alley running in back of the factory at Des Plaines Street between Lake and Randolph moments before the bomb fell. Look closely and you will see the bricked alley, but there is no plaque or marker to designate this area as a spot of historical significance. Neither the city nor organized labor can reconcile past differences or reach a consensus as to the final historical rendering of those eventful times. All that remains is the remodeled Crane's factory (now home to the EDDD Architecture firm) and the former Zepf's Hall (serving a more functional purpose these days as the Grand Stage Lighting Company) at 630 Lake Street.

The Haymarket Square bomb and its tragic aftermath had an enduring impact upon generations of young radicals and idealists, such as Joe Hill and Bill Haywood, whose activism helped shape the future destiny of the labor movement. Never would this event be forgotten. The Haymarket "Affair" directly led to the enactment of the mandatory eight-hour workday and a gradual recognition of the right of workers to organize trade unions to safeguard their interests.

An ideological, cultural, and economic rift between Yankee capital and a largely foreign-born workforce had been festering in Chicago since the end of the Civil War. The troubles down at the McCormick Reaper Works in the early spring of 1886 formed the battleground in what many members of the mercantile class believed to be the opening shot of a "red war."

A mass meeting of workers was called for Tuesday evening, May 4, 1886, to protest recent police actions against striking employees at the McCormick Reaper Works on Blue Island Avenue, who were agitating for an eight-hour workday. The Haymarket was a logical location because of its size and proximity to downtown. A crowd of 20,000 was expected to fill the square, but the night was cool and drizzly. Less than 2,500 tired and despondent spectators showed up to hear the speeches of Albert Parsons, Samuel Fielden, and August Spies.

The rally was the culmination of a weeklong protest with rising tensions out on Blue Island Avenue, then known as the "Black Road."

The incendiary nature of the pamphlets issued in support of the strikers by the Socialist Labor Party (SPL) and the International Working People's Association (IWPA, forerunner of the IWW, Industrial Workers of the World) greatly alarmed the business leaders of the city. The leaders of the movement were denigrated as "anarchists," a designation they accepted with defiant pride.

August Spies, editor of the German-language newspaper *Arbeiter Zeitung,* put out a call to arms, in the mistaken belief that six workingmen were killed by police in an armed confrontation at McCormick's on May 1. A compositor added the word *revenge* to the handbill, which provided a compelling motive for the police and state prosecutors to ponder in the next few days.

Mayor Carter Henry Harrison, a reasonable man with no ax to grind against Spies or the other IWPA leaders, issued a parade permit, believing there was no cause for alarm.

Others saw matters differently. Police Inspector John Bonfield, a failed fertilizer salesman who lost his business through bad planning and carelessness before joining the department at age forty-one, recognized that the "anarchist" scare was a way to feather his own nest. He inexplicably ordered six hundred police reserves called into duty at the West Chicago, Harrison, and Central stations in anticipation of a citywide riot occurring the night of May 4. One hundred more bluecoats were added to the Des Plaines station, less than half a block from Haymarket.

The rally was called to order at 8:30 P.M. The crowd's spirits were damp, and Albert Parsons, one of the speakers, was not even present and accounted for when Spies mounted the wagon. Mayor Harrison rode by on his mount. Satisfied that all was well, he ordered Bonfield to send the reserves home, but the inspector was hearing different reports from his detectives who had been mingling with the crowd.

At 10:20 P.M., Bonfield ordered three divisions to form up on the double quick and go in and disperse a meeting that was just about ready to end. Spanning the street, the police columns halted three paces from the wagon where Fielden was speaking. Captain William Ward commanded the meeting to disperse in the "name of the people of Illinois." Fielden replied, "We are peaceable."

Before he could say another word, a crudely manufactured dynamite pipe bomb, the kind known to be used by the radicals, was thrown from a vestibule at Randolph and Des Plaines Streets. The bomb exploded with fearful intensity in the midst of the two-hundred-man police column. Officer Mathias Degan was killed instantly. Six others were mortally wounded.

Momentarily stunned by the bomb's blast, the dazed officers regrouped and began shooting wildly into the fleeing throng. A volley of bullets tore through the front door at Zepf's Hall where Albert Parsons and Adolph Fischer sought refuge. Gunfire rang out for a full five minutes.

The broken and bleeding officers were dragged into neighboring saloons and drugstores. Those police officers that were able to maneuver under their own power hobbled back to the stationhouse.

While the mayor pleaded for calm, Bonfield and Police Inspector Michael Schaak of the North Division took it upon themselves to get to the root of this dastardly crime. The two officers initiated a reign of terror, creating a state of emergency and suspending civil rights, such as they were in 1886. Hundreds of suspects were interrogated at all hours of the day and night. False confessions were beaten out of men and women thought to be "anarchists," or sympathetic to the aims of the IWPA. The bomb thrower, however, disappeared into the fog of history.

On November 11, 1887, August Spies, Albert Parsons, George Engel, and Adolph Fischer were hanged inside the Criminal Courts Building on Hubbard Street. Their trial had been a sham and their guilt predetermined by the state long before the closing gavel on August 20, 1886. As the rope was fastened to his neck, Parsons issued a prophetic warning that would echo down through the ages, "There will come a time when our silence will be more powerful than the voices you strangle today!"

It is doubtful that any of the hanged men had any knowledge of a bomb plot, or knew who might have perpetrated such an outrage. The state's hysterical desire to avenge the slain police officers turned these rather plain and ordinary men, who might otherwise have been forgotten, into martyrs of the labor movement recognized worldwide. "The anarchists will understand that they cannot do as they please in this country," whispered Schaak moments after the "drop."

The City of Chicago erected a statue of a police officer—the first monument to law enforcement in the nation—and dedicated it in Haymarket Square on May 4, 1889. For many years thereafter, the police, and not the Haymarket men, were seen as society's true martyrs. With the rise of the big labor unions, however, that perception began to slowly erode.

Each year up until 1947, when Officer Frank Tyrrell succumbed to old age, the Haymarket Veteran's Association marched proudly down Des Plaines Street every May 4 to lay a wreath at the spot where their comrades had fallen. Tyrrell was the last surviving member of Captain Ward's column.

During the turbulent 1960s, the statue was defaced, blown up twice, repaired, and finally had to be removed to the Chicago Police Training Academy at 1300 West Jackson Boulevard by an indignant Mayor Richard J. Daley. Until recently the broken pedestal of the statue remained anchored to its original location. But when the Randolph Street Bridge over the John F. Kennedy Expressway was constructed, much of the Haymarket Square area was obliterated. The concrete base of the Haymarket statue, a crumbling eyesore, was eventually demolished.

To continue, go west to Halsted Street and turn left (south). Proceed south on Halsted Street to Van Buren Street.

THE WEST SIDE LEVEE:
"THE DARKEST CORNER OF CHICAGO"
1900–1910

At the turn of the last century, the overcrowded tenement neighborhoods west of Halsted Street were a maelstrom of vice, violent crime, prostitution, and dope addiction. Jane Addams and Ellen Gates Starr opened the Hull House mission at Polk and Halsted Street in 1889 to educate, uplift, and improve the lot of the newly arrived immigrants pouring into the district from the pogroms of Russia, the Greek islands, and the craggy mountains of Sicily. Addams was a prodding voice of humanity on the West Side, enriching the lives of unfortunates in a relaxing atmosphere of tolerance and understanding inside her settlement house. Eschewing the concerns of the community for his own treacherous self-interests, Police Inspector Edward McCann chewed the bone of the "Tenderloin," collecting monthly tribute from the resort keepers, dope peddlers, and all-night "druggists" up and down Sangamon, Green, Peoria, Curtis, Carpenter, and Morgan Streets in the heart of the West Side Levee. McCann's word was nonnegotiable in the "terror" district bounded by Madison Street on the south end and running north to Lake, east to Halsted and west to Center Street (now Racine Avenue). Industrial warehouses, loft apartments, Oprah Winfrey's Harpo Studios on Washington Boulevard, parking lots, and a smattering of ethnic restaurants in the remnants of the old Greek Delta stand on the graves of buildings where women openly solicited for sex in the doorways and the pounding of the ragtime pianos in the concert saloons ran day and night.

Grizzled in appearance, with a neck approaching that of a corn-fed young steer, Edward McCann checked into the Des Plaines Street police station as the new West Side divisional inspector on March 10, 1908, fresh from a tour of duty in the South Side Levee.

Bluntness was McCann's most striking characteristic. "I will say this—the day of the man with the pull has passed at this station. I'm not allowing poor ignorant foreigners to be robbed by grafters who say they have pull!" There was fire in his eyes and an air of conviction. He seemed to be a principled man, and for the moment the officers under his command vested their confidence in the abilities of Ed McCann.

The district was awash in vice. "That part of Chicago had little in it that merited the term civilization," commented a *Tribune* reporter. Exiled hoodlums from other parts of the city sought refuge in the West Side Levee. Vina Hall's disorderly house at 46 Sangamon Street was a place for them to drink, fornicate, and hide from the cops.

Cops and community residents objected to the open solicitation that went on from the windows of the dives, and as a compromise, owners of bordellos within the "segregated" district painted out their windows with red paint. The prostitutes, their livelihoods threatened, simply rubbed the paint off and winked at passersby through the peepholes.

Cocaine, laudanum, and over-the-counter patent medicines spiked with opium were available for purchase at Adolph Brendecke's drugstore on Randolph Street near Sangamon. Junkies from the half-world thronged the counter night and day, their emaciated faces bearing the visible horrors of untreated addiction as they passed quarters over the counter to the "druggist" for a hit. There were more drug addicts roaming the streets of Chicago in the year 1900 than at the end of the millennium.

Acting on repeated complaints from residents, McCann sent a plainclothes man into Brendecke's to investigate. Brendecke was driven out of business soon after, as the Des Plaines Street cops turned up the heat.

A string of whorehouses situated between Monroe and Lake Streets quickly fell into line. McCann informed Louis and Julius Frank, emissaries of the underworld who owned four of the district's objectionable sporting houses, that if they wanted a prayer of staying open they had better cooperate and pay their protection as McCann decreed. It was arranged that on the second day of every month a representative of each house of ill repute would hand-deliver an envelope to McCann containing $440 pinned to the name and address of the business.

Deliveries were made to the Frank brothers' saloon at Madison and Halsted Streets. Louie Frank would carry a satchel full of money over to McCann's home each month. Payoffs were based on a head count of prostitutes in each of the houses, a fixed number usually, but sometimes there were variances. When McCann found out that he wasn't being dealt with honestly, and that the number of inmates had increased and their names had not been recorded in his index file at the Des Plaines Street station, he upped the fees to $550 per month.

Morrie Shatz, who owned a place at 108 South Peoria Street, squawked to State's Attorney John Wayman, "I'm being driven into a hole by this man! I can't operate!"

Wayman initiated a grand-jury probe that resulted in twelve indictments. Waving a beefy hand at reporters, McCann denied that he took graft money. He lovingly spoke of his nine children and his devotion to his second wife and the church. "I'd say I was glad to be suspended and have a chance to stay home and play with the kids," he said, evoking measures of sympathy from the *Chicago Tribune,* which supported him along strict party lines.

Ed McCann was a Republican police officer in those partisan days when the two-party system thrived in Cook County and police promotions were brokered to loyal political hacks. It was pointed out in McCann's defense that he had returned 350 "erring" girls to their parents. He had enforced the one o'clock closing and regulated the hotels, refusing to approve permits to disreputable places. "He has done wonders," the paper concluded, pointing to a spate of lawsuits filed against him by Vina Hall, whose place was shut down by Inspector McCann as evidence of his anti-vice vigilance.

Working overtime, William Randolph Hearst's *Chicago American* excoriated McCann as a dangerous grafter who defiled virtue and encouraged immorality. The West Side Levee was as bad as ever, the *American* argued. So who was right? The opposing camps sparred in the editorial columns for weeks over his guilt or innocence.

Crossing strict party lines, Wayman built a strong and convincing case against the police inspector before Judge Albert C. Barnes, who had to contend with an incident of jury-tampering on the part of McCann's defense team.

Social workers from Hull House and a coalition of downtown business leaders rallied to his cause, but McCann was convicted on September 24, 1909. After fighting his conviction for nearly a year and a half, McCann was thrown into the Joliet penitentiary. He was known as convict number 1,070 and assigned to the yard-raking detail.

From New York, former President Theodore Roosevelt wrote Governor Edward Dunne, pleading with him to pardon McCann, in the belief that crooks sometimes invent a trumped-up charge in order to discredit a good man's reputation. Of course, McCann's pension eligibility was scheduled to expire in thirty days, which may have had something to do with Colonel Roosevelt's pleadings on behalf of a man he had never laid eyes on.

The letter was read aloud to the pardon board and acted upon. McCann's release was only a formality at that point, given the political currents. McCann strolled past the prison gates a sadder but wiser pensioner.

Bouquets of American Beauty roses lined the parlor of his home. One hundred well-wishers filled the front yard. But after hugging the kids and kissing his wife, McCann retreated to the back porch where the cribbage game was waiting. Eddie McCann was a champion cribbage player. He had learned the game in his old hometown of Lincoln, Illinois, and the police chief of Lincoln was waiting on the porch with a sly grin on his face.

Continue south on Halsted Street to Polk Street.

FROM THE FILES OF THE SUPERNATURAL: THE GHOST AT HULL HOUSE

Charles J. Hull built his residence at Halsted and Polk Streets in 1856 in what was then one of the finest residential sections of the city. After the Chicago Fire of 1871, the "better classes" moved to other sections of the city, and the Near West Side became the magnet for the large immigrant Italian, Greek, and Jewish population that arrived daily as a result of political upheaval in Europe.

Jane Addams and Ellen Gates Starr took control of the property in September 1889 and opened their world-renowned settlement house in the former Hull mansion at 800 South Halsted Street. Addams was granted a twenty-five-year, rent-free lease by Hull's confidential secretary, Helen Culver, and the heirs to the family fortune, who were enthusiastic about her ambitious undertaking on behalf of the poor and unfortunate. Only a few years earlier, Mrs. Hull had died of natural causes in her second-floor bedroom. Following her husband's death in 1889, the home was shuttered.

Within months, strange and unearthly noises, believed to be the restless spirit of the late Mrs. Hull, began disturbing the slumber of overnight guests. Mrs. Hull's bedroom was first occupied by Jane Addams, who was awakened one night by the sound of footsteps. After a few nights, Addams confided her story to Ellen Gates Starr, who heard the same unmistakable steps when she decided to investigate the phenomenon and spend a night in the bedroom.

Helen Campbell, author of *Prisoners of Poverty,* reported seeing a "white figure" standing next to the bed after spending a night in the haunted room at the invitation of Addams. When Campbell lit a gas jet, the apparition disappeared as quickly as it had come.

The same peculiar sounds were heard by Canon Barnett of London's Toynbee Hall, who was a visitor to the 1893 World's Fair, and Florence Kelley, a state factory inspector.

The ghost of Hull House was a benign ghost, however, and the residents and mansion guests became accustomed to its nocturnal wanderings. Of course, there are more sinister legends surrounding the Hull House settlement, including the widely circulated urban folktale about a devil-child born to an immigrant woman who had defied her family and neighbors by marrying outside her nationality. The apocryphal story, grounded in ancient tribal prejudices, was a means of keeping young women bound to a caste system cloaked in ignorance and superstition.

Continue south on Halsted Street and turn right (west) on Maxwell Street. Go west on Maxwell Street to Morgan Street.

BLOODY MAXWELL
1889–1997

Urban renewal nearly destroyed another important chunk of local crime history. The historic Maxwell Street police station at 943 West Maxwell Street (Maxwell and Morgan) serving Taylor Street, the Greek Delta, and the old Jewish West Side, closed its doors in December 1997. The intelligence unit, the department of licensing, and the gang crimes, gambling, organized crime, prostitution, and narcotics divisions were transferred to the former Sears Roebuck headquarters at Homan and Arthington on the West Side. The battered red-brick and limestone relic on Maxwell Street is best known to a generation of television watchers as the fictional Hill Street Blues *precinct. The opening credits of the long-running dramatic series were filmed here. The Maxwell Station, a dark and gloomy fortress masking terrible secrets and ghastly legends, stands rather forlornly amid empty weed lots and tennis courts belonging to the University of Illinois. Once there was a thriving community, with rows and rows of tenement housing, surrounding the police station, but now there are only parking lots. The Near West Side Greeks, Jews, Italians, and late-arriving Mexicans, who forged strong community identities against the hardships of poverty and want, were forced to make way for the University of Illinois Chicago Circle campus in the late 1950s. Now the UICC campus police have claimed this last vestige of the past as their new headquarters building.*

The history of the Maxwell Street station mirrors the steady growth of Chicago and the evolution of its tough ethnic West Side neighborhoods, and it unfortunately recalls a brutally violent era of policing.

George Hubbard was the superintendent of police when the old Second Precinct station—then located at Twelfth Street (Roosevelt Road) and Johnson Street (now called Peoria Street) in the heart of the "Terror District"—was abandoned in 1889. The district shifted to the larger, more modern facility at 943 Maxwell, which cost the city $50,000 to build. Captain William Ward, who commanded the column of police officers who were blown to bits by the Haymarket bomb on May 4, 1886, was placed in charge of Maxwell during the first year.

As a consequence of Haymarket and the growing paranoia of an impending "red" revolution about to erupt at any moment, the Chicago Police Department strengthened its manpower resources from 1,145 uniformed officers to 1,624— an increase of more than 40 percent. Two new stations, including the one on Maxwell Street, were opened to counter worker unrest and buffer the densely populated immigrant enclaves encircling the central business district from the south and west. Following the 1890 reorganization, which divided the city into five proximate geographic divisions with an inspector in each responsible for local crime conditions, Maxwell Street was designated as the Sixteenth Precinct of the Second District, Third Division, then later as the Twenty-first Precinct.

Thousands of poor Russian Jews, Italians, Slovaks, Greeks, Poles, and other refugees from Eastern Europe poured into the crowded chaotic neighborhoods hugging Roosevelt Road, Taylor Street, and Halsted during the peak years of the great immigration from 1880 to 1920. During the Black Hand dominance of the neighborhood, around 1905, the district became known as "Bloody Maxwell" because of the escalating murder rate, the terrorists who preyed on immigrant Italians, and the white-knuckle fear that the immigrants had of being arrested on a pretense and thrown into the rat-infested basement dungeon of the station with its inch-deep troughs in the stone floor that served as the jail urinal.

The term "Bloody" was loosely applied to many Chicago police districts in the old days, but on the West Side it took on a special significance. "Murderers, robbers, and thieves of the worst kind are here, born, reared and grown to maturity in numbers that far exceed the record of any similar district anywhere on the face of the globe," the *Tribune* editorialized on February 11, 1906. "But most of all it is the wickedest district to be found within the confines of civilization!"

A policeman's job was no sinecure, especially at night when the tavern lights flickered on and the toughs made their first appearance on the stoops of the tenements.

Taylor Street, located in the heart of the old Nineteenth Ward, was the production and distribution center for bootleg alcohol in the city of Chicago. Bootlegging was a vast criminal enterprise controlled by the "Terrible" Genna brothers who made their payoffs to police every Friday from their warehouse at 1022 West Taylor Street.

Captain William Russell, who was promoted to superintendent in 1928 (just in time for the St. Valentine's Day Massacre), commanded Bloody Maxwell when the first of many bribery scandals broke and two hundred men were hastily transferred to less problematic districts.

Prisoners lacking the resources to buy their way out of the "hole" were often savagely beaten; their blood flowed freely into the sewer connected to the urinal trough. In 1921, Health Commissioner Herman Bundesen declared the place unfit for human habitation and the Maxwell Street dungeon the worst in the city.

The occasional fresh coat of paint and obligatory cleanup, which usually accompanied the arrival of a new captain or watch commander eager to make a name for himself, did little to erase the fearsome reputation of the place. When it finally closed its doors in December 1997, the 110-year-old station was the oldest in the city.

Return to

Halsted Street

and go north to

Taylor Street.

Turn left (west)

and go to Racine

Avenue.

A TERRIBLE BREW: INSIDE THE GENNA WAREHOUSE
1919–1926

The Genna brothers' liquor depot was located at 1022 West Taylor Street in the heart of the Italian quarter, just north of the Maxwell Street police station. An empty lot marks the spot today.

On the eve of Prohibition, the six "Terrible" Genna brothers (Angelo, Pete, Tony, Jim, Sam, and Mike) were granted a special dispensation by the government to sell industrial alcohol from inside their Taylor Street depot.

Relying on a formula invented by their brother-in-law Harry Spignola, the Gennas paid neighborhood residents $15 a week to cook up a home brew of deadly toxins and rotgut, colored with caramel or coal tar. The formula killed inquis-itive rats that invaded the filthy casks stored inside the Taylor Street ware-house, where the cops collected their weekly envelopes. Mike Genna, the Taylor Street political fixer, paid $500 a month to lieutenants and captains from neighboring districts, with weekly payments due every Friday. The cop on the beat was not forgotten either. Payouts ranged from $15 to $125 a month.

The Gennas sold their deadly swill for three dollars a barrel, which was half the going rate charged by Dion O'Banion, who hated these Sicilian "alky" cookers from Marsala. Maintaining an uneasy neutrality with Al Capone and a Mexican standoff with O'Banionites, the Genna gang grossed $300,000 a month. When they began selling the potent blend to North Side barkeeps, a shooting war erupted, and the Genna gang was laid to waste within a few short years.

With assembly-line precision, the Gennas and their allies perished before the blazing guns of rival gangs—first Angelo, then Mike, Tony, and Harry Spignola in rapid succession. Mike Genna, the toughest of the bunch, kicked an ambulance attendant in the face moments before leaving the world and all of its attending miseries behind. His last words before dying: "Take that you bastard!"

The Genna liquor depot closed in 1926. The surviving brothers fled Chicago, thankful to be alive.

Continue west on Taylor Street to Loomis Street. Turn left (south) and go half a block.

DEAD MAN'S TREE
1905–1921

At Loomis Street, half a block south of Taylor in Little Italy, notes with the names of the men marked for death by the Black Hand were tacked to a poplar tree to scare and intimidate fearful Italians into compliance. If there was a tree, and many historians believe that it is an urban folk-tale spun from the fertile imagination of local crime fiction writers, in all likelihood it sprouted here, where violence in the two Italian quarters on the North and West Sides was a daily occurrence.

Between January 6, 1910, and March 16, 1911, fourteen immigrant Italians were beaten, slashed, or shot by death merchants belonging to the Black Hand, the secret society of extortionists and killers that crept into Chicago during the 1890s.

The Black Hand foreshadowed the rise of the modern crime syndicate in the 1920s. Most of the victims lived up on the North Side in "Little Hell," near the intersection of Milton Street (now Cleveland Street) and Oak Street. The street corner came to be known as "Death Corner." (See Tour 2.)

Violence was not confined to the North Side, however. The Black Hand was active along Taylor Street as well.

Ten unsolved murders in fourteen months stymied the police. They received little help from the neighborhood residents, who remained close-mouthed about their troubles.

The killings in the Taylor Street neighborhood were confined to a residential area lying east of Halsted Street near Polk Street and Jefferson Street. A decade later, during the Johnny Powers–Tony D'Andrea feud of 1919–1921, the poplar tree at Loomis and Taylor would be put to use as a bulletin board announcing the name of the next intended victim. Johnny Powers was the Irish alderman who had controlled the Nineteeth Ward since 1888. His political base slowly eroded with the arrival of the Italians who demanded greater access to the political process through D'Andrea, a defrocked priest with Mafia connections. Thirty men died during the protracted war, including D'Andrea, who had become a pimp and counterfeiter and later sought respectability through elective office.

In 1911, a Black Hand death threat was sent to Federal Judge Kenesaw Mountain Landis, from the Kinzie Street Post Office. Landis was warned of the consequences of convicting extortionist Gianni Alongi, but the white-haired jurist was unperturbed. "Oh I guess I won't be bothered," chuckled Landis, who twirled his shillelagh with unconcern. "Letters of this sort make me tired. Don't worry about me."

Judge Landis convicted Alongi. He was also the judge who banned from baseball the eight White Sox players who threw the 1919 World Series. Landis managed to offend many more evildoers in his time without recrimination. He died of natural causes in 1945.

Return to Taylor Street and take Taylor Street west to Ashland Avenue. Turn right (north) on Ashland Avenue and go north to Grand Avenue. Turn right (east) on Grand Avenue and proceed to 1117 West Grand Avenue.

THE MARK OF CAIN
December 20, 1973

Gentrification has overtaken the near West Side, the area where generations of immigrant Italians and their children struggled for survival early in the twentieth century. Abandoned warehouses have been converted into condominiums, film studios, ad agencies, and music houses. Thirty-something yuppies, who poured in during the 1990s, christened this area the East Village and jacked property values sky high. It is a quiet, cerebral neighborhood, but it wasn't always that way. The wiseguys and the good-hearted paisanos who ruled this turf in the raucous days of old would probably laugh or cringe, or maybe both, if they could see Grand Avenue now. At 1117 West Grand, a pleasing little bakery with a maroon awning tempts the neighborhood yuppies and dog walkers. Patrons are probably unaware that in its former life, the Anna Ida & Me Gourmet Bakery was once Rose's Snack Shop, where the shadowy Dick Cain, a man of enduring mystery, was assassinated one cold winter morning.

Al Capone used to say that newspaper guys and the cops blamed every bad thing on him, including the Chicago Fire. Dick Cain was no Al Capone. But many retired police officers and investigative journalists have suggested that this short, stocky little man wearing horn-rimmed glasses was a "black ops" specialist who had something to do with the ill-fated Bay of Pigs operation and the assassination of President John F. Kennedy. Cain did indeed train Cuban pilots at the Glenview Naval Air Station here in Illinois, and anti-Castro insurgents in Miami. The rumors regarding his role in the Kennedy assassination are less precise, though there is a strong suspicion that his ties to the Mafia were used during the planning and execution of the crime.

The Dick Cain mystique grows year after year. Enigmas and riddles. Myths built upon rumor.

Richard Cain (the son of John and Lydia Scalzetti) was a powerful figure in the Cook County Sheriff's Police Department from 1962 to 1964. Before that, he was a vice detective in Chicago who was in constant trouble with his superiors. Many believe he was a mob plant controlled by First Ward Alderman John D'Arco, a friend to the syndicate.

In 1959, Cain murdered a street bookie named Harry Figel. The charges were dropped, but Figel's many friends pressured the city to do something, which of course turned out to be nothing.

A year later, Dick Cain's partnership with Gerry Shallow was dissolved after a janitor caught the pair eavesdropping on Irwin Cohen, Mayor Daley's $22,500-a-year Commissioner of Investigations. The pair had been hired by the State's Attorney's office to get the goods on Cohen, whom they believed was white-washing assorted acts of malfeasance by Mayor Richard J. Daley's department heads and payrollers down at City Hall.

Dick Cain may have looked like an out-of-shape accountant, but he was tough-minded and unafraid, scheming and manipulative.

Richard B. Ogilvie, a spotlessly clean reformer, was elected Cook County sheriff in 1962. Against the advice of top-ranking Republicans, Ogilvie hired Dick Cain as chief investigator and turned a blind eye when Cain traipsed across the vast reaches of suburbia protecting syndicate dice games, shaking down abortionists, and looking after strip joints and outfit hoods who were being inconvenienced by his men.

Cain was finally dumped from his $10,000-a-year job by Ogilvie on December 9, 1964, after his role in the $250,000 robbery of a Louis Zahn Drug Company warehouse was exposed. Dick Cain avoided jail time and turned to Sam Giancana for a job when his application to the Illinois Legislative Investigating Commission was ignored. (Rumors persist that Cain was Giancana's natural father.) Thereafter, until 1967 when he was indicted with twenty-three other mobsters and sentenced to jail for the robbery of a Franklin Park, Illinois, Savings and Loan, Cain traveled with the snarling Chicago crime boss through Mexico, the Caribbean, and South America as his chauffeur and flunky.

These embarrassments nearly cost Richard Ogilvie the 1968 Illinois gubernatorial election and tarnished his otherwise exemplary career in public service. Years later rumors surfaced that Ogilvie was approached by the mob offering assistance during his 1962 election bid for Cook County Sheriff. Cain had a nimble mind, and he harvested people's darkest secrets and used them to his own advantage.

The scales of justice were tilted against Cain, but he benefited from positive press coverage from one of the most influential and well-regarded journalists of the day. Former *Chicago American* columnist Jack Mabley stands by his friend to this very day.

Days after his 1964 conviction, Cain penned a short note to Mabley. Cheerful but resigned, he summed up his views on life. "I think I've at last found the answer to Lenin's famous question: 'What can we do?' We should do the best we can. Thanks friend, Dick."

Emerging from prison in 1971, Dick Cain, desperate to break out of his downward spiral, was rebuffed by Giancana when he came looking for a job.

Time had about run out for this tenacious former investigator, who was fluent in five languages and possessed a near-genius 145 IQ. But he had gone about as far as anyone could through clever manipulation of the system of justice and sheer guile. He was seated in Rosa's Snack Shop conferring with four other men when two gunmen, wearing ski masks and carrying a shotgun and pistol, entered and lined the seven patrons against the wall. The four men Cain was talking to moments earlier hustled out the door, fueling speculation that Cain was set up.

Receiving an "all clear" high sign from outside, the shooters pumped two blasts into Cain's head at point-blank range before disappearing out the door and down Grand Avenue.

The first break in the case came nearly a decade later when a witness close to the mob bosses accused Joey "the Clown" Lombardo and Vincent "the Saint" Inserro of complicity. However, like other sordid aspects of Cain's life, this one was also based on rumor and supposition.

Return to Ashland Avenue. Take Ashland Avenue south to Roosevelt Road. Turn right (west) and proceed to Central Park.

BALLOTS TO BULLETS: THE BEN LEWIS MURDER MYSTERY
February 28, 1963

The Community State Bank, or what remains of its classic white-stone façade, Roman columns, and crumbling interior, is a boarded-up relic in a troubled neighborhood. It is situated on the northwest corner of Roosevelt Road and Central Park in the Douglas Park neighborhood, three miles west and a world away from downtown Chicago. Hours before his death, Alderman Benjamin F. Lewis celebrated his stunning election victory by opening the Twenty-fourth Ward headquarters on the second floor of this once stately building that now shelters the homeless and displaced from the elements.

His story plays like a Greek drama. A poor boy from the Jim Crow South rises to spectacular heights, only to be cut down in the prime of life.

Benjamin Lewis fought his way out of poverty. When he took his seat on the Chicago City Council in April 1958, an inquiring reporter couldn't help but notice the poor cut of his clothes. "I just keep this one because it was the first suit I ever paid more than $100 for," he chuckled. "Now I pay $200 all the time."

Lewis was born in Georgia, but his parents moved to Chicago's West Side when he was just a boy. Following service in World War II, he went to work for the Chicago Transit Authority as a bus driver. It wasn't much of a job, but it was a pathway of opportunity for young African-American men overcoming the grind of poverty and northern racism.

Ben Lewis was one of the first African-Americans to cross over into Douglas Park, a tough Jewish neighborhood controlled by Democratic county chairman Artie X. Elrod, national committeeman Jacob Arvey, and Lenny Patrick, the outfit's point man and Arvey's political "muscle" along Roosevelt Road.

The ward delivered tremendous pluralities for the Democrats at election time. Douglas Park was a syndicate bastion, and Lewis understood that for an ambitious black politician to make his bones in the Twenty-fourth Ward, it was necessary to form "alliances."

For the moment Lewis courted the favor of Mayor Richard J. Daley and Lenny Patrick—an unlikely pair, but one controlled patronage and appointments, the other, illegal gambling and shakedowns.

In 1961, Daley nominated Lewis to be his next ward committeeman after adding up the numbers and concluding that Jewish Douglas Park was a thing of the past. Emboldened by his growing political strength, Lewis replaced thirty-seven white committeemen with African-Americans. Adding insult to injury, Lewis peddled insurance policies to Elrod's established customers along Roosevelt Road.

Lewis was also an outspoken supporter of political maverick Leon Despres, at the expense of Congressman William Levi Dawson and other old-time African-American political leaders, whom he referred to as "Uncle Toms" and dupes of the Daley "plantation" machine.

The alderman's streak of independence disturbed and angered his former sponsors, who felt a sudden, overwhelming sense of betrayal.

When Lewis handily disposed of a political novice in the 1963 city election, thus earning a stunning mandate from the Twenty-fourth Ward voters, the syndicate sprang into action.

The final vote count was not yet in when the cops found him lying facedown under the desk in his second-floor office. Lewis had been dead for two hours by the time Coroner Andrew J. Toman signed the certificate ordering removal of the body to the morgue.

Near the body were four spent .32-caliber cartridges. A cigarette had burned down to his ring finger, and Lewis's hands were manacled with a pair of handcuffs manufactured in New York, which led to speculation that the outfit brought in someone special for this particular job.

Stating the obvious, Republican Alderman John Hoellen blamed the mob. "This murder proves once again that the syndicate is still very much alive in Chicago." Police Superintendent O. W. Wilson called the Lewis slaying "a dastardly crime." Mayor Daley praised Lewis as a "good alderman," believing otherwise.

The killers of Ben Lewis, of course, were never found.

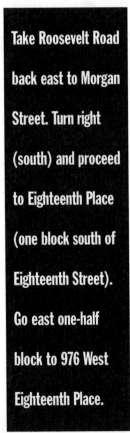

Take Roosevelt Road back east to Morgan Street. Turn right (south) and proceed to Eighteenth Place (one block south of Eighteenth Street). Go east one-half block to 976 West Eighteenth Place.

VANISHED: THE CLEM GRAVER SNATCH
June 11, 1953

In the heart of the Pilsen neighborhood on the city's teeming West Side, a row of sagging one- and two-story workers' cottages dating back to the last century line Eighteenth Place. The only residence in this Mexican-American enclave that has failed to survive the onslaught of time and changing city demographics is the property at 976 West Eighteenth Place. There is a conspicuous hole in the ground where the home of Celinus "Clem" Graver once stood. A half a block west, where Morgan Street intersects Eighteenth Place, a new garage has been erected at the 1824 address, where Graver was "snatched" in June 1953, when this story unfolds. It is rather curious that this particular garage among the many dilapidated garages still standing on Morgan was the only one to be demolished and rebuilt. But it seems to follow that where infamous acts occur, the land becomes tainted. In 1953, Graver's Pilsen was undergoing a subtle demographic shift. The Bohemians

and Czechs who settled Pilsen a half century earlier were slowly being uproot-
ed by a post-war immigration from Mexico. Graver was still the boss, but his
ethnic power base was being chipped away. Today Eighteenth Street is the
"Main Street" of the Mexican "barrio," a colorful collage of storefronts, artists'
lofts, churches, and some of the oldest housing stock in the city—a place where
the past meets the present in startling, unexpected ways.

The cops searched high and low for Clem Graver. They searched the back
alleys of the Pilsen, Lawndale, Fillmore, Deering, Des Plaines, and Central police
districts, the districts that comprise the "River Wards" of the greater West Side. It
was a frustrating and, at times, maddening hunt for a man who had simply vanished into thin air.

For years these neighborhoods were a battleground of organized crime,
the home base of the notoriously corrupt "West Side Bloc" of state legislators,
bagmen, and ward healers at the beck and call of the Chicago crime syndicate.
The city politicians were Democrats. Most of the state representatives were
Republicans. Chicago politics and crime sometimes cut both ways, and partisan alliances are largely meaningless. It's results that count.

Clem Graver was a wheeler-dealer who rose from the ranks of
Republican precinct captain, hustling votes for his political sponsors in the
Twenty-first Ward, to state representative. In 1950, the voters of the Fifteenth
District sent him to Springfield where he was expected to expand the influ-
ence of the "Bloc" and bring home sorely needed jobs to his Bohemian
constituency.

In May 1952, he was fired as a sewer and cement contractor for the
Sanitary District for nonperformance. Today the press would call such a man a
"ghost payroller." But in 1952, reporters merely wondered how it was possible
for an inspector to show up at a work site sporting a cashmere overcoat, a
tailor-made suit, and a gray fedora. It was enough evidence to spark an investigation.

Clem Graver's connections to Harry Hochstein, a former city sealer and an
ex-chauffeur for Frank "The Enforcer" Nitti, were a matter of public record.
Hochstein, who was indicted for perjury in a motion picture shakedown scheme
years earlier, was Graver's brother-in-law.

Despite underworld connections and a spotty career in public service,
Graver was generally well thought of by both county politicians and the people of the neighborhood. He was proclaimed top precinct captain of the state

after the judicial elections of 1951 when he brought in 369 Republican votes compared to only 4 for the Democrats. No one could possibly have suspected at the time that Graver was in trouble with the Chicago "outfit" or its satellite gangs.

After a long day down at the state capitol and a hearty nightcap with "the boys" at Pilsen ward headquarters the night of June 11, 1953, Graver returned home in good spirits. He pulled his car into a rented garage at 1824 West Morgan Street, down the street from his modest two-story frame house at 976 Eighteenth Place. Before he could close the door, two men leapt out of a stolen black 1950 Ford sedan bearing license plate number 919-566. The kidnappers were dressed in suits.

Before Graver had time to react, the men grabbed the state representative and pinioned him from behind, while his wife, Amelia, and a Republican political hack named Walter Pikelis stood transfixed on the front door stoop of the Graver home across the street less than three hundred feet away.

Graver was shoved into the back seat of the car. The unknown abductors sped south down Morgan.

That was the last anyone ever saw of State Representative and all-around good fellow Clem Graver.

Two hundred cops, directed by Captain William Balswick of the Scotland Yard detail, rousted the usual suspects from their known haunts in the "Bloody Twentieth Ward," and the "Valley," where crimes of this nature were daily occurrences. The FBI was put on alert, and they waited and waited for a ransom note that would never come. The family soon lost hope.

In 1958, a thirty-five-year-old jailbird named Raymond Williams was questioned at the federal penitentiary in Terre Haute, Indiana. Williams confessed that Graver had performed various political "favors" for the West Side Frank Vito mob over the years, but there was little else to go on.

The Graver case officially remained open until 1958, when the special detective detail assigned to follow up on leads was disbanded.

Clem Graver was not the first Chicago politician to be cashiered by the mob, nor would he be the last. In fact, his was the second politically motivated murder to occur in less than eighteen months, following close on the heels of the Charles Gross slaying in 1952. What was the true motive? To this day, no one can say for sure.

Continue south on Morgan to Twenty-second Street (Cermak Road). Turn right (west) and continue to California Avenue. Turn left (south) on California Avenue and proceed to Twenty-sixth Street.

26TH AND CAL: THE CRIMINAL COURTS BUILDING

1929–Present

The sprawling courthouse and jail complex at Twenty-sixth Street and California Avenue (west of the Pilsen neighborhood) stands as a shrine to pork-barrel politics and the vision of one man, Anton J. Cermak, principal architect of Chicago's invincible Democratic Machine in the 1930s. Designed by Hall, Lawrence & Ratcliffe, the original Criminal Courts Building adjoining the existing Bridewell House of Correction opened in the Spring of 1929, providing employment to vast numbers of West Side Czechs and Bohemians, all loyal political supporters, who helped elevate Cermak to the presidency of the Cook County Board, then mayor of Chicago three years later. Today the Department of Corrections facilities are inadequate, outmoded, and strained beyond their capacity. For years, the jail was plagued by escapes, rioting, the terror of the "barn bosses," and a legal boondoggle that dragged on in the federal courts for nearly a decade. Inmates slept communally on mattresses spread across the floors of the prison tiers. Sanitary conditions were so bad that inmates reportedly plugged their ears with tissue paper to keep the cockroaches out. Judge Milton I. Shadur eventually approved a consent decree calling for an immediate solution to the mess. The overcrowding crisis has eased up in the last few years with the addition of a new Division XI facility. Innovative boot-camp rehabilitation and home monitoring programs introduced in the 1990s by Cook County Sheriff Michael Sheahan have curbed sporadic outbreaks of violence.

Returning from a whirlwind European tour in the summer of 1928, Anton Cermak promised the residents of Cook County a new courthouse and jail that was comfortable, spacious, and sophisticated in its forward-thinking design concepts. Cermak, who was accompanied by Judge Hugo Pam, personally inspected correctional institutions across the continent.

While newspaper editorialists sympathetic to the Republican agenda criticized the West Side complex as inefficient, costly, and an example of careless tax-and-spend strategies to bolster the aims of the Democratic Party in its most partisan bailiwick, Cermak remained calmly composed.

"The meal service in the new building is comparable to the best hotels," Cermak informed his critics. "The sleeping quarters for jurors are adequate. As for courtrooms they are unexcelled. This jail combines the best features of the most modern institutions of America and Europe."

It didn't remain that way for long. By the 1950s, the jail compound was nasty, brutish, and out of control. For more than forty-five years, the barbed-wire compound has been a festering sore on the West Side.

Major issues confronting the Department of Corrections date back to 1954, when Twenty-sixth and California experienced its first major insurrection—a seven-hour riot that was effectively quelled by Jack R. Johnson of the Cook County Sheriff's Police. A year later Johnson was appointed warden by Sheriff Joseph Lohman. At age thirty-eight, he was the youngest man to head the institution up to that point.

Johnson banned correctional officers from wielding blackjacks and brass knuckles, and installed television sets for inmates. By 1967, Johnson was under fire from civil libertarians who charged him with abuse of prisoners and showing favoritism to incarcerated, but politically connected, syndicate hoodlums. Following the release of a critical grand jury report, Republican Sheriff Joseph Woods replaced Johnson with Winston Moore, the first African-American to serve in this sensitive position. With an eye on easing escalating racial tensions, Moore set out to cure the abuses of the "barn boss" system—where the toughest and most resourceful prisoner exercised supervisory control over the entire inmate population.

It was said that convicted murderer Paul Crump ruled 26th and Cal during the 1950s. Crump was a moral contradiction. Convicted of killing Theodore Zukowski, a guard at the Libby McNeill stockyards plant during a $20,000 payroll robbery on March 20, 1953, Crump passed the time of day studying Socrates, Nietzsche, and the Bible under the guiding hand of Warden Johnson. He was scheduled to die on fourteen separate occasions, but each time he was spared at the eleventh hour. In 1962, following publication of his novel *Burn, Killer, Burn,* and just thirty-six hours before he was to be escorted to the electric chair, his sentence was commuted to 199 years without parole. In spite of his sentence, however, Crump received parole in February 1993, after serving forty years in prison. Only William Heirens has served a longer stretch. (For details of the Heirens case, see Tour 3.)

Later, the "barn boss" at Twenty-sixth Street was said to be Jeff Fort, founder, organizer, and undisputed ruler of the Blackstone Rangers–El Rukn street gang.

Director Moore ended the rule of the "barn bosses" during his first three years in office. After a highly publicized tiff with the John Howard Association and the Chicago Crime Commission following a mass escape of seventeen inmates on May 14, 1975, Moore's troubles mounted. A criminal indictment was issued against him for the alleged beating of an inmate in the security room. Acquitted of these charges, Moore was replaced by Cook County Sheriff Richard Elrod in 1977. Elrod, a loyal cog in the West Side Democratic organization, was assailed by Republican challengers as an out-of-touch, windbag politician who didn't have a clue what was going on inside his jail, but he racked up impressive vote totals in every election, serving a record sixteen years in office.

Despite periodic escapes, relative calm descended over the institution until August 1992, when Director J. W. Fairman ordered a six-day lockdown following the escape of suburban drug kingpin "Fast" Eddie Kurap from Division V. The inmates responded violently to the edict and assaulted the guards with mops, buckets, and wringers until order was restored.

The Cook County Jail was originally built to house 1,302 inmates for temporary detention. During Sheriff Joseph Lohman's administration in the mid-1950s, the seasonal population fluctuated on average between 1,600 and 2,400. At that time, it was the third largest penal institution in the country.

By 1996, the Cook County Department of Corrections housed 9,285 inmates. Cynics contend that it is beyond the power of mere mortal politicians to correct overcrowding and the myriad of security problems at 26th and Cal. Outbreaks of violence are inevitable, and only a matter of time.

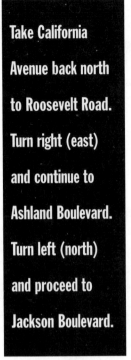

Take California

Avenue back north

to Roosevelt Road.

Turn right (east)

and continue to

Ashland Boulevard.

Turn left (north)

and proceed to

Jackson Boulevard.

A CITY IN MOURNING FOR ITS MAYOR
October 28, 1893

In years past, a stretch of Ashland Boulevard (formerly Reuben Street) between Monroe Street and Harrison Street was the city's finest and most expensive residential district. Carter Henry Harrison took up permanent residence in this West Side neighborhood in 1866. In the immediate vicinity of the future Mayor's mansion at 231 South Ashland (after the 1909 renumbering, the address was changed to 314 South Ashland), there resided numerous families, who, like the Harrisons, were well-to-do former Kentuckians figuring prominently in the city's business, social, and civic affairs during the Gilded Age. Real estate speculator Samuel J. Walker had developed Ashland Boulevard and widened the street in 1864 for the comfort and ease of the wealthy commercial men and their wives, who sought a quiet retreat, shade trees, spacious lots, and stately homes on the isolated prairie. It is anything but that today. The Rush-Presbyterian St. Luke's Medical Center, on land once owned by the Harrison family, obliterated the last gentle reminders of refined Chicago living. The Carter Harrison home, touched by the unexpected tragedy that stunned Chicago the evening of October 28, 1893, is also gone. Months after the fatal shooting of Mayor Harrison, his two sons, Preston and Carter Harrison II, along with the younger Carter's wife, their children, and the servants, closed Ashland Avenue and moved to Schiller and Astor Streets on the Gold Coast. The 1858 mansion, which stood for all those years on the southwest corner of Ashland and Jackson Boulevard, is now park lawn fronting "Teamster City," the regional headquarters of the International Brotherhood of Teamsters (IBT).

Leaning forward to a group of city officials who had come to hear Mayor Carter Harrison address an admiring throng of well-wishers at Jackson Park's Music Hall on the last day of the World's Columbian Exposition, Nineteenth Ward Alderman Johnny "de Pow" Powers said, "The old man is at his best this morning!" First Ward Alderman John "Bathhouse" Coughlin smiled proudly, as he watched

Harrison spellbind his listeners with a dash of his famous homespun southern wisdom and occasional balderdash. "See how straight the old man holds himself up?"

The mayor was a friend to the liberal thinkers. He was revered by the saloon trade, Mike McDonald's gang of downtown cardsharps and river pirates, red-light steerers, the fallen women they represented, and the lost souls of the Levee flophouses, all of whose interests were protected in the City Council by the "Bath" and his spry little henchman Michael "Hinky Dink" Kenna.

Wearing his famous slouch hat, a new necktie, and a heavy overcoat to shield him from the brisk autumn wind, Harrison spoke of the coming glories of Chicago as it approached the dawn of the twentieth century. The World's Fair had been a grand triumph for Chicago, a tour de force of commerce, culture, and midwestern social graces that Harrison had put on parade before the watchful eyes of the world. Chicago passed the test and now looked forward to the future with a renewed sense of purpose.

"I intend to live for a half century yet! I myself have taken a new lease on life. I shall live to see the day when even London shall be looking to its [Chicago's] laurels," beamed the exultant Harrison, his hands thrust in his pockets and his shoulders thrown well back.

In a few short weeks the twice-widowed, six-term mayor of Chicago was to travel by rail to Biloxi, Mississippi, to exchange marital vows with Annie Howard, a genteel New Orleans society woman from a good family who had agreed to become the third Mrs. Harrison.

MAYOR CARTER HENRY HARRISON I.

With thoughts of his beloved Annie running through his mind, the mayor spent the entire day on the Midway, greeting World's Fair visitors and old friends who congratulated him for Chicago's spectacular triumph. Mayor Harrison returned to his Ashland Avenue residence late in the afternoon, exhausted from his labors, but content and at peace with the world. He informed Mary Hansen, the family maid, that he would retire to his bedroom for a nap before suppertime. It had been a long and tiring day.

A few minutes after eight, a clean-shaven young man presented himself at the front door, asking to speak to the mayor about an urgent matter. "I am Eugene Patrick Prendergast," he announced. Recognizing the name, but unsure of the nature of the inquiry, Mary Hansen admitted him into the hallway, then summoned Carter Harrison from the rear of the home where he was puttering with a broken window.

The two men spoke only briefly. And then three shots were fired at point-blank range in rapid succession. Carter Harrison collapsed to the floor, bleeding internally and growing weaker by the second. Hearing the crackle of gunfire, Preston and Sophie Harrison rushed to their father's side. William Chalmers, the mayor's personal valet, bolted out the front door in hot pursuit of the fleeing gunman.

Firing shots over his shoulder, Prendergast raced north on Ashland Boulevard and was soon out of reach. The assassin paused at Madison Street, where he holstered his weapon and flagged down an eastbound cable car, later alighting at Des Plaines Street. Fifteen minutes after murdering the mayor of Chicago, Prendergast sauntered into the police station where he surrendered his four-dollar revolver to the desk sergeant and threw his hands up in the air.

Meanwhile, Preston Harrison attempted to elevate his prostrate father. "Don't move me boy, I'm fatally hurt," the mayor gasped. "I'm hurt to death. Where is Annie?" Annie was, of course, in New Orleans, finalizing plans for the coming nuptials.

Before a doctor could arrive, Mayor Harrison expired, less than twenty minutes after the hostile exchange with Prendergast.

Outside the streets were filled with people, horses, and carriages. Panic set in as word of the murder of the beloved Chicago mayor began to spread across the city. "Could it be true?" "Have the police got him?" "Why did he do it?" "Was he a crank?" Fearing that a lynch mob would soon form, the police doubled the size of the guard outside the Des Plaines lockup.

Alderman John McGillen, a friend of the mayor, was led into the cellblock where he sized up the killer. "They ought to do with him as they do with criminals in China, chop his head off!"

Eugene Prendergast was a talkative but unrepentant killer, who supplied the essential facts of the crime to Inspector John Shea. Prendergast explained that he had been promised a position in the mayor's cabinet, but Harrison had gone back on his word and betrayed him by appointing another man as corporation counsel. "I had a scheme for the elevation of the railroad tracks so that it would cost the railroads but little and the city nothing," he explained. "I wanted to be corporation counsel so that I could push this scheme, and he said I should have the office. I was justified in what I did."

Eugene Prendergast was, in reality, a delusional sociopath who had grown to manhood in abject poverty in a small frame house on June Street. Probing deeper, investigators learned that young Prendergast had suffered a serious injury that seemed to have impaired his mental health. His sanity was the central issue through two exhausting criminal trials. Prendergast's grandfather had been confined to an insane asylum in Ireland. Much was made of the difficult circumstances of his early boyhood by his attorneys and Clarence Darrow, who spoke for two hours at the sentencing hearing pleading with the court to spare the life of the unfortunate.

In moving and eloquent oratory, Darrow recalled the killer's early years. When, at the age of twelve, Prendergast read *Poverty and Progress,* he vowed from that day forth to make something of himself, but his carefully laid plans soon went awry through bad luck, poor timing, and lack of family prominence.

Carter Harrison humored Prendergast's foolish whim by introducing the young man to several Democratic chair-warmers when he first buttonholed the mayor in the corridors of City Hall about the availability of the position of Corporation Counsel. He took Harrison's jest as a clear indication of his intention to appoint him to the cabinet. The mayor knew nothing about this lad, and never gave it another moment's thought until Prendergast unexpectedly turned up at his door with a gun in his pocket.

The accused was by day employed as a newspaper distributor in the Lincoln Park neighborhood. He preached temperance and expressed a metaphysical devotion to God, but he annoyed his neighbors with rambling monologues in defense of Henry George's single tax nonsense. Prendergast was a peculiar man. The press considered him a lunatic.

Inside his jail cell at the Hubbard Street lockup, Prendergast laughed and joked with his fellow inmates. His pungent sarcasm was evident to police and reporters when one of the prisoners crooned a verse of *A Bicycle Built for Two.* "I wish I was on a bicycle built for one!" he quipped.

The assassin remained flippant and unconcerned through two contentious trials, while his attorneys futilely tested the insanity defense for the first time in Illinois criminal history. Acquiescent without being humble, Prendergast was marched to the gallows of the Criminal Courts Building on Hubbard Street, July 13, 1894, by Sheriff James H. Gilbert. Prendergast made the sign of the cross and was then hanged on the same gibbet used to execute the four Haymarket men—Spies, Parsons, Fischer, and Engel—seven years earlier.

Nineteenth-century justice was devoid of remorse for lunatics and "cranks." A newspaper reporter gleefully commented that Prendergast had gone to his death "like an ox going to the shambles."

A Kentucky Dynasty Takes Root in Chicago

SIDE TRIP

Carter Henry Harrison was born in a log hut in a Fayette County, Kentucky, canebrake. The family line extended back to the days of Oliver Cromwell, when, according to ancient family legends, a Harrison led an unhappy King Charles I to the chopping block.

In 1855, following completion of his studies at Yale, the future Mayor settled in Chicago with his first wife. Harrison dabbled in real estate before entering political life. He purchased a small rooming house at the southwest corner of Clark and Harrison Streets just south of downtown. (The street, incidentally, was named for President William Henry Harrison, a relative.) He reopened the place as the Adams Hotel. At the time it was the tallest building outside the central business district.

His son, Carter Harrison II, a five-term Chicago mayor who served alternate two-year terms between 1897 and 1915, was born inside the Adams in 1860. During the Chicago Fire, the five-story hotel was in flames a dozen times, but Carter Harrison the elder, who retained ownership of the property after he moved to Ashland Avenue, beat off the deadly sparks and saved his building. By 1880, a gradual deterioration had begun in this area. The district bounded by Harrison, Twelfth Street, Dearborn, and Wells was known as "Cheyenne," then later as the Custom House Place Levee, after the newly arrived purveyors of vice, gambling, and liquor pierced the residential tranquillity of the neighborhood. It soon became the city's most vicious crime area. (See Tour 1.)

The Adams Hotel was demolished in May 1929 to make room for an open-air parking lot. Carter Harrison II, ancient and brittle, lamented the changing times as he watched the wrecker's ball lay waste to what was believed to be the oldest surviving building in the city at that time. "It is hard to believe that this neighborhood was once a community of fine homes," Harrison sighed, momentarily overtaken by the steady, unrelenting advance of the twentieth century.

The mayor, were he alive today, would find that yet another parking lot, albeit an indoor one, occupies the site, sandwiched between former printing and engraving factories.

To continue our tour, take Ashland Boulevard one block north to Adams Street. Turn left (west) on Adams Street and go to Ogden Avenue. Turn left (southwest) on Ogden Avenue and go to Rockwell Street.

EDDIE O'HARE CASHES IT IN FOR HIS SON

November 8, 1939

Ed O'Hare was gunned down in the "Valley" District, near the intersection of Ogden Avenue and Rockwell Street, due west of the Cook County Hospital complex, just beyond Western Avenue. The light pole at the divided intersection of Rockwell Street, a few hundred feet north of the Ryerson Steel Company, marks the spot where this nefarious mob hit occurred.

Edward Henry "Butch" O'Hare single-handedly saved the U.S. Navy carrier *Lexington* from certain destruction during the early months of World War II. The lone pilot, flying his Grumman F4F-3 fighter into the heart of danger, attacked a wing of Japanese bombers. Wreaking havoc on the enemy craft, young O'Hare prevented a devastating aerial bombardment of the fleet. For conspicuous gallantry, he was awarded the Congressional Medal of Honor.

A year later, in November 1943, Butch O'Hare disappeared near Tarawa Island while pioneering night radar flights. There is a growing opinion among military historians that young O'Hare was a casualty of friendly fire.

Orchard Depot, an isolated landing strip at the far northwest corner of Chicago, was formally dedicated as O'Hare Field on September 18, 1949, in recognition of Butch O'Hare's gallantry.

Ten years before the ceremonies honoring the fallen war hero, Butch's father, Edward Joseph O'Hare, fell victim to the decidedly unfriendly fire of the Al Capone mob.

A maze of mysteries surrounds the ambush-murder of O'Hare at 2601 West Ogden Avenue on November 8, 1939. Did he die a martyr's death in order to further his son's career, or was he just another hustler in a woolen suit sucked into the glamour and allure of mob life?

Born and raised in the tough Kerry-Patch neighborhood of St. Louis, Ed

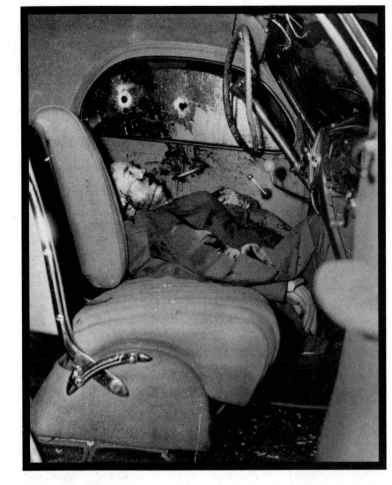

ED O'HARE, MOMENTS AFTER BEING GUNNED DOWN AT TALMAN AND OGDEN AVENUES.

O'Hare associated with O. P. Smith, inventor of the mechanical rabbit for dog racing. When Smith died, O'Hare assumed control of the patent and became a major player in the racing world. Smith's amazing metal rabbit made Eddie O'Hare an overnight millionaire.

Arriving in Chicago in the 1920s, O'Hare opened the Thornton dog track, positioning himself to become the czar of the greyhounds. When Capone and other Chicago mobsters sensed that O'Hare was securing a whirlwind of profits, they decided to cut themselves in. O'Hare, who was convicted of hijacking medicinal whiskey from a bonded warehouse during Prohibition, merged his Lawndale Kennel Club with Capone's Hawthorne Kennel Club. He understood that there was no percentage in defying the overseers of gangland, so he agreed to continue on as legal counsel, track manager, and "front man" for the criminal syndicate.

O'Hare had friends in high places. His association with Judge Eugene J. Holland of the Rackets Court spared 12,624 defendants from serving serious prison time. Holland dismissed all but 28 of those who were arrested and charged with violations of gambling statutes. In mob parlance, Ed O'Hare was a "well-connected" fellow.

After dog racing was outlawed by statute in 1931, O'Hare was named president of Sportsman's Park, the new thoroughbred track built on the grounds of the Hawthorne Club in Cicero. Sportsman's was a Capone operation from start to finish, and a huge financial success. Trusted with the gang's secrets, O'Hare also managed dog tracks in Massachusetts, Pennsylvania, Ohio, Oregon, California, and Florida.

Unbeknownst to his mob overseers, Ed O'Hare became a secret government informant. For nearly eight years, he had been funneling information about Al Capone to Internal Revenue Service agent Frank J. Wilson, who built a solid case against the Chicago gang chief resulting in Capone's conviction on charges of income tax evasion. O'Hare agreed to inform on the mob in order to obtain an appointment to the Naval Academy at Annapolis for his son.

The appointment was brokered by newspaper reporter John Rogers of the *St. Louis Post Dispatch.*

Butch O'Hare graduated from the Academy in 1937. He launched his naval career at the U.S. Naval Training Center in San Diego and was sent overseas the day after Pearl Harbor.

Meanwhile, the bill for tuition was forwarded to the "Al Capone collection agency" in care of Alcatraz.

"Scarface" Capone, a patient man with an unflinching memory, ordered Ed O'Hare's removal after learning of his treachery only weeks before finishing his sentence. The hit team was recruited from the Egan's Rats gang of St. Louis, and they were lying in wait at Twenty-second Street and Ogden Avenue as O'Hare made his way from the dining room at the Illinois Athletic Club on Michigan Avenue to his office at the track.

Suspecting that his life was in danger, O'Hare started carrying a gun. Several hours before he was killed, he cleaned and polished his loaded revolver. He did not know that earlier that same evening a call was placed to his residence at 221 Franklin Road in North Suburban Glencoe, warning the family maid that a bomb was about to explode on the property.

Exposed as a stool pigeon, O'Hare was marked for death. The bogus bomb threat was a cold-hearted diversionary tactic.

When the gunmen pulled abreast of O'Hare's car as he motored east at 2601 West Ogden, O'Hare fumbled for his weapon but it was already too late. A shotgun blast tore through his face and head. The new Lincoln Zephyr automobile he was driving jumped the curb, rolled over the streetcar tracks, and careened into a trolley pole in the center lane. It was a well-planned, perfectly timed murder, the kind the Chicago syndicate specialized in. In a biblical sense, the O'Hare murder was analogous to the sacrifice of Abraham, running in reverse.

Put another way, a veteran Chicago cop observed, "They don't kill people in Chicago for nothin.'"

Inside the wrecked automobile, the police located Eddie's handgun and a mash note written in Italian to a woman named Margie, believed to be a secret girlfriend. In his Glencoe home, detectives retrieved a poem that might well have been O'Hare's own epitaph.

> *The clock of life is wound but once—*
> *And no man has the power*
> *To tell just when the hands will stop—*
> *At late or early hour.*
> *Now is the only time you own.*
> *Live long, toil with a will.*
> *Place no faith in time*
> *For the clock may then be still.*

```
Nov. 8, 1939

Edward O'Hara, 47, 221 Franklin, Glencoe, race
track owner.

Gang killing.

    Shot by one or more persons who drove

abreast his car front 2601 W. Ogden. Received

instantly fatal wounds of face and head from
shotgun blast. Wealthy race track owner, operat-
ed tracks in three cities, as well as real estate
  broker. Was former associate of Al Capone. Love
  angle also investigated, but girlfriend could8n't
                           reveal clue.
```

POLICE REPORT OF THE O'HARE MURDER ON A 3 x 5 INCH INDEX CARD.

Return to

Western Avenue

and go left

(north) to

Monroe Street.

"IT WAS A HELL OF A NIGHT!" THE BLACK PANTHER RAID

December 4, 1969

Until very recently, an empty, weather-beaten five-room apartment house that had come to symbolize racial divisions in troubled times occupied a desolate corner lot at 2337 West Monroe Street, at Western Avenue. The events that played themselves out there the night of December 4, 1969, when fourteen Chicago police officers raided the apartment of Black Panther leader Fred Hampton, symbolized police overreaction and a nation divided. As recently as 1989, Burdett Griffin, the owner of the decaying building, tried to sell the property, but there were no takers. Nor were preservationists interested in memorializing old and contentious memories of that painful, divisive time. The building was razed without much fanfare. A townhouse was later built on the site, and a cul-de-sac was added at the end of the block, perhaps to discourage sightseers, drug runners, and gangbangers. A Black Muslim flag flapping in the breeze next door is the only reminder of a grim and disquieting moment in Chicago history.

On the twentieth anniversary of the shooting deaths of Black Panther leaders Fred Hampton and Mark Clark, mourners staged a candlelight vigil outside the apartment house. By this time, the owner of the building had removed the bullet holes—all ninety-nine of them—in order to make the place "habitable."

There was little chance of that happening. The pockmarked building was a festering wound on the soul of the city. Who could possibly live in such a place ever again?

Fred Hampton was only twenty-one years old, but he was a persuasive and eloquent spokesman echoing the frustrations of Chicago's African-American community. Local law enforcement and the vast majority of the white middle class did not view Hampton or the local chapter of the Black Panthers, which he helped found, in quite the same heroic terms, but rather saw them as a dangerous and disruptive radical fringe bent on turning the streets of Chicago into bloody mayhem.

Cook County State's Attorney Edward V. Hanrahan, the principal player in this drama, was a loyal soldier in Mayor Richard J. Daley's urban political machine. He was a figurehead for the establishment during these unpredictable times, representing the fondest hopes of the law-and-order advocates. Hanrahan was also a tough, calculating politician, and the "Great Silent Majority" of bungalow-belt voters loved him. Within the Cook County Democratic Party, there were those who believed that Daley was grooming the slight-of-build Hanrahan as a possible successor.

However, his budding political career was damaged beyond repair the night of December 4, 1969, when he ordered a predawn raid on the Panther building.

Intelligence reports indicated to Hanrahan that the Panthers were stockpiling a cache of firearms inside Hampton's apartment. Armed with a search warrant and given their marching orders, the Chicago Police swooped down upon the silent, darkened building where Clark and Hampton were sleeping.

With guns blazing, the cops burst into the bedroom. When the smoke cleared, and the police guns were finally holstered, Hampton and Clark lay dead. Three other Panthers and two police officers were wounded in the fray, which reminded next-door neighbor Joseph Murphy of his recent tour of duty in Vietnam. "It was a hell of a night," Murphy told a *Sun-Times* reporter. "It seemed like it lasted a lifetime, the shooting. But it probably didn't last more than five minutes."

Hanrahan defended the actions of his men against the swift and harsh criticism emanating from the press and the minority community. "As soon as Sergeant Daniel Groth and Officer James Davis, who were leading our men, announced their office, occupants of the apartment attacked them with shotgun fire," he said.

The State's Attorney tried the case in the press. He reenacted the raid before the television cameras of WBBM-TV, pointing unconvincingly to Panther "bullet holes," which on closer examination turned out to be the heads of nails. Forensics experts confirmed that only one bullet was fired by the victims, that one shot coming from Mark Clark's gun.

Sealed indictments were returned against Hanrahan and thirteen police officers on June 25, 1971, charging them with obstruction of justice. Chicago Police Superintendent James Conlisk was named as an unindicted coconspirator; but after thirteen weeks of testimony, all of the defendants were acquitted in a bench trial by Judge Phillip J. Romiti.

Civil litigation followed. The families of Hampton and Clark sued Hanrahan and twenty-seven others for $47.7 million in compensatory damages, but it would be years before there would be any closure to this case. The parties eventually agreed to a $1.85 million settlement in 1983. By this time Eddie Hanrahan was gone from public life. He lost his reelection bid to Bernard Carey in 1972. It marked the first time in memory that Chicago's large African-American community turned out in record numbers to vote a Republican into office.

Go north on Western Avenue to Madison Street. Turn left (west) and go to Homan Avenue. Turn left (south) and go to Monroe Street.

THE HOUSE OF WEIRD DEATH
November 21, 1933

The Wynekoop mansion at 3406 West Monroe Street was razed many years ago. The weed-strewn vacant lot at the corner of Homan Avenue and Monroe Street on the city's West Side, where Dr. Alice Wynekoop took the life of pretty Rheta, is a scene of quiet desolation amid ghostly remnants of past elegance. Farther down the block, several residential dwellings dating back to the early years of the century provide clues as to what this neighborhood might have looked like when the well-to-do once lived here. The buildings now stand forlornly amid the gloom of economic deprivation that is the West Side.

Dr. Alice Lindsay Wynekoop was an early advocate of women's rights, a dyed-in-the-wool suffragette, loved and admired for her many charitable deeds. She was a pillar of her community; a well-respected civic leader and a pioneer in the movement for children's hygiene; and, quite possibly, a murderess.

The daughter of a distinguished physician, who at one time served as the city bacteriologist, Dr. Alice Wynekoop graduated from the Women's Medical School of Northwestern University in 1895 and was admitted to general practice that same year.

Her son, Earle J. Wynekoop, the light of her life, was a good-for-nothing and a source of continual embarrassment to the family's good name.

Earle, at age twenty-seven, lived in his mother's fashionable West Side brownstone with his young bride, the attractive, auburn-haired Rheta Gardner Wynekoop. The young man was a poor choice for Rheta. He was an absentee husband who had fallen out of love with his well-to-do Indianapolis heiress wife not long after the honeymoon. Rheta, who played the violin and had designs on a musical performance career, tried to make the best of living in her mother-in-law's gloomy dark-paneled mansion among an odd assortment of hangers-on.

Earle's little black book, cleverly concealed from Rheta's reproachful eye, contained the names and addresses of fifty young women that he had picked up on the grounds of the 1933 World's Fair—the "Century of Progress," celebrating Chicago's cultural and technological achievements in the international arena.

Earle, a devilishly handsome young rake, proposed marriage to several of these poor but lovesick girls, who were working the concession stands at the fair. He escorted them about the grounds buying them cotton candy, calling them "sweetheart," and spinning yarns about a future life together. All the while, he carefully avoided areas of the promenade where his other "sweethearts" happened to be working that day. When the details of Earle's secret life were bared in the press, his "fiancées" accused him of making love in strange ways that were both "shocking and repulsive."

The after-hours intrigues of this young Lothario, dubbed "the automobile Romeo" by jaded police reporters, does not easily explain away the death of twenty-three-year-old Rheta on the afternoon of November 21, 1933. According to Earle's version of events, he was motoring west to take color publicity photographs of the Grand Canyon for the Santa Fe Railroad when he was notified of his wife's sudden and mysterious death.

The weird, but coldly calculated, circumstances of the murder would baffle detectives for months, even years to come.

Police officers from the Fillmore Street station, summoned to 3406 West Monroe Street, found Rheta lying facedown on Dr. Alice's emergency operating table in the basement. Partially nude, she had been shot in the back, just below the left shoulder. Nearby, police found a chloroform mask made of wire and cotton batting. The murder weapon, from which three shots were fired, lay directly above the girl's head.

Dr. Alice, a tall, spare, sixty-two-year-old widow, who wore her graying hair in long pigtails, kept changing her story, confusing the police, the coroner, and even members of her own household. She advised Rheta's father, Burdine H. Gardner, to tell others that his daughter's death was due to the complications of tuberculosis.

Gardner, a wealthy flour and salt broker who rushed to Chicago moments after hearing the news, said he considered the living arrangements at the Wynekoop household odd, and Dr. Alice even more so. "I never did like the Wynekoop family for some reason or other," he said. "They seemed queer and unusual to me."

As crowds milled around outside the home, Dr. Alice, her son Walker, daughter Catherine, and sister-in-law Jesse, and Jesse's daughter Frances were transported to the police station, along with Enid Hennessey, a spinster schoolteacher who rented a room in the mansion. They were questioned for several hours. The Wynekoops were a curious group, but loyal to Dr. Alice, matriarch of the household where they all lived. Miss Hennessey, a zoology teacher at Marshall High School, screamed, "It's a lie! It's a lie!" The woman was accused of impeding the investigation, but she stood faithfully by Dr. Alice all the way through the subsequent trial, when she invented an alibi in order to protect her friend in this ordeal.

"She [Rheta] was a lovely child," sobbed Dr. Alice. "She was like a daughter to me." Wynekoop suggested that the crime was committed by drug fiends. In recent months her basement office had been broken into several times, and her drugs stolen.

Captain John Stege, a fearless gumshoe who battled the Prohibition bootlegging gangs in the 1920s to a standoff, relentlessly grilled Wynekoop for hours at the police station. "She is one woman in 120 million," sighed Assistant State's Attorney John Long, who assisted in an around-the-clock interrogation. "She is a woman of stone."

The existence of a $5,000 life insurance policy taken out on Rheta's life just ten days earlier provided a compelling motive and a possible clue. But it was Alice's concerns for Earle that finally caused her to crack. She had been worried about her boy all along, and was understanding and sympathetic to his philandering. Earle was not happy with his living arrangements, yet his mother desired to protect his reputation and his life.

Dr. Alice finally confessed that it was she, and not Earle, who pulled the trigger, but only after Rheta expired from the deadly anesthetic. Wynekoop explained that she had been about to perform a painful surgical procedure on her daughter-in-law—possibly an abortion. There were whispered rumors to that effect.

In slow, measured sentences, Dr. Alice said she asked Rheta to pour some chloroform into the mask if she wanted to ease the pain of surgery, but the dosage proved to be too powerful and minutes later the girl lapsed into a coma. Fearing public humiliation and a blot on her reputation, Wynekoop panicked and fired the fatal shot. She would blame the crime on imaginary "dope fiends" who invaded her home.

"Under identical circumstances I would do the identical thing again," she told a reporter. The sensational confession raised doubts. The cops believed that Earle masterminded the crime, and that Mama was willing to take the rap in order to save the life of her darling boy. Love letters written from the mother to the son revealed a relationship that strained the bounds of conventional maternal relations. It suggested something far more unnatural. "Precious, I'm choked," Alice wrote in an unmailed correspondence two days before Earle set off for Arizona.

"I want to hear your voice again tonight—would give anything I have to spend an hour of real talk with you." Psychiatrists of the time believed that an "Oedipus complex" existed between the two.

Hearing of his mother's sacrifice, Earle demanded to see Captain Stege. "I will tell him I was in Chicago at the time of the killing," he said gallantly. "I don't believe a word of it." He told police that he had snuffed out the life of his unhappy wife, hours before sneaking out of town with one of his new girlfriends dangling on his arm.

Now there were two confessed murderers to deal with. "A mother's sacrifice is no greater than that of such a child who offers himself to save that mother, even though falsely accused," Alice gently replied.

Earle consistently failed his polygraph tests concerning his whereabouts the day of the murder, but the state looked past him. Alice was in debt, maintained the state's attorney . . . and she hated her daughter-in-law for making her son's life so miserable.

Despite the young man's protestations and a compelling motive, the state indicted Dr. Alice on charges of murder and she was brought to trial. The case dragged on for many weeks, holding the public spellbound. Nearly six months after the strange murder, the jury came back with a guilty verdict against the elderly doctor, but no one could say with any certainty whether or not justice had prevailed. Dr. Alice Wynekoop was sentenced to twenty-five years in prison. She was granted a parole from the Women's Reformatory at Dwight, Illinois, in 1949 at the ripe old age of seventy-nine. She died two years later.

Earle, who struck and killed a nine-year-old boy while driving his automobile during trial deliberations, faded from view. At last report he was working as a garage mechanic. By now he is probably dead.

The house of weird death is long gone, but the memory of these unhappy events haunts a devastated landscape.

Frank and Alice Wynekoop built their red-brick mansion in 1901 in anticipation of raising their children in a happy, loving environment. The couple supervised every last detail of construction and looked forward to the years ahead. But in many ways the building and the surrounding properties were strangely cursed. Alice's daughter Marie Louise died there. Dr. Gilbert Wynekoop, Alice's brother-in-law, brought scandal down on the family when he attempted to choke his estranged wife during divorce proceedings, then went mad and had to be institutionalized.

Today the West Side Fillmore District is a crime-ridden no man's land. Where elegant mansions once stood, there are only empty spaces, broken sidewalks, discarded wine bottles, and boarded-up crack houses. The ghosts of the Wynekoop house dwell in a tragic, eerie setting where there is little or no hope of recovery.

"A Horrible Case"

SIDETRIP

The following notice appeared in the Chicago Tribune *on October 6, 1858:*

> *A hoary wretch named Edward Wilson, with one foot in the grave and about seventy years of age, and Eliza Wilson, his daughter, a woman of forty years of age, were brought before Justice Stickney yesterday on a charge of having maintained incestuous cohabitation for some months past. They have resided in a small tenement on Wolcott; near Hickory Street (present-day Augusta Boulevard) and have been notorious in their infamy for some time past. They were committed to jail in default of $500 bail.*

To continue the tour, go north on Homan Avenue to Chicago Avenue. Turn left (west) and proceed to Avers Avenue. Turn right on Avers and go one block to Iowa Street.

"A GREAT INESCAPABLE SORROW": THE OUR LADY OF ANGELS FIRE

December 1, 1958

In this old and historic neighborhood, the Lady of Angels fire cast a permanent shadow upon a community whose wounds would be slow to heal. The tragedy that occurred on December 1, 1958, claimed the lives of eighty-seven children and three nuns. The memory of the event lingers, even today. It seems that every Chicagoan who lived, worked, or attended school in the city in the late 1950s has a story to tell, or knew someone whose life was personally touched in a sorrowful way by the terrifying blaze that erupted at 3820 West Iowa Street. In 1958, the parish registry listed 4,500 families, mostly Italians and Irish who lived in identical two-flat apartments and mortgaged brick bungalows lining the quiet side streets of Avers, Hamlin, Iowa, etc. After the fire, many of the grieving families abandoned the neighborhood. Today, the Lady of Angels Parish attends to the religious devotions of the faithful in a predominantly African-American neighborhood. It is a poor and economically deprived community, but the housing stock is solid and the properties have *been maintained. The newcomers have heard the stories of the fire that refused to die. It is interwoven into the history of this West Side neighborhood. The two-story red-brick parochial school adjoining Our Lady of Angels Church at Iowa and Avers Streets was a smoldering ruin when the flames were finally extinguished. A new parish school was built by the Chicago Archdiocese in 1960, but declining enrollment forced its closure in 1999. The only memorial to the innocent victims of the third worst school fire in the nation's history is located twelve miles west in the Queen of Heaven Cemetery in suburban Hillside, where twenty-five of the victims were laid to rest. A stone shrine was erected there in 1960 through private donation. One would almost think that in the interest of the surviving family members and for the sake of history, there would have been a more enduring shrine put in place by now.*

In routine fire drills, the kind that have commonly been practiced in every public and parochial grade school by generations of children, the Our Lady of Angels School was emptied out in less than three and a half minutes.

Investigators were at first puzzled by the sudden and terrible swiftness of the fire that erupted at the base of the stairwell at the northeast corner of the school. As they sifted through the charred ruins and debris on the second floor, a clearer picture of what had happened slowly emerged.

Thick smoke and intense heat had spiraled upward into the second-floor corridor, blocking the normal path of escape, rendering years of preparedness drills totally ineffectual.

"Nothing killed those kids but smoke and heat," said Robert J. Quinn, who described the Our Lady of Angels fire as the worst conflagration he had witnessed in his lengthy career as Chicago fire commissioner. "And may there never be another like it."

There was no direct evidence of arson, but Quinn did not rule out the possibility after hearing rumors that a boy had been playing with matches in the stairwell. The FBI and a private detective were called in to investigate, but the consensus of opinion was that the fire had started as a result of a carelessly tossed cigarette landing in a pile of accumulated trash in the shallow basement.

Probing deeper into the mystery, it was agreed that simple safety precautions were ignored, and the loss of life might not have occurred if only the second-floor landing doors of the 1910 building had been kept closed to prevent smoke and gases from flooding into the corridors.

"In all likelihood, every classroom could have been emptied out in time," a staff investigator from the National Fire Protective Association concluded. Installation of a metal fire-retardant door at the top of the stairwell would have blocked the surge of heat and prevented a repeat of the Collinwood, Ohio, disaster of 1908, in which 176 youngsters perished under nearly identical circumstances, or the school fire in New London, Texas, that killed 294 pupils and teachers on March 18, 1937.

The Our Lady of Angels fire broke out inside the forty-six-year-old classroom building at 2:42 P.M., exactly eighteen minutes before the close of the school day for 1,400 students.

Precious minutes were lost when the fire department trucks pulled up in front of the church rectory and not the school. Emergency dispatch had been given the wrong address by the person who phoned in the first report.

Inside the smoke-filled classrooms, students heard the distinct wail of approaching sirens, but as the seconds ticked off, the trucks were nowhere in

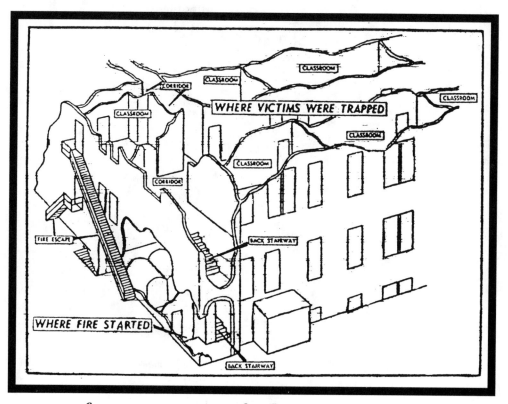

CUTAWAY DRAWING OF THE OUR LADY OF ANGELS SCHOOL.

sight. At that point the nuns asked the children to bow their heads in prayer.

As the flames roared out of control, the alarm was upgraded to a 5-11, meaning that all available police and fire personnel in the vicinity were summoned to Iowa Street to battle the blaze in the bone-chilling cold. Before it was over, forty-three pieces of fire equipment had converged on the scene.

From the second-floor windows, screaming children fell to the frozen ground twenty-five feet below. Many had been pushed by trapped and panic-stricken classmates standing behind them. The dazed and confused survivors who were fortunate enough to escape with their lives, or who had fallen into the arms of the volunteers standing below the windows, were comforted by the neighbors living across the street.

Barbara Glowacki owned a candy store at 919 North Avers Street. The side door of her business opened onto the school yard. "Never will I be able to look out that door again without seeing them as I did yesterday," she said, "those little faces at the windows with the fire and smoke behind them."

A FIRE TRAGEDY

THAT SHOCKED THE

NATION: THE LADY

OF ANGELS INFERNO.

(Chicago Daily News)

Our Lady of Angels had three staircases and a fire escape leading to the street, but once the smoke had overtaken the hallways, the only way out was through the windows.

Spectators poured out into the streets, testing the resolve of the firefighters and police, who had their hands full fighting the fire, the bitter cold, and hysterical parents who attempted to run into the building.

The Cook County Morgue at 1828 West Polk Street was a mass of confusion and human despair as, one by one, the parents showed up to identify the remains of their children. Most of the fathers were ordinary blue-collar tradesmen attired in workmen's clothes. They had come directly from the factories and construction sites of the city in the company of their wives. A policeman stationed at the door repeated the same question to each person having business with the coroner, "Relative?"

And so it went, long into the night.

Messages of condolence were received from across the world. In Rome, Pope John XXIII sent his personal message to the archbishop of Chicago, the Most Reverend Albert Gregory Meyer.

Four days later, Archbishop Meyer conducted a solemn pontifical High Mass for the victims and their families before a portable altar at the Northwest Armory.

In simple but mournful terms, he referred to the devastating loss of life as "a great inescapable sorrow."

In the morally rigid and conservative Eisenhower '50s, it would have been unthinkable for the grieving survivors to initiate tort litigation against the archdiocese of Chicago in the courts of Illinois. The official position coming from the church that it was "God's will" was accepted as a universal and ecumenical truth.

The children whose lives were turned upside down by the wrenching ordeal were told by the nuns that only "the good ones were taken by God." No one in higher authority questioned the emotional cruelty or the lifetime of guilt these women needlessly inflicted on impressionable children through their thoughtless words. No one dared challenge the church on these matters or ask the hard questions that needed asking.

But was it *really* God's will for the doors on the second-floor landing to remain open at the moment of peril?

Go back to

Chicago Avenue.

Turn right (east)

and proceed to

Kedzie Avenue.

Turn left (north)

and go to North

Avenue.

"THEY'LL HAVE TO KILL ME TO GET ME OUT!"

February 6, 1952

Fearing the imminent invasion of the syndicate-controlled West Side Bloc into his Thirty-first Ward bailiwick, Acting Committeeman Charles Gross struck a defiant pose. "Nobody is going to push me around!" he snapped, aware that there was already a bounty on his head. The murder of a politician was becoming a rather commonplace occurrence in post–World War II Chicago, and the execution-style shooting of Gross on the sidewalk outside the Scandinavian Evangelical Church on the southwest corner of Kedzie and North Avenues was just another plague brought down upon "syndicate city." The Scandinavian Church building at 1544–1548 North Kedzie is now the Iglesia Bautista Peniel, reflecting the significant ethnic changes that have overtaken the Humboldt Park community since Gross went out for a stroll that cold Wednesday night in 1952.

Political leaders and civic do-gooders bitterly denounced the criminal tie-ins between gangsters and politicians that paralyzed the city of Chicago in the important election year of 1952. Virgil W. Petersen, the executive director of the Chicago Crime Commission when the Crime Commission was still a strident voice for the common good within this workingman's town, demanded immediate action. "How many more killings and how much more violence must the people of Chicago tolerate before the leaders of both parties clean their ranks of the hoodlum gangster element?"

The ambush murder of Republican committeeman Charlie Gross focused attention on the activities of the West Side Bloc, a vicious cabal of city and state politicians under the thumb of the Chicago outfit.

Gross, a retired soft-drink executive who dabbled in politics the way some men take up golf or bowling to wile away their leisure hours, was advised to stay out of the public arena. "Don't be a fool, Charlie. You've got a good thing going in business. Why fool around with politics?" It was sound advice, and Gross should have heeded the warning and read between the lines, but Gross was a fighter and he refused to cave in. He would defy the nay-sayers and run for Republican committeeman in the April primary, letting the chips fall where they may.

Lately he had taken to carrying a gun, but Gross was unarmed the night of February 6. As he passed by a dark stretch of street in front of the Scandinavian Church, a sudden beam of light from a slow-moving automobile blinded him. A moment later, Gross was cut down in a barrage of seven shotgun blasts coming from two men who emerged from the interior shadows of a 1949 Ford sedan. Charlie Gross never made it to his political meeting that night. He was dead before he hit the sidewalk.

The hunt for the killers filled the newspapers for weeks to come. Police Commissioner Timothy O'Connor called on Frank Pape and his streetwise major crimes squad to round up the top hoodlums, but Pape drew a blank. "This is the queerest case ever," he said. "Gross didn't seem big enough to cause the syndicate much concern, except politically."

Public opinion spurred action against the West Side Bloc and their syndicate allies. An investigative body of city politicians known as the "Big Nine" conducted an inquiry that dragged on over the next three years. Though they were unable to finger the killers of Charlie Gross, the Big Nine stepped up the pressure, and slowly over the next twelve years the power of the Bloc finally eroded.

To continue our tour, keep going west on North Avenue to Sayre Avenue. Turn right (north) and go one block to Wabansia Avenue.

DEATH OF THE EXECUTIONER
April 14, 1973

"Mad" Sam DeStefano was one of those unbelievable Chicago gangland characters who could have easily been plucked from among a legion of walking stereotypes biding their time in Hollywood central casting for the first Godfather *movie. When he wasn't causing mayhem in the federal courts with his lunatic antics, DeStefano lived in a sandstone brick ranch-style home at 1656 North Sayre Avenue (at the corner of Wabansia). This orderly upper middle-class enclave brushes up against the boundary line of West Suburban Oak Park, not far from the mansions of the hoodlum bosses of the 1950s and 1960s. DeStefano, who was awaiting trial for the murder of loan shark Leo Foreman, said that he was "not afraid to die in the street." Instead the master extortionist perished inside the garage, with a clear view of the street just before his last dying gasp.*

Sam DeStefano murdered his brother Michael in 1955, then washed the body with soap to "cleanse his soul." Michael was a drug addict, and DeStefano helped him make his peace with God before dying. Sam hated drug addicts.

According to the late Bill Roemer, who shadowed Sam Giancana and his henchmen for nearly a decade, DeStefano once invited the family of a deadbeat juice collector to a Cicero restaurant so they could "reunite" with the man, who had been missing for a few weeks. The family sat down to an extravagant Italian feast and were enjoying Sam's hospitality, when suddenly their loved one was dragged into the room naked, dazed, and covered with burns all over his body. Sam and his boys circled the table and allegedly ordered the entire family—wife, mother, and children—to urinate all over the body.

It is hard to keep track of the dozens of heinous tortures, atrocities, and mob executions hatched in the fertile mind of Sam DeStefano and carried out with ruthless, almost gleeful abandon. The ice pick was Sam's preferred weapon. When he wasn't chaining his delinquent borrowers to a radiator, he was poking them in their vitals with his trusty pick. There were two kinds of borrowers to Sam's way of thinking, those who were quick to pay, and those who were dead.

An alumnus of the old "42 Gang," who drifted into mob circles in the 1920s, DeStefano was a master of disrupting the legal system with his buffoonery. On May 4, 1964, wearing a silk dressing gown over his silk pajamas, DeStefano was brought into Judge Daniel Ryan's court on a hospital gurney. As he was pushed through the corridors, DeStefano flicked the switch of a bullhorn and announced his dissatisfaction with the criminal justice system. "We are now living in a Gestapo country!" he yelled. "We have lost our civil rights!"

DeStefano reveled in the publicity surrounding the gangster life, and he never stopped bragging about his charity and good deeds on behalf of fellow convicts he knew in southern Illinois, where, believe it or not, he was born.

Anita DeStefano, Sam's long-suffering wife of forty years, was always on edge. According to Sam, "She worries because I always say what I think. I get into trouble but I won't shut up."

It was his big mouth, and his veiled threats to publish an exposé about life in the Chicago rackets, that convinced the racket bosses to silence Mad Sam once and for all.

DeStefano, sixty-four, was sweeping out his garage on a cloudless Saturday morning in April. Wife Anita went to visit her mother at 9:30, leaving Sam, who was clad in an old jacket, a pair of Hush Puppy shoes, and workpants, to tinker and putter about as men like to do. When she returned around noon, Sam was not in sight, but a swarm of reporters, photographers, gapers, and cops were gathered on the sidewalk. She soon learned the awful truth. Her husband had been killed by two shotgun blasts. The body was found by burglary detectives who had come out to the house on an unrelated matter at 11:15 A.M.

Anita pointed an accusing finger at the police and sobbed to reporters. "You people killed him!" she wailed. "Take every picture, make sure you don't miss a goddamn thing!"

Return to North Avenue and go west to Harlem Avenue. Turn left (south) and go to Madison Street. Turn left (east) and continue past Central Avenue to Lotus Avenue. Turn north on Lotus Avenue to 125 North Lotus.

THE STOLEN YEARS
December 16, 1959

The Austin neighborhood where Roger Touhy came to a sudden and violent end in 1959 was once a quiet middle-class area bordering suburban Oak Park. Today the community struggles to overcome the ravages of high crime and gang violence. While change has overtaken much of Austin, the Lotus Avenue address, where Roger Touhy died, looks the same. It is located on a tree-lined residential street a half a block south of Washington Boulevard near West End Avenue.

Roger "the Terrible" Touhy deserved a far better fate than to die on his front porch with his shoes on.

Touhy was murdered just twenty-three days after he had been paroled from the Illinois State Penitentiary, where he had served twenty-five years for the kidnapping of Jake "The Barber" Factor—a crime he didn't commit.

During Prohibition, Touhy headed a bootlegging gang whose operations extended across the far Northwest Side of Chicago into the suburbs of Morton Grove and Niles Center (now known as Skokie). Touhy and his four brothers—Tommy, James, John, and Joe—kept to themselves and never intended to cross swords with the Al Capone gang. Their only aim was to make money plying the suburban roadhouses along Dempster Street with illegal beer.

There was no evidence that Roger ever committed a capital crime; snatched Jake Factor, international swindler and rogue; or even tried to "muscle" Capone, from whom he kept a respectful distance.

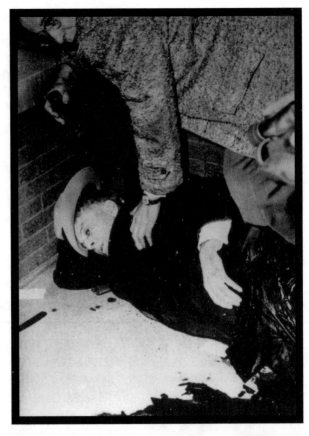

ROGER "THE
TERRIBLE" TOUHY
MORTALLY WOUND-
ED ON THE FRONT
PORCH OF HIS
HOME.

As a youngster, Touhy grew up at Ogden Avenue and Roosevelt Road, at the southern edge of the West Side "Valley," a veritable spawning ground for gangsters. His father, James Touhy, was an immigrant Irish police officer from County Sligo, who tried to keep his brood of rambunctious boys in line after their mother perished in a fire.

But lacking proper supervision, the Touhys fell in with a bad lot. One of their boyhood chums was Dan "Tubbo" Gilbert, former Teamster boss, Chicago cop, and the unscrupulous chief investigator in the state's attorney's office who schemed with his boss, Thomas J. Courtney, to capitalize on Touhy's mounting misfortunes.

The Touhys held their ground against the bullets and intimidation of the Capone forces. Roger's brother John was gunned down in 1927 while running beer in Niles. A second brother, Joseph, was trapped in a hail of machine-gun bullets two years later, and Roger's partner and second in command, Matt Kolb, was murdered outside the Club Morton in 1931. When violence failed to dislodge Roger Touhy from his bootlegging bailiwick, Al Capone decided it would be far easier to simply deliver his rival into the arms of the ambitious state's attorney.

Shortly after 1:00 A.M. the night of July 1, 1933, international con man Jake Factor, half brother of cosmetics tycoon Max Factor, was abducted outside the Dells roadhouse in Morton Grove and was allegedly taken to a safe house in neighboring Glenview. "How soon can you get $500,000?" the kidnappers demanded.

Factor's wife paid a $75,000 ransom twelve days later, and her husband was "released." It was later established that Factor had spent the entire twelve days hiding out in a Wauconda, Illinois, home. The kidnapping was a fraud all along.

Jake Factor swore that he heard Roger Touhy's voice in the confusion. Based on this flimsy piece of evidence, Touhy and several members of his gang were convicted in the Cook County Criminal Court a year later and sentenced to ninety-nine years in Stateville. It was a carefully orchestrated frame-up engineered by the Capone mob, Dan Gilbert, and Tom Courtney, a William Powell look-alike whose obsessions for higher office railroaded an innocent man into the Stateville prison.

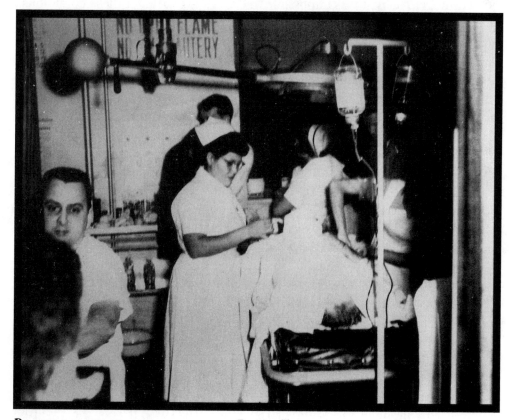

DOCTORS FIGHT TO SAVE THE LIFE OF ROGER TOUHY.

(Bill Helmer collection)

Courtney was wily, ruthless, and without conscience. Gilbert, whose well-documented underworld connections and personal fortune drew the attention of the Kefauver organized crime investigating committee in 1950, was an even more dangerous and unpredictable figure. These men controlled the Cook County judicial apparatus in the mid-1930s, and their clout reached into the court system, the police department, and City Hall.

When a trio of gunmen fired eight errant shots at Courtney's automobile the morning of March 23, 1935, orders were sent down from the mayor's office to find the men responsible for the despicable act and "deal" with them appropriately. This was interpreted by the Chicago police detail assigned to the case as an order to kill the suspects on sight—no questions asked. The cops were never able to track down the hoodlums who tried to kill Courtney, but public sentiment was on the side of the state's attorney. He was praised as a hero and called a crusading public servant—Chicago's version of New York rackets-buster Thomas Dewey. But the case smelled, and Courtney's political career eventually stalled.

For Roger Touhy, it was impossible to catch a break under these conditions. Taking matters into his own hands, he busted out of Stateville on October 9, 1942. Less than two months later, he was recaptured and an additional 199 years were tacked on to his sentence.

During these "stolen years," Touhy waged a long legal battle trying to prove that the Jake Factor kidnapping was an elaborate hoax designed to prevent Factor's extradition to England. Finally, Republican Governor William G. Stratton commuted Touhy's sentence, paving the way for his parole on November 13, 1959.

Humbled and contrite, Touhy sought refuge in a bungalow owned by his sister Ethel Alesia at 125 North Lotus Avenue in the Austin neighborhood on the far West Side. "This freedom is wonderful," he remarked to his biographer Ray Brennan, a reporter for the *Chicago Sun-Times*. But Touhy, now sixty-one, was constantly fearful, and he never strayed too far from the family home.

Expecting deadly reprisals from his former enemies in the Capone mob, Touhy hired Walter Miller, a former police investigator on Gilbert's staff in the 1930s, to serve as his personal bodyguard. Miller had found the Wauconda "vacation" house where Factor hid out during his twelve-day abduction, and tried to set the record straight. Gilbert ordered him to tell no one about it, or risk the consequences. But over the years, Miller continued to speak up, time after time, but no one listened or cared.

Roger Touhy and Walter Miller returned home from a downtown dinner meeting with Brennan the night of December 16, 1959. It was shortly after 10:30 P.M. As Touhy fumbled for his house keys on the front porch, shotgun and pistol blasts from a passing car shattered the calm of this once serene neighborhood. Miller was only slightly injured, but Roger Touhy's wounds were fatal. He expired at St. Anne's Hospital less than an hour later.

Jake the Barber was dining at the Singapore Steak House, a hood joint at 1011 North Rush Street, when he was informed of Roger Touhy's murder. He had just filed a $3 million libel suit against Touhy and author Ray Brennan over allegations contained in the book, *The Stolen Years,* and was probably wondering if he would ever be able to collect his dough.

"This is such a shock," he said in feigned sadness. "I hope they find the killers. That's my only comment." The final chapter of *The Stolen Years* was never written. Roger Touhy's killers vanished into the night, and Factor's spurious lawsuit against Brennan was settled out of court.

Jake Factor received a pardon from President John F. Kennedy in 1962. He was a generous contributor to JFK's 1960 campaign and a friend of the Las Vegas "Rat Pack," and was justly rewarded. Factor reportedly ran the Stardust Casino in Las Vegas for the mob in later years.

Residences of Organized Crime:

The Western Suburbs

The movement of heavy industry out of crowded Chicago neighborhoods in the early years of the twentieth century heralded a population exodus from the city to the suburbs.

The opening of the Western Electric Hawthorne plant in Cicero in 1903 sparked the soon-to-be unstoppable suburbanization of working-class families, who abandoned the deteriorating West Side of Chicago and took up residence in the emerging western suburbs, most of which were railroad towns hugging the Chicago, Burlington, & Quincy right of way.

The same economic and social forces that drove thousands of Chicago families out of the central city also compelled organized crime to abandon its West Side roots for the wide-open spaces of the western suburbs. (Horace Greeley's famous admonition, "Go west, young man!" must have imparted a lasting impression on the gangland minions who fled the old neighborhoods, when the old neighborhoods were no longer safe for the wise guys.) By the 1950s, the uprooting of the Chicago mob was nearly complete. In many respects, Taylor Street, the Valley, and Douglas Park were safer places to live once the mob vacated its traditional strongholds to follow the trail of money.

Cicero became the business address for most of the mob-run enterprises, but the more affluent western suburbs of River Forest, Oak Park, Elmwood Park, and North Riverside beckoned the syndicate leaders to their leafy-green side streets and extravagant manses built to specification.

Paul "the Waiter" Ricca, Chuckie English, and Tony Accardo lived like British noblemen in their expensive River Forest digs. "Milwaukee" Phil Alderisio, who was Sam Giancana's most capable enforcer during the 1960s, took up residence on Byrd Street in North Riverside. Oak Park beckoned "42 Gang" alumnus Sam "Teetz" Battaglia; Marshall Caifano, a Las Vegas player in Chicago; and Sam Giancana, whose modest family bungalow belied his ostentatious lifestyle. Jackie

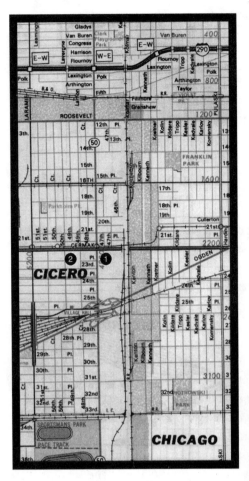

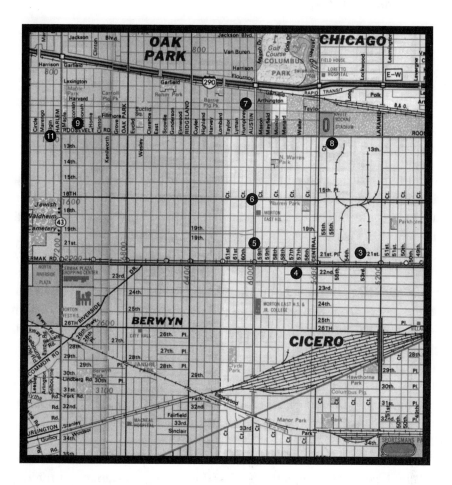

1. Frank Capone killed outside the Hawthorne Works, Twenty-second and Chicago.
2. Former site of the Hawthorne Hotel, 4833 West Twenty-second Street.
3. Former site of the Cotton Club in Cicero, 5342 West Twenty-second Street.
4. Klas Restaurant, where Al Capone dined.
5. Tony Lombardo's former residence, 2111 West Austin Boulevard.
6. Al Capone's crash pad, 1600 West Austin Boulevard.
7. Ralph Capone slept here, 1117 West Austin.
8. The Pony Inn (now Sarno's Restaurant) at Roosevelt and Fifty-sixth Court.
9. Sam Giancana's residence at 1147 Wenonah Avenue.
10. Tony Accardo's second mansion at Ashland and Greenfield.
11. The Armory Lounge (now Andrea's), 7427 West Roosevelt Road.

Cerone, onetime chauffeur for Accardo, a scratch golfer, and juice-loan extortionist, was a longtime resident of Elmwood Park.

Crime not only paid, it paid handsomely, as one look at the sumptuous homes of the syndicate leaders will attest.

Cicero: Welcome to Potterville

Cicero, a town that has come to symbolize the rustbelt decay of the industrial North in the second half of the twentieth century, has at various times in its long and uniquely colorful history been called the most corrupt municipality in America and the "Main Street of the Mob."

Cicero lies along the ragged western boundary line of Chicago, extending from Roosevelt Road on the north to Pershing Road on the south. Although scarred by its reputation as a racially intolerant and dangerous "border town," Cicero has been home to generations of law-abiding Czechs and Bohemians, many of whom worked at the Western Electric Hawthorne plant until the industrial giant, once the world's largest manufacturer of telephone equipment, pulled up stakes a quarter of a century ago.

Town pioneers will tell you with understandable community pride that Cicero is a safe and decent place to live. In many respects that is probably true, but for many years Cicero's power structure was in the tightly clenched fist of the Chicago "outfit." Twice in this century, the first time in 1924 and again in 1964, an outside police agency was ordered to occupy the Town Hall after the inertia of mob-controlled cops threatened the peace and stability of the community.

Incorporated in 1867, the town achieved a dubious notoriety in the 1920s when local officials welcomed the incursions of the Capone mob and the introduction of open gambling; 161 rip-roaring, all-night saloons; and a string of two-dollar brothels. In 1926, three years after Al Capone pulled out of Chicago and transferred his headquarters to the western suburb, Cicero was the fourth largest community in Illinois. Its puppet government, headed by Town President William Z. Klenha, formerly the town dogcatcher, and Police Chief Theodore Svoboda, was firmly under the thumb of organized crime.

Over the years, Cicero has waged a continuous, but unsuccessful, public relations campaign to clear its reputation and good name. Street-lamp banners, placed there in the 1990s at the suggestion of political strategist Ray Hanania, proclaim Cicero as the birthplace of Ernest Hemingway, bending the truth a little bit perhaps, but recrafting the town's image requires imagination as well as patience. Another Hanania banner makes reference to Cicero, "the Great Roman Orator." Cynics chuckle at the unintentional irony and suggest that the banner should rightfully proclaim "the Great Roman Orgy," for the wild saturnalia carried on inside the notorious dives lining Twenty-second Street during Prohibition.

In an effort to wipe clean the stains of its mob heritage, town officials authorized the demolition of the Hawthorne Smoke Shop, the Stockade, Eddie Tancl's saloon, the "Ship," and other less comfortable reminders of troubled times. But as long as there is a "mob-ocracy" at work and the charges continue to percolate, Cicero is doomed to revisit the sins of its "Potterville" past. (Potterville, of course, is what became of idyllic Bedford Falls after it was poisoned by political corruption and greed in Frank Capra's *It's a Wonderful Life*.)

It's hardly a "wonderful life."

CICERO HECKLERS GREET OPEN-HOUSING MARCHERS ON CICERO AVENUE NEAR EIGHTEENTH STREET IN ONE OF CHICAGO'S FAMOUS "LONG HOT SUMMERS" OF THE MID-1960S. A RIOT WAS AVOIDED AFTER IT WAS LEARNED THAT THE REVEREND DR. MARTIN LUTHER KING WOULD NOT BE PARTICIPATING IN THIS DEMONSTRATION.

We will begin our gangland tour of the western suburbs in Cicero at Twenty-second Street and Cicero Avenue.

"YOU NEVER GET NO BACK TALK FROM A CORPSE!"
April 1, 1924

Al Capone's younger brother Salvatore (Frank Capone) was cut down in a volley of police bullets outside the Hawthorne Works, the massive Western Electric plant located at the southeast corner of Twenty-second Street and Cicero Avenue, on April 1, 1924. It was primary day in Illinois, probably the bloodiest in Illinois history, and Capone marshaled his forces in an all-out bid to elect a slate of candidates favorable to his interests. Frank Capone was on hand to make sure that Cicero residents "voted right." The Hawthorne Works provided steady employment for Ciceronians from 1903 until its closing in the 1980s. The ancient factory fell to the wrecker's ball a few years after the last worker punched his time card for the final time. A numbing collection of budget chain stores and a vast parking lot now comprise the former factory site. There are no visible clues pointing to the earlier infamy of this famous Cicero street corner. A White Castle hamburger restaurant covers the ground where Frank Capone's blood was spilled.

Unafraid of gangsters, murder threats, and the sinister presence of Al Capone, William K. Pflaum challenged Max Haucek for town clerk of Cicero. The night before the Illinois primary, Pflaum's offices at 5709 West Twenty-second Street were raided by syndicate goons. An elderly man of rather frail comportment, Pflaum was no match for the Capone gunmen who bloodied his face and slammed his wife against the wall.

William Pflaum headed the Civic Democratic Club, a splinter coalition of reformers and laypeople enthusiastically supported by Robert St. John, the crusading editor of the weekly *Cicero Tribune*. St. John decried the violence, savagery, and loose moral conditions infecting Cicero ever since Al Capone had stumbled across the border from Chicago in 1923 and claimed Cicero as a trophy.

Interestingly, Cicero has voted the Republican ticket since 1918, and it still does to this day. It is perhaps the last Republican "machine" town in America.

Democrats are not welcome on Twenty-second Street, and attempts to build a solid opposition party have, over the years, been met with fierce resistance.

In the spring election of 1924, Democratic precinct workers suddenly began to disappear. Polling places were raided by gangsters. Election judges, clerks, and opposition supporters were chased out the door by Capone strongmen. Automobiles filled with gunmen raced up and down the streets slugging and kidnapping in a campaign of terror without equal in the long history of Illinois politics.

Outraged by reports of preelection violence, Cook County Judge Edmund K. Jarecki ordered 120 Chicago police officers into Cicero to be sworn in as Cook County deputy sheriffs for the purpose of protecting the twenty-thousand-member Western Electric workforce from intimidation. It marked the first time that Chicago police officers had crossed city limits in an official capacity since 1870. The situation was desperate, and it demanded extreme measures.

Outside the factory on the afternoon of April 1, 1924, a caravan of fifty police "flivvers" from the Lawndale precinct and other city jurisdictions on the West Side drove single-file down Cicero Avenue under the command of Detective Sergeant William Cusack. The procession came to a sudden, tire-screeching halt when the lead driver spotted a trio of gangsters emerging from the shadows. The police, thinking they were about to be fired upon, jumped out of the cars and took cover.

Charles Fischetti, Dave Hedlin, and Frank Capone, believing that a rival faction of gangsters bent on killing them had invaded their turf, opened fire on the plainclothes Chicago cops. Silhouetted against two sidewalk billboards, Frank Capone was hit in the crossfire from shots fired by Sergeant Phillip McGlynn.

"I walked up to him as he lay there," McGlynn explained at the inquest. "His hand still clutched the gun. He tried feebly to rise and fire but was too weak and fell back."

After hearing McGlynn's version of events, Al Capone, purple with rage, said his brother was an innocent bystander, who had come to Cicero that afternoon merely to discuss the purchase of a Cicero coffee shop with business "associates" at the Hawthorne Hotel.

Charles Fischetti, a cousin of the Capones, ran into an open field but was captured almost instantly. He told police that he didn't even know there was an election going on. Dave Hedlin escaped with a bullet wound.

Al Capone's older brother died later that day. The body was identified by family at the Cook County Morgue, and $20,000 worth of floral arrangements was hastily ordered from Dion O'Bannion's flower shop.

John and Harry Madigan, owners of the notorious Pony Inn roadhouse on

Roosevelt Road, were arrested and charged with abducting Democratic poll watchers, who were taken to a garage at 3614 West Harrison Avenue where they were bound and gagged until after the election results were in.

When the smoke cleared, the votes counted, and the bodies laid out neatly in the morgue, Al Capone's entire slate of candidates won the election by narrow margins.

Cicero belonged to Capone at long last, but it cost him the life of his brother Frank, who once remarked, "You never get no back talk from a corpse."

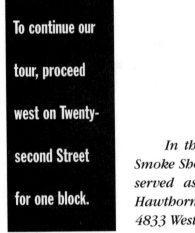

To continue our tour, proceed west on Twenty-second Street for one block.

THE HAWTHORNE SMOKE SHOP, THE HOTEL ANTON, AND THE HAWTHORNE HOTEL, FORMERLY LOCATED IN THE 4800 BLOCK OF TWENTY-SECOND STREET

In the heart of Al Capone's Cicero, the Hawthorne Smoke Shop, Ted Anton's Hotel, and the Hawthorne Hotel served as the gang's compound and sanctuary. The Hawthorne Hotel stood on the south side of the street at 4833 West Twenty-second Street, one block west of Cicero Avenue. A men's clothing store separated the hotel from the smoke shop and Anton's Hotel, one door west. The Hotel Anton was remodeled and the name was changed to the Hotel Alton after the Capones moved out. By the late 1980s, the building was on its last legs. It had become a squalid transient hotel and public eyesore destined for the wrecker's ball. The Hawthorne Hotel later changed its name to the Western Hotel, and in its final days was called the Towne Hotel. Sold to mob boss Joseph Aiuppa on February 17, 1970, the Towne Hotel burned to the ground as a result of a fire of suspicious origin. Today, the First Federal Savings building occupies a portion of the lot where the Hawthorne stood. Cook County police investigators, familiar with the interior layout of the mob-owned hotel, reported finding metal cages, just large enough to imprison a grown man, in the basement of the building.

Entrenched in Ted "the Greek" Anton's modest, but affordable, hotel in the spring of 1924, Al Capone decided his rising status in local politics and Cicero's "civic life" demanded a more ostentatious display. Anton's place was the organi-

THE HAWTHORNE SMOKE SHOP AND ANTON'S HOTEL: COMMAND POST OF THE
CAPONE MOB IN CICERO DURING THE 1920S. AN EMPTY LOT FLANKED BY A BANK
BUILDING AND A RESTAURANT IS HOW THIS SECTION OF TWENTY-SECOND STREET
APPEARS TODAY.
(Photo by author)

zation's gambling flagship, and when the owner had had enough, he turned the operation over to gangster Frankie Pope, the "Millionaire Newsboy." Frankie Pope peddled the afternoon *American* on the streets of Chicago as a boy, only to go on to make a fortune in the rackets a quarter of a century later.

The Hawthorne Hotel, a three-story, brown-brick building, was a legitimate business front for Capone's mentor Johnny Torrio. When Capone took up residence at the hotel, he installed bulletproof steel shutters and arranged the furniture in such a way that a stranger entering the lobby was immediately recognized from all sides by watchful bodyguards who took up positions along the walls.

The Hawthorne Smoke Shop was the place where bets were accepted for a twenty-four-hour wire room inside Anton's hotel next door. The proprietors clocked bets and sold seventy-five-cent drinks despite recent, feeble attempts to close the place by statute.

Capone's heavily armed compound came under deadly attack from a cavalcade of machine gunners arriving in massed formation shortly after 1:00 P.M. on September 20, 1926. A caravan of six automobiles, coming from the west, proceeded slowly down Twenty-second Street. Only the barrels of the machine guns poking through the curtained windows of the cars were visible to eyewitnesses. The lead car, equipped with an alarm bell on the front, resembled a police flivver.

The streets were crowded when the shooting started outside of Anton's Hotel. Machine-gun fire raked the windows of Angelo Gurdi's barbershop, where Capone received his daily shave; a delicatessen; a laundry; and the Hawthorne Restaurant. In a final, murderous volley, a man dressed in khaki overalls stepped from the running board of one of the cars and approached the main entrance of the Hawthorne Hotel. With the machine gun resting on his knee, he sprayed the interior lobby the way a gardener might aim the nozzle of a hose at a dry lawn. Then the attack cars sped off, crossing the city limits back into Chicago.

Amid the incredible fury of a thousand whizzing bullets, only two persons sustained injury. A woman from Ft. Worth, Texas, who was in town for the horse races at the Hawthorne Race Track, was grazed by a stray bullet. (According to widely circulated reports, Al Capone paid Mrs. Freeman $10,000 in compensatory damages.) Gunman Louis Barko, who had fired on Hymie Weiss outside the old Standard Oil Building on Michigan Avenue only a few months earlier, was struck in the neck and shoulder. At the Jefferson Park Hospital where he was taken, Barko listed his occupation as "gambler."

Capone was seated inside the Hawthorne Restaurant, with bodyguard Frank Rio, sipping his coffee when the first shots were fired. Capone dove under his table and escaped unharmed.

It was an open secret that the gunmen belonged to George "Bugs" Moran's North Side mob, and the man in the khaki overalls was probably Peter Gusenberg, who would perish inside the S.M.C. Cartage Company on Valentine's Day, 1929.

The "Strip Molls" of Cicero

S I D E T R I P

In a sworn affidavit read before interested members of the McClellan U.S. Senate Committee investigating organized crime, Roswell T. Spencer, Chief Investigator for the Cook County Sheriff's Police, introduced the Washington crowd to Al Capone's crowd.

On June 15, 1962, Spencer demonstrated in a prepared statement before Congress that in the forty years following Capone's invasion of Cicero, mob franchises were in firm control of three of the wickedest sin spots draping the commercial district of Twenty-second Street (Cermak Road)—Rose's Magic Lounge at 4820 Cermak; the Frolics Lounge at 4813 Cermak; and the Turf Lounge, a center for prostitution and gambling inside Joey Aiuppa's Towne Hotel at 4827 Cermak.

"The Magic Lounge and the Frolics Lounge have been notorious for years as clip joints and the worst kind of strip joints where lewd and obscene dancing, stripping to complete nudity, 'B' drinking, prostitution, and every kind of immorality and public indecency have flourished without interference from Cicero authorities despite a constant barrage from the pulpit, the press, and public. Establishments such as the Magic Lounge and the Frolics Lounge are not legitimate places of business or of entertainment and refreshment, but are, in fact, an integral and important part of the crime organization's establishment and facilities pandering to the base appetites and desires for enticing victims under the pretense of entertaining them and giving them a good time, but with the real purpose of cheating, robbing, and gouging them and of taking their money from them by any means necessary, from exorbitant prices and 'B' drinking to jack-rolling and knockout drops."

Sheriff Richard B. Ogilvie, following up on a suggestion made by Art Bialek and accompanied by a uniformed army of Cook County cops, invaded the town of Cicero in 1964. ABC newsman Frank Reynolds was on the street with a microphone and a camera crew filming Ogilvie's every move as his raiders herded scores of young women sleazily attired in leopard-skin coats, six-inch heels, and bouffant hairdos into a waiting paddy wagon, past grim-faced detectives in fedoras and the usual gaggle of newsmen. Cicero had once again become a national news item and a metaphor of modern organized crime's stranglehold on our cities.

In time, Ogilvie lost interest in the crusade, and life returned to its nor-
mal routines. By the 1970s and 1980s, the action had shifted to a narrow strip
of Cicero Avenue extending from Roosevelt Road south to Twenty-first Street.
The "twenty-minute" motels provided all the necessary amenities for a man on
the go: a mattress, a plastic sheet, and a condom. Vacant-eyed women prowled
the street in search of "Johns." While this was going on, the wise-heads in Town
Hall were in self-denial until raids and a storm of negative publicity from the
Chicago newspapers resumed.

In the 1990s, town President Betty Loren-Maltese took a bold step to curb
escalating gang crime and vice in her domain. She published the names of
fifty-seven men who had solicited hookers on Cicero Avenue in the pages of her
political paper, the Cicero Observer, *and ordered the police to force arrested*
gangbangers to wear pink aprons while in detention.

We will continue the tour by going five blocks fur-ther west on Twenty-second Street.

THE COTTON CLUB, FORMERLY AT 5342 WEST TWENTY-SECOND STREET

A Home Center and tile warehouse stands on the site of the old Cotton Club.

Five blocks west of the Hawthorne Hotel, Ralph Capone owned and operated Cicero's best-known speakeasy, the Cotton Club, at 5342 West Twenty-second Street. The walls inside the rustic log cabin exterior were covered with expensive murals. It was one of the premier show spots of the western suburbs. It was here that Milton Berle was paid $2,000 by Al Capone to perform one night before Chicago Mayor William Hale Thompson.

Jazz greats King Oliver, Duke Ellington, Jelly Roll Morton, and Walter Bond played at the Cotton Club, but none of these African-American entertainers would have dared sign a lease agreement or mortgage for property in all-white Cicero. They understood, as most blacks understood, that a brick through the window or a burning cross on the lawn would begin the welcoming party.

Continue west on Twenty-second Street.

THE KLAS RESTAURANT
5734 WEST TWENTY-SECOND STREET

Serving authentic Bohemian-Czech cuisine, the Klas Restaurant is a family restaurant that dates back to 1922 when patriarch Adolph Klas opened his establishment. During the years of the "Cicero occupation," Al Capone played gin rummy with his gang in the Moravia Room on the second floor. According to a Klas waitress who is familiar with Cicero history, the original owner built "closets" or small rooms off the main room for the private use of the gangsters and their girlfriends. Capone's deck of cards is on display in a glass case in the lobby of the restaurant.

Continue west on Twenty-second Street to Austin Boulevard and turn right.

TONY LOMBARDO'S RESIDENCE
1928

Tony Lombardo, head of the Unione Sicilione, and his wife lived at 4442 West Washington Boulevard in the Austin neighborhood on the city's West Side until the Chicago police uncovered a plot to assassinate him in 1927. The young couple fled to the relative safety of suburban Cicero and the protection of their benefactor, Al Capone. The red-brick bungalow at 2111 West Austin Boulevard where they took sanctuary is located north of Twenty-second Street just a few blocks south of Al Capone's party house. On September 7, 1928, Tony Lombardo's wife, feeling secure in her new surroundings, was preparing dinner when she received word that her husband had been killed.

Tony Lombardo, a penniless immigrant from Italy who washed up on U.S. shores with $12 in his pocket, controlled the wealthy and ruthless Unione Sicilione, a midwestern fraternal society that required Italian merchants to buy goods from a prepared list drawn up by Lombardo.

Between 1925 and 1929, the North Side gang systematically murdered four presidents of the Unione Sicilione, believing that the key to "decommissioning" Al Capone was to remove his power base and install Joe Aiello, an Italian they believed they could "work with." Tony Genna, Samuzzo "Samoots" Ammatuna, Tony Lombardo, and Patsy Lolordo all fell in the line of fire.

Lombardo and Lolordo were particularly close to Capone and were men of respect within the Italian-American community, symbolizing immigrant triumph over the hardships of poverty and intolerance. When disputes arose, Italian-Americans turned to Lombardo in their hour of need. In such times, his criminal alliances were forgotten or ignored.

Continue

north on

Austin

Boulevard.

AFTER A HARD DAY AT THE OFFICE: AL CAPONE'S CRASH PAD IN CICERO
1928

Al Capone's after-hours party house is located at 1600 West Austin Boulevard (the southwest corner of Austin Boulevard and Sixteenth Street) in Cicero.

Al Capone purchased the tan-brick apartment house, with ornamental masonry and an imposing eight-foot-high brick wall encircling the backyard, as a place to kick back and cavort without being bothered by the intrusions of family life or the prying eyes of reporters. The front door was fashioned from bulletproof steel, and a getaway tunnel connected the garage at the rear of the property to the house.

And of course, Al Capone was the sole proprietor and resident. He was the lord of his manor and keeper of the secrets. Mama Teresa, wife Mae, and Sonny boy kept a safe, respectful distance. They knew better than to stray too far from the family abode at 7244 South Prairie Avenue. If the family members had caught a glimpse of what really went on inside Capone's Cicero dwelling, they would have been appalled by the spectacle of sex orgies, drug use, and wild bacchanalia. What must the neighbors have thought?

AL CAPONE IN A MUG
SHOT AND WITH HIS
MEN. JACK McGURN
IS SEATED TO THE
LEFT OF AL. THIS
PHOTO MAY HAVE
BEEN SHOT AT THE
AUSTIN AVENUE
"CRASH PAD."

Continue

north on

Austin

Boulevard.

RALPH "BOTTLES" CAPONE SLEPT HERE
1925

Al Capone's older brother Ralph purchased a three-story brick dwelling at 1117 West Austin on the boulevard of gangsters, just blocks north of Al's party house. The private residence can be seen on the east side of the street just south of the Father & Daughter Remodeling Company. Ralph Capone, who originally lived up on the North Side at Farwell and Sheridan, moved here to be closer to his base of operations and the seat of Cicero town government.

Lacking the charisma and flare for self-publicity that consumed his younger brother's waking hours, Ralph Capone supervised the gang's bottling operations, which inspired his famous nickname. During the 1933 Century of Progress Fair, two years after Al was incarcerated in a federal penitentiary, brother Ralph ran a soft drink concession on the fairgrounds. It was quite a comedown for a Capone, who had worked quietly behind the scenes as the "political fixer" of Cicero during the heyday of his brother's regime in the western suburbs.

Ralph Capone began a two-year prison sentence for income tax evasion at McNeil Island in 1931, but he lived quite anonymously thereafter, until the Chicago newspapers announced his passing in 1974.

Continue north

on Austin

Boulevard to

Roosevelt Road

and turn right

(east).

WHO KILLED McSWIGGIN?
April 27, 1926

Harry Madigan's Pony Inn, where the sensational slaying of Assistant State's Attorney William McSwiggin occurred, is now Sarno's Restaurant at 5613 West Roosevelt Road (on the south side of the street at Fifty-sixth Court, near the Cicero-Chicago boundary). Look closely. It is the same two-story building—there is no doubt. However, the original brickwork has been replaced, burying the notoriety of years in the past.

The *Chicago Tribune* and State's Attorney Robert Emmet Crowe thought they had it all figured out. According to the *Tribune,* May 2, 1926, "Scarface Al Brown, whose real name is Caponi [sic], was the machine gunner who killed William H. McSwiggin, assistant state's attorney; Thomas Duffy and James J. Doherty according to the best information...."

Al Capone, who was commonly known as Al Brown during his Chicago heyday, demurred, "I didn't kill McSwiggin. I liked the kid." A special grand jury studied the matter, but there was no evidence against Capone, who was released three days later.

The cynical world-weary view that it is a great public service when gangsters kill fellow gangsters began to change with the shocking death of young William Harold McSwiggin, who was known around town as Cook County's "hanging prosecutor" after obtaining seven death sentences in eight months. He was the son of Anthony McSwiggin, a thirty-year veteran of the Chicago Police Department's detective bureau, who was escorting a prisoner back from Iowa when word of the shooting reached him by telephone.

Sergeant McSwiggin was especially proud of Bill's accomplishments securing indictments and zealously prosecuting such public enemies as John Scalise and Alberto Anselmi. It made no sense to the beleaguered cop or, for that matter, the entire city. Why was this twenty-six-year-old wonder boy in the company of unsavory hoodlums at Harry Madigan's Pony Inn, a Cicero dive frequented by West Side bootlegger William "Klondike" O'Donnell and other gangsters? Who killed McSwiggin and why? The public demanded answers.

O'Donnell and his brother Myles were undercutting the cost of Capone's "needle (near) beer" in Cicero to dangerously low levels. Their bravado helped seal warrants for their execution.

On the night of April 27, 1926, Al Capone was dining at the Hawthorne Inn when he was tipped that Klondike and Myles O'Donnell were lurking inside the Pony Inn. Capone was probably correct in saying that he did not know of Bill McSwiggin's saloon-hopping escapade. If he had, the whole thing would have in all likelihood been called off.

McSwiggin had left the family dinner table at 4946 West Washington Boulevard shortly after 7:00 P.M., telling his mother that he was going to Berwyn to play a hand of cards with his boyhood chum, Thomas "Red" Duffy. But the plan changed, and the two men ended up at Harry Madigan's place. Duffy, another police officer's son in the wrong place at the wrong time, was Madigan's former business partner.

A five-car caravan hastily departed the Hawthorne Inn a few minutes past eight o'clock, bound for the Pony Inn to settle old scores. Al Capone, it is widely believed, cradled a Thompson submachine gun in his lap. The convoy arrived at the precise moment McSwiggin, Klondike, and Myles O'Donnell, bootlegger Jimmy Doherty, Edward Hanley, and "Red" Duffy stumbled out of Madigan's joint in their cups.

It was 8:15 and the boys were not through for the evening. They turned and walked toward Doherty's Lincoln, parked a few feet west of the Pony Inn, to drive to the next neighborhood tavern—forgetting that Prohibition was still the law of the land and that the voters of Cook County might not look kindly on one of the "white knights" of local law enforcement celebrating with gangsters.

Before McSwiggin's group could climb into the Lincoln sedan, Capone and his men, driving west on Roosevelt Road, turned the choppers loose. McSwiggin was felled by twenty bullets and dead on the spot. Doherty was literally cut in half by a volley of bullets. The O'Donnell brothers and Ed Hanley survived the ambush. They propped the severely wounded Duffy up against a tree and left him there to die, but he held out for a few more hours before expiring at West Suburban Hospital.

The O'Donnell brothers made short work of McSwiggin and Doherty. They emptied the pockets of the dead men, and dumped their bodies on the side of the road on the outskirts of Berwyn. A passing motorist spotted the still warm bodies in the glare of his automobile headlights a few hours later.

When the story of the slayings hit the papers the following day, the city was thrown into an uproar. "I am going to root out this booze and gang killing business if we have to use all the peace officers in Cook County on the one task," vowed State's Attorney Robert Emmet Crowe. "Of McSwiggin's character, I cannot say too much. He was one of the hardest workers on my staff. We have had plenty of threats, many have come to me, but we have laughed them off—until now."

The fighting words of a Republican state's attorney had an empty ring. Crowe's record was spotty. He was a political hack cut from the same soiled political cloth that foisted the blustering, cartoonish Mayor William Hale Thompson on the city of Chicago.

No one was ever brought to justice for the murder of one of Crowe's top trial aces. A grand jury whitewashed the deadly affair and ruled that McSwiggin was an innocent bystander caught in the crossfire between warring gang factions.

The prosecutor was laid to rest in Mount Carmel cemetery, not far from the gravesites of Dion O'Banion and other underworld legends of the 1920s. Bill McSwiggin was just another casualty of Prohibition, and symbolic of the moral hypocrisy of the age.

Oak Park

Oak Park, a part of Cicero Township for many years, reached maturity as a residential suburb by the 1960s. Besides being the boyhood home of Ernest Hemingway, who never mentioned the village in any of his published works, Oak Park was the mailing address for Sam Giancana, "Chairman of the Board" for the Chicago outfit, until his death in 1975.

To continue the tour, go west on Roosevelt Road to Harlem Avenue. Turn right on Harlem and go north to Lexington Street (three blocks). Turn east (right) and go three blocks to Wenonah Avenue. Turn right again, back south, and proceed two blocks to Fillmore Street.

THE DARK SIDE OF CAMELOT
June 19, 1975

Sam Giancana was cooking up a late-night repast of Italian sausages and spinach in the basement kitchen of his red-brick bungalow at 1147 South Wenonah Avenue (at the corner of Fillmore Street) in Oak Park when an unknown gunman entered through a side door. The sausages were still simmering in the kettle when Giancana's eighty-one-year-old caretaker found his boss lying faceup on the floor. Six spent shell casings were retrieved nearby. The Giancana bungalow, purchased for $22,500 in the mid-1940s, looks much the same today as it did in 1974, when the feared Chicago mob boss returned home to die. There is nothing garish or ornate about the solidly built one-and-a-half-story residence. It blends in perfectly with the surrounding 1920s brick bungalow architecture. In Giancana's lifetime, as now, this tree-lined section of Oak Park was a nice place to live and raise a family.

Without the benefit of a warm, engaging personality, movie star good looks, and that certain indefinable aura surrounding our cultural icons, Sam "Momo" Giancana, a weaselly, unlikable gangster during his lifetime became a cause célèbre in death. The fedora hat. The sunglasses. His famous gangster scowl. It was all part of a cleverly crafted image that enchanted Hollywood, captivated the Kennedys, and won the heart of his little "canary," Phyllis McGuire.

"Seven out of ten times when we hit a guy, we're wrong," Momo said in a rare moment of philosophical reflection. "But the other three guys we hit, we make up for it." There were seventy-nine mob murders during Giancana's brutal nine-year reign (1957–1966) as boss of the Chicago outfit. During the next eight years, there were only twenty-four, which speaks volumes about the character of the man that Frank Sinatra referred to as "Sam Flood."

Momo dined on chateaubriand with his Rat Pack "pallies" at the Sands in Las Vegas, provided the margin of victory to Jack Kennedy in 1960, and tried to knock off Fidel Castro in an event-filled life.

A product of Taylor and Halsted Streets on the near West Side, Giancana was a protégé of "Machine Gun" Jack McGurn. Giancana had a reputation on the streets as an expert "wheel man" for the old "42 Gang" of toughs, who ran errands for Al Capone during Prohibition. When asked by the draft board what he did for a living, Giancana replied, "I steal." Years later he embellished the recounting even more. "They thought I was crazy. But I wasn't crazy. I was telling the truth."

Twice arrested for murder before his twentieth birthday, Giancana muscled in on Edward "Teenan" Jones's South Side "policy" rackets after World War II. One by one, the old policy kings were executed, as Giancana, the leader of a faction of "young Turks" who served their apprenticeship in the "42 Gang," spread terror far and wide.

Sam and his family lived in a red-brick three-flat at 2822 West Lexington Street on the Near West Side before moving to 1028 South Monitor Avenue in 1945. As his gangland status and reputation grew, Giancana bought the comfy little bungalow on Wenonah Avenue in Oak Park. It was nothing outrageous, just a modest family home. Giancana wanted to blend in and be left alone. Being Sam Giancana, that was, of course, impossible.

Shoving Tony Accardo aside in 1957, the newly crowned Chicago mob boss became an unlikely ally of the Kennedys, but his friendship with Sinatra, McGuire, Dean Martin, and songbird Keeley Smith had overruled common sense.

Against his better judgment, Momo's political fixers put John F. Kennedy in the White House. The syndicate-controlled river wards (the 1st, 25th, 28th, and 29th), along with the South and West Side black wards (the 2nd, 3rd, 4th, 6th, 20th, 21st, and 24th), delivered to Kennedy 60 percent of the vote and the margin of victory. In return, the "grateful" Camelot crowd unleashed Bobby Kennedy and six years of unrelenting FBI "heat" on Giancana and the outfit.

Driven into a self-imposed nine-year exile in Mexico, the Caribbean, and Peru in 1966 as a result of JFK's double-cross and the attorney general's hypocritical crusade against organized crime, Giancana's high-profile lifestyle continued to draw unwanted attention to the goings-on in Chicago. While traveling abroad, Giancana lived like a Roman emperor and invested millions of dollars of mob money in offshore accounts.

In the mid-1970s, the government began poking into his dealings with the Kennedys, their girlfriends, the CIA, and the Cubans and his cash pile of laundered money. Suffering from blood clots and barely able to walk, Giancana was rousted from his villa by the Mexican authorities and put on a jetliner bound for Houston in his pajamas. The Mexicans didn't even allow him the chance to pack a toothbrush. A year later, in 1975, an assassin's bullets tore through his neck.

"He was a walking dead man at the time he was killed," said one investigator.

Some believed the mob chieftains feared that Giancana would spill secrets to the "G" about his "investments." Others believed that he was trying to usurp power from Tony Accardo, the grandfatherly "Godfather," who was far more clever and self-effacing than the foul-tempered "Momo." Giancana's longtime companion and his bodyguard, Dominick "Butch" Blasi and Charles "Chuckie" English, were strongly suspected. Earlier that evening they had both greeted their former boss at an informal welcome-home party inside the bungalow.

Subpoenas were issued, suspects were grilled, but no one was talking. Blasi served eighteen months in the slammer for refusing to discuss the Giancana murder and other mob hits with a grand jury.

Two months later, detectives discovered the murder weapon—a .22 automatic with a silencer—that had been hastily discarded and left lying in a ditch in neighboring River Forest.

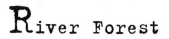

River Forest

Affluent River Forest was settled in 1836 and was known as Thatcher until it and neighboring Forest Park became part of the Town of Harlem. In the 1890s, River

Forest was a whistlestop on the Galena Division of the Chicago and Northwestern line. It is the home of Rosary and Concordia Colleges and has a number of Frank Lloyd Wright homes within its boundaries.

To continue the tour, return to Harlem Avenue and go north (right) past Chicago Avenue to Greenfield Street. Turn west (left) and proceed to Ashland Avenue.

DINING IN WITH THE DON: THE SECOND TONY ACCARDO RESIDENCE

Tony Accardo's secluded, fortresslike ranch house at 1401 Ashland Avenue (the northeast corner of Ashland Avenue and Greenfield Street, seven blocks west of Harlem Avenue) in River Forest is not nearly as ostentatious as one might expect from the most powerful and influential organized crime boss in the post–Al Capone era. In fact, by River Forest standards, it is quite modest.

When Paul "the Waiter" Ricca went to prison in 1943, control of the Chicago outfit passed to Anthony "Big Tuna" Accardo, a soft-spoken career criminal, who chauffeured Al Capone around town in the 1920s. An associate once remarked that "Tony Accardo had more brains before breakfast than Al Capone had all day."

Accardo was a "man of respect," remembered in law enforcement circles as a perfect gentleman, refined in manner, but cagey and utterly ruthless when provoked. Accardo consolidated his power by seizing control of Chicago bookmaking by eliminating powerful rivals like James M. Ragen and a score of African-American policy bosses who presided over penny-ante South Side gambling games in the early 1950s.

Tony Accardo ruled the outfit for two decades, possibly even longer. In old age, he was still "Chairman of the Board," an elder statesman of crime, who took the Fifth Amendment 152 times rather than betray secrets of the underworld to Estes Kefauver and his congressional subcommittee investigating organized crime in 1950.

Longing for the semblance of respectability and domestic tranquillity of the distant crime-free suburbs, Accardo purchased a sprawling $500,000 Tudor-style mansion at 915 Franklin Avenue in the upscale bedroom community of River

Forest. He stocked it with priceless antiques, installed a two-lane bowling alley, and called his new digs "The Palace."

A few blocks away, Paul Ricca lived in sartorial splendor at 1515 Bonnie Brae. No fewer than fifty-four gangsters settled in the affluent River Forest suburb in the 1960s. It was the highest concentration of organized crime figures in one residential community in the United States.

These hoodlums, who had risen from the poverty of the West Side slums, now lived among millionaires and the pillars of society, but their movements were constantly tracked by the FBI's Top Hoodlum Squad. And the Fourth of July, when Tony invited all the top mobsters and their families over for his annual barbecue, was no exception.

The wise guys drifted in and out of Accardo's mansion. On Sunday mornings, it was customary for "Mad Sam" DeStefano to drop in for a game of gin rummy and an informal talk.

The attention the media lavished on Accardo and his famous backyard soirees finally convinced him to give up the mansion, as much as he loved all of the delightful amenities. After selling his house at 915 Franklin Avenue for a cool million in 1964, Tony took up residence in the sixteen-room, custom-built ranch house at 1401 Ashland Avenue. Construction costs for the new place were pegged at $160,000.

An aside: The contractor who built Accardo's new home, Van Corbin, otherwise known as "Sam Panveno," was executed as he left his room at the Country Club Motel at 8303 North Avenue in the early morning hours of July 19, 1966. Corbin had been observed by the FBI at many of the mob's social functions over the years, but the Feds were at a loss to explain his sudden departure from this world. Was it, perhaps, the quality of the construction? Or did the mob accuse him of spilling secrets to the FBI?

The years rolled by quietly for the Accardos until January 1978, when their second home was broken into and ransacked by a burglary gang while the "chairman" and his wife were out of town. It was an extremely foolish thing to do, and the seven men, led by one Bernard Ryan, sealed their death warrants with their greed. Within a month, five members of the crew, their throats slashed and their bodies stuffed in the trunks of automobiles, were present and accounted for—in the county morgue. The other two burglars were found in much the same way in April.

Tony Accardo, who bragged that he never spent a night in jail, lived out the last few years of his life in Palm Springs, California. He died on May 27, 1992, from heart disease and the complications of old age. With his passing, the last link to Al Capone and his era disappeared. Since 1978, when the Accardos moved away, four succeeding owners of the property have all filed for bankruptcy. Is it cruel fate, or is the house cursed? You decide.

Forest Park

Forest Park was founded in 1856 by German settlers. For a time, Forest Park and River Forest comprised the town of Harlem. In 1907, Forest Park was given its name from the two adjacent suburbs, River Forest and Oak Park. A decade before the two suburbs established separate boundaries and individual identities, a syndicate of gamblers opened a racetrack, known as the Harlem Jockey Club, in what would become Forest Park. The track was a haven for a gang of touts, bookies, and handbook operators clocking wagers on often crooked races. Race results were dispersed by the gambler Mont Tennes with a telegraph link-up to the major thoroughbred tracks across the United States from a Forest Park "wire room." While Tennes funneled racetrack information to Chicago gamblers, "Blind" John Condon, an early business partner of downtown crime boss Mike McDonald, supervised the day-to-day operations at the track. Forest Park is also the home of the historic Forest Home and German Waldheim Cemeteries, the final resting place of the Haymarket men who were executed in Chicago in 1887 and several victims of the 1915 Eastland capsizing.

Return to Harlem Avenue and proceed south to Roosevelt Road. Turn right (west) and proceed to Thomas Street (five blocks).

THE MOB COMMAND POST
1950s–1960s

It's hard to believe that such an inconspicuous little restaurant like Andrea's at 7427 West Roosevelt Road in Forest Park (at the corner of Thomas Street, two blocks west of Circle Avenue) could occupy such an important place in mob folklore. In the 1950s and 1960s, Andrea's was under different ownership and infamously known as the Armory Lounge, because in earlier days weapons and ammunition were manufactured in a real armory that stood across the street. Surprisingly small and out of the way, what was the Armory Lounge is a very ordinary-looking brick building. It was, however, a symbol of the Chicago mob; it rep-

resented to the wise guys what the White House or the Kremlin represents to visiting heads of state. For it was here, in the famous "back room," where some of the major news events of the 1960s implicating the Chicago mob (the Kennedys, Marilyn Monroe, and Fidel Castro), were discussed, planned, and acted upon.

Chicago gangsters frequented many famous show spots and restaurants along the glittering white way extending from Chicago Heights to Cicero to Rush Street and out again to the Mannheim Road "strip" and points farther west. None was more famous in its day than the Armory Lounge, owned by Carmen Fanelli, a pal of Tony Accardo.

The cops and the Chicago Crime Commission had known about the Armory Lounge for years. A high-level conference of mobsters and executives from the Fox Head Brewing Company of Waukesha, Wisconsin, was held here on April 14, 1956, for the purpose of securing gainful employment for Tony Accardo as a distributor for Premium Beer Sales, Inc. His annual salary was pegged at $65,000.

Meeting in the famous "back room," where FBI agent Bill Roemer later planted a secret listening device on August 8, 1961, the executives reluctantly consented to add Tony to the payroll. Nervously adjusting his tie and mopping away the sweat from his brow, company president Henry Morgen suggested that Accardo would make a fine beer salesman, especially with all of his wonderful contacts in the resorts of Las Vegas. Syndicate heavies Murray "the Camel" Humphreys, Jackie "the Lackey" Cerone, and Dominick Volpe grunted their assent. Yes, they said. Tony knew everyone, but most of all he loved Fox DeLuxe beer and endorsed the product. What better testimony could there be? Humphreys and Cerone even bought shares of company stock to cement the deal.

From that day forward, a check in the amount of $1,250 was handed over to Howard Rice, the company treasurer, for delivery to Tony Accardo each week. But under questioning, none of the warehouse employees could ever recall seeing Mr. Accardo inside the plant.

It was not uncommon for the mob bosses to gather at the Armory Lounge to discuss business deals of this nature. In the 1920s it was a Prohibition speakeasy and a hangout for the hoodlums. By the 1960s, Sam Giancana held court here each evening. The location was convenient. It was only minutes away from 1147 South Wenonah, and the food was always magnifico. Sam's bodyguard Butch Blasi kept a watchful eye on the front of the restaurant through a tiny peephole drilled into the wall.

With Roemer and his colleagues listening in, the FBI learned the full extent of Giancana's ties to President John F. Kennedy and Frank Sinatra, while keeping a running log of his phone calls to his girlfriend, singer Phyllis McGuire.

The myths of Camelot turned to ashes inside the Armory Lounge, a place that Jack Kennedy probably never even heard of.

South Side Sinners

Whatever else one may say about Chicago's South Side, it is an undeniable historical truth that the importance of the Windy City as a commercial hub for manufacturing, meatpacking, and transportation was shaped by the forces of urbanization unleashed in the mid–nineteenth century south of Madison Street.

The Near South Side filled in quickly after 1830. Wealthy entrepreneurs desiring to live in secluded privacy in spacious surroundings followed the lead of Henry Clarke and built their "country homes" on the Near South Side close to the site of the Fort Dearborn massacre. The Henry B. Clarke house, originally built at 1700 South Michigan before being moved twice, now stands in the Prairie Avenue Historic District and is Chicago's oldest residential dwelling, built in 1836.

Potato-famine Irish settled in Bridgeport in the 1840s, then built the Illinois-Michigan Canal, linking Chicago to the Illinois and Mississippi Rivers before the Civil War. The nautical link to the great rivers of the Midwest opened up Chicago to the rest of the country and firmly established the city as an important part of the commercial life of the nation.

On Christmas Day of 1865, John Sherman opened his stockyards for business, spurring rapid economic development and continuous immigration into the

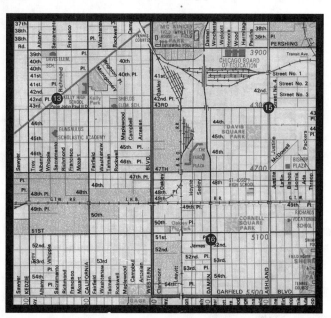

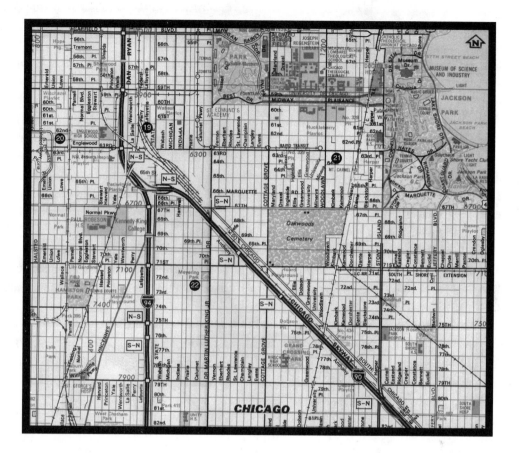

1. Prairie Avenue and Eighteenth Street, site of the Fort Dearborn Indian massacre.

2. Marshall Field Jr. mansion, 1919 South Prairie Avenue.

3. The South Side Levee district, Twenty-second and Dearborn.

4. Everleigh Club location, 2131 South Dearborn.

5. Former site of the Lexington Hotel, Twenty-second and Michigan.

6. Former site of the Metropole Hotel, Twenty-third and Michigan.

7. Former site of the Four Deuces, 2222 South Wabash.

8. Former Prohibition liquor depot raided by Eliot Ness, 2108 South Wabash.

9. George Silver's Maxim Cafe, 2107 South Wabash.

10. Former site of Scotland Yard Police Station, Canalport and Eighteenth Street.

11. Stephen A. Douglas monument, site of Camp Douglas prisoner of war camp, Cottage Grove Avenue and Thirty-fifth Street.

12. Site of James Ragen shooting, Thirty-ninth and State.

13. Brighton Theater, near where the Grimes girls were abducted, Archer and Sacramento.

14. Former site of the Union Stockyards, Halsted and Exchange.

15. Officer Lundy killed here, Forty-third and Ashland.

16. Residence of Joe Majczek, Damen Avenue near Fifty-second Street.

17. Bobby Franks abducted by Loeb and Leopold at Forty-ninth and Ellis.

18. Former Franks residence at Hyde Park Boulevard and Ellis.

19. Site of the Green Hornet trolley crash, Sixty-second and State Street.

20. Former site of Holmes murder castle at Sixty-third and Wallace, west of the railroad tracks.

21. First Presbyterian Chruch, where the Blackstone Rangers once operated, Sixty-fourth and Kimbark.

22. Al Capone's family home, 7244 South Prairie Avenue.

23. Town of Pullman, 111th and St. Lawrence.

24. Former site of the Ness bakery, 112th and Champlain.

25. Richard Speck murdered eight student nurses here in 1966.

South Side. The Yards provided Chicago with the unenviable—or enviable, depending on how you looked at it—reputation as "Hog Butcher to the World." For the next 100 years, the unsavory aroma of cow manure and the stench from the offal and dregs flowing out of "Bubbly Creek" blanketed the areas of Canaryville, Bridgeport, Back of the Yards, and McKinley Park.

For much of its history, the South Side was a dark landscape: a gritty, tough environment predicated on racial unease and ancient ethnic hostilities. Conditions were hard on everyone, and Upton Sinclair, a writer of dime novels, aptly named the Stockyards district *The Jungle*, in his 1906 muckraking serialization for the Socialist magazine *An Appeal to Reason*. Reaching a wider audience as a published novel, Sinclair's angry polemic exposed the evils of industrial Chicago to the eyes of the world.

The criminal underworld of the South Side was well defined by the 1840s, and the downtown press railed against the Irish toughs of Bridgeport, masking their nativist prejudices under the guise of civic concern for the well-being of Chicago citizens.

Street gangs, based on ethnic, religious, and social identifiers, were formed for the purpose of protecting neighborhood boundaries. Ragen's Colts, a Halsted Street "social-athletic club," was one such organization that tapped into ward politics as its source of strength, spreading terror near and far. Before the gang had run its course in the 1920s, one of its leaders was elected a Cook County commissioner. Another controlled the dissemination of racetrack information, until syndicate torpedoes got the best of him in a deadly ambush near Thirty-ninth and State Streets.

The unholy alliance between politicians and criminals allowed vice, gambling, and interstate prostitution to flourish in the Twenty-second Street Levee, a dangerous cauldron of vice and moral turpitude that defied the staid conventions of the late Victorian era. The Levee, in turn, enhanced career opportunities for Al Capone and a legion of followers who applied modern business principles to a continuing criminal enterprise that still exists today as the Chicago "outfit."

African-Americans, who were an important swing vote for the Democratic Party in later years, began arriving in Chicago in significant numbers before World War I, settling into the narrowly defined "Black Belt" (or Bronzeville) fronting Cottage Grove Avenue and running west to Wentworth Avenue. After the war, the growth of the African-American community and its institutions was explosive. Trainloads of blacks coming up from the Mississippi Delta on the Illinois Central displaced whites in Washington Park, Kenwood, and other formerly white South Side immigrant communities.

And just as the white ethnic gangs had capitalized on the moral vagaries of the age, so too did black gangsters, satisfying a growing demand in their communities for gambling and other forms of vice. Bronzeville hosted the largest and most successful policy racket in America, run by Teddy Roe, Edward "Teenan" Jones, and Winston Howard until Sam Giancana and the outfit muscled in on the action in the late 1940s.

The battle for control of the rackets led to endless shooting wars and assassinations. Years later, after Capone and the policy kings died or moved away, the South Side neighborhoods were taken over by inner-city drug traffickers and street gangs, which are organized on a scale that defies comprehension. The size of the gangs on the South Side parallels that of standing armies, and they impose their will upon the blighted communities of Washington Park, Woodlawn, and Englewood, where a once stable and prosperous middle class was forced out decades ago.

Organized crime preys on all races and social classes, respecting no social distinctions or boundaries, but today the South Side still remains stigmatized by its history and reputation.

We will begin our tour at Prairie Avenue and Eighteenth Street on Chicago's Near South Side.

THE FORT DEARBORN MASSACRE
August 15, 1812

Pavement markers on the four corners of Michigan Avenue and Wacker Drive (on the south bank of the Chicago River) commemorate the location of Fort Dearborn, a lonely military outpost erected by the U.S. government on this site in July 1803. On the occasion of the ninetieth anniversary of the founding of Fort Dearborn, industrialist George Mortimer Pullman, founder of the Pullman Palace Car Company, commissioned sculptor Carl Rohl-Smith to execute a bronze sculpture commemorating the 1812 massacre and the heroic rescue of Mrs. Helm by Black Partridge, a tribal leader on friendly terms with the white settlers. Pullman unveiled the monument on the grounds of his sprawling thirty-five room Second-Empire mansion at 1729 Prairie Avenue (on the northeast corner of Prairie and Eighteenth) in the most fashionable residential section of the country west of Fifth Avenue. At the height of the late Victorian era, no fewer than twenty millionaires lived along this majestic thoroughfare. By the 1930s, however, the industrialists and captains of industry had abandoned Prairie Avenue. The neighborhood was already in sharp decline by World War I. The incursions of heavy industry and the Levee vice district to the immediate west drove the patricians to safer, more agreeable neighborhoods on the North Side. Fearing that one of the wealthier vice merchants would lay claim to the property and convert it into a bordello, Pullman's daughter ordered the demolition of her father's home in 1922. Most of the other mansions, relics of another age, were demolished one by one. Pullman's Fort Dearborn statue was presumed to stand on the exact spot where legend placed the massacre, but the lakefront shallows had been filled in earlier, so it is virtually impossible to make an accurate determination of whether or not this is the same hallowed ground where Mrs. Helm was saved. The Pullman statue, which remained on public display at the Pullman property for the next thirty-seven years, was taken down in 1931 after vandals chipped away the cement base. The curators of the Chicago Historical Society later transferred Pullman's creation to the first floor of the museum at Clark Street and North Avenue. It is now part of a permanent exhibit on frontier Chicago. The purported massacre site is represented by a brass plaque affixed to the exterior wall of a brutishly stolid, one-story factory building standing on the former Pullman property.

By the terms of a peace treaty signed in Greenville, Ohio, in August 1795, following General "Mad" Anthony Wayne's successful engagement with the Miami tribe at the Battle of Fallen Timbers near present-day Toledo, Ohio, the native people ceded to the U.S. government the Northwest Territory. Later, by dint of a stunning military victory, the government added a small, six-square-mile parcel at the mouth of the "River Chicagou," which emptied into the southwest end of Lake Michigan.

Long before these developments, agents of the governor of Pennsylvania were sent in 1718 across the broad expanse of frontier to explore access routes to the Mississippi River. James Logan, a representative of the governor, claimed to have visited a military encampment at the aforementioned river's bank, but Logan's recollections are suspect. Questioned about this earlier "fort" years later, Potawatomi tribal elders could not recall the presence of white men in the region earlier than 1800.

Rumors of a new military garrison planned for the Chicago portage began to circulate in 1795, but it wasn't until 1803 that Captain John Whistler and a company of forty men were dispatched from Detroit to build a twelve-foot-high palisade and two blockhouses. The resulting fort was named in honor of the

THE FORT DEARBORN MASSACRE IS BELIEVED TO HAVE OCCURRED HERE—AT THE INTERSECTION OF PRAIRIE AND EIGHTEENTH, SHOWN IN AN 1886 DRAWING WITH A PORTION OF THE PULLMAN MANSION IN THE LEFT-HAND CORNER AND AN ANCIENT TREE DATING BACK TO 1812 IN FRONT.

BY THE 1830S, THE CITY OF CHICAGO WAS GROWING WELL BEYOND THE STOCKADE OF THE FORT.

American Secretary of War, General Henry Dearborn (1751–1829). By 1808, Chicago's first public building was completed. Passing through the area in 1809, traveler William Johnston reported that Fort Dearborn "was the neatest and best wooden garrison in the country," reflecting "great honor to Captain John Whistler who planned and built it."

Under Whistler's command, the military installation also flourished as a trading center. Relations with the ten native tribes in the area were generally good. The government maintained cordial relations with the dominant tribe, the Potawatomi, and peace settled in until British agents in Canada fomented an uprising against the frontier outposts along the Great Lakes.

The War of 1812 was at hand, and the slaughter of farmer Charles Lee at the south branch of the Chicago River in April of that year signaled a period of unrest. Captain Nathan Heald replaced Whistler after Whistler quarreled with John Kinzie, the most influential member of the community of settlers, over Kinzie's stubborn refusal to cease selling intoxicants to the natives.

At age thirty-seven, Heald found himself in a hopeless position. He was in charge of a garrison of sixty-six enlisted men, nine women, and eighteen children, all of whom had been placed in harm's way.

A military disaster at Fort Mackinac made Heald's position untenable. At any moment, the combined forces of the Miami, Ottawa, Winnebago, Chippewa, and Huron could descend upon the fort and kill all of its inhabitants. Apprehension gave way to panic.

On the morning of August 7, 1812, orders from General William Hull (1735–1825), Commander of the Army of the Northwest, reached Captain Heald. Heald was ordered to abandon the Fort and flee the region "if practicable." Hull's vague and imprecise directive sealed the fate of the settlement.

At nine o'clock on the morning of August 15, Captain William Wells took his place at the head of the column of soldiers and a wagon train carrying the women, children, and provisions of the fort to a safe haven in the east. Wells was a frontier Indian fighter who had come from Fort Wayne with thirty friendly Miami tribesmen to lead the Fort Dearborn settlers out of danger.

Hours before their departure, John Kinzie advised Wells that To-Pee-Nee-Be of the St. Joseph's tribe had conveyed the news that an attack by an unfriendly band of Potawatomi, led by Chief Leopold Pokogon, was imminent.

The warning came too late and Wells set out. Riding ahead of the rest, Wells spotted an army of four to five hundred warriors in full battle regalia forming over the sand hills and marshy banks in the distance, about two miles south of Fort Dearborn. He turned his horse and raced back to his slowly advancing column. Waving his hat in a circle above his head (the universal symbol of distress in frontier America), Wells called out in a frantic voice, "We are surrounded by Indians! They are about to attack us! Form instantly and charge upon them!"

The actual attackers were in fact members of the Potawatomi escort who accompanied the Wells party out of the fort under a flag of friendship. As the wagon train moved farther away from the safety of the wooden stockade, the Indians fell behind, re-forming behind the sand berms west of Lake Michigan as a hostile force.

Heald's men fell quickly under the withering fire of the Potawatomi warriors. Separated from the soldiers, the civilian party was at the mercy of the Indians. Twelve children who cowered in terror in the back of one of the transport wagons were tomahawked by a single brave. "Is that their game? Butchering women and children?" Captain Wells cried out, seconds before a bullet pierced his lungs.

In the heat of battle, Black Partridge, a friendly Potawatomi chieftain, dragged Lieutenant Helm's wife (Kinzie's daughter-in-law) into Lake Michigan. He held the hysterical woman underwater until she understood that he was shielding her from a certain death.

Once it was clear that the troops were in a hopeless position, the Potawatomi chief Blackbird ordered his men to desist. Captain Heald agreed to surrender in return for guarantees of safety for the survivors. Blackbird agreed, but then decided to torture and kill the wounded soldiers without pity or remorse. The slaughter might have lasted through the night if not for the friendly intervention of the half-breed Billy Caldwell, whose Indian name was Sauganash.

Caldwell, respected by the Indian tribes, dissuaded Blackbird from inflicting further acts of savagery. The Indians put away their weapons and retreated northward, burning Fort Dearborn to the ground before dawn.

Three days later, the massacre survivors were delivered to Colonel McGee, the British Indian agent in Detroit, as prisoners of war—each of them soberly reflective as the last horrific images of Chicago blazed in their memories.

John Kinzie and his family crept back into Chicago from Detroit in 1816 only to make a grisly discovery. The bleached skeletal remains of the slaughtered men, women, and children had been left unburied along the south shore of the Chicago settlement. The Potawatomi chiefs denied responsibility for the actions of the marauding warriors, blaming the Winnebago tribe instead.

Under the command of Captain Hezekiah Bradley, Fort Dearborn was rebuilt on a larger scale in July 1816 and more strongly garrisoned. Illinois entered the union two years later, but the Indian victory inflicted a greater misery upon the natives who had peacefully coexisted with the settlers up until that awful moment in 1812. Memories of the massacre stiffened the resolve of the white men to displace the Indian tribes from the Great Lakes region, and their forced exodus from Chicago was complete by 1833.

Haunted Memories at 1919 South Prairie Avenue

S
I
D
E
T
R
I
P

The dilapidated and desolate Queen Anne mansion at 1919 South Prairie Avenue was designed and built in 1884 by architect Solon S. Beman. The building has been altered so many times that it caused novelist Arthur Meeker to comment, "it's impossible to say any longer what it thought it was originally trying to be." It has remained unoccupied for many, many years. Towering over the Prairie Avenue Historic District, this now crumbling red-brick shell was purchased by Marshall Field Jr. in 1890. His father, the czar of dry goods retailing, lived only a few doors north at 1905 South Prairie Avenue and undoubtedly helped finance his son's acquisition of the $65,000 honeymoon house.

Long before young Field and his bride, the lovely Albertine Huck, set up housekeeping, the mansion was commonly known in the neighborhood as the William H. Murray house.

What stories this old house could tell us now, if only the past could come alive and speak to the living from inside the drafty, barren rooms. What magical parties were given here on chilly winter evenings punctuated by the gentle clip-clopping of horse-drawn carriages upon cobblestone? How gaily did the servants decorate this manor, when the Fields welcomed the crème de la crème of the social register to their gala Gilded Age affairs? As we silently gaze up at the boarded windows, overgrown grass, and the tree sprouting grotesquely from the roof, we can only imagine this grand estate in better days than these, before its master was taken in the prime of life.

Shortly before the evening dinner bell tolled on November 22, 1905, Marshall Field Jr. fired a bullet into his left side while comfortably seated inside his dressing room. It was a wound that would eventually prove fatal. The morning Tribune *was careful to explain to its readers that it was an unfortunate accident. Mr. Field was examining a loaded revolver in anticipation of his upcoming hunting expedition to the Wisconsin woods when it accidentally discharged, or so it was stated. Others were not so sure.*

In similar circumstances, Cook County State's Attorney John W. Wayman had blasted a hole through his chest while examining a handgun he planned to introduce as evidence in a pending murder trial. As in Field's case, it was

THE MARSHALL FIELD

JR. MANSION AT 1919

SOUTH PRAIRIE AVENUE

IN RUINS, 1999.

(Photo by Christina Carlson)

maintained that Wayman was only "examining the gun" when it inadvertently fired. It was a common excuse offered by would-be suicidal men given a chance for second thoughts, and not entirely believable.

It has long been whispered that young Field had been involved in some disreputable behavior involving gunplay inside a Levee resort earlier that afternoon, and was dragged back to his mansion to avoid a newspaper scandal. Drug-related deaths, accidental suicides, wayward girls, and contract murder in the Levee district along Twenty-second were routine during the district's wild and untamed years. But if there were a kernel of truth to the scandalous allegations surrounding the death of Marshall Field's son, it would seem reasonable that sooner or later the true facts of the case would have surfaced.

The police were summoned to 1919 Prairie Avenue, and the domestic help were questioned at length by detectives. Neither the footman, the children's nurse, nor any other servant on the household staff witnessed the shooting. Mrs. Field was conveniently away—out for an afternoon canter with the three children. The parents of the critically wounded man were vacationing in New York at the time.

Satisfied with the wounded man's version of events, the police pursued the inquiry no further.

Marshall Field Jr. was eulogized by his colleagues as a man of gentle refinements possessing a quiet and retiring disposition. Sickly for much of his life, he was an enthusiastic sportsman, Harvard-educated, and above all a family man in good stead. At least that was what was reported.

Lurking in the shadow of death, reporters and photographers swarmed through the corridors of Mercy Hospital snapping photographs, chasing rumors, and hounding family members for bits of information. Shaking his walking stick at a young reporter with a trembling hand, eighty-seven-year-old Marshall Field I upbraided the gentleman of the press. "What paper are you with? Aren't you ashamed? Haven't you a pretty low opinion of yourself?"

"Why yes, Mr. Field, I have," the reporter timidly replied, as he backed away.

His liver pierced, Marshall Field Jr. expired on November 27, 1905. A private wake was held at the family's residence at 1919 Prairie. Young Field

THE 1905 BLUE BOOK SOCIAL REGISTER LISTS MARSHALL FIELD JR. THE FIELDS RECEIVED CALLERS ON TUESDAYS.

was accorded a lavish funeral, and buried with due solemnity at Graceland Cemetery on the North Side.

On January 16, 1906, the family patriarch, in mourning for his son, died from complications of pneumonia and old age. Not long afterward, the younger Field's widow and the family heirs disposed of the house on Prairie, which represented only grief and sorrow.

Years passed. The Gatlin Institute for Alcohol Rehabilitation converted the vacated Field mansion into a boarding house for inebriates, a move that undoubtedly hastened the departure of the remaining residents of Prairie Avenue during this period of rapid, irreversible decline.

The Gatlin Institute moved out of the mansion in the 1920s, turning the property over to the Monterey Nursing Home, a private elder-care provider attending to the needs of the aged and infirm in the spacious, high-ceilinged bedrooms.

In the 1970s the Cenco Care Corporation took control of the house, but they were unable to do much of anything to improve appearances. It was as if there was a curse attached to the place.

Within a few years the mansion was sold again. The new owners embarked on an ambitious plan to open an upscale restaurant. They stripped away the original wood paneling as the first step in a long overdue renovation. But the venture failed, and the investment group ran out of money. The mansion was boarded up for good in 1981, despite unsuccessful efforts by the Prairie Avenue Foundation to secure title to the property and add it to the historic district.

The stately old Field mansion, battered by time, continued to be neglected and allowed to deteriorate by the private ownership group who held title to the building. A rotting floor collapsed. Windows were shattered, and debris was scattered across the yard on the side of the manse. Scavengers applied the finishing touches, leaving only the coach house at the rear of the lot in relatively good condition.

The preservationists who maintained Glessner House added a cul-de-sac to the middle of the street, effectively cutting off pedestrian access to the blighted red-brick Victorian relic at 1919 South Prairie, in an attempt to shield the delicate eyes of tourists who come to view the restored nineteenth-century homes from an eyesore they are powerless to do anything about.

There is a strong sense that when a dark and deeply defining tragedy occurs, there can be no inner peace or reconciliation with the events of the past, so it is wise to destroy the evidence or cover it up as best as we can.

Turn west and proceed to State Street. Turn left (south) and go to Twenty-second Street (Cermak Road).

THE TAJ MAHAL OF VICE: THE SOUTH SIDE LEVEE
1893–1912

The Levee was officially closed by decree of the Cook County State's Attorney in September 1912, but it never completely disappeared, not really, even after this incredible menagerie of door-to-door call houses, opium dens, cigar stands, wine rooms, brothels, penny arcades, and bordellos were ground into dust. Roman circuses like this one never completely vanish, and so the Levee of legend lives on in memory. Today, portions of Dearborn, Federal, Cullerton, and Twenty-first Streets are overgrown with weeds, broken sidewalks, and auto junkyards—another high crime area evolved into a brown

DETAILED MAP

OF THE SOUTH

SIDE LEVEE IN

ITS HEYDAY.

(Illustration by Bob Deckert)

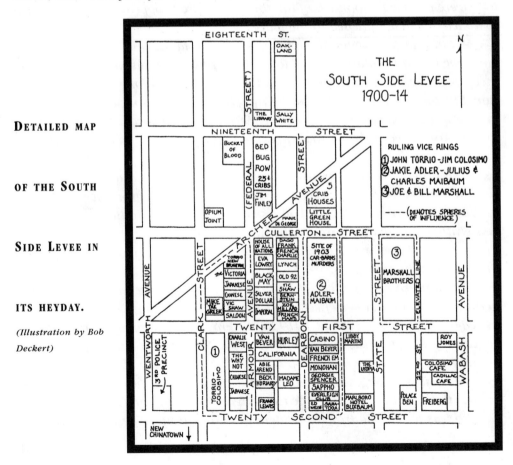

URBAN RENEWAL CLAIMED THIS FORMER LEVEE BUILDING AT EIGHTEENTH
AND STATE STREET IN 1994. THE DAN RYAN EXPRESSWAY SLICED THROUGH
THE HEART OF THE OLD LEVEE IN THE 1950S.

*field. The Dan Ryan Expressway bisects the district, and only a few buildings
from the original Levee remain. Amid the desolation and ruin, one senses the
lasting presence of broken lives, despair, and infamy. Ghosts seem real here,
and if they do walk among these ruins, they will soon have company. The
building boom of the 1980s and 1990s is slowly reclaiming the deserted Near
South Side "badlands," which vanished from the map decades ago. Almost
overnight, the gated townhouse communities of Dearborn Park and Central
Station have sprung up in the vicinity of Roosevelt Road and Clark Street, and
real-estate speculators continue their relentless march southward into the
Levee.*

*South of Twenty-second Street along Wentworth Avenue, bustling
Chinatown moves along at its own pace. When the Custom House Levee dispersed in 1905, the fragmented Asian community at Harrison and Clark
Streets were forced to follow the trail of the flesh peddlers down to Twenty-
second Street. They started their own community just south of the Levee.*

Tourists and food fanciers who stroll past the many restaurants and gift shops on Wentworth Avenue should take note of the functional architecture, for it is the last faint reminder of the presence of the Levee in this area.

In the unfettered days of yesteryear, the midnight hours were clamorous with the revelry of the giddy patrons of the underworld and their female consorts. Ragtime music tinkled in every brothel and "dipping house" along the side streets and back alleys north of Twenty-second Street. Patrons drank and caroused until dawn in the twenty-four-hour saturnalia that was the Levee, a seedbed of crime that existed for less than a quarter of a century but long enough to spawn Al Capone, Johnny Torrio, and the generations after them who have comprised the modern Chicago "outfit."

The Levee took shape as a commercial center of vice during the World's Fair of 1893, when thousands of tourists from around the world invaded the South Side to celebrate the accomplishments of man and technology.

The coming of the vice mongers who beckoned the tourist trade shocked and horrified the millionaires and merchant princes who lived in solemn dignity along Prairie Avenue near the intersection of Eighteenth Street. Fearing the imminent and long-term decline in South Side property values, Potter Palmer spared no expense in building his wife, Bertha Honore Palmer, a turreted castle on North Lake Shore Drive, safely removed from the illicit goings-on. His Prairie Avenue peers did not linger much longer in the neighborhood. They had no desire to suffer personal embarrassment or lose their Blue Book listing by having to exchange pleasantries with lowlifes. Prairie Avenue fell into gradual ruin as the Levee grew and prospered at the beginning of the twentieth century.

Three vice rings formed the nexus of the criminal organization that brokered police protection and courted the favor of Michael "Hinky Dink" Kenna and "Bathhouse" John Coughlin, the thoroughly corrupt First Ward aldermen who controlled patronage, zoning, and liquor licensing in the district.

James Colosimo, an old-world Italian brothel keeper fond of Caruso, Verdi, and Tetrazzini, controlled the street-sweeper's union and was linked to the Black Hand. After striking it rich selling the services of young women inside his two "Tenderloin" brothels (one of them called the Victoria, in honor of his first wife), Colosimo branched out. He opened a famous cafe at 2124–2128 South Wabash Avenue, beckoning society sophisticates, show people, and gangsters to its now fabled doors.

Italian opera stars dropped by to sample Colosimo's famous bowls of steam-

"A MAIDEN'S PLIGHT." FLORID 1910 NEWSPAPER DEPICTIONS OF A VIRTUOUS

MAIDEN BEING LURED INTO A LIFE OF PROSTITUTION AND DEPRAVITY BY A SMOOTH-

TALKING LEVEE PIMP.

NEW TOWNHOMES

EMERGING ON THE

EMPTY AND ABAN-

DONED FIELDS OF

THE OLD LEVEE IN

1999.

*(Photo by Christina
Carlson)*

THIS 1919
ADVERTISEMENT
EMPHASIZES THE
"REFINED"
ASPECTS OF THE
NOTORIOUS CLUB
OWNED BY THE
FORMER BROTHEL
KEEPER.

COLOSIMO'S RESTUARANT IN THE LEVEE WAS CLOSED ONLY TWICE DURING

PROHIBITION. THIS WAS ONE OF THOSE OCCASIONS.

ing Chicken Vesuvio and rub elbows with dangerous Levee characters. It was an exciting experience, an unforgettable public adventure, shared by Chicagoans of modest and affluent means from across the city. Only twice during Prohibition was Colosimo's closed, and then only briefly. As the years rolled by, the restaurant attained a flashy prominence in the pantheon of famous Chicago nightclubs, continuing long after its famous Italian proprietor departed the world.

Enjoying his new found respectability, Colosimo was momentarily distracted by Dale Winter, a winsome choir singer from Grand Rapids, Michigan, who sang and danced her way into the rotund gangster's heart. Miss Winter agreed to become the second Mrs. Colosimo in the spring of 1920. Three weeks after their hastily arranged elopement, the bellicose Colosimo expired from gunshot wounds, fired by killer or killers unknown inside the vestibule of the restaurant on May 11, 1920. Three judges and nine aldermen were counted among the pallbearers in a funeral procession that scandalized Chicago.

The legacy of the club bearing the Colosimo name would live on. Mike "The Greek" Potson, a former Gary, Indiana, saloonkeeper, whose real name was Mihail Bodoglou, kept the restaurant going. After Big Jim was killed, Potson reportedly got a new business partner—Al Capone.

An even more pernicious Levee vice ring was controlled by Maurice Van Bever and his wife Julia, criminal panderers whose interstate white slavery ring extended from St. Louis to Chicago and inspired passage of the Mann Act in 1910.

Charley Maibaum, owner of Buxbaums, an after-hours hotel where a streetwalker could take a client for a tête-à-tête was the third most influential Levee boss.

Outside the three main rings, there were scores of "independents" and extremes of bad taste. The Levee arcade featured a succession of "dollar-a-girl" joints where the girls sold their services on a "volume" basis. Many of the poor unfortunates were lured into the life by smooth-talking con men (called "cadets" or "ropers"), who induced them to flee the drabness of small-town life in the Midwest with the promise of romance and marriage. Instead of discovering an idyllic existence in the city, they were robbed, beaten, and "broken in" at the Levee dives.

The Everleigh Club, nearly everyone agreed, was the most garish, opulent bordello west of the Hudson River. Ada and Minna Everleigh recruited cultured and refined young ladies and charged their well-heeled clientele $500 a night for an evening of merriment at 2131 South Dearborn Street.

On January 10, 1910, the police were summoned to Madame Victoria Shaw's place at 2012 South Dearborn, where they found the lifeless form of Nathaniel Ford Moore, the twenty-six-year-old heir to the Rock Island Railroad fortune.

Moore had died of a morphine overdose while in the company of one of Vic Shaw's honeys. The brothel madam and her man, Roy Jones, had planned to sneak the remains over to the Everleigh sisters' doorstep in the wee hours of the morning. Hearing of the devious intrigue, the sisters called the Twenty-second Precinct and were spared a press embarrassment.

The clergy, the media, and certain Republican politicians deprived of the harvest of graft that steadily poured into the pockets of the Democratic ward organizations railed against the Levee as a great "social evil" and defiler of virtue. A Vice Commission was empowered to strike hard at commercialized vice. Their final report, coming in 1910, was considered pornographic for the times and deemed too hot to handle by the U.S. Postal Service.

RUINS OF THE CHICAGO COLISEUM AT FOURTEENTH STREET AND WABASH (1985). THE COLISEUM HOSTED NUMEROUS NATIONAL NOMINATING CONVENTIONS, INCLUDING THE 1920 REPUBLICAN CORONATION OF WARREN G. HARDING. IT WAS ALSO THE SITE OF THE NOTORIOUS FIRST WARD BALL, WHERE THE LEVEE LOWBROWS DRANK AND DANCED TILL DAWN, AND THERE WASN'T A THING THE COPS OR POLITICIANS COULD DO ABOUT IT. IT IS A PARKING LOT TODAY.

(Photo by author)

Rare photo of the South Side Levee district in 1910. All of these buildings were torn down by 1925 (above). Maurice Van Bever ran his St. Louis-to-Chicago "white slave" ring from inside this notorious Levee dive at Twenty-first and Dearborn (below).

There had been great moral crusades foisted on Chicago before. The English evangelist Gipsy Smith led twelve thousand psalm-singing Christians in an old-fashioned revival meeting on Twenty-second Street, October 18, 1909. It was reported that business in the bawdy houses was never more brisk than in the days and weeks that followed Gipsy Smith's sermonizing.

On September 29, 1912, a massive civic welfare parade, led by Reverend Elmer Williams of the Grace Methodist Church, proceeded down Michigan Avenue past thousands of well-wishers and ordinary Chicagoans, who were just as fed up with continuing newspaper coverage of the Levee as a future generation would be with the exhausting media accounts of Bill Clinton and Monica Lewinsky.

One of the floats in the parade featured a ten-year-old boy attired as a "vice fiend." The boy held a banner aloft bearing the message "Swear off or I'll get you!" The moralists had finally won over the political support of the community.

The climax to the growing anti-vice sentiment occurred three days later, when the grand jury, cooperating with an ambitious Republican State's Attorney named John Wayman, filed complaints against the property owners. Wayman shuttered the dens of iniquity and challenged his successor, Maclay Hoyne, to keep them closed once Wayman's term was concluded.

John Wayman, a practical, level-headed officeholder, closed the page on an era of "segregated vice" in Chicago, but the Levee did not magically disappear with the wave of the politician's wand. While it was true that many of the famous resorts from the Gaslight era were bulldozed because they stood in the path of an important east-west rail corridor, many more remained and evolved into the jazz and gin cabarets of the 1920s.

In the 1940s, crooner Vic Damone recorded "The South Side of Chicago," a nostalgic ballad that paid tribute to the "living breathing heart" of the jazz kingdom—Twenty-first and Wentworth Streets. Damone remembered smoky cafés and innovative New Orleans–style jazz. The bordellos, opium dens, and white slavery rings of yesteryear were conveniently ignored or forgotten.

There were more deadly occurrences—garrotings, contract killings, and the like—after September 29, 1912. The Levee gang was amazingly resilient, and the cops looked the other way as long as the prostitutes registered their names in the index file at the Twenty-second Street Precinct and the "swag" (bribery money) was paid.

Chicago police detective Stanley Birns was shot to death by a private morals investigator in a case of mistaken identity on July 16, 1914, on the sidewalk between Michigan Avenue and Wabash (on the south side of Twenty-second Street). A riot nearly erupted as the streetwalkers and riff-raff pelted the city morals investigators with stones and bricks. Chicago was thrown into a chaotic uproar, until this too passed.

It wasn't until after 1945, when "The Greek" Potson closed Colosimo's Restaurant following his conviction on income tax evasion charges, that the final sordid chapter of Levee history was written.

The building that housed Colosimo's, a dismal reminder of Chicago's seamy nightlife, was condemned in November 1957 after vandals gained access to the interior of the club and plundered the contents, leaving an empty shell. The cost of the demolition of the old nightclub was borne by the city. In the condemnation suit filed against Potson's widow, city inspectors described the place as "dangerous and unsafe" and "a public nuisance."

Turn right (west) on Twenty-second Street and continue to Dearborn Street.

EVERLY YOURS
1900–1911

The world-famous Everleigh Club at 2131–2133 South Dearborn Street was demolished in 1933. From the outside, the club was a modest-looking three-story walkup sandwiched between a row of similar-looking buildings, all leased for immoral purposes during the heyday of the South Side Levee. In its last years before the city condemned the property, the former bordello was a transient rooming house. Then the 2100 block of South Dearborn vanished altogether when the land was cleared for the construction of the Raymond Hilliard Homes, a high-rise apartment complex for low-income residents.

Born in Evansville, Indiana, and raised in the genteel Kentucky bluegrass region of the mid-South, Ada and Minna Lester later changed their name to "Everleigh" because their affectionate grandma signed her letters "Everly yours."

The Lester girls were steel magnolias, strong-willed independent women who fled their loutish, vulgar husbands for careers as touring actresses.

In 1898, their theatrical dreams shattered by bad reviews and the deadly grind of vaudeville's "C" circuit, Ada and Minna opened a brothel near the Trans-Mississippi Exposition in Omaha with a small inheritance left to them by their father. It was only supposed to be a temporary situation, but the money was better than they expected, so when the fair ended, the sisters drifted to Chicago—the "A" circuit of Midwestern vice and corruption.

The Everleigh sisters leased the property at 2131 South Dearborn and two adjoining buildings from Christopher Columbus Crabb, who was Carrie Watson's "fancy man" until the famous madam was too old and too sick to care. After Watson passed away, Crabb took up with Lizzie Allen, a notorious Custom House panderer, who constructed the Dearborn bordello in 1890 for the unheard-of sum of $300,000. Allen died in 1895, and Crabb carried on as best as he could, but without a strong woman telling him what to do he found that he had neither the stomach for the trade nor a head for business.

The Everleighs took charge of the building on February 2, 1900, agreeing to pay Crabb $500 a month. For their gilded palace of vice, the sisters hired their own chefs, porters, and servants. Six parlors and fifty bedrooms were magnificently furnished with fine damask tapestries, regal ornamentation, imported French champagnes, and impressionist paintings. There was a vast library for the education and refinement of the beauteous courtesans. Ninety girls, the "elite" of the trade, worked three shifts, each girl working thirty hours a week.

There was a waterfall in one room and orchestras positioned in the large, imposing drawing rooms. Upstairs, the Gold Room featured gold-rimmed fishbowls, a miniature gold piano, and gold spittoons. The basement of the Everleigh Club was arranged to duplicate the sleeping compartments of a Pullman coach.

Sex was incidental to the overall experience. "It's not the ladies they like best . . . really," opined the lovely, auburn-haired Minna. "They like cards. They like

A PALACE OF SIN: THE EVERLEIGH CLUB (WHITE BUILDING) AT 2131 SOUTH DEARBORN WAS THE NATION'S MOST FAMOUS BROTHEL.

dice and horseracing the best. If it wasn't unmanly to admit it, they'd rather most of the time gamble than screw."

The Everleighs circulated brochures all over the Midwest, inviting affluent gentlemen to call "Calumet-412" if they happened to be passing through the Windy City. "We only serve the best people," cooed Minna.

Indeed, the registry book was a veritable "Who's Who" of the late Victorian age. Crown Prince Henry of Prussia and John "Bet a Million" Gates, and even the black heavyweight prizefighter Jack Johnson spent many a riotous night in the Everleigh Club. So did Marshall Field Jr., scion of one of Chicago's most famous and respected mercantile families. Field was rumored to be enjoying the amenities of the club the night he inflicted his fatal gunshot wound in 1905.

The Everleigh sisters paid extravagant sums for police protection. That was one reason why Captain Patrick J. Harding deferred a direct order from Mayor Carter Harrison II to padlock the bordello to his divisional inspector John Wheeler. The inspector did not lift a finger until he had received the high sign from Aldermen Mike "Hinky Dink" Kenna and "Bathhouse" John Coughlin. The Mayor by then was purple with rage.

The Mayor had been handed one of the Everleigh Club's descriptive brochures while traveling outside the city, and was deeply embarrassed—ashamed if the truth be known—for Chicago.

"I'll close the ship and walk out of the place with a smile on my face," Minna said on the last day, October 24, 1911. "If the ship sinks we'll go down with a cheer and a good drink under our belts." Of course, there was more to it than the whim of the mayor. Ike Bloom, proprietor of the notorious Freiberg's Dance Hall, thought the Everleigh sisters "uppity" and a threat to his business. He demanded a staggering payoff from them in order to keep their store open, but the Everleighs said no and retired to private life.

The sisters amassed a personal fortune in jewelry, stocks, and bonds. They gathered their mementos and cash holdings and sought refuge on the city's West Side, but they were soon driven out by indignant neighbors. Their journeys eventually took them to New York, where they lived out their days under assumed names. Minna died in 1948. Ada then moved to Virginia, where she passed away in 1960.

The Hilliard Homes is a public housing project, designed by Bertrand Goldberg and inspired by his earlier Marina City design, that opened in 1966. Standing on the former site of the Everleigh Club and lesser known bordellos of South Dearborn Street during the Gaslight Era, the Hilliard Homes towers are being considered by the City of Chicago for landmark status. It would mark the first time a Chicago Housing Authority building has been so designated.

Turn around and go east on Twenty-second Street to Michigan Avenue.

AL CAPONE'S VAULTS AT THE LEXINGTON HOTEL
1928–1932

In 1986, Geraldo Rivera (born Jerry Rivers) provided a nationwide television audience of sixty million viewers with a rare glimpse inside one of Chicago's most sinister but enduring landmarks—the Lexington Hotel on the northeast corner of Michigan Avenue and Twenty-second Street. Rivera was in search of buried treasure, the presumed lost fortune of Alphonse Capone, but the building was already a deserted, empty shell, picked clean by vandals and souvenir hunters long before the film crew inflicted the final indignity on this once majestic building, once forced to endure the slings and arrows of Capone's outrageous fortunes. Rivera blasted away a seven-thousand-pound concrete wall in a basement chamber that he believed to be shielding a secret compartment. The Internal Revenue Service was on hand to claim its share of the loot, but, alas, there were only a few empty gin bottles and an old sign hidden behind the massive slab. Rivera and his viewers had been had. The ten-story, four-hundred-room hotel, dangerous and unstable from years of neglect, was torn down in November 1995. The empty lot awaits redevelopment.

Al Capone and his brigands maintained offices inside the Lexington Hotel for a period of only four years (1928–1932), but that was enough to infect a wonderful old landmark from the Gay Nineties with a notorious reputation, which ultimately contributed to its final appointment with the wrecker's ball.

Designed by Clinton Warren, architect of the Congress Hotel (a hotel that has been magnificently preserved for the enjoyment of future generations), the brick and terra cotta Lexington opened in 1892 to accommodate the crush of World's Fair visitors. These were boom years on the Near South Side, and the Lexington was a symbol of economic stability and achievement, even as the Levee district began to take shape two blocks to the west. President Benjamin Harrison once addressed an audience from its balcony.

Al Capone, the Lexington's most famous resident, abandoned the Metropole Hotel, just one block south, for a luxurious fifth-floor suite of rooms at the Lexington in July 1928. Capone registered as "George Phillips" and ran his empire

No treasure in Al Capone's vaults. The Lexington Hotel in 1990: ready for the wrecker's ball (above). Al Capone is sentenced to eleven years following his conviction on income tax evasion charges, October 23, 1931 (right).

from the hotel until he was escorted off to prison following his conviction on income tax evasion in October 1931. Capone greeted friend and foe from his office overlooking Michigan Avenue. In the lobby, Capone gunmen sat in easy chairs keeping a watchful eye on the door. Should an unwanted intruder get past this imposing security gauntlet, a Capone machine gunner was hidden away in an inside closet.

In the 1980s, when a local women's construction company investigated the possibility of restoring the hotel, a shooting gallery used for target practice and a dozen secret stairways, including one behind Capone's medicine chest, were found. The building was honeycombed with secret passageways, which in turn led to a maze of underground tunnels connecting the taverns and whorehouses of the Levee to the immediate west. The tunnels were elaborate escape routes from police raids. They were dug into the earth by the proprietors of the houses of ill repute lining Dearborn and Federal Streets and Wabash Avenue before 1912.

After the Capone gang vacated the premises in the 1930s, the ownership of the hotel changed hands numerous times, and the character and reputation of the place declined with the neighborhood. Renamed the New Michigan Hotel in the 1950s, it became a bordello, a flophouse, and then, finally, a public nuisance.

Turn right (south) on Michigan Avenue and go south one block to Twenty-third Street.

FORMER SITE OF THE METROPOLE HOTEL
1925–1928

The Metropole Hotel, another luxurious but vanished landmark, stood on the now vacant weed lot on the southeast corner of Twenty-third Street and Michigan Avenue. Al Capone maintained his headquarters here from 1925 to 1928.

Realizing that it was impossible for reform mayor William Emmet Dever to enforce the Volstead Act and chase the bootlegging gangs out of Chicago, Al Capone crept back into the South Side of Chicago in 1925 with renewed confidence after two years of self-imposed exile in west suburban Cicero.

Capone and his lieutenants booked five rooms on the fourth floor of the terra cotta trimmed Metropole Hotel, its many bay windows affording a fine view of the Levee to the west.

The hotel was, for many years, the home base of the two First Ward scoundrels, Aldermen Michael "Hinky Dink" Kenna and "Bathhouse" John Coughlin. The Dink and the Bath were caricatures from a past era and out-of-touch political has-beens by 1928. Capone paid them no mind, for the graft flowed through his own organization now, not theirs. On Sunday mornings, police, prosecutors, and city officials discreetly knocked on the door of Room 409, Capone's office suite, and received their weekly payoffs.

In 1927, a good revenue year for the South Side gangsters, Capone modernized and expanded the Metropole. He added a gymnasium and took over for his own use fifty rooms, spread across two floors. That same year, Capone entertained actor George Jessel at the Metropole following the Chicago premiere of the first "talkie," *The Jazz Singer.* Then shifting politics blew in an ill wind. In 1928, police harassment forced Capone to move his headquarters to the Lexington Hotel.

Poisoned by the sins of the Levee and Al Capone's presence, this crime site, like so many others scattered across Chicago, has been abandoned by time. Only weeds grow there now.

Turn right (west) on Twenty-third Street and go to Wabash Avenue. Turn right (north) on Wabash Avenue and go to Twenty-second Street.

FORMER SITE OF THE FOUR DEUCES
c. 1914–1924

Crossing over the eastern boundaries of the old Levee leaves the interested observer with the eerie sense that these abandoned and neglected properties cry out for a reckoning with history in order to square past infamies with modern times. The Lexington and Metropole Hotels and the Four Deuces, a saloon and whorehouse where Al Capone murdered "Ragtime" Joe Howard on May 8, 1924, stand as mute testaments to the corrupting influence of organized crime. By the 1960s, the Four Deuces and the adjacent buildings on South Wabash were poorly lit, unsafe, and crumbling tenement housing rented to poor southern blacks. Today there is only an empty lot at 2222 South Wabash (on the southwest corner of Twenty-second Street) where the Four Deuces once stood. There is nothing left to see but a broken sidewalk where Capone and his minions once strolled. The property is all but overrun with high grass and weeds. A "For Sale" sign stands forlornly in the midst of the neglect, but there are few takers.

AL CAPONE'S "FOUR
DEUCES" (THE BUILDING
ON THE LEFT) WAS
REDUCED TO SLUM HOUS-
ING IN 1963 WHEN THIS
PHOTO WAS TAKEN, AND
DEMOLISHED A FEW YEARS
LATER.
*(Courtesy of the Chicago
Historical Society)*

THE SITE OF
THE FOUR
DEUCES IS
TODAY ANOTHER
CRIME "BROWN-
FIELD." THE
HILLIARD
HOMES STANDS
IN THE BACK-
GROUND.

Johnny Torrio opened the Four Deuces during World War I, a couple of years before his paternal uncle, Jim Colosimo, was murdered in the vestibule of his Wabash Avenue cafe.

The four-story, red-brick building replaced the notorious Freiberg's Dance Hall as the command post of Levee criminal operations following police crackdowns in 1912 and 1914.

The Four Deuces was a rabbit warren of iniquity supervised by Charlie Carr, who bought and sold Thompson machine guns for his employers, the Capone gang. A saloon occupied rooms at street level. The bookkeeping offices were on the second floor; a secret gambling den was hidden behind a steel door on floor three; and the fourth floor brothel housed thirty girls.

In 1919, Al Capone went to work as a $35-a-week saloon bouncer and sidewalk "capper," whose principal responsibility was to draw single men into the action.

"Got some nice-looking girls inside, Mister. What do you say?"

In his lean and hungry years, Al Capone adopted the alias "Al Brown." For the next few years, or until they understood the character of the man, the reporters around town referred to him in this way. Capone's first brush with notoriety occurred on May 8, 1924, when he pumped six shots into "Ragtime" Joe Howard, a Levee con man who dared to slap the business manager Jake Guzik in the face. The shooting occurred at Henry Jacob's saloon, a few doors down the street from the Deuces.

As his fame and stature in gangland continued to rise, Mr. Brown outfitted an empty storefront adjoining the Four Deuces at 2220 South Wabash. He hung a shingle outside that read "A. Brown: Antiques Dealer," but there was very little buying and selling of old furniture going on inside. To keep up appearances, Capone's men carried in a piano, three tables, a planter, some rugs and an aquarium.

The Four Deuces earned a seamy reputation during the early years of Prohibition, and it was the target of several raids during the William Dever mayoralty (1923–1927). During these years, when the reform administration threatened his operations, Capone moved to Cicero, abandoning the famous café that launched his career in organized crime.

Continue north on Wabash Avenue to Twenty-first Street.

ELIOT NESS RAIDS AN AL CAPONE BREWERY
June 13, 1930

Amazingly, several buildings dating back to the Prohibition Era have managed to survive the onslaught of urban renewal ... for the moment at least. In 1930, the Wabash Automobile Accessory Shop at 2108 South Wabash Avenue (north of Twenty-second Street halfway up the block on the west side of the street, now 2100–2110 South Wabash Avenue) was a "blind" for a Capone liquor depot supplying beer to the downtown speakeasies. Eliot Ness launched his career and the reputation of the "Untouchables" on June 13, 1930, when he smashed through the warehouse doors of this building. Now it is just another anonymous brick building on a boulevard forgotten by time.

Eliot Ness was a broken figure late in life, drowning in booze and failed ambitions. In death, he became something of a national hero, enticing generations of documentary filmmakers and Hollywood studios to spin a fairy tale that has been blindly accepted as truth.

The Desilu Studios in Hollywood strung together a few of Ness's blurry recollections of Chicago in the 1920s for their 1959 anthology series *The Untouchables* (recollections that were exaggerated beyond belief in Oscar Fraley's book of the same name), thus creating another celluloid myth for twentieth-century popular culture.

The real Eliot Ness had the good fortune of profiting from family connections. A Norwegian immigrant's son from the Scandinavian section of Kensington on Chicago's South Side, Ness's sister married Alexander Jamie, an FBI agent who hired the lad in 1928, when Ness was just three years out of college.

During Prohibition, at a time when it was apparent that the great national experiment was going up in smoke and those charged with enforcement had become objects of scorn and ridicule, Alexander Jamie, Chief Special Prohibition Agent, and U.S. Attorney George E. Q. Johnson outlined an ambitious strategy. Their plan was to attack the sources of supply—with fifteen hand-picked federal agents the world would come to know as the "Untouchables."

In his first toe-to-toe encounter with organized crime, Assistant Chief Special Agent Eliot Ness was ordered into wicked Chicago Heights, where he seized the financial records of slot-machine boss Oliver Ellis and produced evidence that 3,500,000 gallons of alcohol were being produced each year. Somewhere behind these disclosures, Johnson reasoned, was the answer to the Capone riddle. The government needed more evidence to indict—bookkeeping ledgers, receipts, and safes full of money.

Johnson unleashed Ness on Chicago bootleggers in June 1930. From his offices in the Transportation Building, the earnest young University of Chicago graduate relied on wiretaps and informants to develop the intelligence that the biggest Capone beer depot of them all was in a warehouse at 2108 South Wabash Avenue. The plant was churning out one hundred barrels of lager a day, with a street value of $55 per barrel. The beer cost $4 a barrel to produce, and after bottling retailed for about $20 a case.

The agents battered down the door of the beer depot with a rented ten-ton truck, catching the warehouse employees off guard. The agents impounded two hundred thousand gallons of beer and mash. It was Ness's first foray into the South Side badlands, and it was a successful one. Jamie was in line for a promotion, once the responsibility for enforcement of the Volstead Act was transferred from the Prohibition Bureau to the Justice Department on July 1, 1930.

Intoxicated by the press notoriety accompanying his first splashy raid, the twenty-six-year-old Ness immediately ordered wiretaps placed on Al Capone's family residence at 7244 South Prairie Avenue. Capone responded by paying linemen to bug the telephones of the Treasury agents. Ness was offered a $2,000-a-week bribe, and when he refused, his car was stolen.

Despite the flattering attention, the historical record suggests that Eliot Ness, a notorious Romeo in his off-hours, was only a minor irritant to gangland in the fading days of Prohibition. The real unsung hero of the 1920s booze wars for the enforcement side is a man lost to history—Prohibition agent Major A.V. Dalrymple, who destroyed 2,500 working stills in less than one year and confiscated $4,000,000 worth of liquor. When Dalrymple grew weary of this futile battle, he retired and moved to Texas to drill for oil, leaving the limelight for the publicity-seeking Ness.

During his 1931 trial on income tax evasion, Al Capone leaned over and asked his attorney to point out a man he never met—Eliot Ness.

GEORGE SILVER'S "MAXIM CAFE"
1903

A building that housed a famous Levee café—perhaps the only building left standing that was home to a cabaret and wine room of the "red-light era,"—stands directly across the street from the Al Capone liquor depot at 2107-2111 South Wabash Avenue. George Silver's "Maxim Café, " a "Greek temple" of vice, is now the Moran Equipment Company.

In the spring of 1903, a Citizen's Vigilance Committee from the First and Second Wards went to court to put a stop to the incursions of the "disorderly houses" into their respectable neighborhoods. The Near South Side was a quiet, desirable place to live until 1900, when the resort keepers and brothel owners drove out the Palmers, Fields, and Leiters of Prairie Avenue and gained a permanent foothold north of Twenty-second Street. When George Silver, the politically privileged dive keeper, opened his new "Maxim Cafe" in June 1903, the Prairie Avenue aristocrats were aghast, and they vowed a fight to the finish. They found little popular support, however.

It was the character of George Silver that was so objectionable, they pleaded. Indeed, Silver flouted societal convention and repeatedly strained Mayor Carter Harrison's patience with suggestive exterior advertising and provocative street-front façades adjoining the saloons he owned and operated.

Harrison, a liberal, even-handed politician, was neither a puritan nor a moralist. He subscribed to the prevailing view that vice contained within geographic boundaries was eminently preferable to vigorous suppression and subsequent dispersal into outlying neighborhoods.

His chief objection to Silver's "palace of delight" was the "immoral" architecture. Harrison thought the Greek temple style, featuring a recessed and pillared façade, an affront to community standards. Silver covered the tympanum and received his license to operate—for a $20,000 down payment.

On opening night, Silver issued stern warnings to his goons to keep a sharp eye out. "The place has got to be run right, see? I put you on your honor to help me conduct a moral place. If you see anyone getting gay you must remonstrate with him. No flirting goes here and no high jinx."

The *Chicago Tribune* sent a reporter down to record his observations of the opening night festivities. "All Silver's old friends from his Dearborn street dives were there, including several city hall politicians, and as one blonde creature expressed it, as she stuck her gum under the table and departed, 'a lovely time was had.'"

By contemporary standards of morality, the Maxim was probably not nearly as Bacchanalian as we might imagine such a place to be. It was a saloon in which to co-mingle with furtive fighters, ballplayers, Flora-Dora girls, politicos, song pluggers, and the demimonde of the street. It was an essential Chicago tavern up against the moral constraints of the day.

In respect to the sensibilities of the neighbors nearby, a soloist sang an opening night chorus of *Jerusalem* with real religious fervor in every note.

Return to Twenty-second Street (Cermak Road) and turn right (west). Continue to Halsted Street. Turn left (south) and continue to Canalport Avenue.

IF ALL ELSE FAILS—THE CLENCHED FIST, THE RUBBER HOSE, AND THE POINTED SHOE. THE SCOTLAND YARD DETAIL
1931–1956

A drab, forbidding two-story police building once stood on the now vacant corner lot at 2075 Canalport Avenue at Halsted Street. The vintage 1880s police station served the residents of the Twenty-first District for many years until June 1931, when its functions were taken over by the Twenty-second District, then headquartered at the Maxwell Street Station nearby. Thereafter, until the changing political winds of Chicago rendered the building and its occupants obsolete, the Canalport Station was the home of Scotland Yard, an elite, hand-picked police detail whose methods of prying a confession out of a suspect could only be whispered about. Once the building was demolished, the lot, like so many other locations in Chicago where infamy occurred, remained an empty brown field, cursed by its very nature. Happily, the city is redeveloping the site as a public park.

With a verbalized shoulder shrug, the foreman of the coroner's jury announced the findings of his panel, "The deceased came to his death at the hands of person or persons unknown."

In the 1920s, murder was on the rise in Chicago. The Prohibition gangland wars were only part of the story. Armed robbers were shooting their victims in cold blood and getting away with it. Everyone, it seemed, owned a gun and had a motive.

The Chicago police department was held accountable for the intolerable crime conditions and had become the laughingstock of the nation. Swift action was demanded to end the epidemic rise in crime.

Mayor Anton J. Cermak took office in 1931 with a mandate to "clean up" the city after four wild and woolly years of unchecked crime and corruption under his predecessor, the cartoonish William Hale Thompson. The World's Fair was coming in two years, and people had to begin to feel safe in the streets.

Acting on the advice of Commissioner John P. Alcock, the mayor authorized the formation of a unique investigative unit to gather intelligence, interrogate criminal suspects, and bring closure to the headline crimes that caused embarrassment and brought public censure to the department. "No murder or other major crime will ever be dropped," vowed Captain William Schoemaker, regarded by Alcock as one of the "gamest" and most incorruptible men on the force. "The detail has men enough and will have the time to stay on an investigation until it is completed."

Named after metropolitan London's legendary detective department, Scotland Yard's precise duties were vague and its *modus operandi* maintained in highest secrecy. It was rumored, and later confirmed in several lawsuits filed by ranking Chicago hoodlums, that on the second floor of the weather-worn brick station, the clenched fist, the rubber hose, and maybe even a rolled-up telephone book or two were applied to the skulls of reluctant suspects.

Telephone books leave no telltale scars.

Slot-machine boss Eddie "Dutch" Vogel and Jake Guzik, proprietor of a string of Levee whorehouses before being elevated to a position of importance in Al Capone's mob, filed suits against the personnel of Scotland Yard for violating their civil rights.

Captain William Balswick, who commanded the elite detail from 1940 to 1952 (longer than anyone else), defended the brutal methods of interrogation. "They just don't know and we can't tell them how greatly productive the unit has been through the years."

Scotland Yard earned muted praise from FBI Director J. Edgar Hoover for the investigation of suspected Nazi spies and collaborators during World War II. "I can only say this much," Balswick recalled. "Our men would adopt any disguise— they'd dress like workingmen to get what they were after, and what they were after was a chain reaction, little links leading to a bigger one."

The glory days ended with the stroke of a pen on June 15, 1956. Commissioner Timothy O'Connor was ordered to abolish Scotland Yard and disperse the seventy-eight men in the unit to new regional detective bureaus. Scotland Yard had gone too far. The elite unit had incurred the wrath of Mayor Richard J. Daley by installing listening devices at Democratic headquarters in the Morrison Hotel.

Continue south on Halsted Street to Thirty-fifth Street. Turn left (east) on Thirty-fifth Street and proceed to Cottage Grove Avenue.

CAMP DOUGLAS—EIGHTY ACRES OF HELL

Senator Stephen A. Douglas passed away quite unexpectedly on June 3, 1861, at the Tremont House in Chicago. The "Little Giant," as he was known, was a towering figure in Illinois politics for nearly twenty-five years. In 1860, two years after he engaged Abraham Lincoln in a series of landmark debates that shaped the issue of popular sovereignty in the public mind in the months leading up to the Civil War, Douglas won the Democratic nomination for president but lost the general election to his old rival, Lincoln. During the last fourteen years of their lives together, Senator and Mrs. Douglas resided at Okenwald, their South Side estate located due east of the present-day intersection of Cottage Grove Avenue and Thirty-fifth Street. Following Douglas's death, the government took control of the property. They constructed a training base and a prisoner-of-war camp named in honor of Douglas, whose appeasement of the South clouded an otherwise exemplary career in public service. Camp Douglas was bounded on the north by Ridgley Place (now Thirty-first Street), fronted Cottage Grove Avenue, and extended south to College Place (now Thirty-third Place). Rumors of the disease-ridden barracks and crowded conditions within the wooden stockade of Camp Douglas were widely circulated in the Confederate press. Camp Douglas and its eighty acres were situated four miles south of downtown Chicago. The prison camp was closed in 1865 and demolished immediately after the cessation of hostilities. Today, the Lake Meadows townhomes and high-rise condominiums fill in much of the site. A statue of Senator Douglas is perched high atop a 104-foot obelisk over his burial crypt on the grounds of Okenwald at 636 East Thirty-fifth Street, between Lake Park Avenue and the Illinois Central Railroad tracks to the east. The cor-

nerstone of the Douglas Monument was dedicated by President Andrew Johnson and General Ulysses S. Grant on October 6, 1866, but the tomb, designed by Leonard W.Volk, was not fully complete until 1881, because of the inability of its backers to collect scarce private funds and public subscriptions. The cost of the Douglas Monument was ultimately borne by the state of Illinois. The monument is the last visible reminder of Chicago's hidden role in the War Between the States.

The incalculable misery of the Civil War, and the attending horrors of starvation, scurvy, lack of proper medical attention, and squalor brushed up against Chicago's back door when Camp Douglas received between eight and ten thousand disheartened Confederate prisoners captured at the battle of Fort Donelson in February 1862.

In the months following the bombardment of Fort Sumter, the lakefront property belonging to Henry Graves and Stephen Douglas served as a military training outpost, where Union troops under the command of Colonel Joseph H. Tucker bivouacked before moving south to engage the enemy troops of Jefferson Davis.

Finis Farr pegs the death toll at Camp Douglas in the last three years of the Civil War at 6,129, slightly less than one-third of the entire inmate population housed inside the stockade during the course of the war. Most perished from the dreaded scurvy or smallpox, despite the intentions of good Samaritans and relief workers in the city who administered to the sick and dying through a relief fund organized in the winter of 1862. In 1864, 1,156 inmates died at Camp Douglas.

Others managed to escape through ingenious means. Seventy-five ragged and starving men tunneled their way out of the camp in November 1863. In response, eight companies of the Veteran Reserve Corps and a regiment of Michigan sharpshooters were ordered to Camp Douglas as additional garrison. There were no more "gopher" escapes at the heavily guarded compound.

The fear of insurrection at Camp Douglas weighed heavily on the minds of city officials. Early in the war, an unruly band of paroled Union soldiers, returned north by the Confederacy in a prisoner-of-war swap, attempted to burn down the barracks rather than accept reassignment in the other theaters of war. Chicago was filled with Copperheads, spies, and southern gamblers who fled northward along the Mississippi River to escape conscription in the early days of the war. What would these disruptive secessionists do were they to be properly armed

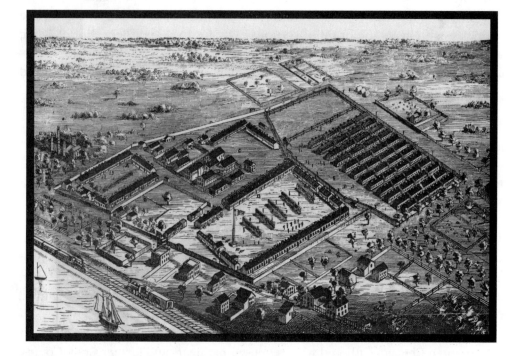

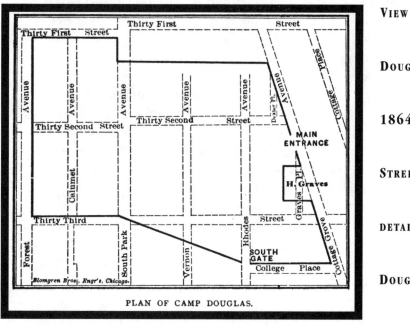

PLAN OF CAMP DOUGLAS.

VIEW OF CAMP

DOUGLAS IN

1864 (ABOVE).

STREET MAP

DETAILING CAMP

DOUGLAS (LEFT).

and directed? The Camp Douglas compound was guarded by 450 enlisted men and officers, a number barely adequate to manage so large a population.

In July 1862, former mayor Levi D. Boone, the discredited know-nothing politician who bears the brunt of responsibility for the Lager Beer Riot of 1855, was jailed at Camp Douglas for supplying money and material comforts to escaping prisoners. The Copperheads had powerful supporters in Chicago's civic and political life.

Buffer zones were established outside the camp by the military authority and a decree of martial law was imposed to circumvent further escape attempts following this serious breach of security.

The threat of a Confederate revolt in Chicago resurfaced in May 1864 when Jacob Thompson, the former secretary of the interior during the lamentable administration of President James Buchanan, organized an expedition to free Confederate prisoners languishing in Northern camps.

Thompson raised a large sum of money and enlisted a brigade of northern secessionists known as the "Knights of Liberty" in the Southern cause. The plan of battle was formulated in Canada. The armed insurrection was all set to begin on August 29, 1864, just as the opening gavel of the Democratic National Convention dropped in Chicago.

As the eastern delegates arrived, the Camp Douglas escapees who had been hiding out in Chicago gathered with rebel sympathizers and former Cook County Sheriff Charles Walsh inside the Richmond House Hotel, a downtown haven for "blacklegs," vagabonds, and Southern-leaning Democrats.

Walsh was a Copperhead who commanded a secret order of two thousand armed men calling themselves the "Sons of Liberty."

Luckily, Colonel Benjamin Sweet, the post commander at Camp Douglas, had received intelligence reports about the impending disruptions and wisely sent for reinforcements from Ohio and Pennsylvania. Walsh and his Confederate sympathizers, hearing of the massive troop buildup at Camp Douglas, lost their nerve and a catastrophe was averted. Without the help of the Canadian benefactors, the prisoner uprising inside the stockade fizzled.

After the threat subsided, Chicago came through the remainder of the Civil War remarkably unscathed. Camp Douglas closed in the summer of 1865, and the remaining prisoners were released after taking an oath of loyalty to the United States. The former military post was used as a rendezvous point for returning Federal troops through the early fall, but after that it was practically deserted. In November 1865, the government property was sold and Camp Douglas ceased to exist.

For many an undernourished and poorly clothed wretch, who awaited the arrival of a warm blanket or the letter from home that never arrived, a quiet resting place underneath an anonymous grave marker in the Oakwoods Cemetery was to be his final benefaction.

Turn around on Thirty-fifth Street and go west to Lowe Avenue (three blocks east of Halsted Street).

A MAYORAL SIDE TRIP

The opening of the Illinois & Michigan Canal in 1848 signaled Chicago's ascent to a viable center of commerce and trade. The canal connected the lakefront city to the Mississippi River. However, the enormity of the twelve-year construction project demanded a large and pliable work force. The fortuitous arrival of thousands of potato-famine Irish into Chicago around that same time ensured that the shallow waterway would be completed according to the timetables set forth by the politicians. It was no small coincidence that Bridgeport, the northern terminus of the Illinois & Michigan Canal, where the vast majority of immigrant Irish lived in squalid conditions, was once called "Hardscrabble." Bridgeport has remained a densely populated Irish-American enclave through most of its history, and the political home base of Chicago's invincible "Democratic Machine."

Politics is more than just a way of life in Bridgeport. It is a special passion. Six mayors, none of them more famous or abiding than the late Richard J. Daley, came out of Bridgeport. The elder Daley matriculated into this rough-and-tumble world from the "Hamburg Athletic Club," a gang of roughnecks said to be active in the defense of the neighborhood during the worst days of the July 1919 race riots. Daley, a party stalwart who fortified the machine during his four terms of office, achieved manhood, prominence, and fame within Bridgeport's surreal boundaries.

Mayor Daley, his wife Eleanor ("Sis"), and their children eschewed the comforts of a more stately mansion, befitting the most powerful big city political boss of the post–World War II era, in favor of a common brick bungalow situated four blocks west of Comiskey Park at 3536 South Lowe Avenue (just south of Thirty-fifth Street).

The Daley home is distinguishable by an iron fence ringing the tiny front yard and an American flag flapping in the breeze. Outside, Chicago police officers maintain an around-the-clock vigil, reminding gawkers, curiosity seekers, White Sox fans, and picture takers to keep moving. Sis Daley, now in her nineties, cherishes the comforts of home, the warm affection of her neighbors, and most of all, her privacy.

Residents still recall, with feelings of disgust, anger, and horror, the civil rights marchers who descended upon Lowe Avenue and disturbed their tranquility in July 1965, a tense week of racial discord on two fronts—on the South Side of Chicago and in the corridors of power in Washington, D.C. In the nation's capitol, the Reverend Dr. Martin Luther King Jr. described Chicago as "the most ghettoized city in this country."

At the heart of the controversy was the black community's unrelenting opposition to Chicago Public Schools Superintendent Dr. Benjamin C. Willis, whose reappointment caught civil rights leaders and grass-roots community organizers off guard. The embattled Willis presided over a public education system that was branded by the U.S. Civil Rights Commission and the Chicago Urban League in a 1961 study as the most segregated in the nation. (In 1988, William Bennett, secretary of education during the Reagan administration, labeled Chicago's public school system the worst in the nation.)

Four years later, very little had been done to alleviate the dangerously overcrowded conditions in the inner-city schools. The cramped and uncomfortable mobile classrooms installed in the parking lots and school playgrounds were desultory moves that inspired deep enmity. They were sarcastically referred to as "Willis Wagons."

As the clatter in the streets escalated to a deafening crescendo and the cops donned their riot gear in anticipation of a showdown, Daley blamed the escalating tensions on communist subterfuge. "They participate in anything like this because that is their line," the all-knowing Daley announced. He backed up his assertions with a veiled allusion to secret intelligence compiled by the Chicago Police "Red Squad" in a fact-finding mission, but he refused to say how he came by this information or divulge the contents to the media and the public.

The marches and protests continued throughout that summer and into the next. They were dramatic signposts of the 1960s, jarring Daley's sense of invulnerability. He sincerely believed he understood the black community and had their best interests at heart, and he could not understand that their frustrations with the system led them in other directions.

Surrounding himself with old-line political warriors like William Levi Dawson, who faithfully delivered his South Side constituency to Daley each and every election day, the mayor could not fathom the reasons behind the militancy exhibited by the comedian Dick Gregory, who accused Daley of "fixing" Willis's reappointment.

Every night for a week, Gregory and seventy sign-carrying civil-rights picketers supported by the Chicago chapter of the NAACP paraded past Daley's residence in all-white Bridgeport. The neighbors hung signs from their picture windows that read: "We Support Our Mayor!"

With 170 stone-faced Chicago cops on full alert and poised to respond to the slightest sign of trouble, the Bridgeporters stood silently and menacingly in front of their bungalows as Gregory and his followers passed. Meanwhile, Daley pleaded for patience and asked that his friends show "courtesy" to the visitors.

In befuddled "Daley-ese" that was at times both charming and annoying, Daley nervously issued a statement with regard to Willis. "I haven't minced any words as to what my position was regarding the Board of Education, and that is my position today."

A committee was formed to consider the ways and means of integrating the Chicago Public Schools through busing—a goal accomplished by the late 1970s, but with mostly disappointing results.

Benjamin Willis, a symbol of the racially divided northern city, agreed to retire on his sixty-fifth birthday in 1966. Dr. King's arrival in Chicago later that week finally calmed the nerves of a jittery city.

The Nobel Prize–winning civil rights leader toured the ravaged inner-city neighborhoods before articulating his views to a respectful audience of ten thousand gathered on the village green of Winnetka, a North Shore suburb of upper-income whites that hardly resembled one of the beachheads of the civil rights movement.

Dr. King did not accept an invitation to meet with Mayor Daley, however. There just was not enough time.

Turn around and go east on Thirty-fifth Street to State Street. Turn right (south) and continue to Thirty-ninth Street (Pershing Road).

A RACE TO THE WIRE
June 24, 1946

James Ragen was slain in the middle of the intersection of Pershing Road and State Street in the "Bronzeville" community—for many years the living, beating heart of Black Chicago. A block north on the east side of State Street, the newspaper offices of the old Chicago Bee *have been restored to their former luster as a branch of the Chicago Public Library. New townhomes are being built and older units restored. Bronzeville is on the move once again, but Pershing and State remains a desolate location. The elevated line still trundles by a half a block to the east, but the corner buildings Ragen observed as he motored south toward his final destiny vanished a long time ago.*

In 1945, when the city was in the throes of a deadly crime wave, a vicious gambling war suddenly erupted over the future control of Continental Press. Continental Press was the leading purveyor of racetrack odds, track conditions, and race results to the operators of illegal wire rooms and handbooks in subscribing cities across the United States.

In Chicago, it was estimated that the "outfit" was earning $50 million in yearly revenues from illegal wagering on the ponies through the lucrative wire services.

Continental published the *Midwest Press,* a Chicago scratch sheet also owned by James M. Ragen, an aging gambler and odds maker whose brother Frank was elected commissioner of the Cook County Board during the World War I era. In their younger years, the Ragen brothers organized a gang of Halsted Street toughs into a formidable political organization. Ragen's Colts "AC" (athletic club) jealously guarded their turf from the incursion of blacks who lived east of Halsted, and terrorized the poor, the weak, and the indigent who crossed their paths.

"Hit me, and you hit two thousand!" South Siders, especially poor southern blacks, understood the implications of defying members of the Ragen gang. The Colts and similar South Side "AC's" were active during the 1919 race riot, which was sparked by the death of a young African-American boy who strayed too far onto the segregated beach at Twenty-ninth Street.

Jim Ragen reformed in his later years, renouncing the gang he forged with his brother. He avoided smoking, drinking, and the gambling games he had supplied to his customers. In 1939, Ragen purchased a controlling interest in Continental from Moe Annenberg, who had, in turn, inherited the service from Mont Tennes, a turn-of-the-century North Side gambling boss who was the first to utilize the electronic transmission of race results from out-of-town tracks to amass a fortune. Tennes was squeezed by Al Capone and forced to sell to Annenberg in 1927.

Ragen, an elder statesman of the gambling rackets, valiantly fended off the attempts of Jake "Greasy Thumb" Guzik, Tony Accardo, Paul Ricca, and their political sponsor in Springfield, State Senator Dan Serritella, to muscle in on the business. Bribes, a promise of a one-time cash payment of $100,000, and threats of direct intimidation did not shake Ragen. In a moment of candor, he confided to one Chicago political crony that the Capone gang was "as strong as the United States Army."

Acting as conciliator for the Capone gang, Serritella proposed a meeting with Accardo, but Ragen wasn't buying it. "Dan made five attempts to get me to meet him," Ragen recalled. "He wanted to arrange hotel rooms where I could come up and nobody would see me, and I said I didn't want any part of him in any way, shape, or manner."

When Ragen refused to bargain in a polite sit-down, the outfit thought they could sidestep him by establishing a rival racing wire, Trans American Publishing and News Service. When that tactic failed, syndicate overseers simply decided to kill him. Sensing his vulnerability, Ragen hired bodyguards. "I like to live just as well as anyone," he said.

James Ragen was homeward bound the afternoon of June 24, 1946. He was driving south on State Street, with his usual chauffeur following close behind in another car, when a stolen delivery truck loaded with orange crates pulled up even with Ragen at Pershing Road. The driver of the gray sedan immediately in front of Ragen's car slammed on his brakes, thereby blocking the only means of escape. Shotgun blasts roared from the tarpaulin-covered truck, mangling Ragen's arms and shoulders. The truck sped away.

Ragen remained coherent and calm through his ordeal. Family members expected him to recover from his wounds until someone slipped past a police cordon at Michael Reese Hospital and finished the job by administering a lethal injection of mercury.

Before Ragen expired on August 14, from what doctors described as uremic poisoning, he revealed the existence of an affidavit given to State's Attorney William Touhy claiming that Guzik, Murray "the Camel" Humphreys, and others were plotting to take over his business. The affidavit conveniently disappeared.

Witnesses were threatened. A newsboy was placed in protective custody. Chicago police captain William Drury, whose shotgun murder inside his Addison Street garage in 1950 by syndicate gunmen was foreshadowed by the Ragen hit, was suspended for refusing to sign an immunity waiver before his grand jury appearance. And though the brass hotly denied it, Drury's nervy arrest of syndicate boss Jake Guzik broke the rules. The murder of the racing czar had far-reaching implications.

Ragen's heirs assumed control of the contentious racing wire, but within a few months, the outfit was in charge of bookmaking citywide and the South Side policy rackets.

The identity of the killers remained a puzzle to everyone except Drury for the next forty-five years until Lenny Patrick, the North Side crew boss of sports bookmakers and the leader of the outfit's "Jewish faction," turned federal informant in the early 1990s. Patrick shed new light on a well-worn saga of mob treachery, murder, and deceit.

In return for a promise of leniency from the state and federal government (a broken promise, as it later turned out), Patrick cleared up nine unsolved mob hits. James Ragen's murder was allegedly carried out with the help of Willie Block and Dave Yaras.

Block was ordered to Los Angeles by Patrick, where he reportedly opened up a liquor store in the Watts neighborhood.

Turn right (west) on Pershing Road (Thirty-ninth Street) and proceed to Archer Avenue. Turn left (southwest) and continue to Sacramento Avenue.

LAST SEEN ON THE ARCHER BUS: THE HAUNTING MYSTERY OF THE GRIMES SISTERS
December 28, 1956–January 22, 1957

Back in the 1950s, Chicago's southwest side was a melting pot for many nationalities. In those years, the working classes of Brighton Park, Canaryville, Bridgeport, and Back of the Yards fought their way up through poverty. In the best and worst of times, in times of happiness, and in times of hardship and sorrow, neighbors united. Amidst the burgeoning economic prosperity of the 1950s, there was a growing sense of optimism that the children born in the post-war baby boom would lead better and more wholesome lives than their parents, who came up through the Great Depression and World War II. A gentle complacency settled over Chicago, as it did over other cities and small towns across the country. The accompanying unshakeable confidence in our government, its institutions, and the ability of law enforcement to protect all citizens was altered by a set of jarring and senseless child murders that began in 1955 with the abduction-murder of the Schuessler-Peterson boys. Then came the bizarre disappearance and murders of Barbara and Patricia Grimes. The city was thrown into a state of shock from which it was slow to recover. The two teenage girls were abducted after leaving the Brighton Theater at 4223 South Archer Avenue (now a performing arts center located just south of Sacramento Avenue, 3000 West). To this day, no one knows with certainty where they were taken or for what evil purposes. Their cause of death remains a puzzle, and the discovery of their unclad bodies lying in a snow-covered, twenty-foot culvert two hundred feet east of the Cook–DuPage County dividing line along German Church Road (Eighty-third Street, a remote two-lane highway) raised fresh questions in the minds of forensic pathologists. With the passing years, the mystery has only deepened. The bizarre aspects surrounding this infamous murder case have fueled wild speculation among armchair detectives, police personnel, journalists, and even a renowned Chicago ghost hunter, whose bus tour swings past the isolated forest area west of Wolf Road and the suburb of Willow Springs. The ori-

THE

BRIGHTON

THEATER

AS IT

APPEARS

TODAY.

gins of the hauntings, he points out, begin at Devil's Creek, a sluggish water-
way that bisects the property at odd angles. Over the years there have been alle-
gations of satanic rituals, ghostly sightings, and unworldly goings-on, partic-
ularly around Halloween. The cops who patrol Willow Springs have their own
pet theories, as does everyone who is familiar with the case. Law enforcement
insiders are naturally reluctant to talk about the case in anything but a whis-
per, adding the familiar cop rejoinder, "Of course what I'm going to say is off
the record!" Since the 1950s, police policy has always been one of containment.
Keep the kids, the crackpots, the crime buffs, and the curiosity seekers out and
allow the residents to carry on with their lives. But is that possible?

Between the romantic idealization of a time and place long past and the hard-edged cynicism of the modern age, there exists a subtle truth. No age can claim moral supremacy over another.

Idealists tend to view the 1950s as America's last golden age. Through the rose-colored glasses of nostalgia, we mourn the passing of innocence and lament the moral breakdown of society that has permeated our society since that time. In truth, the Eisenhower years were never as blissful as depicted in the popular media.

In the city of Chicago, crime and police corruption were on the rise. The homicide bureau of the Chicago Police Department listed 192 unsolved murders that occurred between 1952 and 1957, pointing to lax law enforcement and a pattern of inefficiency. The disappearance of the Grimes sisters and the failure to conduct a diligent murder investigation free of jurisdictional rivalries between city and county police exposed the vulnerabilities of law enforcement and the politics of policing under which it labored.

Barbara Grimes was a sophomore at Kelly High School. Her sister Patricia was a seventh grader at St. Maurice School, located in the heart of Brighton Park on Hoyne Avenue. The girls lived with their divorced mother, who worked as a file clerk and struggled to keep a roof over their heads and food on the table.

Loretta Grimes and her family were beset by continuing hardship and tragedy. Two years earlier, the eldest daughter, Leona, had died from kidney failure. The grim struggle of daily living was made endurable by the love and affection within the family, which was looking forward to celebrating Patricia's thirteenth birthday.

The party was scheduled for Sunday, December 30, 1956, just two days after the girls traipsed happily down the steps of their mother's home at 3634 South

POLICE AND REPORTERS SWARM AROUND THE GERMAN CHURCH ROAD CRIME SCENE AS THE NUDE BODIES OF THE GRIMES SISTERS ARE PHOTOGRAPHED (ABOVE). A MAP SHOWS THE GRIMES CRIME SITE (BELOW).

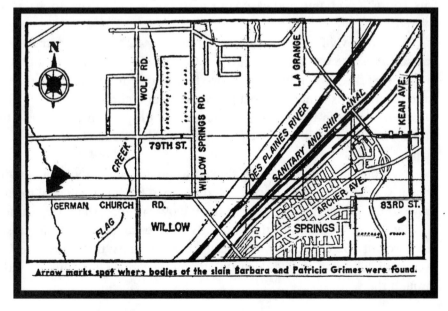

Arrow marks spot where bodies of the slain Barbara and Patricia Grimes were found.

Damen Avenue on their way to see Elvis Presley's *Love Me Tender* at the Brighton Theater. They left home with $2.15 in their pockets.

The sisters were devoted Presley fans. They had gone to the same neighborhood movie house a dozen times to see the same film.

Schoolmates told police that they remembered seeing Barbara and Patricia standing in the popcorn line at 9:30 P.M., laughing and joking. The movie let out at 11:00 P.M., and what happened to them at that point is less certain. In several accounts, the girls boarded an eastbound Archer Avenue CTA bus. Motorman Joseph Smok was certain that two girls matching the description of the Grimes sisters rode his bus down to Western Avenue, but there was no way of knowing for sure.

A classmate said she saw them pass by Angelo's Restaurant at 3551 South Archer Avenue twenty-four hours after their reported disappearance. A Chicago North Shore and Milwaukee railroad conductor told police that he was certain they had hopped on board a train near the Great Lakes Naval Training center in north suburban Glenview.

The police theorized the girls had been chasing after two Navy men they had met downtown a month earlier, but that was only supposition born out of mounting frustration. Hearing these rumors, the tearful mother expressed her outrage. The search for clues, a motive, and possible suspects intensified. By the time it was over, the search for the missing Grimes girls became the greatest missing-persons hunt in Chicago Police history.

From Memphis, Elvis Presley issued a statement. "If you are good Presley fans, you will go home and ease your mother's worries." The appeal went unanswered.

The long vigil ended suddenly on January 22, 1957. Construction worker Leonard Prescott was driving south on German Church Road to a grocery store in Willow Springs when he spotted two figures resembling discarded department store mannequins lying next to a guard rail over a culvert within five feet of the road. Ten feet from the guard rail, the ground dropped precipitously to Devil's Creek. The ninety-acre, privately owned, wooded subdivision was not on the map.

Nervous and edgy, Prescott slowed to take a closer look. Uncertain of just what it was he had seen, Prescott raced home to fetch his wife and together they drove to the crime site and then to the Willow Springs Police Department.

Once the identities of the two girls were established, a multi-jurisdictional task force of 162 officers from Chicago, Cook County, the Forest Preserves, and five south suburban police departments mobilized their resources and plowed through the woods.

Medical examiners, reporters, photographers, and cops swarmed around the murder site trampling precious clues underfoot. The investigation was botched from the moment the first squad car pulled up.

A coroner's jury returned a murder verdict, but they could not explain to anyone's satisfaction the precise cause of death. The Grimes sisters had been sexually assaulted during their captivity, but this information was deliberately withheld from the media so the suffering of family members would not be compounded. However, there was no evidence to show that the girls died as a result of stabbing, shooting, suffocation, or poison. After a fruitless five-hour autopsy, a top pathologist threw up his hands in frustration and said that maybe, when all was said and done, the girls had died of fright.

Coroner Walter McCarron believed the bodies were exposed to the elements for nearly a month before Prescott's gruesome discovery. Why hadn't anyone noticed them lying there before, if that was the case?

Medical experts concluded that the Grimes girls suffered "death by exposure," but it was a questionable verdict that was easily challenged. When Chief Investigator Harry Glos disputed the findings, he was fired by the peevish McCarron, a political hack with a low ignition point who presented weak job credentials for the weighty tasks of his office. The city's first elected Republican coroner since 1928 owned an Oak Park trucking company.

Eager to crack this case in order to save face and further his political ambitions, Cook County Sheriff Joseph Lohman arrested a twenty-one-year-old skidrow drifter from Tennessee named Benny Bedwell. The suspect wore long sideburns and worked as a dishwasher at an all-night Madison Street greasy spoon. In his confession, Bedwell related a lurid tale of drunken debauchery with two underaged girls he had picked up inside the restaurant. But were they the Grimes girls? Everyone except Joe Lohman doubted Benny's story.

"Benny is the best suspect we have so far. We won't make the same mistakes we made in the case of the boys," vowed Lohman, whose career had gone into an irreversible decline after failing to bring the Schuessler-Peterson killers to justice. (See Tour 4.) Solving this latest set of murders was priority number one and an opportunity to cement his place in local law enforcement history.

Lohman booked Bedwell on a charge of murder, but Bedwell's testimony was vague and contradictory, and the confession was probably coerced.

Harry Glos, an investigative pit bull who left no stone unturned in his search for the truth, believed Bedwell was implicated in some mysterious way, but Bedwell was a dubious suspect. Unconvinced of Bedwell's guilt, State's Attorney Benjamin Adamowski ordered him released. While the cops bickered over technicalities and refused to share their information, a turf war erupted between the politicians, whose interests were grounded in partisan politics. The integrity of the investigation was compromised throughout.

Lohman was a Democrat, and Adamowski a Republican. One had his eyes set on the governor's chair, the other entertained notions of unseating an old foe, Mayor Richard J. Daley, who turned to his police chief Timothy O'Connor for answers in times of crisis. O'Connor was a well-intentioned and sincere line officer, but his reach exceeded his grasp and, allegedly, he owed his appointment to a warm, personal friendship with Cardinal Samuel Stritch of the Chicago archdiocese.

Lohman, Adamowski, McCarron, and O'Connor represented the faint hope of getting to the bottom of this deepening mystery.

Glos believed the girls were beaten and tortured by a sexual predator who lured them into the kidnap car on a pretense. Four decades later, experienced detectives who have studied every angle of this provocative murder case agree with the Glos hypothesis. They are firmly convinced that Barbara and Patricia Grimes were abducted by the front man for a "white slavery" ring and taken to a remote stable, farmhouse, or hovel nestled deep in the woods surrounding Willow Springs. They are convinced the sisters were strangled after refusing to become prostitutes.

Over the next few years, various suspects were interrogated from as far away as Lincoln, Nebraska. A $100,000 reward was posted, but the trail went cold and only the kooks and cranks, who recounted prophetic dreams and claimed special psychic powers, came forward to volunteer information. One of them telephoned police headquarters hours before the bodies were found, saying that in a psychic dream he saw the bodies being dumped in Santa Fe Park, a stockcar racetrack located in Tiedtville, a mile and a half south of Willow Springs.

The 1995 conviction of Kenneth Hansen on a charge of abducting and murdering the Schuessler-Peterson boys exactly forty years earlier in a Northwest Side horse stable offered a glimmer of hope that the accused killer might shed light on the decades-old South Side murder case. What connection, if any, did Hansen have to this case?

On the surface it appeared there was no connection at all. The Schuessler-Peterson murders were committed in a desperate act of lust and rage by a homosexual hustler residing at the opposite end of the county. Dismissing the obvious similarities between the two sets of murders, no one bothered to conduct a thorough link analysis, an investigative technique used by investigators to establish commonality between seemingly unrelated crimes.

In 1995, the trail was as cold as ice once again.

Steeped in intrigue and tragedy, the Grimes murders will perhaps never be solved. It remains one of the most tantalizing murder mysteries of the twentieth century.

Near the location where the bodies were found stood the concrete foundation and rubble of what had once been a private family residence. Thick underbrush obscured the former driveway, and the exposed cement bore the unmistakable graffiti of vandals and Satanists who came here because they are familiar with old legends and superstitions surrounding Devil's Creek and the Indians who once roamed these woods.

According to a Willow Springs cop and several journalists who have closely monitored breaking developments in this case over the years, a local resident living off of the main road fled in terror not long after the Grimes girls were found, leaving much of the family furniture, an automobile, and his worldly belongings behind. The five-acre property went to seed. The house eventually burned down in a fire of mysterious origin, and only the slab flooring covering the basement remained. Scribbled on the cement were the words "Pink Floyd, Nobody's home!"

Chicago ghost hunter Richard Crowe, the foremost expert on supernatural phenomenon in the area, is convinced that the unearthly screeching of tires and the late-night slam of a car door heard by local residents are the restless apparitions of an unknown killer reenacting the violent events of the week when innocence died.

Return to Halsted Street via Archer Avenue. Turn right (south) on Halsted Street and go to Exchange Avenue (4136 South).

FIRE IN THE STOCKYARDS
May 18–20, 1934

The essential identity of Chicago as "Hog Butcher to the World" was forged in the dismal landscape of the hog pens, slaughterhouses, and rendering plants of the Union Stockyards, opened by meatpacker John B. Sherman on Christmas Day, 1865. Here, at Halsted Street and Exchange Avenue, was the center of America's meatpacking industry, a vivid kaleidoscope of the nation's industrial might . . . and its shame. Here was where generations of immigrant Czechs, Slovaks, Poles, Lithuanians, Swedes, Ukrainians, Irish, and Jews living nearby in Bridgeport, Canaryville, McKinley Park, and Back of the Yards earned their daily sustenance amid brutal hardship and continuous labor strife. Here journalist Upton Sinclair in his

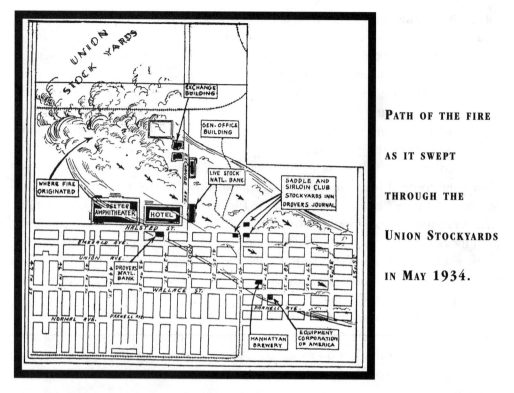

PATH OF THE FIRE

AS IT SWEPT

THROUGH THE

UNION STOCKYARDS

IN MAY 1934.

landmark 1906 novel, The Jungle, *recorded the daily horrors and the hideously unsanitary conditions the workers of packing town endured. By the mid-1950s, the Union Stockyards began losing market share to Kansas City. The big packinghouses quickly abandoned Chicago and, with that, a way of life fast disappeared. The beginning of the end was already in sight. Armour & Company closed its plant in 1950. Swift discontinued their slaughtering operations in 1958. The end of the Stockyards came, as expected, on August 1, 1971. Since then, the Yards have been paved over and reincarnated as a warehouse and industrial park. The Streets and Sanitation Department of Chicago opened a spacious facility on these historic grounds. The last of the packinghouses was razed in 1991. In fact about all that is left from former times is the ancient stone arch located one block west of Halsted on Exchange. The stone steer perched at the top of the arch is believed to be carved in the image of Sherman, a prize-winning animal named for John Sherman. Through this entranceway passed thousands of anonymous workers in good times and bad. One of those bad times occurred in the deadly dry and stifling heat of 1934, when the Yards suddenly burst into flames. In terms of economic loss, it was Chicago's worst conflagration since the entire city was leveled in October 1871.*

The fire began quite unexpectedly in the Swift & Company stock pens at Forty-fifth and Morgan Streets. Before the last ember was extinguished two days later, thousands of heads of cattle were lost. Eleven hundred people were injured. The economic loss was pegged at a staggering $10 million.

More than three square miles were enveloped in the flames that raged through the night of May 18, 1934, and into the next day. Along the east side of Halsted Street from 4159 South to 4233 South, every business and residential dwelling lying in the path of the flames was destroyed. Entire blocks were obliterated, and hundreds of South Side families were left homeless.

The famed Stock Yards Inn and the Saddle and Sirloin Club were early casualties. Dexter Park Amphitheater, a block-long iron and glass pavilion, one of many Daniel Burnham and John Root commissions at the Stockyards, stood in the path of the advancing flames and was lost.

A FRONT PAGE EXTRA:

THE STOCKYARDS FIRE

OF THE "DUSTBOWL"

SUMMER.

North of Exchange Avenue, the fire swept away the entire district east of Halsted Street and north to Forty-first Street, taking with it the Drovers Bank, the firehouse, and several warehouses.

The swiftness with which the flames engulfed the sun-baked structures brought about the grim realization that the Midwestern drought of that "Dust Bowl" summer posed a deadly fire threat to the entire city.

If not for the rapid response of the Chicago Fire Department, it is conceivable that the devastation might have been much worse—possibly repeating the Great Fire of 1871. Within two minutes of Watchman James Fuller's alarm, every Chicago engine company from South Chicago to Rogers Park as well as those in the western suburbs were deployed. The emergency communications system in place in 1934 was considered to be among the finest in the world.

Fire Commissioner Arthur Seyferitch told reporters that 1,500 men from 138 companies battled the blaze, utilizing 75 percent of the city's entire equipment. For a time, large areas of the city were left unprotected, as fire companies raced to the South Side from all directions.

High winds fanned the intense flames. Scores of firemen were overcome by the billowing smoke and the deadly heat. Efforts were hampered by low water pressure, but it was a tribute to the indomitable spirit of Chicago that this and other problems were overcome. The scorched ruins of the Live Stock National Bank, a replica of Philadelphia's Independence Hall, were still smoldering when workmen began the arduous process of rebuilding. Incredibly, the bank was open for business the next day.

Meanwhile, hundreds of workmen were pressed into service constructing pens, chutes, and barns. It was business as usual in Chicago.

The origin of the fire was never determined. William J. O'Connor, Assistant General Manager of the Union Stockyards and Transit Company, was vigorous in his denial that union agitators were responsible. "We have no labor difficulties," he said.

State Fire Marshal Frank E. Doherty Jr. wasn't so sure. He refused to rule out the possibility of arson. "It is a very peculiar coincidence that all of them [the last four Stockyard fires] occurred either on Saturday or Sunday afternoons."

It should be recalled that twenty-four firemen, including Fire Marshal James Horan, met their deaths battling another inferno, which broke out in the hide storerooms of Morris & Company on December 22, 1910. The 1910 disaster represented the worst loss of human life in the history of the department.

Continue south on Halsted Street to Forty-seventh Street. Turn right (west) and go to Ashland Avenue. Turn right (north) and go to 4312 South.

CALL NORTHSIDE 777
December 9, 1932

Hollywood Director Henry Hathaway and his seventy-member 20th Century Fox film crew descended upon Chicago, September 22, 1947, to begin work on a gritty motion picture about the unsolved murder of a policeman, the wrongful conviction of an innocent man, and a mother's desperate plight to free her son from the Stateville Penitentiary with the help of a crusading reporter played by Jimmy Stewart. Call Northside 777 *premiered the next year and was praised by the critics for its "docu-drama" approach to storytelling. Like most cinematic treatments of real life incidents, however, the true facts of the case and the principals in the drama were blurred or distorted by imaginative scriptwriters. As a result, the true story behind the screenplay is virtually lost in the fog of history.* Northside 777 *is really a South Side story set in the Back of the Yards neighborhood. The murder of Officer Lundy occurred not in a "speakeasy," as some writers mistakenly believe, but inside a delicatessen belonging to Mrs. Vera Walush at 4312 South Ashland Avenue. The deli is gone. Danny's Hollywood Diner stands next to an asphalt parking lot where Lundy was shot down in cold blood. A few doors south, however, a collection of shabby two-story buildings gives you a pretty good idea of what this poor working-class area must have looked like in the winter of 1932. Joe Majczek (Joe Wiecek in the film) lived in a two-story wood-frame house at 2038 West Fifty-second Street. Fifty-second Street dead ends one block west of Damen Avenue. The heavy concentration of Poles and Slavs who earned their livelihood working in the Stockyards slaughterhouses during the years when Joe's mother fought a long and hard battle to clear her son's name have long since moved on. Today, Damen Avenue south of Fifty-first Street is a mixed Hispanic–African-American community, and the boarded-up house at 2038 West Fifty-second Street bears an ominous sign warning would-be trespassers to* Keep Out.

William D. Lundy, a fifty-five-year-old Chicago police officer assigned to the Stockyards District, was contemplating retirement, the possibility of which was now only a year away. Like most cops, Lundy looked forward to wiling away his later years at home with his wife and three children. Lundy, however, understood that there are no guarantees in life, and he had grimly resigned himself to working past his retirement in order to bring in a few extra dollars.

These were hard times that were exacting a toll on city workers. Lundy had not received a paycheck in several weeks. Payless paydays were becoming increasingly common in the cheerless winter of 1932.

Officer Lundy entered Vera Walush's Polish delicatessen the morning of December 9 for a cup of coffee. He sat at the rear of the room keeping an eye on things while Mrs. Walush paid a deliveryman for a load of heating coal. Just then, two gunmen entered, one of them shouting, "It's a stickup! Put 'em up!"

The police officer lunged at the robbers from the shadows. In a panic, Mrs. Walush grabbed her four-year-old daughter and hid in the closet. While Lundy wrestled on the floor with the first holdup man, the second armed robber drew his weapon and pumped six shots into the policeman.

The two men then raced out the front door and into a waiting getaway car driven by an accomplice. John Zagate, the deliveryman, told police the car bore an Ohio license plate, but only the first two numbers—unlucky 13—were identifiable. In the scuffle that had ensued, a pair of colored glasses had been left behind. It was the only crime-scene clue the police had to work with.

The murder of Officer Lundy tugged at the heartstrings. There was a great public outcry, as well as pressure emanating from State's Attorney Thomas Courtney, to clear this case up right away, execute the cop killers, and save face for the city.

Courtney was never one to let truth stand in the way of securing a headlining conviction. In 1933, he framed gangster kingpin Roger Touhy on a bogus kidnapping charge in order to feather his own political nest. The Majczek case was just a warm-up for the biggest prize of all.

Detectives pinned the Lundy murder on Joe Majczek and Theodore Marcinkiewicz, who had been lodging with the Majczek family, based on Mrs. Walush's eyewitness testimony. Of late, the woman had been selling pints of illegal hooch under the counter, and she was scared. Pressured by the cops to make a positive identification on the basis of flimsy evidence and in fear of losing her license, she fingered Majczek, who already had a police record. It was another classic Chicago frame-up.

The young men were indicted on January 18, 1933, but the case was not heard until November 7 of that year. "We needed time in which to collect evidence," Courtney said. "It is now in our possession and we are ready to go ahead."

The case was assigned to Judge Charles P. Molthrop, who, after hearing the evidence, believed Majczek innocent.

The defense team was headed by a shyster named William P. O'Brien, a former member of the legal team that represented gangster Hymie Weiss. O'Brien, an inebriate mouthpiece serving the criminal underworld, made a spectacle of himself in court and represented his clients poorly. The pair was convicted on November 10, but spared the death penalty. "No lesser punishment would fit the crime," complained Prosecutor John Murphy, speaking on behalf of Courtney.

Judge Molthrop pulled Majczek aside and in a sympathetic, reassuring tone promised him a new trial, but Courtney and the Cook County Democratic Party hacks would hear nothing of the sort. They threatened Molthrop with removal from the bench if he pursued this matter any further. Molthrop agreed to their demands, but was skipped over by slate makers anyway. He died two years later.

The doors of Stateville slammed shut on Joe for the next thirteen years. Majczek was convict #8356E, forgotten by just about everyone except his mother, Tillie Majczek, a cleaning woman. Tillie took an after-hours job scrubbing the floors of the Commonwealth Edison building downtown in order to raise reward money. For the next eleven years, she scrubbed floors on her hands and knees in an empty office building, until the fateful day in October 1944 when she took out a personal ad in the *Chicago Times*. "Five thousand dollar Reward For the killers of Officer Lundy on Dec. 9, 1932. Call Gro. 1758, 12–7 p.m."

Karin Walsh, the big-hearted city editor, was intrigued. He assigned James McGuire to interview the woman. Jack McPhaul, the rewrite man who authored several books about Chicago crime lore, dusted off the police reports and began asking the hard questions the cops and prosecutors had overlooked in 1932. The *Times* men established that the cops had arrested Majczek the day *before* Mrs. Walush made her positive identification. The sordid political aspects of this case bubbled to the surface, and with this new evidence, the newspaper pressed the state pardons board for a review.

State Senator Walker Butler, with Governor Dwight H. Green's hearty support, made an impassioned plea to the board in April 1945. In August, as the bells tolled signaling the end of the Pacific war, Joe Majczek left the formidable walls of Stateville behind. Warden Joseph Ragen was sorry to see him go. "He was the best hospital clerk we ever had here!"

Holding no grudge against Courtney or any of the shady politicians and jurists responsible for this disgusting perversion of justice, Majczek returned to his old neighborhood. "I'm going to live and let live and conduct myself so that my mother, Governor Green, and others who have helped me will never regret their actions," he said.

Joe Majczek made good on his vow to lead a clean life. He died in 1982. The real killer of Officer Lundy was never found.

<table>
<tr><td>

Take Ashland Avenue to Garfield Boulevard (5500 South). Turn left (east) and proceed to Cottage Grove Avenue. Turn left (north) and go to Hyde Park Boulevard. Turn right (east) and go to Ellis Avenue.

</td></tr>
</table>

COMPULSION!

May 21, 1924

The scars have almost disappeared. In the quiet orderliness of Kenwood–Hyde Park living, the murder of fourteen-year-old Bobby Franks by "thrill" seekers Richard Loeb and Nathan "Babe" Leopold on May 21, 1924, are faint echoes from a time long past. So many of the sprawling nineteenth-century mansions belonging to the millionaire philanthropists and industrialists of former days have disappeared. But there remains in Kenwood–Hyde Park a certain exclusivity that will certainly continue to define the neighborhood as long as the University of Chicago dominates the local economic, cultural, and social scenes. While much of Kenwood looks the same as it did in 1924, the residence of Nathan Leopold at 4754 South Greenwood Avenue was razed and the property subdivided. The garage at the rear of the home, where Leopold stored his automobile, was converted to a carriage house. The Loeb mansion at 5017 South Ellis Avenue was torn down in the 1970s. Nearby, at the southwest corner of Forty-ninth Street and Ellis Avenue, a huge, impressively detailed terra cotta mansion (4848 South Ellis Avenue) dating back to the turn of the century looms over the street. On the sidewalk outside this palatial estate, Loeb and Leopold accosted Bobby Franks as he walked home from the Harvard School, a somber-looking institution still standing on Ellis Avenue between Forty-seventh and Forty-eighth Streets. The Franks home at 5052 South Ellis (at the corner of Hyde Park Boulevard and Ellis Avenue) remains, though it bears the visible scars of deterioration and benign neglect. The DeLena Day School at 932 Hyde Park Boulevard operated out of the house in the 1970s, but it is gone and the paint is peeling away from the sign.

At a quarter past five on May 21, 1924, Bobby Franks was heading home for supper when a gray Winton automobile pulled up alongside him at 4848 South

Ellis Avenue on the west side of the street. Franks was only three blocks from the safety and comfort of his family home when the boy was lured into the death car on a pretense.

The fourteen-year-old Franks was an honor student at the Harvard School for Boys, a private institution for the privileged sons of the wealthy commercial men of the South Side. Jacob Franks, Bobby's father, was the president of the Rockford Watch Company and dabbled in downtown real estate during the stock market boom of the early 1920s.

The following morning, just as the police were fishing the lifeless remains of the boy out from a soggy ravine, Franks received a special delivery letter mailed from inside Zak's drug store at 2357 West Lake Street. The typewritten ransom note demanded $10,000 in vintage unmarked bills. The kidnappers instructed Franks to procure old money, carefully seal it in bundles with white paper, and place the stacks of green inside a cigar box. Franks was told to deliver the ransom to the Van de Bogert & Ross pharmacy at 1465 East Sixty-third Street near the Illinois Central's Woodlawn Station.

"As a final word of warning—this is strictly a commercial proposition and we are prepared to put our threat into execution should we have reasonable grounds to believe you have committed an infraction of the above instructions," cautioned the kidnapper—who was articulate and obviously well-educated.

"Robert knew them, I must know them," said Franks in a barely audible whisper. "I have been racking my brain trying to think who they might be."

By the time Franks collected his thoughts and was able to comply with the ransom demand, his son was already dead. Bobby's body was thrown into a culvert under the Pennsylvania Railroad tracks at 121st Street near the Calumet River. The swift current floated the body into a two-foot main in the shallow waters of Wolf Lake. The cause of death was ascribed to blunt trauma. Franks was struck in the back of the head with an iron chisel while seated next to the driver of the car. Just who administered the fatal blows is not known.

A pair of tortoise-shell eyeglasses was found near the body. The police were able to trace ownership of the spectacles to Nathan "Babe" Leopold through Almer & Co. opticians. Only three people in Chicago owned this particular style of eyewear, but the other two had ironclad alibis.

Leopold, a gifted young ornithologist and Phi Beta Kappa student at the University of Chicago, had graduated from high school at age fifteen. Possessing a grand intellect and a sociopath's capacity for reinventing the truth, Leopold explained that he was bird watching that afternoon and had carelessly misplaced his glasses. "Babe" Leopold was glib and defiant under questioning.

Leopold and his worshipful companion Richard "Dickie" Loeb had used an

ONE OF THE "CRIMES OF
THE CENTURY." *DAILY NEWS*
REPORTERS JAMES MULROY
AND ALVIN GOLDSTEIN
HELPED FINGER NATHAN
LEOPOLD AND RICHARD LOEB
AS THE KILLER OF BOBBY
FRANKS. THE BOBBY FRANKS
HOME IN HYDE PARK AS IT
APPEARS TODAY (BELOW).
(Photo by Christina Carlson)

Underwood typewriter to record their ransom demand. A reporter from the *Chicago Daily News* compared samples of the type in a note written by Leopold to a law student with that of the ransom note. Leopold alibied that he worked with a second typewriter—a Hammond model. The experts were summoned and a microscopic examination of the fonts offered convincing proof that the same Underwood owned by the accused had been used in writing the ransom note.

Exactly ten days later, State's Attorney Robert Emmet Crowe pried separate confessions from the boys, each blaming the other. They said that they had originally targeted Armand Deutsch, grandson of Sears Roebuck Chairman Julius Rosenwald, as their intended victim but ransom money was incidental to the "thrill" of committing the perfect crime in order to thwart police dullards and convince a skeptical world of their "superior intellect."

With two signed confessions in hand, Crowe prepared to square off against Clarence Darrow, the cagey criminal defense attorney, in what many legal experts acknowledged to be an open and shut case. The families of Loeb and Leopold spared no expense to save their boys from the gallows.

As expected, Darrow managed to outmaneuver Crowe at every turn. He entered a guilty plea in order to waive a jury trial that the defense was certain to lose. Darrow's passionate plea to the court to spare the lives of these troubled young men, who could not have committed the crime acting alone, brought gallery spectators to tears.

Clarence Darrow was masterful. He succeeded in diverting attention away from the heinous crime and shifted the focus toward a moral indictment of capital punishment. In his long career, Darrow had saved Charles Healey, a thoroughly corrupt and despicable Chicago police chief, from the penitentiary along with many other bottom-dwelling rogues, con artists, anarchists, and criminals. His passionate courtroom oratory, dramatic eloquence, and sense of moralistic outrage against the injustices of society blurred the portentous record of crimes some of his clients had committed.

Spared the death house, Loeb and Leopold were delivered to the Joliet penitentiary to begin serving life sentences that afforded them time to reflect upon the consequences of their actions.

Dickie Loeb was stabbed to death in a shower room twelve years later by a prisoner who resisted his untoward sexual advances.

Leopold, on the other hand, was an exemplary prisoner. In 1949, he was declared eligible for parole, but he needed a public relations boost. He got it in 1956 with the publication of Meyer Levin's best-selling book *Compulsion,* which was later made into a long-running Broadway play and a 1959 motion picture starring Orson Welles as Darrow and Dean Stockwell and Bradford Dillman as the killers.

Nathan Leopold was paroled in 1958. He fled to Puerto Rico where he began a career as an X-ray technician. He died of natural causes in 1971 at age sixty-six.

Return to Garfield Boulevard and take Garfield Boulevard west to State Street. Turn left (south) on State Street and proceed to 6200 South.

THE DEATH TROLLEY
May 25, 1950

At the time, the crash of a Green Hornet trolley and a gasoline truck at Sixty-second and State Street was described as the "worst loss of life involving a motor vehicle in America." Thirty-three people were instantly incinerated, and four apartment buildings standing in the 6200 block of South State Street, across the road from the railroad embankment, exploded with the force of the Nagasaki atomic bomb. On a quiet Sunday morning in 1998 when I first visited this site in Woodlawn, which is east of the Sixty-third Street exit of the Dan Ryan Expressway, I found only vacant lots where buildings once stood and an eerie calm transcending the usual bustle of city life. The trains still rumble past, though not as many as before. The rusting, paint-chipped beams supporting the viaduct spanning Sixty-third Street as you

A GREEN HORNET TROLLEY CAR LUMBERS SOUTH DOWN STATE STREET

approach from the west are as they appeared to Chicago Transit Authority motorman Paul Manning seconds before impact.

T he night before, a sudden and violent rainstorm flooded the low-lying Sixty-third Street underpass at State Street, making the road impassable to the electric CTA trolley cars. All day long, a flagman detoured the southbound cars toward a CTA turnaround track on the east side of State Street. For the moment, Sixty-third Street marked the end of the line.

The Green Hornet driven by Paul Manning in the early evening rush hour of May 25, 1950, was one of the newest and sleekest cars on the CTA line. The trolley was determined to be in perfect working order, and only a terrible mis-calculation could be blamed for what happened next.

Manning, forty-three, was clipping along at thirty miles per hour, way too fast for conditions, when the flagman standing at Sixty-second Street frantically signaled the driver to slow down. In the opposite lane heading north, a semi-tractor trailer driven by Mel Wilson approached the viaduct.

Wilson hauled eight thousand gallons of Standard Oil gasoline, earmarked for South Side filling stations.

When Manning realized that he had ignored the flagman's signal, he slammed on the brake, forcing the car to swerve sharply to the left and directly into the path of the oncoming semi.

Every seat on the Green Hornet was occupied. The aisles were filled with standing passengers who were thrown to the floor by the sudden jolt. Upon impact, a burst of flame shot through the car. Manning threw his hands up and screamed in agony. He was consumed in the flames.

In the terror and confusion that followed, trapped victims pushed against the side exit doors in desperation, but they would not budge. The windows were covered with steel bars, cutting off an escape route for the thirty-three trapped victims. Thirty others managed to crawl away from the inferno and were treated for severe burns at Provident Hospital.

Meanwhile, flames soaring two and three stories high erupted in the build-ings along State Street. Luckily, they were uninhabited at the time, but fire dam-age exceeded $150,000.

The smell of scorched flesh hung in the air long after the debris was cleared and the bodies removed to the morgue. According to published reports, twenty thousand people lined the streets for a glimpse of the carnage.

Paul Manning, who had been involved in ten minor accidents during his

THE CHARRED RUIN

OF THE GREEN

HORNET STREET CAR

(ABOVE), WITH PAS-

SENGERS STILL

TRAPPED INSIDE.

THE INCINERATED

GASOLINE TRUCK

(LEFT).

(Photos by Art Bilek)

NEARBY BUILDINGS WERE DESTROYED INSTANTLY BY THE FORCE OF THE BLAST.

(Photo by Art Bilek)

career, was held accountable by his supervisors for the tragedy. "The poor guy is dead," said CTA attorney James Dwight, who remained guarded in his choice of words. "Let's not make it too hard on him."

"There isn't a thing in the world the CTA wants to hide, but we want the facts to come out and no distortion of the facts," added Ralph Budd, CTA chairman.

The facts were obvious. The Green Hornet's design flaws were the real scandal. The Green Hornet cars lacked safety pulls (now standard equipment on all busses and elevated lines). CTA engineers were immediately ordered to remove the offending metal bars from the trolley lines and install the necessary safety pulls. But hindsight is largely meaningless amid such senseless slaughter.

Continue south on State Street to Sixty-third Street. Turn left (east) and go to Kimbark Avenue. Turn right (south) on Kimbark and go to Sixty-fourth Street.

THE KILLING FIELDS
1965–1969

Ravaged by gangs, poverty, and a sense of hopeless despair, the Woodlawn community on Chicago's South Side stands as mute testament to the pernicious power of urban street gangs. One such gang, known as the Blackstone Rangers, wreaked havoc on a neighborhood whose wounds have been slow to heal. The First Presbyterian Church, due east of St. Gelasius Parish at Sixty-fourth and Kimbark, was an integral component of that story.

Dick English, the former Deputy Director of the Illinois State Department of Corrections, remembers when Eugene "Bull" Hairston and Jeff Fort organized 250 Woodlawn youths, who hung out at Blackstone Avenue and Sixty-seventh Street, into a gang called the "Rangers," in honor of the elite U.S. Army military unit. Members of the Rangers wore red berets and struck fearsome, defiant poses.

"Eugene Hairston was a little older than Fort, who was the number two man at that time," English recalled. "Fort became number one because Hairston was in jail for using drugs. When I first met Jeff Fort he was thirteen years old and in the Illinois Youth Department of Corrections. He was quite shrewd, very manipulative with a strong personality and mannerisms. He's tough physically. I knew that, because I used to teach him boxing and wrestling."

In 1965, the Rangers initiated a "recruitment drive," fueled by a savage gang war with their arch rivals, the Vice Lords, an older, more entrenched street gang headquartered in Lawndale. Within three years, Hairston and Fort ruled a stratified criminal organization with eight thousand members. Woodlawn merchants were forced to pay "street taxes" to gang representatives under the guise of "community development." Businesses, receiving little or no help from the police, gave up and moved out. The neighborhood was severely blighted by the end of the decade.

The human toll was incalculable. Police statistics recorded forty-five gang-related homicides in the first nine months of 1968. Heavily armed teenagers roamed the South Side streets leaving behind a ragged trail of death and mayhem. The Rangers battled the Vice Lords and later the Disciples of Englewood, led by David Barksdale and Nicholas Dorenzo, from inside their command post at the Joyland Ballroom on East Sixty-third Street.

Well-intentioned ecumenical leaders like the Reverend John R. Fry of the First Presbyterian Church at 6400 South Kimbark Avenue provided access to social workers. Reverend Fry opened up his church to the Rangers to solicit the Office of Economic Opportunity (OEO) for federal grant money for job training. The OEO funded a $927,341 grant to The Woodlawn Organization (TWO), which was fronted by the Rangers and Disciples. The scam, perpetrated by the gangs against a respected community outreach organization founded by the Reverend Arthur M. Brazier to benefit disenfranchised neighborhood youth decades earlier, nearly worked.

Jeff Fort purchased a new Ford Mustang with money coming from the Board of Missions of Reverend Fry's church. Over one thousand separate acts of fraud relating to the disbursement of checks to the job training centers were uncovered by examiners, touching off a Senate probe that forced cancellation of the program.

With the fraud in high gear, thirty-seven Rangers and Disciples were hired to "teach" Woodlawn youth in a classroom setting. "Those gang members were paid at that time, more money than what I was earning as a shift commander in the Illinois Youth Department of Corrections," English chuckles.

During the 1968 Democratic Convention, a mysterious fire gutted Reverend Fry's Church office, which was always kept under lock and key. The bomb and arson squad was called in to investigate.

Meanwhile, gang recruitment spread into South Shore, Essex, Grand Boulevard, and points further south and west. The ambitious social welfare agenda, supported by Chicago insurance magnate and philanthropist W. Clement Stone, was adjudged a failure.

In one murderous rampage, which received scant attention from the downtown newspapers, whose editors simply refused to acknowledge such daily carnage, 135 youths were shot in the first six months of 1969. Cornell Steele, a well-known Ranger leader, was convicted of one murder but is thought to be responsible for twenty-seven more. If true, it is a record of slaughter unmatched by H. H. Holmes, Ted Bundy, or the worst of serial killers.

For the students of Hyde Park High School who attended classes between 1966 and 1968, the chances of being shot before graduation day was one in twenty.

Federal grants, intervention programs, police crackdowns . . . nothing seemed to stem the violence. Fort changed the name of the gang to the El Rukn Tribe in 1978, renounced violence, and proclaimed himself Chief Prince Malik. But the end result was always the same—making money and extending gang influence at the expense of human life. The El Rukns were finally destroyed by significant government prosecutions in the late 1980s, but their legacy was powerful and enduring.

Borrowing on the organizational model charted by Fort in the 1960s, stronger and more resourceful gang leaders emerged to fill the power vacuum. Larry Hoover, the eldest of four children reared on the South Side, joined a gang at age twelve and had been shot four times by his sixteenth birthday. By 1969, he had molded the Supreme Gangsters into a five-thousand-member criminal force by studying the methods employed by Jeff Fort, his mentor. "As he walked through, the church was getting quiet," Hoover said of Fort. "You could hear a pin drop. I told myself I can have a mob like that."

Hoover spurned Fort's offer to join the Rangers when Fort refused him a seat on the gang's ruling commission known as "the Main 21." Instead, Hoover merged the remnants of David Barksdale's smaller and less organized Disciples gang, following Barksdale's death in 1975, with the Black Gangsters. They became the Black Gangster Disciple Nation and were estimated to be thirty-thousand strong during the height of their power.

Convicted on a gang-related homicide charge in 1973, Hoover commanded this large imposing force from inside his jail cell at the Vienna Correctional Center in downstate Illinois. Up to that point he had never read a book in his life—not even a comic book. When he finally got around to it, Hoover borrowed a copy of Mike Royko's *Boss,* the life story of the late Mayor Richard J. Daley and the attainment of political power in Chicago.

The police calculate that there are forty-one major gangs operating in Chicago with a combined membership pegged at a staggering one hundred thousand. It is not a new phenomenon. Sociologist Frederic Thrasher identified 1,013 kid gangs in 1929, but at their very worst, the neighborhood toughs belonging to the ethnic gangs of former times represented a temporary passage from youth to manhood. It is not that way now, and hasn't been since the 1960s when the Rangers laid waste to a once stable African-American community.

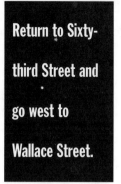

Return to Sixty-third Street and go west to Wallace Street.

THE MONSTER OF SIXTY-THIRD STREET
1887–1894

At the end of the nineteenth century, Englewood was a quiet, suburban community formed by the convergence of three railroad routes and known as Junction's Grove. Newcomers, seeking affordable housing after the Chicago Fire, poured into Englewood. The community gradually shed its suburban identity. In 1884, eight railroads connected Englewood with downtown Chicago, bringing the village that much closer to the central city and its attending horrors. Herman Webster Mudgett (aka "Henry Howard Holmes") came down from Chicago in 1887 to stake a claim in the community and ply his diabolical schemes upon the simple, trusting folk who encouraged imaginative entrepreneurs from the city to help them grow the commercial district along Sixty-third Street. Mudgett signaled his intention to build a large comfortable hotel in nearby Jackson Park to accommodate the crush of visitors to the World's Colombian Exposition. He acquired a large lot at Sixty-third and Wallace Streets adjacent to the Western Indiana railroad tracks, and he hired crews of workmen to build an oddly shaped, incongruent structure that his horrified neighbors would come to call "Murder Castle" once the fiendish secrets buried in the cellar were exposed. The Englewood of Mudgett's day has disappeared. A U.S. Post Office stands nearest the site of the Castle. Plagued by years of unending gang violence, high crime, and the gradual disappearance of a thriving retail corridor, the Sixty-third Street commercial district stretching west from the Dan Ryan Expressway (I-94) is void of the natural amenities of Chicago's most vibrant neighborhoods. It is as if the ghost of Mudgett dwells within this vast South Side slum, clutching this neighborhood by the throat.

Herman Webster Mudgett was America's first interstate serial killer and a study in moral depravity. America was not quite sure what to make of him. The memory of his crime spree, extending as it did from New England to the Midwest in the closing years of the nineteenth century, has inspired authors and essayists to search for a way to reconcile the odd contradiction between the carefree "Gay Nineties" and the mounting horrors of urbanization symbolized by Herman Webster Mudgett.

When his last hope of escaping the gallows faded, Mudgett confessed to twenty-seven murders. The arch-criminal said he was "born with the devil in him." Franklin Geyer, the Philadelphia detective who shadowed the madman from city to city, was skeptical. "He always was an expert liar and on the scaffold his instincts were too strong for him. He did not kill all the people he is charged with killing, for some of them are still alive, but he killed many and now he is dead himself."

Born in Gilmanton, New Hampshire, in 1858 (1861 according to other accounts), Holmes entered medical school shortly after his marriage to Clara A. Lovering, a beautiful young woman of eighteen who helped support him while he attended classes in Burlington, Vermont. The sight of dead bodies amused and fascinated him. He studied dissection and made it his hobby. To satisfy his craving for blood, he murdered his first son, a crime that went undetected for many years. He then set out for the Midwest, leaving his broken-hearted and grieving wife behind.

Mudgett led the life of a rover, turning up here and there, only staying long enough in one place to ply his trickery on the unsuspecting. In St. Paul, Minnesota, he was appointed receiver for a restaurant but absconded with the proceeds of a fire sale that he engineered on behalf of his financial backers. The itinerant con man passed through South Bend, Indiana, and the small towns of Pennsylvania before settling in Wilmette, Illinois, and marrying a wealthy local girl named Myrtle C. Belknap in 1887.

Stoop-shouldered, deliberate in speech, and an otherwise modest man by all outward appearances, Mudgett quickly wore out his welcome in Wilmette. He tried to kill Jonathan Belknap, granduncle of his second wife, after forging his name to a $2,500 note and insuring his life. Insurance fraud was Mudgett's criminal specialty.

In 1887, Mudgett left the quiet North Shore suburb and the Belknaps in a state of shock in order to resume his larceny in Englewood. Preying on a naive widow woman, Mrs. E. S. Holden, Mudgett took control of a family-owned drugstore. She disappeared shortly after turning over the books to the charming stranger.

The drugstore was mortgaged in 1889 so that Mudgett, who by this time called himself H. H. Holmes, could build his famous "castle" at 701 West Sixty-third Street, across the street from the Holden property. "From cellar to garret [it] was designed for the commission of crime," observed the *Chicago Tribune*. "It had hidden doors, concealed staircases, secret rooms, traps, shafts, paraphernalia for disposal of the bodies. He planned the building and superintended its erection."

The Castle was three stories of shoddy construction, measuring 162 feet

HERMAN WEBSTER

MUDGETT (AKA H.H.

HOLMES) ON DEATH

ROW AT MOYAMENSING

PRISON.

Trap door on the second floor.

Vault and quicklime grave.

TRAP DOORS AND

EARLY DEATH INSIDE

THE HOLMES MURDER

"CASTLE."

Castle stove that furnished clues.

Holmes' private laboratory.

long by 50 feet wide. The second floor contained thirty-five rooms with fifty-one doors cut into walls at every imaginable place. Workmen were hired and fired with numbing regularity. That way, no one but Holmes really understood the intricacies of the layout.

The 160-room Sarah Pardee Winchester home in San Jose, California, is the only other private residence in America that is reflective of Mudgett's nightmare visions. In the Winchester case, a seemingly mad *woman* tormented by the walking spirits of all who were killed by the weapons of death manufactured by her father-in-law, the inventor of the repeating rifle, kept building and building right up to the moment of her final reckoning in 1922.

How many people perished inside the Englewood house of horrors has never been accurately determined. Chicago Police estimated that Holmes killed nineteen people, including young children. He subjected men and women from all walks of life to unspeakable horrors—businessmen who were a party to his crooked, windfall schemes; his pretty young fiancée; a personal stenographer; and a number of vacationers who had come to Chicago to visit the 1893 World's Fair. Their deaths were agonizing. Chloroform poisoning, slow strangulation, and asphyxiation inside secret air-tight chambers designed and operated by the devious Holmes awaited the innocent and unsuspecting. When he was finished with his victims and the fleshy portions of their bodies were boiled in acid, their skeletal remains were sold to downtown medical colleges, who paid cash and asked no questions.

Holmes was arrested in Boston on November 17, 1894, on a charge of insurance fraud and the murders of his dim-witted sidekick, Benjamin Pitezel; Pitezel's wife, Carrie; and their three children, Nellie, Alice, and Howard, whom Holmes suffocated in a trunk. The crimes did not occur in Chicago, which made it impossible for Cook County prosecutors to extradite Holmes back to the Midwest.

By this time, Chicago Police had unearthed the skeletal remains of five women and a child from Holmes cellar. The police discovered that Holmes had equipped his chamber with a butcher's table, surgical tools, and vats of acid and quicklime to speed the process of decomposition.

The Holmes Castle was destroyed by fire on August 19, 1895, just eight days after Detective John W. Norton opened the place up for public inspection, charging admission for a personally guided tour. There was a settled belief among the police who refused to be a party to such nonsense that a confederate of Holmes had deliberately torched the building in order to hide the misdeeds of others who had taken salacious delight in participating in the blood rituals.

Holmes was convicted of murder in Philadelphia and sentenced to die by the rope on May 6, 1896. The killer was calmly composed and contemplative as he faced his own death inside a dank cell inside Moyamensing Prison. To his warders and members of the press, Holmes presented a stolid, impassive front. "I was born with the devil in me," he said. "I could not help the fact that I was a murderer no more than the poet can help the inspiration to sing."

It was only a minute's walk from the cell to the gallows, and as the hangman covered Holmes' face with the black hood, the killer turned to him and said, "Aleck, don't be in such a hurry!" When asked if he was ready to die, Holmes nodded his assent. "Don't bungle," he cautioned the executioner. Then a simple goodbye, before the specially handmade rope dropped the Monster of Sixty-third Street and other places into eternity.

A couple of years passed, and the awful memories receded. Then a Wilmette woman told the Evanston Police (Wilmette did not yet have a police agency of its own) of a strange recurring dream she had about the buried remains of a human being lying at the root of a large oak tree in a coppice of woods. Police unearthed a skeleton buried in the shadow of a church spire and a rambling, wooden home with a spacious front porch. It didn't take them long to figure out that Herman Webster Mudgett had once lived nearby.

Continue west on Sixty-third Street to Halsted Street. Turn left (south) and go to Seventy-first Street. Turn left (east) and go to Prairie Avenue. Turn right (south) to 7244 South Prairie.

AL CAPONE'S FAMILY RESIDENCE
1920s–1930s

Far from the hurly-burly of the South Side "Levee," Al Capone purchased a quiet, unassuming home at 7244 South Prairie Avenue for his widowed mother Theresa; wife, Mae; sister Mafalda, who attended Lucy Flower High School; and younger brothers. The red-brick, fifteen-room house is located one block west and a block south of St. Columbanus, where Capone's mother attended mass several times a week. Recalling the quiet tranquility of Seventy-first Street, poet and novelist Nelson Algren, who lived in the neighborhood as a boy, wrote, "The cross above St. Columbanus caught the light of a holier daybreak than ours while the wan gas-flares still wavered. Then the bells of early mass rang, for our own morning had lightened the alleys at last." The wide, spacious street with its well-maintained brick bungalows reflects a sense of orderliness and suburban domesticity, which even Al Capone, a symbol of urban evil in the 1920s, desired for his family, away from the tumult of public life. In 1989, the former Capone property on Prairie Avenue came within one vote of being considered for inclusion in the National Register of Historic Places. State officials voted down the petition for all the usual reasons, and the campaign to celebrate a unique slice of Chicago stalled.

The rather conventional looking building at 7244 South Prairie Avenue was a source of pride for Al Capone, and an unending curiosity for police who wondered what the "Big Fella" was up to inside of his South Side residence. At one point during Capone's short but violent reign, squad cars maintained an around-the-clock vigil outside the house waiting for Capone to emerge so they could harass him, arrest him, and presumably drive him out of town. The order came down from Police Chief Michael Hughes, appointed by Mayor William Hale Thompson in 1927. "Go get 'em, Mike!" Thompson chortled. Hughes was hailed as a rackets buster and his boss a gangster pal. It was a curious dichotomy, but in Chicago the usual rules rarely apply.

Al Capone managed to slip away to Florida, not wanting to continue to put his wife son, and mama Capone through the daily grind of police surveillance. Prairie Avenue was a family sanctuary, and Capone purchased fine imported Chinese rugs, Dresden candelabra, elegantly woven tapestries, and other accoutrements to make his house truly a home. To protect his investment from the cops and rival gangsters, he installed horizontal bars across the ground-floor windows.

When he was at home on Prairie Avenue, and not at one of his Chicago Heights whorehouses or making "whoopee" at the gang's party house at 1600 West Austin Avenue (where the boys went to "relax" with their teenage girlfriends from the exertions of running a criminal empire), Capone was something of a culinary master, known for his steaming pasta with tomato sauce. A reporter who dropped by one afternoon caught him in a pink apron stirring the spaghetti.

To continue the tour, go south on the Dan Ryan Expressway. Exit at Ninety-fifth Street and proceed east to Van Vlissingen Road. Turn right (south) and go to 100th Street. Turn left (east) and proceed east to Luella.

"BORN TO RAISE HELL!"
July 13–14, 1966

The Calumet Harbor section of Chicago is tucked away in a remote corner of the Southeast Side. Its saloons, crumbling steel mills, shipping docks, and decaying infrastructure are hidden from view by the Dan Ryan Expressway (I-94) and an east-west rail corridor belonging to the Chicago & Western Indiana. The railway serves to isolate the western boundary of the community from the rest of the city as it whisks commuters and goods to and from Northwest Indiana. Once, this area was an important commercial shipping center. Over the years a great number of nationalities checked in and out of the neighborhood, but all that has changed. In 1966, 7,500 people, about half of them Jewish, lived in Jeffery Manor, south of Burnside and a mile west of the docks. Today the townhouses and post–World War II, neatly arranged, suburban-style ranch houses are mostly owned by African-Americans. The exodus of heavy industry hit the area hard. The area is depressed and in need of economic redemption.

The addresses associated with the Richard Speck murders are still standing. However, the National Maritime Union hall is now the Greater Morning View Church, and its façade has been rebricked. In the long, hot summer of 1966, when escalating racial tensions threatened to turn the West Side of Chicago into a bloody battleground, there occurred in this hidden corner of Chicago a crime of such epic proportions that it jolted the nation and diverted attention away from the Vietnam War, race riots, and a myriad of other political and social problems challenging the complacency of middle America. In a small townhouse at 2319 East One Hundredth Street, leased by the South Chicago Community Hospital as a dormitory, eight student nurses were dragged from their beds in the sweltering heat of a July night and brutally slaughtered by a shambling Texas drifter, who had tattooed on his arm a cryptic warning to society. The tattoo read, "Born to Raise Hell."

In the spring of 1966, Richard Franklin Speck, a depressed loner possessing an IQ of ninety and a string of forty-two arrests for serious crimes in Dallas and its surrounding neighborhoods, blew into Chicago like an ill wind.

Tall, gaunt, and stupid, Speck set up housekeeping with Gene Thornton, his brother-in-law, and Speck's older sister, Martha, in a second-floor apartment at 3966 North Avondale on the city's Northwest Side. It was his announced intention to search for work as a merchant seaman, but work was contrary to Speck's nature. From the moment he arrived, it was an uncomfortable fit. Richard Speck was shiftless and prone to obsessive-compulsive behavior. Neither the sister nor her husband knew that Speck was wanted by police in two states.

Tiring of Speck's lazy, unpredictable ways, Thornton drove his unwanted houseguest down to the National Maritime Union (NMU) Hall at 2315 East One Hundredth Street, a few doors away from three residential townhouse dormitories rented by the South Chicago Community Hospital for 24 of its 115 student nurses.

Thornton was hoping against hope that there was an open berth still available for Speck on a slow-moving scow bound for Vietnam. As it turned out, the assignment went to another man with greater seniority, leaving Speck to his own devices. Wishing him well, Thornton handed Speck $25 and drove off. Whatever happened next, Richard Speck was on his own, and Gene Thornton was thankful to be finally rid of his malevolent in-law.

In early May, Speck secured a position aboard the SS *Clarence Randall,* an iron ore ship traversing the Great Lakes. Stricken with appendicitis during the final leg of the voyage, Speck was hospitalized in Hancock, Michigan, a copper-mining town in the Upper Peninsula. When Speck returned to Chicago in mid-June, he was fired by his employer, Inland Steel, for drunk and disorderly conduct. He had been repeatedly warned that his combative behavior would not be tolerated, but the threat of job loss was something he took very lightly.

Speck spent the next three weeks in flophouses and seedy taverns, financing his drinking and occasional romps with waterfront whores and barflies through whatever odd jobs he could scrounge.

The twenty-four-year-old drifter and ex-con was marking time in the scorching ninety-degree Chicago heat. At night he slept in the park. By day he prowled the dimly lit air-conditioned bars reeking of stale beer and bad memories.

Sullen, angry, and depressed over his prospects, Speck was drinking heavily in the Shipyard Inn the night of July 13, when he was possessed by a sudden and demonic compulsion to raise a little hell. He had ingested a combination of pills, booze, and narcotics and would later say he didn't remember a thing beyond that point.

Armed with .22-caliber pistol (supplied by a woman twice his age), a hunting knife, and a pocketknife, and seized by a sudden and uncontrollable impulse, Speck left the bar and approached one of the student nurse dormitories. For the past few weeks Speck had observed the young women coming and going from the pastel green and buff brick townhouse. He had watched them sunbathe in nearby Luella Park across the alley from the rear of the townhouse, and was familiar with their schedules and daily routines. It was nearly 11:00 at night, and he knew that they were in bed or preparing to retire for the night.

Hearing a knock at the door of the second-floor bedroom she shared with two other young women, Corazon Amurao, an exchange student nurse from the Philippines, responded. She peered out at a tall, lean stranger who smelled of liquor and was brandishing a gun in one hand and a knife in the other. "I'm not going to hurt you," the man said. "I'm only going to tie you up. I need money to go to New Orleans."

Richard Speck pushed his way inside the townhouse and ordered the three Filipino students, Valentina Pasion, Merlita Garguilo, and Amurao, into a bedroom in the rear of the dwelling, where Pamela Wilkening, Nina Schmale, and Pat Matusek were preparing to turn in for the night. Speck cut the bed sheets into three-foot strips and used them to bind each of the student nurses by their wrists and ankles. At 11:30, a seventh nurse, Gloria Davy, returned home from a date. Then, a half-hour later, Suzanne Farris and her friend, Mary Ann Jordan, appeared at the front door. Richard Speck ushered them into the back room at the point of a gun.

Speck had systematically bound and gagged nine women. How he accomplished this with minimal to no resistance is one of the enduring mysteries in the annals of Chicago crime. At one point, as he was leading one girl at a time into an adjoining room, he must have lost count of the victims.

By 3:30 A.M., eight student nurses were already dead or dying. Speck, his lust finally satiated, pocketed his weapons and slipped out of the townhouse.

Only Corazon Amurao had survived the ordeal. She had managed to roll under the bunk bed, remaining there in a state of petrified terror and shock until the following morning at 6:00 A.M. At last, emerging from her hiding place, Amurao pushed her way out of the apartment through a window screen and climbed onto a ledge and shouted down to passersby. "My friends are all dead! I'm the only one alive. Oh, God, I'm the only one alive!"

Hearing the woman's screams, police officer Daniel Kelly of the South

Chicago District entered through an open door at the rear of the building, where he found the naked body of twenty-two-year-old Gloria Davy, the only one of the eight women Speck had sexually molested. For Kelly, the discovery was all the more horrifying. He had once dated Davy's sister.

The residential unit resembled a charnel house. The horrors encountered by soldiers in Vietnam could not have been much worse. "I found bodies all over the place," Kelly later remarked. Cook County Coroner Andrew Toman, whose father served as Cook County Sheriff back in the 1930s, described the revolting scene as "the crime of the century."

Less than six hours after the crime scene was cordoned off, six detectives from Area 2 Burglary, working in teams of two, were already on the trail of Richard Franklin Speck.

Police sketch artist Otis Rathel composed an amazing likeness of Speck from the descriptions provided by the heavily sedated Amurao. The FBI crime lab in Washington compared fingerprints taken from the Chicago townhouse with those in the Dallas police files and determined they were a match. The casual reference Speck made to Amurao about his New Orleans trip established his connections to the maritime union hall, leaving little doubt in the mind of the veteran Chicago detectives who they were after.

The tracking job was described by State's Attorney Daniel P. Ward as the "finest bit of police work" he had ever seen. Without the interference of outside agencies, the Sheriff's Police, the Coroner, and a host of other amateur investigators, the Chicago Police demonstrated remarkable aplomb and a level of competency few other big city departments could ever hope to emulate. Chief of Detectives Otto Kreuzer coordinated a methodical investigation free of error and the usual political acrimony that seems to surround so-called "heater cases."

The detectives traced Speck's movements to Room 306 of the Raleigh Hotel, a dismal flophouse located at 648 North Dearborn (at Erie Street) on the Near North Side where Speck had shared a room with a prostitute after a night of dancing and drinking at the Twist Lounge on Clark. (*Author's note:* Gentrification quickly overtook this former Near North nightclub district. In the late-1970s, the Raleigh Hotel became the Hotel Mentone, providing hookers and their Johns a place to crash until a fire gutted the interior of this vintage nineteenth-century walkup in 1983. After the fire, the Mentone was cleaned up. Neighborhood rents soared sky high, and by the late 1980s Speck's overnight hideout had become a stylish boutique and office complex . . . incredible as all this may now seem.)

The crime of the century attracted universal attention and demands for fast answers and swift action from the cops. Police Superintendent O. W. Wilson did

RICHARD SPECK SPENT THE NIGHT HERE AFTER MURDERING THE STUDENT NURSES. IN 1966 IT WAS A FLOP-HOUSE KNOWN AS THE RALEIGH HOTEL.

(Photo by Christina Carlson)

what he could to ease public concern by announcing that Speck had been positively identified, though he was not yet in custody.

Around midnight on the evening of July 16, 1966, Michael Gregrich, a resident of the Starr Hotel at 617 West Madison Street just west of the Chicago Loop, was rousted from his slumber by what he called a "hillbilly's moaning." Gregrich, who said he mistrusted hillbillies, discovered Richard Speck lying in a pool of his own blood in a six-foot by nine-foot cubicle.

The Starr Hotel was the last stop on the line, a temporary refuge for the mostly elderly Madison Street stew bums and winos stumbling past the all-night clerk in alcoholic stupors. A symbol of human misery and personal failure since before the Great Depression, the hotel was torn down in 1982. It was sacrificed for the luxurious Presidential Towers apartments. Nowadays, homeless shelters scattered across the city provide the same lack of amenities and perilous dangers as the Starr.

Plywood partitions separated the cubicles. The front door of each cubicle was a chicken wire net. For the going rate of ninety cents a night, a transient was provided a cot bed, a wall locker, a metal stool, and a fifteen-watt light bulb dangling from a frayed wire in the ceiling. The flickering neon marquee overlooking the street promised overnight guests a "Fireproof Room," but not much more. In the suffocating heat of July, the fetid odors emanating from the rat-infested fleabag were appalling. Anonymity and shelter from the storm was about all this rabbit warren of filth and despair provided. Once inside, a man had to survive by his wits and his willingness to employ a jagged shank, if threatened. What went on upstairs was of no concern to the clerk at the front door.

When asked by the police how Speck ended up in his dive, clerk Joseph Jokubauskas nonchalantly shrugged his shoulders. "It's hard for me to say how long he has been here. This is skid row. If you start asking questions, pretty soon you don't have any customers."

The man who checked into the fifth-floor space registered under the name "B. Brian." He had come there with the intention of killing himself. Speck shattered a wine bottle and used a shard of glass to open his left elbow and right wrist, but privacy was nonexistent and his timing bad. Taken to Cook County Hospital, the mass murderer was identified by Dr. LeRoy Smith, an emergency room surgeon who recognized the tattoo from reports he had heard over the TV and radio.

Speck was in police custody hours later. From Texas, relatives of the mass murderer bitterly denounced the Chicago

Police. "Everyone is telling lies," snapped Richard Speck of Dallas, a cousin of the accused. "That boy couldn't have done all the things they said he did. Sure, he got into a few scrapes, but who hasn't?"

This was more than just a "scrape," and it was up to William J. Martin, an earnest and hard-working young assistant state's attorney, to prove the essential facts of the case. Martin based much of his case on the testimony of Corazon Amurao, who had to be persuaded to linger in the states long enough to secure the conviction of the man who had killed her friends. The courtroom drama pitted Gerald Getty, a seasoned criminal defense lawyer who represented the "Babbling Burglar" Richard Morrison in 1961, against Martin, who headed the state's team of prosecutors.

In the face of such incontrovertible evidence, it took only forty-nine minutes for a jury in Peoria to convict Speck. He was sentenced to die in the electric chair, but once the death penalty was voided by the Illinois Supreme Court in 1971, the killer had to go before the courts again. This time he was sentenced to 400 to 1,200 years in the Stateville Penitentiary at Joliet. It was the longest prison term given an Illinois inmate up to that time.

During his long period of incarceration, Richard Speck never admitted his guilt. He painted still-life watercolors and involved himself in the invisible subculture of the prison until a sudden heart attack claimed his life on December 5, 1991.

Speck's secret world did not become a matter of public record until much later when television journalist Bill Kurtis went behind the walls of Stateville and came back with a secret videotape showing Speck and fellow inmates whooping it up in sex and drug orgies. Segments of the shocking spectacle, originally filmed on the sly in the mid-1980s, were aired on *American Justice,* a nationwide cable TV program seen on the Arts & Entertainment Network. Viewers were repulsed by the grotesque appearance of Speck, who had been ingesting female hormones. The murderer had happily consented to become the "female" drone of street-gang members during his confinement, and was made up to look the part.

The Illinois Department of Corrections (IDOC) was wrapped in denial from the moment the scandal broke, and responded angrily to the press sensationalism. "The tape was staged by a small group of inmates for maximum impact and revulsion," Brian Fairchild, spokesman for the IDOC told the author in a 1996 interview. "It was smuggled out of the prison and was shopped around for several years by gang members who hoped to use it to pay legal fees with no luck-until Bill Kurtis and his people purchased it for use during a television sweeps period."

To reach Pullman take the Dan Ryan Expressway (I-94) to the Calumet Expressway (I-94) and exit at 111th Street. Take 111th Street west to Champlain Avenue.

THE COMPANY TOWN EXPLODES
July 1894

George Mortimer Pullman's factory town is a living museum to the misshapen utopian vision of a nineteenth-century idealist who failed to grasp the entrepreneurial spirit of the human animal. Built between 1880 and 1885, the Village of Pullman was designed by architect Solon S. Beman, who also fashioned the 1919 South Prairie Avenue residence of young Marshall Field Jr. George Pullman offered his workers (his "children," as he called them) the opportunity to live in solid but modestly appointed common brick row houses flanking the Florence Hotel (the centerpiece of the planned community), a public park, and a church far removed from the slum dwellings of Chicago. The living environment was hardly ideal, but Pullman believed he had rescued his workers from the daily grind of unpleasant city living. "I have always held that people are very greatly influenced by their physical surrounding," he said. "Take the roughest man, a man whose lines have always brought him into the coarsest and poorest surroundings and bring him into a room elegantly carpeted and furnished and the effect upon his bearing is immediate." Pullman housing featured indoor plumbing and gas. There was much to be said about Pullman, not all of it a ringing endorsement of the founder's philanthropy. Tension between labor and capital boiled over in May 1894, after the company reduced wages following a downturn in business predicated by the national recession of 1893. By the end of August 1894, Pullman succeeded in breaking the strike. His temporary victory was an illusory one, because he lost both the affection of his daughters and the respect of his workmen and a large segment of the national press. In 1898, a year after the distraught and broken "palace car" magnate died, the Illinois Supreme Court ordered the company to sell off its housing stock, a task that was accomplished between 1907 and 1909. The town of Pullman was designated a state landmark in 1969, and a City of Chicago landmark three years later. The Historic Pullman Foundation has preserved the beautiful Queen Anne–style Florence Hotel, named for Pullman's favorite daughter, and much of the surrounding properties. The model town remained largely untouched by outside interlopers until early December 1998, when a homeless man named Anthony Buzinkas torched the historic railcar factory at 111th Street and St. Lawrence Avenue. The Foundation had planned to turn the building into a transportation museum. Now it is a glorious ruin, an eerie echo from the nineteenth century. Buzinkas told the police that he heard "voices" commanding him to set fire to the building. Perhaps he heard the deep despair of the Pullman workers, chanting their familiar nineteenth-century refrain through the mists of time, "We were born in a Pullman house, fed from a Pullman shop, catechized in the Pullman church, and when we die we shall be buried in the Pullman cemetery and go to Pullman hell!"

On the face of things, industrialist George Mortimer Pullman assembled a utopia for his workers along the Lake Michigan shoreline to uplift mankind and company profits. "That such advantages and surroundings made better workmen by removing them from the feeling of discontent and desire for change which so generally characterizes the American workman; thus protecting the employer from loss of time and money consequent upon intemperance, labor strikes and dissatisfaction which generally result from poverty and uncongenial home surroundings."

Pushed by the wealth of his Pullman Palace Car Company and inculcated with a paternalistic regard for his employees, the company founder journeyed to the Northern England town of Saltaire, where Sir Titus Salt rescued his workers from abject poverty and tenement living by building a company town devoid of crime, disease, and despair.

Utopianism was an old idea. There had been planned communities before, but nothing on so grand a scale as Pullman imagined when he purchased 3,800 acres of land on Lake Calumet, nine miles south of the (then) existing city limits of Chicago, for the sum of $800,000. George Pullman acquired the property in the mistaken belief that the Lake Calumet region would become the next great inland harbor and a magnet for commercial development.

The first shovel of dirt was turned on May 26, 1880. Work progressed rapidly on the long rows of worker's cottages lining Langley, Champlain, and St. Lawrence Avenues south of 111th Street. By 1881, 1,400 housing units were completed. Within three years, 45,000,000 fired clay bricks and 16,000,000 feet of lumber had been used in the building operations. The renowned Chicago architect Solomon S. Beman designed the buildings for the craftsmen, supervisory personnel, and laborers. Landscape architect Nathan F. Barrett supervised the layout of the park, the arcade, and the open spaces.

It was all very beautiful and picture perfect, but George Pullman refused to sell any of it, dashing the dreams of home ownership for the great mass of residents and workers.

The huge car shops mass-produced Pullman sleepers and club cars for every nation on earth with a rail system. The Pullman Company also supplied the workforce to staff the cars—sleeping car porters and dining car waiters. At peak efficiency, twelve thousand people dependent on the benevolence of Mr. George Pullman for their food, shelter, and clothing either lived in his town, were employed by his company, or deposited their money in his bank.

The first inkling of the troubles to come followed an ill-advised, across-the-board pay cut in 1885. Disgruntled workers who voiced protests against this capricious action were fired if the word "strike" even crossed their lips.

The Panic of 1893 hit the nation's railroads hard. The unexpected downturn in business forced George Pullman to close his Detroit plant in order to keep his South Side factories open. Wages were cut 25 percent and, in some cases, much more. However, Pullman refused to reduce the rents or cut food prices in his Market Place galleria. Penny wise, but pound foolish, George M. Pullman refused to negotiate with his "children." His arrogance in the face of starvation and want galvanized the Pullman workforce to militancy.

In the spring of 1894, a majority of the Pullman employees joined Eugene V. Debs's American Railway Union. The union approached George Pullman in the spirit of conciliation on May 9, 1894. Pullman told the delegation of tradesmen represented by the ARU that his company employed 4,300 men at a loss of $20,000 per month. He gently reminded them that sleeping cars were being constructed at a loss of $79 each simply to keep the factories busy.

Pullman paid his unskilled laborers $38.68 per month on average. Journeymen mechanics earned $59.33, and while not exceptional for the times, the wages were slightly ahead of the curve.

George Pullman often said he was not running a charity, but a real estate venture. Therefore, there would be no raise or concessions granted. Those who could not keep up with the $14 per month rent payments were allowed to leave. The company made little effort to collect back rent or evict tenants in arrears. In the face of such generosity, George Pullman could not comprehend the rising hostilities and dissension in the ranks.

On May 11, two thousand tradesmen and unskilled workmen laid down their tools. The direct cause of the job action was the laying off of three members

GEORGE MORTIMER PULLMAN, A CAUTIOUS MAN (LEFT). BELOW, PULLMAN STRIKERS CLASH WITH FEDERAL TROOPS AT FORTY-NINTH STREET AND LOOMIS AVENUE, 1894.

of the arbitration committee, who had received assurances from company executives that they would not be harassed or intimidated.

Pullman's steadfast refusal to accept binding arbitration or negotiate with the ARU sparked nationwide sympathy strikes that spread across twenty-seven states and random acts of mob violence that sparked a Federal injunction and brought forth U.S. troops, dispatched to Chicago by President Grover Cleveland over the vociferous objections voiced by Governor John Peter Altgeld.

Labor historians blamed the mob action occurring the week of July 6, 1894, on hooligans and vandals, not union saboteurs. Almont Lindsey, author of a scholarly study of the prolonged strike and its accompanying mob violence, concluded that "an abnormally large group of hoodlums, tramps, and semi-criminals, some of whom had been attracted to Chicago by the Columbian Exposition [were left] stranded [in Chicago] by the Depression."

The Panic of 1893, the nation's most serious economic downturn before the Stock Market crash of 1929, left thousands homeless, instilling in these rootless men a mean-spirited restlessness and deepening anger toward the symbols of prosperity.

Published accounts suggest that Pullman workers were as culpable for the wanton destruction to property that occurred over a wide expanse of the South Side as the roving gangs of vandals were. Strikers impeded the courageous efforts of firefighters to extinguish arson fires in the rail yards of Burnside, costing the Pullman Company $30,000 in rolling stock. "As the afternoon fire increased in volume, the inhabitants of Pullman and Kensington went out on the prairies and jeered at the fireman," it was reported by the *Chicago Inter-Ocean*. "Before dark there was a crowd of ten thousand people about in the fields."

Pullman residents nervously reported a stockpiling of weapons. Troops were deployed to the car barns at 111th Street in anticipation of sabotage. Meanwhile, the worst of the rioting occurred six miles north of Pullman at 50th Street near the Dan Ryan Expressway (Interstate 94) on July 6. Over 750 standing boxcars were looted for food and provisions.

The violence and mayhem spread west into the Stockyards District, where Captain Francis O'Neill of the Nineteenth Precinct contained them as best he could. (*Author's note:* O'Neill was one of Chicago's most famous and forthright police officers. A collector of Irish folk tunes, O'Neill capably served as superintendent of the Chicago Police Department from 1901 to 1905.)

At Forty-seventh Street, four thousand rioters overturned freight cars, set the rolling stock on fire, and "were dancing in the streets, running across the tracks and shouting in a frenzy of half-maddened joy," reported one newspaper. The crowd was beyond control, and the police sensed it. Wisely they backed off. "You policemen are all right," shouted one striker. "Only keep out of our way. We have not yet begun."

The next night (July 7), a company of militia was attacked by a frenzied mob at Forty-ninth and Loomis Avenue near the Grand Trunk rail line. The rioters pelted a train crew and the soldiers with rocks and stones. When efforts to disperse the crowd failed, the militia fired at will, killing four persons and wounding twenty others. Chicago was in a state of siege. With the trains halted at the city limits, the paralysis created widespread food shortages.

And while all this was going on, the Chicago Police exhibited a remarkably passive restraint even after a suspected arson fire laid waste to the Administration Building and four other remainders of World's Fair architecture in Jackson Park. It began as a small blaze witnessed by several boys who vainly tried to stamp out the flames, but a fierce wind swept the fast-moving flames into the fairgrounds.

Because so many of the Pullman workers were second-generation Irish, German, or Anglo tradesmen and not the dreaded foreign-born "anarchists" so despised during the Haymarket troubles, the Chicago Police holstered their batons and side arms. Police Chief Michael Brennan admitted as much, and the *Chicago Tribune* criticized him for it. "Time and again men who have paid taxes for police protection have asked for it only to be told that none could be given them. The Chief should have left out this confession of sympathy."

The nation's commerce was momentarily paralyzed by a strike of local origins. Meanwhile, the president and company founder hunkered down inside his Prairie Avenue mansion, refusing to negotiate, compromise, or believe this could be happening to *him*.

Following a series of violent episodes that threatened to engulf the entire South Side, Eugene Debs and other ARU officials were arrested, indicted, and held on $10,000 bail. Less than two weeks later, on August 2, 1894, the strike collapsed, Debs was jailed, and the union was broken. George Pullman identified the ringleaders and fired all one thousand of them. The entire work force was compelled to sign loyalty oaths, and the pace of life returned to its normal rhythms in Pullman.

There would be no peace for George Pullman after the seven-week ordeal. Alienated from all his natural children except one, he died of apoplexy on October 19, 1897, and went to his grave believing his "children" had committed the gravest of all sins—the unpardonable sin of ingratitude. His grave at Graceland Cemetery was fortified with railroad ties and reinforced concrete to prevent grave robbers, radicals, anarchists, and crackpots from violating the crypt.

George Mortimer Pullman was a cautious man.

By the 1910s, the model town was sold off; the American worker's utopia—

this paradise on earth—had become just another Chicago neighborhood. The Pullman factory was forced to close its doors in 1982, but the Florence Hotel is still open and the Sunday brunch is marvelous.

Market Hall, 112th Street and Champlain Avenue

SIDETRIP

Conceived as the retail district of Pullman, the Romanesque colonnaded buildings of Market Hall were completed by Solon Beman in 1892 (following a fire that destroyed the original structure). The circular structure, with its soaring archways and twelve retail stores, is boarded up and empty today. But in the heyday of Pullman, storefronts rented for $40 a month. The Ness Bakery, one of the thriving commercial establishments in Market Hall, sold bread and sweets to the residents of Pullman. The bakery was owned and operated by the parents of the indestructible G-man Eliot Ness. Years later, several episodes of the television anthology series glorifying Ness's exploits, The Untouchables, *were filmed at Market Hall.*

"I HOPE WHEN MY TIME COMES, THAT I DIE DECENTLY IN BED. I
DON'T WANT TO BE MURDERED BESIDE THE GARBAGE CANS IN SOME
CHICAGO ALLEY."

George "Bugs" Moran

"I DON'T WANT TO END UP IN THE GUTTER PUNCTURED BY MACHINE-
GUN SLUGS."

Al Capone

PARTING SHOTS

ADDITIONAL READING

Adelman, William. *Touring Pullman.* Chicago: The Illinois Labor Society, 1972.

This handy reference guide, published in pamphlet form by the ILS, is one of a series of tour booklets focusing on places and events that are significant to Chicago's labor heritage. The author's biases preclude objectivity and historical balance with regard to the enigmatic George M. Pullman, whose acts of personal philanthropy (however perceived) through the course of a lifetime are never mentioned in this one-dimensional canonization of the strikers, some of whom committed senseless, malicious acts of vandalism during the 1894 sit-down at the company town.

———. *Haymarket Revisited.* Chicago: The Illinois Labor Society, 1976.

A thorough, at times engrossing, retelling of the Haymarket Affair, which provides a running commentary and a roadmap to the incidents and locales (what little is left to look at) associated with this highly charged episode from labor history.

Allsop, Kenneth. *The Bootleggers: The Story of Prohibition.* New Rochelle: Arlington House, 1961.

An anecdotal history of the "noble experiment" and the rise of modern organized crime.

Andreas, A. T. *History of Chicago from the Earliest Period to the Present Times.* 3 volumes. Chicago: A. T. Andreas, 1884–1886.

A number of civic "booster" histories were published in the latter years of the nineteenth century and well into the twentieth. Some were little more than vanity editions sold by private subscription to the families of the wealthy profiled within the pages of the book. Andreas's handsomely bound editions celebrate the achievements of the titans of industry, commerce, politics, the arts, and civic life. What they lack in historical synthesis and objective reporting is more than compensated for by the presentation of little-known facts and the eyewitness accounts of historic events.

Asbury, Herbert. *Gem of the Prairie: An Informal History of the Chicago Underworld.* New York: Alfred Knopf, 1940.

Herbert Asbury's pioneering survey of Chicago crime conditions, from the city's earliest days through Al Capone's conviction on tax evasion charges in 1931, is studded with colorful figures and lively, but often unverifiable, anecdotes. The book is number four in a series of sixteen Asbury volumes exploring the American urban underworld. It has been reprinted in trade paperback by Northern Illinois University Press.

Baumann, Edward. *May God Have Mercy on Your Soul: The Last Moments of 171 Convicted Killers Who Paid the Ultimate Price.* Chicago: Bonus Books, 1993.

Not every execution is covered. Pre–Chicago Fire court records are lost to history, and only a methodical day-by-day search of the newspapers would shed light on the names of criminals who paid the ultimate price for their treachery prior to 1871. Nevertheless, Baumann has written a useful and engaging reference volume that fills an important gap in local crime history.

Baumann, Edward and John O'Brien. *Chicago Heist.* South Bend, IN: And Books, 1981.

Two veteran Chicago reporters covering the city beat for their respective newspapers turned to writing books in the 1980s, reviving the tradition of big-city crime writing excellence by the legendary newshounds of the fourth estate—Jack McPhaul, Ray Brennan, Lloyd Wendt, Herman Kogan, Jack Lait, and Lucy Freeman. *Chicago Heist* is a detailed look at the Purolator robbery. It is spiced with lively stories and odd characters, and as their later collaborations attest, Baumann and O'Brien are a fun read.

————. *Getting Away with Murder: 57 Unsolved Murders with Reward Information.* Chicago: Bonus Books, 1991.

Interesting glimpses into the famous and nearly forgotten cases of the last half-century by the prolific *Tribune* newsies. It is oddly curious that the publisher offers a paltry $11,000 for the identity of the Grimes girls' killers (which the authors call Chicago's "most baffling crime"), but a $250,000 reward for information that would bring closure to the mysterious disappearance of candy heiress Helen Brach. How does one in good conscience affix a dollar value to such infamous deeds?

Bergreen, Laurence. *Capone: The Man and the Era.* New York: Simon & Schuster, 1994.

An engaging, finely crafted biography, despite several glaring errors of fact traceable to the author's unfamiliarity with the geography of Chicago. Bergreen, a resident of New York, fills in the missing gaps of Al Capone's private life and post-Chicago years that other historians have simply ignored in earlier biographies. Had they dug deeper into the historical record they might have discovered that Capone's brother Vincenzo changed his name to Richard Hart and moved to Homer, Nebraska, where he began a long and distinguished career as a lawman known to the local moonshiners and western desperados as "Two-Gun" Hart. The law-abiding Capone was careful not to reveal his true identity to President Calvin Coolidge, whom he guarded during Coolidge's summer vacation in the Black Hills of South Dakota in 1927.

Better Government Association (J. Terrence Brunner, Executive Director). *"Patent Malarkey": Public Dishonesty and Deception, the Brown's Chicken Massacre.* Chicago: Better Government Association, 1997.

The BGA absorbed a lot of political heat for their courageous stance in exposing the deficiencies of suburban law enforcement following the Palatine murders. The BGA was subjected to a barrage of scorching criticism, most of it personally directed toward Brunner from suburban politicos, police chiefs with reputations to protect, and rank-and-file law enforcement personnel who circled the wagons behind Palatine Police Chief Jerry Bratcher, none of which is surprising to veteran observers. Brunner was condemned as a publicity hound or worse; but the plain truth of the matter is there are few individuals in the public arena today who possess the courage of their convictions to speak as plainly or as openly as this public watchdog and bellringer.

Biles, Roger. *Big City Boss in War & Depression: Mayor Edward J. Kelly of Chicago.* DeKalb: Northern Illinois University Press, 1984.

A worthy political biography coming from a small press. Mayor Kelly was a fascinating figure who served Chicago for fourteen up-and-down years. It was never clear how much of a "Boss" Kelly really was, if at all. The record suggests that it was the machine that made the man, and not the other way around.

Bluestone, Daniel. *Constructing Chicago.* New Haven, CT: Yale University Press, 1991.

A wonderful collection of photographs, many of them rare and unusual, supports a balanced interpretation of architecture, urbanism, and Chicago's development at the midpoint of the nineteenth century. The volume had its origins as a Ph.D. dissertation.

Boettiger, John. *Jake Lingle: Or Chicago on the Spot.* New York: E. P. Dutton, 1931.

This contemporary account of the murder of *Chicago Tribune* reporter Jake Lingle in June 1930 is largely drawn from newspaper clips, but it kept the spotlight of public attention focused squarely on Al Capone at a time when the government was fast closing in on the dispirited gangster.

Cowan, David and John Kuenster. *To Sleep with the Angels: The Story of a Fire.* Chicago: Ivan R. Dee, 1996.

Two authors with divergent backgrounds collaborate on a moving account of the 1958 Our Lady of Angels Fire.

Cromie, Robert. *The Great Chicago Fire.* Nashville, TN: Rutledge Hill Press, 1994.

Originally published by McGraw-Hill in 1958, this illustrated edition by Cromie is acknowledged to be the authoritative work on the Great Fire. A new generation of readers will enjoy the collection of lithographs, photographic images, and maps.

Curley, J. Seymour. *The Story of Old Fort Dearborn.* Chicago: A. C. McClurg, 1912.

As the title suggests, this out-of-print curiosity offers a moving narrative of the evacuation of Fort Dearborn and the subsequent battle along the shores of Lake Michigan. The author does not reveal his sources or the bases for his conclusions.

Davis, Ronald L. *Hollywood Beauty: Linda Darnell and the American Dream.* Norman, OK: University of Oklahoma Press, 1991.

The author is a professor of history at Southern Methodist University. Both Davis and Darnell grew up in the Oak Cliff section of Dallas, which partly explains his fascination with the beautiful Hollywood actress, whose life he describes as an "American tragedy." How many times have we heard that overused phrase bandied about? *Hollywood Beauty* is a workmanlike biography; a straightforward, book-end narrative that lacks the synthesis and interpretation one would normally expect from a university press. If Darnell represented the "American Dream," as opposed to Elizabeth Taylor for example, Davis needs to explain his rationale to his readers, which he does not.

Dedmon, Emmett. *Fabulous Chicago: A Great City's History and Its People.* New York: Athenaeum, 1981.

Originally published in 1953, Dedmon's book paints an idyllic portrait of Chicago on a broad historical canvas. The gamblers, criminals, politicians, and rogues of every stripe escape censure in this sentimental, often amusing account of the Windy City in its formative days.

Demaris, Ovid. *Captive City: Chicago in Chains.* New York: Lyle Stuart, 1969.

Demaris's tell-all account about the criminal-political alliance in Chicago reveals the mob's infiltration of labor unions, legitimate businesses, and the Illinois State House in the years following Prohibition. The book resulted in a tide of lawsuits filed against the author by the libeled gangsters whose Chicago Crime Commission "rap sheets" appear in the appendix of the book. It is still one of the best "documentary" accounts of the Chicago underworld to appear in print.

Dobyns, Fletcher. *The Underworld of American Politics.* New York: Fletcher Dobyns, 1932.

A bruising political indictment and cautionary tale told to Chicago voters by a Republican partisan, who decried the corruption of the bellicose William Hale Thompson but reserved his harshest judgment for the incoming mayor, Anton J. Cermak. Concerning the new administration, which he describes as "Chicago's Tammany Hall," the author writes: "Cermak is therefore, not only one of the most powerful, but one of the most sinister and portentous figures in the political life of America." A year after this self-published tome startled Chicago voters, Cermak fell victim to an assassin's bullet. This is an interesting, and at times portentous political diatribe that is almost impossible to find.

Farr, Finis. *Chicago: A Personal History of America's Most American City.* New Rochelle, NY: Arlington House, 1973.

Written twenty years after Emmet Dedmon's *Fabulous Chicago* first appeared in bookstores, this author's work greatly expands on a tested concept—the grand sweep of city history, bouncing from one era to the next, mixing subjects and metaphors of urban life at will. The difference is, Farr does it so much better than Dedmon.

Ewing, Steve and John B. Lundstrom. *Fateful Rendezvous: The Life of Butch O'Hare.* Annapolis, MD: Naval Institute Press, 1997.

Military historians naturally choose to dwell on bombs, battle tactics, and equipment, but the Ewing-Lundstrom volume explores the young aviator's close family ties, casting his father, Edward O'Hare, in a more favorable light than history records.

Fraley, Oscar and Eliot Ness. *The Untouchables.* New York: Julian Messner, 1957.

Eliot Ness was an obscure, footnote figure of the Prohibition era when the authors resurrected a few good memories of Chicago in the final stages of Prohibition. The book, TV series, and film that followed recast Ness in the role of the crusading, incorruptible G-man.

Fremon, David K. *Chicago Politics Ward by Ward.* Bloomington, IN: Indiana University Press, 1988.

Thumbnail sketches of the political and ethnic demographics of Chicago's fifty wards. The book is strewn with colorful and interesting anecdotes and is the only "guidebook" to city politics that a tourist might actually enjoy.

Giancana, Antoinette and Thomas Renner. *Mafia Princess: Growing Up in Sam Giancana's Family*. New York: Avon, 1984.

Giancana's lively yarn catapulted her to local fame and stardom. Hollywood was intrigued by what she had to say about the "Beauty and the Beast" romance between Phyllis McGuire and the gangster. The mystique of Sam Giancana and the Kennedys kept on growing and growing until it sparked a media feeding frenzy. Sam was never so glamorous in life as he appeared in death.

Girardin, G. Russell and William Helmer. *Dillinger: The Untold Story*. Bloomington, IN: Indiana University Press, 1994.

Russ Girardin was a Chicago ad man who had social ties to Louis Piquett, John Dillinger's attorney. Chicago author Bill Helmer resurrected an original manuscript written by Girardin about the famous stickup man a year after the Biograph shooting in 1934. A half-century later, Helmer published the book with Girardin's blessing. The preponderance of evidence submitted by Helmer debunks the far-fetched theories and unsubstantiated rumors that a John Dillinger double was killed in his place that night.

Gottfried, Alex. *Boss Cermak of Chicago: A Study of Political Leadership*. Seattle: University of Washington Press, 1962.

Vilified by Prohibitionists and Republican "wets" alike, Anton Cermak slowly, and with great precision, built a formidable political organization based in "Cesca Pilsen" along Twenty-sixth Street while the cartoonlike Mayor Thompson ran his party into the ground. Never again, after Cermak's election in 1931 by the largest majority ever given a mayoral candidate up to that time, would a Republican come close to recapturing City Hall. Cermak was the architect of the Democratic machine of legend.

Green, Paul M. and Melvin G. Holli, eds. *The Mayors: The Chicago Political Tradition*. Carbondale, IL: Southern Illinois University Press, 1987.

Not every mayor of Chicago is covered. The book begins with a discussion of Joseph Medill, the city's post-fire mayor, and concludes with a scholarly "ranking" of the most capable and efficient chief executives based on an opinion survey circulated among journalists (who are not historians) and academics. Because there are no contemporary interpretations of Chicago's nineteenth-century political traditions available on the bookshelves, the omission of Levi Boone, "Long" John Wentworth, Monroe Heath, Harvey D. Colvin, and Carter Harrison I, all of whom presided over a raw, wide-open town, in this otherwise encompassing volume is both puzzling and disappointing.

Halper, Albert, ed. *The Chicago Crime Book*. Cleveland: World Publishing, 1967.

Herbert Asbury, Sandy Smith, and LeRoy McHugh are among the journalistic icons who contributed twenty-four true stories about Chicago contract men, kidnappers, stool pigeons, gunmen, and killers, covering seventy years of criminal mayhem in the Windy City from the Gaslight Era through the 1960s. Lively, entertaining tabloid fun, including reprints of material from *Chicago Murders*, a 1945 anthology of Windy City crime originally published by Duell, Sloan & Pierce.

Harrison, Carter II. *The Stormy Years: The Autobiography of Carter Harrison.* New York: Bobbs-Merrill, 1935.

With a wink and a nod to "Hinky Dink" Kenna and "Bathhouse" John Coughlin, his larcenous allies in the City Council for nearly two decades, "Our Carter," as he was affectionately dubbed by his coat carriers and ward heelers, defends his policies of vice segregation; the hiring of Joseph Kipley, one of the most corrupt and venal police chiefs to ever serve Chicago; and the frequent interparty skirmishes that fractionalized the Democrats into two opposing camps for years to come.

Helmer, William. *The Gun That Made the Twenties Roar.* London: Macmillan, 1969.

A concise history of the Thompson submachine gun, a weapon of destruction invented by Brigadier General John Taliaferro Thompson in 1916 to "sweep" enemy trenches during World War I. It was introduced to the streets of Chicago in January 1925 by the Bugs Moran mob against Al Capone's men.

———. Public *Enemies: America's Criminal Past, 1919–1940.* New York: Facts on File, 1998.

Helmer's latest serves up a sumptuous banquet of American crime with rare and unusual photography; colorful, occasionally amusing cartoons and graphics that provide readers with concise historic analysis; and probing insights that go well beyond the standard recitation of facts.

Helmer, William and Mark Levell. *The Quotable Al Capone.* Chicago: Mad Dog Press, 1990.

There is plenty to savor in this monograph recalling the wit and wisdom of Al Capone. "Nobody was ever killed except outlaws and the community is better off without them," observed Big Al. And the following gem: "Don't get the idea that I'm one of those goddamn radicals. Don't get the idea I'm knocking the American system."

Higdon, Hal. *The Crime of the Century: The Loeb-Leopold Case.* New York: G. P. Putnam's Sons, 1975.

The author waited until all of the principal players were dead before penning the definitive account of the Bobby Franks murder. Higdon's book penetrates the layers of misunderstanding and half-truths about this case, but more important, the author refuses to succumb to Clarence Darrow's sentimental malarkey that turned a serious criminal trial focusing on two dry-eyed society killers into a Bughouse Square capital-punishment debate.

Hoffman, Dennis. *Scarface Al and the Crime Crusaders.* Carbondale, IL: Southern Illinois University Press, 1993.

In 1989, Dennis Hoffman, an associate professor of criminal justice at the University of Nebraska, prepared a historical monograph for the Chicago Crime Commission, recounting the watchdog agency's role in "getting" Al Capone, particularly the involvement of the Secret Six investigative group, formed in 1930 by Colonel Robert Isham Randolph, the president of the Association of Commerce and Operations Director for the 1933 World's Fair. The Secret Six, whose political loyalty was with State's Attorney John A. Swanson and a powerful faction of the Republican Party led by former Governor Charles Deneen, was disbanded in 1932 amid charges of vigilantism and collusion with the gangsters themselves. Hoffman's book casts the Secret Six in a more sympathetic light and discusses the other private initiatives—beyond Eliot Ness's celebrated brewery raids—to close down the Capone gang.

Holli, Melvin, and Peter Jones. *Ethnic Chicago.* Grand Rapids, MI: William B. Erdmans, 1975.

A long-awaited second edition, with new chapters on emerging ethnic groups, was published in the last few years. Professor Holli's volume offers a scholarly, but sometimes plodding, academic focus on immigrant settlement and neighborhood dispersal.

Hunt, Henry M. *The Crime of the Century: The Assassination of Dr. Patrick Cronin.* Chicago: H. L. Kochersperger Publishers, 1889.

Better than average "rush-to-print" reportage meticulously pieces together the essential facts of the Cronin case months after the abduction/murder. It would take five more years of legal maneuvering before there would be a final resolution to this multilayered murder mystery that drove yet another wedge in the bitterly divided Irish-American community in Chicago. A contemporary retelling of the Cronin case is long overdue.

Johnson, Curt with R. Craig Sautter. *Wicked City Chicago: From Kenna to Capone.* Highland Park, IL: December Press, 1994.

The title of the book misleads the reader. Al Capone and Hinky Dink Kenna share the footlights with Charles Tyson Yerkes, Louis Sullivan, the Black Sox, Theodore Dreiser, Mrs. Bertha Honore Palmer, "Cash and Carry" Pyle, and other luminaries from the worlds of sport, high finance, society, literature, music, and gangland in this swift-moving survey of Chicago decadence. Johnson and Sautter borrow a concept originally conceived by Herbert Asbury, and copied with less success by Stephen Longstreet, Norman Mark, and others.

Kennedy, Dolores. *William Heirens: His Day in Court.* Chicago: Bonus Books, 1991.

Kennedy has waged a long and unsuccessful battle to convince the courts to retry William Heirens for the 1946 murder of Suzanne Degnan. She presents compelling evidence that defense attorneys conspired to deny Heirens his civil rights, and allegedly coerced him to confess to a crime he never committed. The preponderance of evidence suggests that the Chicago Police engaged in high-handed and often brutal tactics in order to close sensitive murder cases tried in the court of public opinion. Doubts will always exist about this case. I am not entirely convinced of Heirens's innocence based on the author's impassioned plea for justice, but I am sure that most reasonable people would agree that the courts should be willing to reexamine whatever long-suppressed evidence Kennedy and her attorneys can produce to shed new light on the investigation.

Kenney, William Howland. *Chicago Jazz: A Cultural History 1904–1930.* New York: Oxford University Press, 1993.

A wide-ranging study of race, culture, politics, and the musical art form born in the deep South, but nurtured in the smoky Levee dance halls and bagnios of the pre–World War I era. The author moves the story forward through the 1920s with a discussion of the "Black & Tan" cabarets strung along south State Street in Chicago's "Bronzeville." Comprehensive, engrossing, and highly recommended.

Kinzie, Mrs. John. *Wau-Bun: Early Days in the Northwest.* Chicago: Lakeside Press, 1932.

Contemporary narrative of Fort Dearborn and the settlement of Chicago by the widow of the famous Indian trader, who may or may not have committed murder outside the gates of the stockade.

Kobler, John. *The Life and World of Al Capone.* New York: G. P. Putnam's Sons, 1971.

The first published biography of the famous gangster to appear in print since Fred Pasley's 1930 account is an ambitious, well-researched tome, but it has been eclipsed by two recent and more comprehensive volumes authored by Robert Schoenberg and Larry Bergreen. Rereleased in paper by DaCapo Press.

Kogan, Herman and Lloyd Wendt. *Lords of the Levee: The Story of Bathhouse John and Hinky Dink.* New York: Garden City, 1944.

Kogan and Wendt capture the spirit of wide-open, wicked Chicago through the eyes of the hopelessly corrupt, but oddly impressive, aldermen representing the notorious First Ward. The darker side of the Levee—the drug addiction, Maurice Van Bever's St. Louis-to-Chicago white slavery ring, and the broken lives of the downtrodden women whose livelihood was linked to the purveyors of human misery—is deliberately ignored.

————. *Big Bill of Chicago.* New York: Bobbs Merrill, 1953.

Befitting the man, Kogan and Wendt's case study of "Big Bill" is the same larger than life, rollicking political biography that they themselves invented in an earlier volume, *Lords of the Levee.* At times the authors appear to be in awe of their subject, and they often find themselves caught up in Bill Thompson's bluster. The bulk of the research is undoubtedly drawn from the examination of old newspaper copy, but the anecdotal volume is the only real biographical treatment of Thompson for the general reader. It captures the essence of a vibrant time and a political blowhard who was born to raise hell and destined to rule Chicago along with Al Capone.

Lait, Jack and Lee Mortimer. *Chicago Confidential!: The Lowdown on the Big Town.* New York: Crown Publishers, 1950.

John Drummond of WBBM-TV said that he was inspired to become a big-city crime reporter after reading Lait and Mortimer's breezy, "tell-all" account of the gangsters, "B-girls," clip joints, dope dens, and evil doings inside Chicago's notorious after-hours sin spots. The book is a great time capsule of the city in the waning years of Chicago's fabulous downtown night life. The story goes that Lee Mortimer was assaulted by a local gangster after the book was published. Such was the fate of this scandal sheet writer who was punched in the mouth for a similar offense by Frank Sinatra a few years later.

Landesco, John. *Organized Crime: Part Three of the Illinois Crime Survey.* Champaign, IL: University of Illinois Press, 1929.

Chicago's intolerable crime conditions after World War I spurred civic action on two fronts. The Chicago Crime Commission was founded in 1919 as a civilian adjunct to law enforcement. But as the violence deepened in the mid-1920s, business colleagues from the Chicago Association of Commerce, the Crime Commission, and the University of Chicago—working in conjunction with the Illinois State Bar Association—established the Illinois Association for Criminal Justice to examine the root causes and patterns of "organized" lawlessness. The result was this scholarly examination of Chicago's crime problem by John Landesco, a member of the University of Chicago Sociology Department. His book remains a valuable document for researchers and historians attempting to make sense of Chicago in the ragged 1920s.

Leopold, Nathan, Jr. *Life Plus 99 Years.* New York: Doubleday, 1958.

Leopold's memoir of the Bobby Franks "thrill" murder coincided with his parole from the Stateville Penitentiary. The ice-cold intellectual displays little remorse for his crime. His debt to society paid, Leopold retreated into the world of scientific research in Puerto Rico.

Levy, George. *To Die in Chicago: Confederate Prisoners at Camp Douglas, 1862–1865.* Evanston, IL: Evanston Publishing Company, 1994.

The first book-length treatment of Chicago's infamous prisoner-of-war camp—otherwise known as "Andersonville North," for the squalid and contemptible conditions Southern prisoners of war were forced to live in. The book profiles an overlooked episode from Chicago's past given only cursory attention by those responsible for the glut of books dealing with the wonders of architecture, the great "inescapable art," Daniel Burnham, the 1893 World's Fair, and the Great Fire.

Lindberg, Richard. *To Serve and Collect: Chicago Politics and Police Corruption From the Lager Beer Riot to the Summerdale Scandal 1855–1960.* Westport, CT: Praeger Publishing, 1991.

The first published history of the Chicago Police Department since John Flinn and John Wilkie's 1887 volume, which was conceived as a police fundraising vehicle and public morale builder in the wake of the Haymarket Riot. *To Serve and Collect* surveys the major police scandals and defines the corruptive arrangements between the gamblers, Levee vice merchants, and the cops. It is a study of the police cadre, ethnic identity and fraternalism within the department, its response to scandal, and the various attempts at reform, with a hundred pages devoted to the Prohibition era.

———. *Passport's Guide to Ethnic Chicago.* 2nd ed. Chicago: NTC Publishing, 1997.

A travel guidebook designed with the Chicago resident in mind, which explores city neighborhoods and reviews the ethnic history of their settlement. A listing of festivals, restaurants, parades, and ethnic attractions accompany the text.

———. *Chicago by Gaslight: A History of the Chicago Netherworld 1880–1920.* Chicago: Academy Chicago, 1996.

Originally published in hardcover in 1985 as *Chicago Ragtime: Another Look at Chicago 1880–1920,* the recently released paperback volume zeros in with an unvarnished account of the Levee, wrapped around a mosaic of Windy City social history between the Civil War and the war to end all wars.

Lyle, John H. *The Dry and Lawless Years.* Englewood Cliffs, NJ: Prentice Hall, 1960.

An implacable foe of Chicago's Prohibition gangsters, Municipal Court Judge John Lyle was once asked to preside over a secret peace convocation between the warring Capone and Moran syndicates in 1926. Before declining the offer, Lyle jokingly asked: "What's my cut?" Lyle was a close friend of *Tribune* publisher Colonel Robert McCormick, and Lyle's entertaining and crisply written memoir probably exaggerates the historical record, but is nevertheless an enjoyable, eyewitness account of a wild era. Out of print.

McCaffrey, Lawrence J., Ellen Skerrett, Michael F. Funchion, and Charles Fanning. *The Irish in Chicago.* Urbana, IL: University of Illinois Press, 1987.

Another volume in the series of ethnic histories edited by Professor Mel Holli of the University of Illinois profiles the role of priests, politicians, and the literati in the shaping of Chicago's Irish-American identity. The unifying thread, the authors argue, was the pride in the homeland and interest in the cause of Irish nationalism. In the police world, the struggle to free Ireland from British rule was an issue that divided the department down the middle and contributed to long-standing ethnic hostilities between the Irish and the Germans that compromised morale and the quality of street law enforcement in late nineteenth and early twentieth century Chicago.

McPhaul, Jack. *Johnny Torrio: First of the Ganglords.* New Rochelle, NY: Arlington House, 1970.

The only published biography of this important Chicago gangland figure was authored by a famous newspaper reporter of the day employed by the *Chicago Times.*

Mayer, Harold M. and Richard C. Wade. *Chicago: Growth of a Metropolis.* Chicago: University of Chicago Press, 1969.

The photographic images are marvelous, and the discussion of Chicago's emergence from a frontier outpost to a sprawling city ringed by miles of suburbs makes this a classic of the genre—and the inspiration for dozens of pricey cocktail-table picture books celebrating the city's architecture.

Mezzrow, Mezz and Bernard Wolfe. *Really the Blues.* Garden City, NY: Doubleday, 1972.

Clarinetist and sax man Mezz Mezzrow spent most of his formative years in New York and abroad. He left Chicago in 1928. His cynically jaded autobiography provides the reader with a rare glimpse into the Jazz Age as seen through the eyes of one of its most talented but radical impresarios. Mezzrow tips the hat to the denizens of Chicago gangland who loved the new music as much as the boys in the band. Originally published in 1946.

Miller, Russell. *Bunny: The Real Story of Playboy.* New York: Holt-Rinehart, 1984.

Many books have been written about the bedroom high jinks of one Hugh Marston Hefner. And then there are the better written volumes about the boardroom misfortunes of the Playboy Corporation. We can only guess what goes on inside the Hefner boudoir in Holmby Hills, California, these days. Miller's volume presents a broad picture of the Playboy empire and its various misfortunes in the 1970s and 1980s, not the least of which was the Bobbie Arnstein tragedy.

Nelli, Humbert. *Italians in Chicago, 1880–1930: A Study in Ethnic Mobility.* New York: Oxford University Press, 1970.

Still the best ethnic history of the Italian settlement in Chicago. With a historian's discerning eye, Nelli examines the role of the Black Hand and the rise of gangsterism in the 1920s.

Pacyga, Dominic A. and Ellen Skerrett. *Chicago: A City of Neighborhoods.* Chicago: Loyola University Press, 1986.

A self-guided tour of the neighborhoods of Chicago that Wade and Mayer managed to capture from afar in their earlier volume. The neighborhood strolls emphasize aspects of sacred space, the history of Catholic parishes, and the role of religion in the lives of the ethnic people who settled in Chicago. That religion played an integral role in neighborhood development is an important theme that emerges in this valuable reference volume that is so much more than just a travel guide. Chicago is the sum total of all its parts. It is indeed a tapestry of interesting and unique neighborhoods, each with an important story to tell.

Pasley, Fred D. *Al Capone: The Biography of a Self-Made Man.* New York: Ives Washburn Publishing, 1930.

Published a year before Al Capone was convicted of income tax evasion, Pasley's book was titillating reading for the American public, who by this time thirsted for information on its Public Enemies. "Poor little rich boy," Pasley concludes—not knowing the difficulties lying immediately over the horizon for Al Capone. "The Horatio Alger of Prohibition; the gamin from the sidewalks of New York who made good in a big shot way in Chicago. General Al the Scarface!"

Peterson, Virgil W. *Barbarians in Our Midst.* Boston: Little Brown & Co., 1952.

Virgil Peterson served as Executive Director of the Chicago Crime Commission from 1942 until 1969. Mr. Peterson never feared crooked politicians or hesitated to point the finger of blame at lawmakers in connivance with gangsters in his yearly reports to the membership on Chicago crime. This book, a post–World War II wrap-up of Chicago organized crime, is out of print.

———. *A Report on Chicago Crime.* Chicago: The Chicago Crime Commission, various years, 1953–1968.

Peterson's staff of interns clipped news items about city crime and the mob from the daily papers. Mr. Peterson, the driving force behind the Chicago Crime Commission for nearly three decades, interpreted the raw data, prepared his yearly reports, and named names with a no-holds-barred candor that is sorely missing in this era of milquetoast political correctness.

Reckless, Walter Cade. *Vice in Chicago.* Chicago: University of Chicago Press, 1933.

An excellent, scholarly study by a colleague of Frederick Thrasher at the University of Chicago. Reckless ponders the migratory patterns of vice merchants and segregated vice districts fanning outward from the central city. Long out of print, the book was originally a Ph.D. dissertation.

Rights in Conflict: The Official Report to the National Commission on the Causes and Prevention of Violence. New York: American Library, 1968.

Otherwise known as the "Walker Report," the document stirred controversy and an angry denunciation from the mayor of Chicago, when its author, the eternally ambitious Daniel Walker, accused the police of fomenting a convention-week riot.

Roemer, William F. *Man Against the Mob: The Inside Story of How the FBI Cracked the Chicago Mob by the Agent Who Led the Attack.* New York: Donald L. Fine, 1989.

Good-guy Roemer authored a series of books recounting his battles against organized crime in his star-studded career as an FBI agent in Chicago and Arizona. The quasi-novel *War of the Godfathers* misfired, and the biographies of Tony Spilotro and Tony Accardo he authored shortly before his death are mediocre rehashes of his first and very finest work, *Man Against the Mob.* Bill Roemer's memoir revealed the secret inner-workings of the FBI during the early tumultuous days of wiretapping syndicate strongholds. While it is true that Roemer had his share of detractors in law enforcement—he was accused of overstating his importance by a handful of envious Chicago cops—he was a perfect gentleman and will always remain a real American hero. Our "man against the mob" is sorely missed by his longtime friends and colleagues.

St. John, Robert. *This Was My World.* Garden City, NY: Doubleday, 1953.

The son of a pharmacist, young Bob St. John set out to destroy Al Capone and save the Town of Cicero for the decent, law-abiding folk who resented the intrusion of Chicago gangsters into their working-class community. St. John published the *Cicero Tribune,* a muckraking weekly newspaper whose offices at Fifty-second Avenue and Twenty-fifth Street became the target of the Capone mob. St. John was intimidated, harassed, and beaten by Capone thugs, but he refused to compromise his principles. When all else failed, Capone simply bought the newspaper and installed Louis Cowen, one of his flunkies, as the new editor. St. John handed in his resignation and moved to Rutland, Vermont—as far away as he could get from Cicero.

Sawyers, June Skinner. *Chicago Portraits: Biographies of 250 Famous Chicagoans.* Chicago: Loyola University Press, 1991.

A handy reference guide providing thumbnail sketches of the movers and shakers of local politics, commerce, the arts and sciences, sports, and medicine, with a sprinkling of ne'er-do-wells thrown in for good measure. Impressive in scope, and handsomely laid out.

———. *Chicago Sketches: Urban Tales, Stories, and Legends from Chicago History.* Chicago: Wild Onion Books, 1995.

Seventy-two essays and an interesting collection of photographs and sketches draw upon major themes of Chicago social history. Most are familiar, some are not. Sawyers packs a lot of information into the retelling of defining moments in this family album of the Windy City. It is regrettable that the editorial board of Loyola Press made the decision to drop the Wild Onion titles from its line.

Schaak, Michael. *Anarchy & Anarchists: A History of the Red Terror and the Social Revolution in America and Europe.* Chicago: F. J. Schultie & Co., 1888.

Fantastic, long-winded tome written by a Chicago police captain desiring to assure his place in history as the "hero" of the Haymarket Affair. Schaak was a vainglorious windbag and self-promoter—ruthless, brutal, and dishonest. In 1889, following a sensational newspaper exposé, Schaak was suspended from the force for fencing impounded personal belongings of prisoners.

Schechter, Harold. *Depraved: The Shocking True Story of America's First Serial Killer.* New York: Pocket Books, 1994.

Schechter, a professor at Queens College of New York who ought to know better, sensationalized the H. H. Holmes (an alias of Herman Webster Mudgett) murders by conjecturing that Mudgett masturbated to the anguished screams of his gasping victims trapped inside his airtight vault. Otherwise, Schechter borrows heavily from the earlier volumes published by David Franke (*Torture Doctor,* 1975) and Detective Franklin Geyer (*The Holmes-Pitezel Case: History of the Greatest Crime of the Century,* 1896).

Schmidt, John. *The Mayor Who Cleaned Up Chicago: A Political Biography of William E. Dever.* DeKalb, IL: Northern Illinois University Press, 1989.

Mayor Dever drove Al Capone out of Chicago and into Cicero. He ordered his police chief to aid Treasury agents as they attempted to enforce the Volstead Act, not because he happened to believe in the temperance cause, but because it was the law of the land, and Dever, unlike his blustering predecessor William Hale Thompson, was one who upheld the law. Mayor Dever was a silk-hat reformer and a failure—despite initiating great civic works projects and pushing for reform at the cost of his own political career. But it was no coincidence that the Prohibition gun battles escalated during the Dever crackdown. Al Capone (the reporters knew him as "Al Brown" or "Al Caponi"), an up-and-comer in 1923 when Dever moved into City Hall, was the undisputed ruler of the rackets by the time Dever left office four years later. Chicago voters were not ready for reform. Maybe they never will be.

Schoenberg, Robert. *Mr. Capone.* New York: William Morrow, 1992.

Schoenberg places Al Capone in a historical, cultural, and political context, demonstrating how Prohibition played into Capone's hands. The Laurence Bergreen volume and Schoenberg's earlier biography were both published within a year of each other and are written by two out-of-town authors whose unfamiliarity with Chicago neighborhoods is painfully evident to the local reader. Author Schoenberg, a Californian, places Lincoln Park in the heart of downtown Chicago. The Bergreen book, richer in detail and better researched, is the preferred choice.

Sinkevitch, Alice, ed. *AIA Guide to Chicago.* New York: Harcourt Brace, 1993.

This was a joint venture of the American Institute of Architects Chicago, the Chicago Architecture Foundation, and the Landmarks Preservation Council of Illinois. Here's the problem with books about architecture and architectural tours of Chicago. They tell you nothing about the lives of the people who inhabited the Queen Anne mansions or the hopes and aspirations of the businessmen who rented the corner office space on the fortieth floor of the classic terra cotta office building we see before us on Randolph Street. Queen Annes and terra cotta, while pleasing to behold and interesting to read about, are still-life representations without the human dimension. The prose in this book is not colored with lively and provocative yarns, but the book is far from disappointing. Borrowing heavily from an eight-year research study by the Commission on Chicago Landmarks of every building and hovel constructed within the city limits before 1940, the guide condenses voluminous material into a useful paperback reference work appealing to both layman and scholar.

Smith, Anson J. *Syndicate City: The Chicago Crime Cartel.* Chicago: Henry Regnery, 1954.

Anson Smith's previous book, *Chicago's Left Bank,* is a loving and tender account of Chicago's literary golden age. Trolling in unfamiliar and more treacherous waters, his second book is an odd amalgam of Roaring Twenties/Prohibition gangster lore, pop sociology, and off-the-cuff political advice to Mayor Martin Kennelly concerning City Hall grafters. The book is out of print, out of date, and best forgotten.

Solzman, David M. *Chicago River: An Illustrated History.* Chicago: Loyola Press, 1998.

A wonderful excursion up and down the Chicago River recalling footnote episodes from early Chicago history, discussing the flora and fauna of the region, and providing a collection of unusual and arresting photographs. An excellent companion volume to Mayer and Wade's *Growth of a Metropolis.*

Spiering, Frank. *The Man Who Got Capone.* New York: Bobbs-Merrill, 1976.

Frank J. Wilson, the man who "got" Capone, lacked the egotism of the publicity-obsessed Eliot Ness, and never intended to become a rackets buster. The role was thrust upon him by the federal government and President Herbert Hoover, who had grown weary of Al Capone's shenanigans and open defiance of the federal Prohibition laws. Wilson was assigned to Elmer Irey's IRS Intelligence Unit, and was sent to Chicago in 1928 to begin a three-year investigation into Al Capone's finances after the U.S. Supreme Court determined in 1927 that even illegal income was taxable. The Treasury Department could find no tax records for the Chicago gangster. The pencil-pushing Wilson's task was to uncover the evidence. He posed as an out-of-town tourist and lived a modest existence at the Sheridan Plaza Hotel during the whole time, arousing the suspicions of no one until it was time to go to court.

Stead, William. *If Christ Came to Chicago.* Chicago: Laird & Lee, 1894.

English reformer William Stead visited the gambling dens and houses of prostitution in the Custom House Place Levee. He submitted this firsthand report that awakened all of Chicago to the great "social evil," hastening the demise of the downtown vice district.

Stead's scorching condemnation of Chicago in the not-so-gay nineties lists addresses of the
dens of iniquity and names of the owners. The book was an eye opener in its day and had
a prepublication sale of 70,000 copies. Stead's volume was serialized and satirized in the
pages of the *Chicago Reader* and has since been reissued in paperback.

Sullivan, Edward Dean. *Rattling the Cup on Chicago Crime.* New York: Vanguard
Press, 1929.

"This book is not concerned with what should be done to halt or lessen crime," writes
Sullivan, a former newspaper reporter, in volume one of his two-volume saga of the
Chicago gang wars. *Rattling the Cup* covers the years 1924–1928. Its sequel, *Chicago
Surrenders,* was published just after the gangland slaying of *Chicago Tribune* reporter
Jake Lingle in 1930.

Sullivan, Terry and Peter Maiken. *Killer Clown: The John Wayne Gacy Murders.* New
York: Grosset & Dunlap, 1983.

Gacy murdered thirty-three young men, perhaps many more. In 1998, the Better
Government Association, acting on an informant's tip, initiated a sweeping search for the
bodies of additional victims. Digging in the backyard of a Northwest Side apartment house
where Gacy's mother once lived, investigators unearthed a flattened sauce pan and a marble, but no human remains.

Thrasher, Frederick. *The Gang: A Study of 1,313 Gangs in Chicago.* Chicago:
University of Chicago Press, 1927.

Frederick Thrasher's landmark study outlines the history and root causes of juvenile crime
in the squalid, ethnic enclaves of "Little Hell," "Bucktown," the "West Side Wilderness," the
"Patch," the "Valley," and other seedbeds of poverty that spawned the rise of kid gangs in
the 1920s. The greater majority of disenfranchised youth eventually outgrew the gangs
upon attainment of young adulthood. The difference today seems to be that the kids who
join gangs for the usual stated reasons of peer acceptance and social status remain in the
gangs well beyond the onset of adulthood. Instead of the 1,313 independent kid gangs
defending their neighborhood "turf," as Professor Thrasher, a faculty member in the sociology department at the University of Chicago, described in his 1927 volume, there are perhaps fewer than 250 gangs active in Chicago today, but with many thousands of members,
forming a complex and intricate organized crime network that in many ways parallels the
rise of the Prohibition-era mobs in Chicago and New York. This is an excellent companion
volume to Zorbaugh's *Gold Coast and the Slum.* In fact, both books were originally part
of the same series.

Touhy, Roger and Ray Brennan. *The Stolen Years.* Cleveland: Pennington Press, 1959.

If ever there was a "Robin Hood" of Chicago crime, it had to be Roger Touhy, boss of the
Northwest and North Suburban gambling operations and the roadhouse district cen-
tered along Dempster Street in Skokie. Touhy, never a vicious killer or extortionist, but
merely a guy who wanted to make a buck out of Prohibition, was railroaded into prison
by State's Attorney Thomas Courtney on a fabricated charge of kidnapping. Jake "the
Barber" Factor, the alleged kidnap victim in this diabolical scheme, sued Brennan and the

publisher for libel when the book first appeared in print. The author settled out of court. *The Stolen Years* was the first and only volume published by Pennington, a lithograph company driven out of business by Factor's onerous lawsuit.

Washburn, Charles. *Come Into My Parlor.* New York: National Library Press, 1936.

The Everleigh sisters' spectacular rise to fame and infamy in the Levee, and their version of the events leading to the closing of their famous bordello and the demise of the Twenty-second Street Levee are covered in assiduous detail. Out of print, but available for examination in the Chicago Historical Society library.

Whitehead, Don. *The FBI Story: A Report to the People.* New York: Random House, 1956.

J. Edgar Hoover wrote the foreword to this "authorized," and undoubtedly heavily censored history of the Bureau.

Wilson, Samuel Paynter. *Chicago and Its Cesspools of Infamy.* Chicago: Samuel Paynter Wilson, 1910.

A curious blend of scandal and religious fervor, self-published around the time the Chicago Vice Commission released a report listing 1,000 brothels, 1,800 madams, and 4,000 prostitutes dwelling within the Levee. Pawnbrokers, abortionists, proprietors of concert saloons, and the "lost sisterhood" are zealously denounced by Wilson as the vile corrupters of youth. A library volume out of print for many years.

Wright, Sewell Peaslee, ed. *Chicago Murders: True Crimes and Real Detectives.* New York: Bantam, 1947.

An anthology of murder stories by LeRoy "Buddy" McHugh, a famous 1940s crime writer for the old *Chicago Herald-American*; Otto Eisenschiml, who concocted the hair-brained theory that Edwin Stanton hatched a plot to kill President Lincoln; and other mystery genre writers. Out-of-print, this obscure volume is an interesting addition to a collector's library.

Zeller, F. C. Duke. *Devils Pact: Inside the World of the Teamsters Union.* Secaucus, NJ: Birch Lane, 1996.

Good "insider's" account of Jackie Presser and his dislike of Allen Dorfman.

Zorbaugh, Harvey Warren. *The Gold Coast and the Slum: A Sociological Study of Chicago's Near North Side.* Chicago: University of Chicago Press, 1929.

When Zorbaugh began his study in 1928, the boundaries of the Gold Coast and the blighted neighborhoods to the immediate west were easily understood by the existence of a "boundary line" between the Gold Coast "haves" and the ethnic "have nots" residing west of Clark Street—a street called the "rialto of the half world" by the author. It was a dividing line that reflected extremes: the extremes of wealth and poverty. Dating back to the 1880s, Clark Street was a region of honky-tonk saloons and low dives—a North Side "Levee." Traveling farther west, the slum districts of "Little Hell," populated by succeeding waves of Irish, Swedes, Eastern Europeans, and Italians were a setting of social disorganization and crime. East of Clark, hugging the lake front, one found the stately mansions of the elite, limited commercial development, and fashionable hotels—the extravagance of wealth. If Harvey Warren Zorbaugh were alive today, he would discover that the current demographics of the Near North Side are not so very different. Relevant to the modern era, *The Gold Coast and the Slum* reaches across the gulf of time. A masterful volume of urban sociology.

NEWSPAPERS

Chicago American (1951-1969)

Chicago Daily Journal (1900-1910)

Chicago Daily News (1875-1978)

Chicago Herald & Examiner (1922-1940)

Chicago Herald-American (1940-1948)

Chicago Inter-Ocean (1890-1915)

Chicago Sun (1941-1945)

Chicago Sun-Times (1948-)

Chicago Times (1945-1948)

Chicago Today (1969-1974)

Chicago Tribune (1855-)

Crain's Chicago Business (1990-)

Northwest Herald (1983-)

INDEX

R

S

Y

Z

ABOUT THE AUTHOR

Author, historian, and journalist Richard Lindberg was born and raised in Chicago, the city he most often writes about. His ten previous books all deal with aspects of Chicago's history, politics, crime, ethnicity, and sport.

Lindberg served as head writer and senior editor for the Edgar award-winning *Encyclopedia of World Crime* in 1990. For six years, he was the managing editor of *The Illinois Police and Sheriff's News,* a law-enforcement investigative journal. He is currently Marketing Director for Search International, Inc., a private investigation and research firm headquartered in the Chicago suburbs. Over the years Lindberg's byline has appeared in numerous publications including the *Chicago Tribune Magazine, Chicago History, Inside Chicago Magazine, Screen Magazine,* and *USA Today Magazine.* He is a member of the Chicago Crime Commission, the Chicago Press Veterans, and the Illinois Academy of Criminology, and is vice president of the Society of Midland Authors. He lives in Chicago with his wife, Denise.

A FINAL WORD TO THE READER

It is not possible to cover every crime of consequence within one volume. The absence of any notable Chicago criminal cases from the pages of this book has more to do with spatial limitations than deliberate oversight, and these cases will be properly addressed in a subsequent edition if there is sufficient interest on the part of my readership. I encourage feedback and welcome readers to contact me with suggestions and comments.

Please address all inquiries to:
Richard C. Lindberg
c/o Cumberland House Publishing
431 Harding Industrial Drive
Nashville, TN 37211